USING TURBO C++

Herbert Schildt

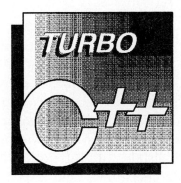

Osborne McGraw-Hill

Berkeley New York St. Louis San Francisco
Auckland Bogotá Hamburg London Madrid
Mexico City Milan Montreal New Delhi Panama City
Paris São Paulo Singapore Sydney
Tokyo Toronto

Osborne **McGraw-Hill**
2600 Tenth Street
Berkeley, California 94710
U.S.A.

For information on translations and book distributors outside of the U.S.A., please write to Osborne **McGraw-Hill** at the above address.

TAB BOOKS is a McGraw-Hill Company. TAB BOOKS offers software for sale. For information and a catalog, please contact TAB Software Department, Blue Ridge Summit, PA 17294-0850.

Using Turbo C++

234567890 DOC 99876543210

ISBN 0-07-881610-6

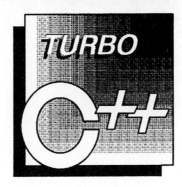

Contents at a Glance

PART III

Using Turbo C++'s Object Oriented Features   455

Contents

Part II
The C Language

Part III
Using Turbo C++'s
Object Oriented
Features

Introduction

As the 1980s drew to a close, a new way to approach the job of programming was beginning to take hold. This new method is called object oriented programming. Object oriented programming (OOP for short) embodies all features of structured programming (its predecessor), but provides the programmer with an exciting new way to analyze and solve programming tasks. In the course of this book, you will learn why OOP is important and how OOP is implemented in Turbo C++.

As you probably know, C++ is the object oriented version of C. C was the preeminent language of the 1980s and is still in wide use at the time of this writing. (In fact, it will most likely be a very long time before C is deemed obsolete.) C is known for its efficiency, power, and elegance. C++ preserves these important qualities but adds support for OOP. It is this combination that makes C++ the single most important object oriented programming language available today.

In 1988, Borland International, Inc. began secret work on Turbo C++. They started with their extremely powerful Turbo C and added to it the C++ OOP extensions. It was not an easy task. C++, although easy for the programmer to use, is a rigorous exercise in compiler construction. In fact, Turbo C++ is the largest and most ambitious language project Borland has undertaken. To create Turbo C++, Borland assembled a group of some of the best compiler programmers available. During the development of Turbo C++, Borland also enhanced the user interface to its interactive development environment.

As you will learn while working through this book, Turbo C++ provides a powerful yet flexible programming environment. It produces tight, efficient code and supports hundreds of library functions and classes. Although Turbo C++ was an ambitious project, it is fair to say that it lives up to its ancestor's reputation and deserves the title *Turbo*!

About This Book

This book teaches the Turbo C++ programming language, beginning with its base language, C. Because C++ is a superset of the C language, you need to know C before you can learn C++. Therefore, if you don't already know C, you can still use this book because it contains all the background information you need. The book also covers the Turbo C++ integrated environment, the editor, and many library functions. By the time you finish this book, you will definitely be able to call yourself a Turbo C++ programmer.

This book is based on the philosophy that learning is best accomplished by doing. Toward this end, the book contains many sample programs that you can compile and run. In fact, virtually every major feature of Turbo C++ has a sample program to demonstrate it.

How This Book Is Organized

This book is organized in such a way that it can be effectively used by two different types of programmers: those who already know C and just want to learn about the C++ extensions, and those who are new to both C and C++.

Part I presents an overview of Turbo C++, introduces the Turbo C++ integrated environment, and discusses the editor. In Part II, the C-like features of C++ are presented. If you don't already know C, be sure to carefully work through Part II. However, if you are proficient at C, you can skip to Part III, in which the C++ extensions to C are fully described.

Organizing the book in this fashion prevents the experienced C programmer from having to wade through reams of material he or she already knows, yet still provides the beginner with sufficient background material.

Conventions Used in This Book

In this book, keywords, operators, function names, and variable names are shown in bold when referenced in text. General forms are shown in italics. Also, when referencing a function name in text, the name is followed by parentheses. In this way, you can easily distinguish a variable name from a function name.

Additional Help from Osborne/McGraw-Hill

Osborne/McGraw-Hill provides top-quality books for computer users at every level of computing experience. To help you build your skills, we suggest that you look for the books in the following Osborne/McGraw-Hill series that best address your needs.

The "Teach Yourself" series is perfect for beginners who have never used a computer before or who want to gain confidence in using program basics. These books provide a simple, slow-paced introduction to the fundamental usage of popular software packages and programming languages. The "Mastery Learning" format ensures that concepts are learned thoroughly before progressing to new material. Plenty of exercises and examples (with answers at the back of the book) are used throughout the text.

The "Made Easy" series is also for beginners or users who may need a refresher on the new features of an upgraded product. These in-depth introductions guide users step-by-step from the program basics to intermediate-level usage. Plenty of "hands on" exercises and examples are used in every chapter.

The "Using" series presents fast-paced guides that quickly cover beginning concepts and move on to intermediate-level techniques, and even some advanced topics. These books are written for users already familiar with computers and software, and who want to get up to speed fast with a certain product.

The "Advanced" series assumes that the reader is already an experienced user who has reached at least an intermediate skill level, and is ready to learn more sophisticated techniques and refinements.

The "Complete Reference" books are a series of handy desktop references for popular software and programming languages that list every command, feature, and function of the product, along with brief, detailed descriptions of how they are used. Books are fully indexed and often include tear-out command cards. The "Complete Reference" series is ideal for all users, beginners and pros.

The "Pocket Reference" is a pocket-sized, shorter version of the "Complete Reference" series, and provides only the essential commands, features, and functions of software and programming languages for users who need a quick reminder of the most important commands. This series is also written for all users and every level of computing ability.

The "Secrets, Solutions, Shortcuts" series is written for beginning users who are already somewhat familiar with the software, and for experienced users at intermediate and advanced levels. This series provides clever tips and points out shortcuts for using the software to greater advantage. Traps to avoid are also mentioned.

Osborne/McGraw-Hill also publishes many fine books that are not included in the series described above. If you have questions about which Osborne book is right for you, ask the salesperson at your local book or computer store, or call us toll-free at 1-800-262-4729.

Diskette Offer

There are many useful and interesting functions and programs contained in this book. If you're like me, you probably would like to use them, but hate typing them into the computer. When I key in routines from a book it always seems that I type something wrong and spend hours trying to get the program to work. For this reason, I am offering the source code on diskette for all the functions and programs contained in this book, for $24.95. Just fill in the order blank on the next page and mail it, along with your payment, to the address shown. Or, if you're in a hurry, just call 217-586-4021 (the number of my consulting office) and place your order by telephone. (Visa and Mastercard accepted.)

Please send me _____ copies, at $24.95 each, of the programs in *Using Turbo C++* on an IBM-compatible diskette.

Foreign orders only: Checks must be drawn on a U.S. bank. Please add $5 shipping and handling.

_____

Name

_____

Address

_____ _____ _____

City   State   Zip

_____

Telephone

Diskette size (check one): 5 1/4″ _____ 3 1/2″ _____

Method of payment: check _____ Visa _____ MC_____

Credit card number: _____

Expiration date:_____

Signature:_____

Send to:
    Herbert Schildt
    RR 1, Box 130
    Mahomet, Il 61853
    or phone: 217-586-4021

This offer subject to change or cancellation at any time.

Why This Book Is For You

If you want to learn to program in Turbo C++ and also learn about the programming philosophy known as object oriented programming, this book is for you. This book is for both beginning programmers and seasoned pros. As you might know, C++ is built upon the C language. In fact, knowing C is prerequisite to learning C++. Because of the way this book is organized, if you are already familiar with C, you can quickly advance to the chapters that exclusively deal with the C++ extensions to C without rehashing topics you already understand. If you are completely new to both C and C++, start at the beginning of the book and work your way to the end, one chapter at a time.

In addition to teaching Turbo C++ language, this book also covers the Turbo C++ integrated programming environment, the Turbo C++ editor, and various compiler options.

One last point: because the information in this book was reviewed for technical accuracy by Borland International, Inc., you can be assured of its quality.

Learn More about Turbo C++

Here is an excellent selection of other Osborne/McGraw-Hill books on Turbo C++ that will help you build your skills and maximize the power of the Borland compiler you have selected.

Turbo C++ DiskTutor, by Greg Voss and Paul Chui, is a book/disk package that features a streamlined version of the Turbo C++ compiler along with a disk of examples and a book that thoroughly covers Turbo C++ and object oriented programming step-by-step. Just load the compiler and the examples disk and follow instructions in the book. It's perfect for C programmers who want a detailed introduction to Turbo C++.

Turbo C/C++: The Complete Reference, by Herbert Schildt, is a comprehensive encyclopedia that lists every Turbo C and Turbo C++ command, feature, function, and programming technique. This lasting reference is great for programmers at all skill levels.

Turbo C++ Professional Handbook, by Chris H. Pappas and William H. Murray III, is for programmers who want to uncover all the components of Turbo C++ Professional, including C, Turbo C++ with object oriented programming, the Turbo Assembler, Turbo Debugger, and Turbo Profiler. After quick-start chapters on each component, Pappas and Murray cover Turbo C++ in careful detail. The final chapters put all the components together for an all-encompassing perspective on Turbo C++ Professional.

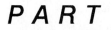

Getting Started

Part I of this book lays the groundwork for your study of Turbo C++. Chapter 1 gives a brief history and overview of the C++ language, including how it relates to its parent language, C. Chapter 2 teaches you how to use Turbo C++'s integrated programming environment. Chapter 3 discusses the Turbo C++ editor.

1

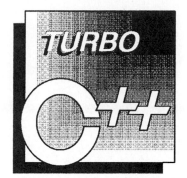

Turbo C++ *in* Perspective

Before you begin to explore the exciting world of Turbo C++, it is important to place it into perspective relative both to other programming languages and to C, the language on which C++ is built. The purpose of this chapter is to present a general overview of the C++ programming language, its origins, uses, and philosophy. If you already know something about C++ and are a fairly experienced programmer, you might want to skip to Chapter 2.

This chapter begins with a short history of C++. If you are completely new to C++ (and C itself) or to programming in general, you will find this background information valuable. The chapter goes on to cover the differences between compilers and interpreters. If Turbo C++ is the first compiled language you have worked with, you should read this section. Finally, the chapter ends with a little information specifically for C users who are moving up to Turbo C++.

The Origins of C++

The story of C++ begins in the 1970s with the invention of C, the language C++ is derived from. C was invented and first implemented by Dennis Ritchie on a DEC PDP-11 using the UNIX operating system. C is the result of a development process that started with an older language called BCPL, developed by Martin Richards. BCPL influenced a language invented by Ken Thompson, called B, which led to the development of C.

As you probably know, C became one of the most widely used (and liked) programming languages. It is flexible yet powerful, and C has been used to create some of the most important software products of the last several years. However, even C reaches its limits when the size of a project exceeds a certain point. While the actual limit will vary from project to project, when a program becomes 25,000 to 100,000 lines long, it becomes hard to manage because it is difficult to grasp as a totality. To address this problem, in 1980, while working at Bell Laboratories at Murray Hill, New Jersey, Bjarne Stroustrup added several extensions to the C language and initially called the new language "C with Classes." However, in 1983 the name was changed to C++.

Most additions made by Stroustrup to C support *object oriented programming*, sometimes referred to as OOP. (A brief explanation of object oriented programming follows in the next section.) Stroustrup states that some of C++'s object oriented features were inspired by another object oriented language called Simula67. Therefore, C++ represents the blending of two powerful programming methods.

Since C++ was first invented, it has gone through two revisions, once in 1985 and again in 1989. The current version is 2.0 and it is this version of C++ that Turbo C++ implements.

What Is Object Oriented Programming?

Although a thorough description of what object oriented programming means will have to wait until Part III of this book, the following short discussion will give you an idea.

The most fundamental underlying purpose of object oriented programming is to allow a programmer to manage and understand larger, more complex programs. The key to achieving this goal is the *object*. Essentially, object oriented programming involves the creation of objects, which combine and encapsulate both data and the code that operates on that data. Objects may contain both public and private elements. When an element of the object is private, then only other elements of that object may have access to it. Public elements may be accessed by any other piece of the program. Using private elements, it is possible to strictly control how an object is accessed. The advantage to using objects is that, when correctly applied, an object is a single, logical entity that is easier to comprehend and manage than the separate elements that comprise the object.

Another feature of object oriented programming is that it allows you to create a hierarchy of objects, moving from most general to most specific. In this hierarchy, each object inherits the traits of those that come before it. The ability to create hierarchical structures allows you, the programmer, to carefully organize parts of your program into neat, self-contained units.

C++: *True to the Spirit of C*

C is often referred to as a middle-level language, lying somewhere between assembler (low-level) and Pascal (high-level). Part of the reason that C was invented was to give a programmer a high-level language that could be used as a substitute for assembly language. As you probably know, assembly language uses the symbolic representation of the actual instructions executed by the computer. There is a one-to-one relationship between each assembly language instruction and the machine instruction. While this relationship makes it possible to write highly efficient programs, doing so is quite tedious and error prone. On the other hand, high-level languages, such as Pascal, are greatly removed from the machine. A statement in Pascal has virtually no relationship to the sequence of machine instructions that is ultimately executed. However, while C retains high-level control structures, such as are found in Pascal, it still allows the programmer to manipulate bits, bytes, and addresses in a way more closely tied to the machine rather than the abstraction presented by other high-level languages. For this reason, C has occasionally been called "high-level assembly code." Because of C's dual nature, it allows programmers to create very fast, efficient programs without having to resort to assembly language.

The philosophy behind C is that the programmer knows what he or she is doing. For this reason, the C language almost never "gets in the way of" the programmer, and you are free to use (or abuse) the language any way you see fit. There is little (if any) runtime error checking. For example, if for some weird reason you want to overwrite the memory in which your program is currently residing, there is nothing the C compiler will do to stop you! The reason for the "programmer as king" approach is that it allows a C compiler to create very fast and efficient code because it places the responsibility for error checking and the like on you.

In short, C assumes that you are smart enough to add your own error checking when needed.

When C++ was invented, Bjarne Stroustrup knew that it was important to maintain the original spirit of C, including its efficiency, its middle-level nature, and the philosophy that the programmer, not the language, is in charge, while at the same time adding the support for object oriented programming. As you will see, this goal was accomplished. C++ still provides the programmer with the freedom and control of C coupled with the power of objects. The object oriented features in C++, to use Stroustrup's words, "allow programs to be structured for clarity, extensibility, and ease of maintenance without loss of efficiency."

What Can C++ Be Used For?

Although C++ was initially designed to aid in the management of very large programs, it is in no way limited to this use. In fact, the object oriented attributes of C++ can be effectively applied to virtually any programming task. It is not uncommon to see C++ used for projects such as editors, databases, personal file systems, and communication programs. Also, because C++ shares C's efficiency, much high-performance systems software is constructed using C++. (Systems software is, loosely, those programs that are associated with the operating system.)

As stated, using C++ you can create a hierarchy of related objects. This feature allows the creation of special object oriented libraries, which may be shared by many programmers. Therefore, even programs that are small enough to be easily managed by C may be written in C++, just to take advantage of the features found in an object oriented library.

Another reason that C++ is beginning to be widely used for all types of programming tasks is that it allows programs to be more easily maintained and expanded. When a new feature needs to be implemented, as you will learn later in this book, it is very easy to add it to the definition of a currently defined object. In essence, C++ provides a well-defined method of expanding the capabilities of an object.

Compilers Versus Interpreters

Turbo C++ is a compiler. By contrast, the standard BASIC that came with your computer is an interpreter. If you have never worked with a compiler before, it will seem different. If compilers are new to you, please read the next few paragraphs.

The terms *compiler* and *interpreter* refer to the way in which a program is executed. In theory, any programming language can be either compiled or interpreted, but some languages are usually executed one way or the other. For example, BASIC is generally interpreted and C++ is usually compiled. The way a program is executed is not defined by the language in which it is written. Interpreters and compilers are simply sophisticated programs that operate on your program source code.

An interpreter reads the source code of your program one line at a time and performs the specific instructions contained in that line. The interpreter must be present each time the program is run. A compiler reads the entire program and converts it into executable code. Executable code is also referred to as *object, binary,* or *machine* code. However, in this context the term *object code* has no relationship to objects defined in a C++ program. Once the program is compiled, a line of source code is no longer meaningful to the execution of your program. The compiler is not needed to run the program once the program is compiled.

Two terms that you will see often in this book and in your Turbo C++ compiler manuals are *compile time* and *run time.* Compile time refers to the events that occur during the compilation process. Run time refers to the events that occur while the program is actually executing. Unfortunately, you will often see them used in connection with the word *errors,* as in *compile-time errors* and *runtime errors.* Happily, as you become a better Turbo C++ programmer, you will see these messages less often.

A Word to C Programmers

If you already know C, then you will be able to start learning the C++ extensions immediately. Virtually everything you know about C is applicable to C++. In fact, since C++ is a superset of C, all C programs are implicitly C++ programs. Keep in mind, however, that to write effective object oriented code, you will need to reshape the way you think about your programs. If you keep an open mind, you will have no trouble.

CHAPTER

2

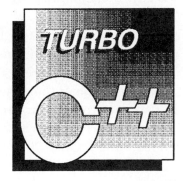

The Turbo C++
Integrated
Development
Environment

Turbo C++ has two separate modes of operation. The first, and the one you will almost certainly want to use in the beginning, is called its *integrated development environment,* or *IDE* for short. Using the IDE, editing, compilation, and execution are controlled by single keystrokes and easy-to-use menus. In fact, the IDE is so easy to use that its operation is almost intuitive. The other method of operation involves the traditional command-line approach where

13

you first use an editor to create a program source file; then you compile it, link it, and run it. The first part of this book will use only the integrated environment because it is easier to work with and its online help is available. Using the compiler from the command line will be covered in Appendix F.

The purpose of this chapter is to show you around the Turbo C++ IDE without going into very much detail at this time. Instead, this introduction to the IDE is simply to get you acquainted with it so that you know what is available. Many of the options that you will see may seem cryptic at first, but as you progress through the book they will become clear. If you are already familiar with how the integrated environment functions, you should proceed to Chapter 3.

The rest of this book assumes that you have properly installed Turbo C++ according to the instructions given in the Borland manual. If you have not, install Turbo C++ at this time.

Executing Turbo C++

To execute the integrated version of Turbo C++, simply type **TC** and press ENTER. When Turbo C++ begins execution you will see the screen shown in Figure 2-1. It consists of these four parts, in order from top to bottom:

- the main menu
- the editor window
- the message window
- the status line

Each of these areas is examined briefly in this chapter.

Figure 2-1.

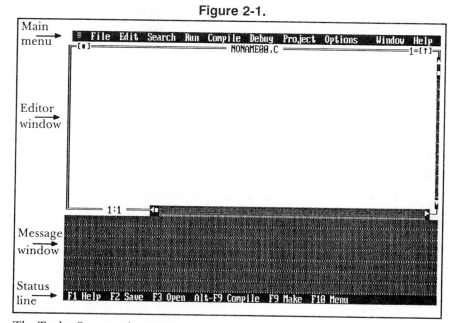

The Turbo C++ opening screen

Using the Mouse

The Turbo C++ IDE can be operated using either the keyboard or the mouse. Although the mouse is not required, mouse support has been carefully integrated into the Turbo C++ IDE, and a mouse is certainly an excellent addition.

To make the discussion of the IDE that follows easier, a few mouse operations and terms are defined now. In general, to select an item, position the mouse pointer over that item and press the left mouse button. Doing this is called *clicking* on an item. Sometimes, you will need to *double click* in order to select something. Double clicking means that you press the left mouse button twice in rapid succession without moving the mouse between clicks. Some objects can be *dragged* about the screen. To drag an object using a mouse, position the mouse pointer at the appropriate part of the object, press and hold down the left mouse button, and then move the mouse. As you move the mouse, the object will move in the same direction. When the object reaches the desired part of the screen, stop moving the mouse and release the left button.

The Main Menu

To activate the main menu, press the F10 key. When you do this, one of the menu items will be highlighted. Press F10 now.

The main menu is used either to tell Turbo C++ to do something, such as load a file or compile a program, or to set an option. Once the main menu is activated, there are two ways to make a main menu selection using the keyboard. First, you can use the arrow keys to move the highlight to the item you want and then press ENTER. Second, you can simply type the first letter of the desired menu item. For example, to select **Edit** you type **E**. You may enter the letters in either upper- or lowercase. If you have a mouse, you can click on the main menu item that you want to activate. Table 2-1 summarizes what each menu selection does.

When you select a main menu item, a *pull-down menu* is displayed containing a list of choices. This menu allows you to select an action that relates to the main menu item. To make a selection using the arrow keys, move the highlight to the item you want and press ENTER. Or, you can type the letter of the option that is shown in a different color (or as boldface on a monochrome monitor). Most of the time, the different color letter is the first letter, but not always. If you have a mouse, click on the

Table 2-1.

Item	Options
≡	Displays the version number, clears or restores the screen, and executes various utility programs supplied with Turbo C++.
File	Loads and saves files, handles directories, invokes DOS, and exits Turbo C++.
Edit	Performs various editing functions.
Search	Performs various text searches and replacements.
Run	Compiles, links, and runs the program currently loaded in the environment.
Compile	Compiles the program currently in the environment.
Debug	Sets various debugger options, including setting break points.
Project	Manages multifile projects.
Options	Sets various compiler, linker, and environmental options.
Window	Controls the way various windows are displayed.
Help	Activates the context-sensitive Help system.

Summary of the Main Menu Items

desired item. You can cancel any menu at any time by pressing the ESC key or by clicking on another part of the screen using the mouse.

Sometimes, a menu entry will not be available in a given situation. When this occurs, no letter is shown in a different color and if you move the highlight to this option (or click on it with the mouse) it will be displayed as a black bar.

Some pull-down menus produce another pull-down menu that displays additional options relating to the first. The secondary pull-down menus operate just like primary menus. When one menu will generate another, it is shown with a dark arrow to its right.

Some menu entries are On/Off selections. To change the state of an On/Off entry, move the highlight to that entry and press ENTER. This will reverse the state. You may also click on it using the mouse or type the letter that is in a different color.

Dialog Boxes

If a pull-down menu item is followed by three periods, selecting this item will cause a *dialog box* to be displayed. Dialog boxes allow input that is not easily accomplished using a menu. Dialog boxes consist of one or more of the following items:

- action buttons
- check boxes
- input boxes
- list boxes
- radio buttons

Let's see what these items do. Most dialog boxes have these *action buttons*: **Delete**, **Cancel**, and **Help**. To activate one of these using the keyboard, press the TAB key until the desired action is highlighted and then press ENTER. If you have a mouse, simply click on the appropriate button. There may be other *action buttons* in a dialog box that relate to the specific function of the dialog box.

A *check box* looks something like this:

[X] *option*

Here, *option* is some option that can be enabled or disabled. When the box has an "X" in it, that option is selected. If the box is empty, then that option is not selected. To change the state of a check box, tab to the box and then press the SPACEBAR. The SPACEBAR acts as a toggle: each time you press it the state of the box changes. You can also change the state of a check box by clicking on it with the mouse.

An *input box* allows you to enter text, such as a filename. To activate the input box either press TAB until the box is active or click on it using the mouse. Once the box is selected, enter text using the keyboard and press ENTER when you are done.

A *list box* presents a list of items from which you can choose. To activate the list box, either press TAB until the box is active or click on it using the mouse. Once the box is activated, select the item you want by moving the highlight to the appropriate item and pressing ENTER, or by double clicking on the item using the mouse.

Radio buttons are a list of mutually exclusive options. The list takes this general form:

( ) *option 1*
(.) *option 2*
   .
   .
   .
( ) *option N*

To activate the radio buttons, tab to them or click on them using the mouse. Use the arrow keys to change the selection or click on the desired selection using the mouse.

An example of one of Turbo C++'s dialog boxes is shown in Figure 2-2. Now that you know how to use Turbo C++'s menus, let's begin a tour of the IDE.

Figure 2-2.

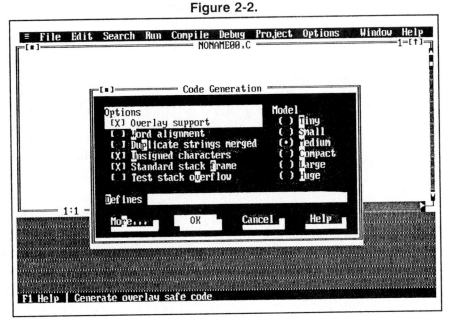

An example Turbo C++ dialog box

Turning On Full Menus

Because Turbo C++ has such a rich and flexible set of options, not all menu items are displayed by default. Instead, only the most commonly used options are presented. However, so that you can see what all the available options are, it is necessary that the full menus be displayed. To do this, activate the main menu (if you have not already done so) by pressing F10. Next, move the highlight on the main menu to the **Options** entry and press ENTER. Your screen will look like the one shown in Figure 2-3. If, by previous usage, **Full menus** is on, then change nothing on this menu. Otherwise, move the highlight to the **Full menus** entry and press ENTER to turn it on. Next, reactivate the main menu by pressing F10.

Figure 2-3.

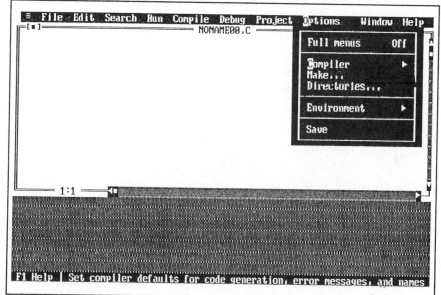

*The **Options** pull-down menu*

Now, using the left arrow key, move the highlight to the system menu entry. (The system menu option is at the far left of the main menu.)

Exploring the Main Menu

In this section each entry of the main menu will be briefly examined.

The System Menu

If you have not already done so, move the highlight to the system menu symbol (on the far left) and press ENTER. The system menu tells you information about your version of Turbo C++. It also lets you clear the work area and redisplay the screen. The reason you might want to redisplay the screen is that sometimes a program will overwrite the video memory when it executes, causing the screen to become messy.

Using the system menu you can also execute some utility programs supplied by Turbo C.

File

Move the highlight to **File**. This activates the **File** pull-down window as shown in Figure 2-4. Let's look at each of the **File** options.

The **Open** option prompts you for a filename and then loads that file into the editor. If the file does not exist, then it is created. The **Open** option also displays a list of files from which you can choose. Use the arrow keys to move the highlight until it is on the file you wish to load and press ENTER to load the file, or double click on the desired filename. **New** opens another editing window and lets you create a new file. The file is called NONAME*n*.C, where *n* is a value between 0 and 99. However, you can rename the file to whatever you want when you save it. The **Save** option saves the file in the active window. The **Save as** option lets you save a file using a different filename. The **Save all** option saves the files in all open windows. **Change dir** changes the default directory to the one you specify. The **Print** option prints the file in the active window. The **Get info** option displays information about the file in the active window. The **DOS shell** option loads the DOS command proces-

Figure 2-4.

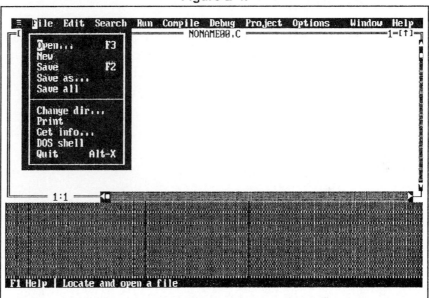

*The **File** pull-down menu*

sor and lets you execute DOS commands. You must type **EXIT** to return to Turbo C++. Finally, the **Quit** option quits Turbo C++.

Edit

At this time, press the right arrow key to select the **Edit** main menu entry.

The **Edit** option allows you to perform several editor operations. These commands and the operation of the editor will be discussed at length in the next chapter.

Search

Press the right arrow key to select the **Search** main menu option.

The **Search** main menu entry allows you to perform various types of searches and search-and-replacements on the text in the active window. Since the **Search** options relate to the editor, they are discussed in the next chapter.

Run

The **Run** option activates a submenu containing these six selections:

> Run
> Program reset
> Go to cursor
> Trace into
> Step over
> Arguments . . .

The **Run** option executes the current program. If the program has not yet been compiled, **Run** compiles it for you. The next four options relate to the execution of a program using the debugger. To use them you must compile your program with the debugging information option turned on, as it is by default. Although the operation of the debugger is covered in Appendix C, the following descriptions will give you an idea of what these options do. The **Program reset** option terminates your program when it is being run in a debug mode. **Go to cursor** executes your program until it reaches the line of code where the cursor is positioned. The **Trace into** option executes your program one statement at a time. If the next statement includes a subroutine call, execution is traced into that subroutine. The **Step over** option executes the next line of code, but does not trace into any subroutines.

The **Arguments** entry is used to pass command-line arguments to a program that is run from the IDE. (If you are new to programming and do not know what a command-line argument is, it will be explained later in this book.)

Compile

Press the right arrow key at this time. This activates the **Compile** menu. You will see the screen shown in Figure 2-5. The first option allows you to compile the file currently in the editor to an .OBJ file. (An .OBJ file is a relocatable object file that is ready to be linked into an .EXE file that can be executed.) The second option will compile your program directly into an executable file.

Figure 2-5.

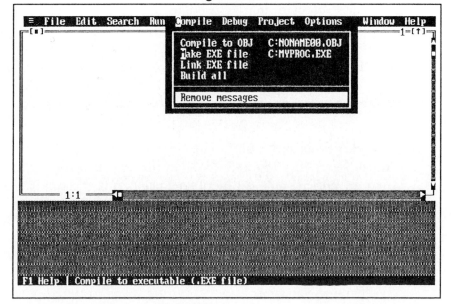

*The **Compile** pull-down menu options*

The third option lets you link your current program. The **Build all** option recompiles all the files related to your program. The **Remove messages** option clears the **Message** window.

Debug

Press the right arrow key to advance to the **Debug** main menu option.

The **Debug** option lets you control the way Turbo C++'s integrated debugger operates. For now, the default settings will work just fine and you do not need to worry about them.

Project

Advance to the **Project** entry of the main menu.

The **Project** option is used to aid in the development and maintenance of large, multifile programs. You can learn more about it in Appendix B.

Options

Select **Options** at this time. The entries in the pull-down menu are shown here. (If you see fewer than these, you probably forgot to turn on **Full menus** as described earlier in this chapter.)

```
Full menus

Compiler
Transfer...
Make...
Linker...
```

```
Debugger...
Directories...
Environment
Save...
```

Except for the first, each of these entries allows you to change the way Turbo C++ operates. You need not be concerned about any of these options at this time because Turbo C++'s default mode of operation is fine for now.

Window

Activate the **Window** option at this time.

Turbo C++'s IDE is based on the window. Turbo C++'s windows are very versatile. The **Window** entry allows you to perform various operations on a window. The **Window** pull-down menu is shown in Figure 2-6.

The first entries let you perform various operations on the active window. The first option is **Size/Move**. If you select this option you will be able to change the size of the active window and/or move it to a new location on the screen. The **Zoom** option increases the size of the active window so that it fills the entire screen. Once a window has been zoomed, selecting **Zoom** a second time returns the window to its normal size.

The IDE allows several windows to be open at the same time. There are two ways that multiple windows may be displayed by Turbo C++: *tiled* or *cascaded*. By default, windows are cascaded; this means that each time a new window is created, it partially overlays one or more other windows. Figure 2-7 shows an example of several cascaded windows. By contrast, if you select the **Tile** option, then no window overlays another. Each is given

Figure 2-6.

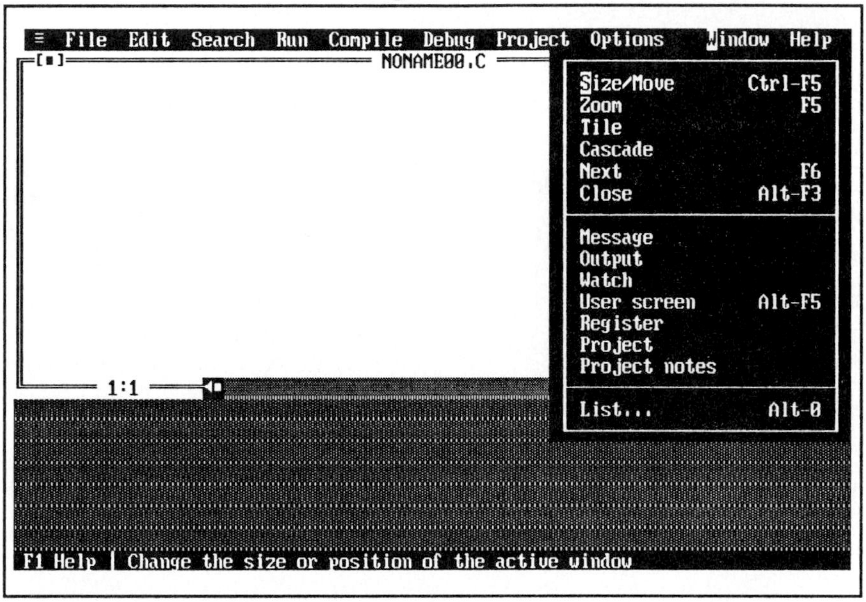

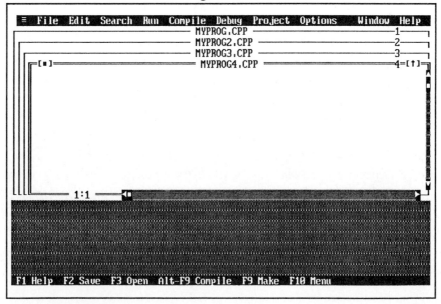

*The **Window** pull-down menu*

Figure 2-7.

Cascaded windows

a reduced part of the screen. Figure 2-8 shows the same windows as shown in Figure 2-7, except in tiled format.

If you have several open windows, then you can progressively jump from one window to the next by selecting **Next**. You can remove a window from the screen by selecting **Close**.

The second part of the **Window** menu allows you to activate one of Turbo C++'s built-in windows. The **Message** window is the one used by Turbo C++ to output information. The **Output** window displays the output generated when a program executes inside a window in the IDE. The **User screen** shows the full screen output of a program. If you select this option, then to return to the IDE screen you must press F5. The **Watch** window is used in debugging. The **Register** window displays the contents of each register of the CPU. The **Project** and **Project notes** windows relate to projects, which are explained later in this book.

Figure 2-8.

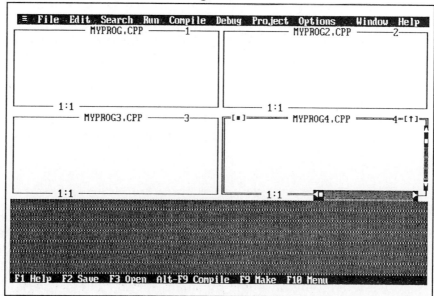

Tiled windows

To list all open windows, select **List**. You can activate a window by selecting one from the list.

Help

Activate the **Help** option at this time. You will see the following menu selections:

Contents
Index
Topic search
Previous topic
Help on help

The **Contents** option displays the table of contents to the Help system. The **Index** activates an index of topics covered by the Help system. To make a selection, move the highlight to the topic you want and press ENTER. You will then see information relating to the topic you selected. To exit the Help system, press ESC.

One very convenient feature of Turbo C++'s Help system is that when you select the **Topic search** option, the keyword that the cursor is currently located on will have information displayed about it. To review the previous topic, select **Previous Topic**. You can receive help about the Help system by selecting **Help on help**.

Press ESC at this time. (This activates the editor window.)

The Hot Keys

Turbo C++'s most common operations can be activated directly without going through the main menu. These operations are activated by use of *hot keys,* which are various key combinations that are displayed to the right of various menu entries. (You probably remember seeing some of these keys on the main menu.) These keys are ready for use whenever you need them. The hot keys are summarized in Table 2-2.

Using Turbo C++'s Context-Sensitive Help

Turbo C++'s Help system works a little differently when the F1 hot key is used to activate it than it does when you use the main menu. The difference is that when activated by pressing F1, C++'s Help system is *context sensitive.* This means that it will display help information that relates to what you are doing. Or, more specifically, it will display information that relates to the current focus of activity. For example, if the editor is currently active, then activating the Help system by pressing F1 causes information about the editor to be displayed. If a menu item is highlighted, then pressing F1 gives you information about the highlighted entry.

To see how this works, activate the main window and highlight the **Options** entry. Now press F1. As you will see, information relating to the **Options** entry is displayed. When you are done with the Help system, press ESC.

Before moving on, you might want to try the context-sensitive help feature on your own. As you will see, it is a powerful aid.

Understanding Windows

The Turbo C++ IDE is based on the *window,* which is a portion of the screen. All windows have similar characteristics. The features

Table 2-2.

Hot Key	*Meaning*
F1	Activates the online Help system
F2	Saves the file currently being edited
F3	Loads a file
F4	Executes the program until the cursor is reached
F5	Zooms the active window
F6	Switches between windows
F7	Traces program into function calls
F8	Traces program; skips function calls
F9	Compiles and links your program
F10	Activates the main menu
ALT-0	Lists open windows
ALT-*n*	Activates window *n* (*n* must be 1 through 9)
ALT-F1	Shows the previous help screen
ALT-F3	Deletes the active window
ALT-F4	Opens an Inspector window
ALT-F5	Toggles between the user screen and the IDE
ALT-F7	Previous error
ALT-F8	Next error
ALT-F9	Compiles file to .OBJ
ALT-SPACEBAR	Activates the main menu
ALT-C	Activates the **Compile** menu
ALT-D	Activates the **Debug** menu
ALT-E	Activates the **Edit** menu
ALT-F	Activates the **File** menu

The Hot Keys

Table 2-2. (*continued*)

ALT-H	Activates the **Help** menu
ALT-O	Activates the **Options** menu
ALT-P	Activates the **Project** menu
ALT-R	Activates the **Run** menu
ALT-S	Activates the **Search** menu
ALT-W	Activates the **Window** menu
ALT-X	Quits Turbo C++
CTRL-F1	Requests help about the item the cursor is on
CTRL-F2	Resets the program
CTRL-F3	Shows the function call stack
CTRL-F4	Evaluates an expression
CTRL-F5	Changes the size or location of the active window
CTRL-F7	Sets a watch expression (debugging)
CTRL-F8	Sets or clears a break point
CTRL-F9	Executes the current program

The Hot Keys

common to most windows are shown in Figure 2-9. All windows have a title, which describes what the window is being used for, and most have a number, which identifies that window. All windows also include a *zoom box* (which can enlarge or reduce the size of a window), a *close box* (with which you can remove a window), and a *resize corner* (which allows you to change the size of a window). The zoom box, close box, and resize corner may only be accessed using a mouse. (If you don't have a mouse, you can still perform the same operations, but you will use special keyboard commands.)

Figure 2-9.

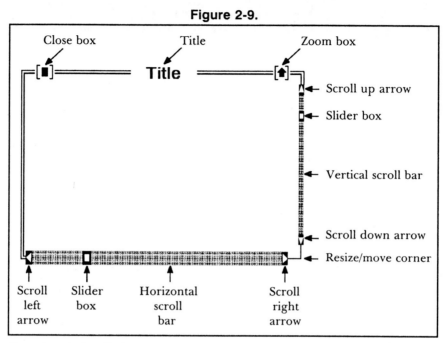

Common window features

Some windows, but not all, also have horizontal and vertical *scroll bars*. The scroll bars allow you to scroll text in the window, and they work only with a mouse. When scrolling vertically, you can scroll one line at a time by clicking on the up or down arrow of the vertical scroll bar. The slider box will move along the scroll bar, indicating your relative position in the file. If you press and hold down the left mouse button while on an arrow, a continuous scroll is produced. You can click anywhere on the scroll bar, and the corresponding location in the file will be displayed. Finally, you can drag the slider box along the bar and the text will scroll accordingly. These operations are paralleled by the horizontal scroll bar except that text is moved from side to side.

When a window is on the screen, it is said to be open. Although there may be several open windows on the screen at the same time, only one will be active. When a window is active, it is the focus of any input you generate from the keyboard. There are several ways to make a window active. First, if you know the number of the window, you can simply hold down the ALT key and press the number of the window you want. The windows are numbered 1 through 9. Pressing ALT-0 causes a list of all windows currently in use to be displayed. You may also activate a window by selecting it from this list. Or, if you have a mouse, you can activate a window simply by clicking on it.

Sizing and Moving Windows

By far the easiest way to resize or move a window is by using the mouse. To move a window, move the mouse pointer so that it is on the top border of the window. Press and hold the left button and drag the window to its new location. To change the size of a window, move the mouse pointer to the resize corner of the window, press and hold the left mouse button, and move the mouse in the appropriate direction.

If you do not have a mouse, then to resize and/or move a window, first make active the window that you want to operate on. Next, activate the **Window** main menu entry and select the **Size/Move** option. Now, using the arrow keys you can move the window around the screen. To change its size, hold down the SHIFT key while using the arrow keys.

Keep in mind that dialog boxes and menus are not windows and they cannot be resized or moved.

The Editor Window

The *editor window* is where you create the source code for your C++ programs. The title of this window is NONAME00.C. The reason for this is that when you executed Turbo C++, you did not specify any filename, so the editor automatically gave the file a temporary name. (You can change it when you save a file.) Notice that the editor window is window number 1. Keep in mind that you can have several editor windows open at any one time.

Because the editor window is a *window,* it may be moved and/or resized. You might want to experiment with changing the size or location of the editor window.

The next chapter will look more closely at the editor window.

The Message Window

The *message window* lies beneath the editor window and is used to display various compiler or linker messages. It is most commonly used to display any error messages generated by the compiler. You may move and/or resize the message window.

The Status Line

The line on the bottom of the screen is called the *status line*, and it displays a short comment relating to whatever you are currently doing. For example, when the **Window** main menu option is selected, the status line displays the following:

```
F1 Help │ Open, arrange, and list windows
```

The value of the information displayed on the status line is that it provides clues about the meaning of whatever is the current focus of the IDE.

Now that you know your way around the basics of Turbo C++'s programming environment, it is time to learn to use the editor.

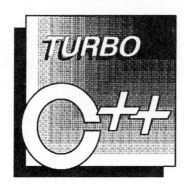

3

Using the Turbo C++ Editor

In this chapter you will learn to use the editor built into Turbo C++'s integrated programming environment. Its operation is similar to the original Turbo C editor. The main additions found in the Turbo C++ editor are that it supports the mouse, that several of the text-manipulation and search commands can be executed using menus, and that multiple edit windows can be created to allow concurrent editing of two or more files. If you already know how to use the original Turbo C editor, you may still want to skim this chapter to learn about these enhancements.

The Turbo C++ editor contains about 50 commands and is quite powerful. However, you will not have to learn all the commands at once. The most important deal with insertion, deletion, block moves, searching, and replacement. Once you have mastered these basic areas, you easily will be able to learn the rest of the editor commands and put them to use as you need them. Actually, learning to use the editor will be surprisingly simple because you will have Turbo C++'s online context-sensitive Help system at your disposal.

If the Turbo C++ IDE is not currently executing, start Turbo C++ once again by typing **tc** at the prompt.

Editor Commands

Before beginning, it is important to understand how you give commands to the Turbo C++ editor. With few exceptions, all editor commands begin with a control character. Many are then followed by another character. For example, the sequence CTRL-Q F is the command that tells the editor to find a string. (This book uses the abbreviation CTRL to stand for control.) To execute this command, hold down the control key, and then press Q followed by F in either upper- or lowercase.

Although all editor commands can be entered from the keyboard, some are also available from the main menu and some can be executed using the mouse. When menu or mouse alternatives exist, they will be pointed out.

Invoking the Editor and Entering Text

When Turbo C++ first begins executing, the editor window is active. When you activate the main menu to perform some operation, you can return to the editor window by pressing ESC.

The top line of the editor window displays the name of the file currently being edited, which is also the title of the editor window. At the bottom left of the editor window, the number of the current line and column position of the cursor are displayed.

When the editor window is active and you are not in the middle of giving it a command, then it is ready to accept input. This means that when you strike keys on the keyboard they will appear in the editor at the current cursor location.

By default, the editor is in *insert mode*. This means that as you enter text it will be inserted in the middle of whatever is already there (if anything). The opposite is called *overwrite mode*. In this mode of operation, new text can overwrite existing text. You can toggle between these two modes by pressing the INS key. You can tell which mode is currently active by the shape of the cursor. In insert mode, the cursor is represented as a blinking underscore. In overwrite mode, it is a blinking rectangle.

Make sure that the editor window is active and type the following lines:

```
This is a
test of the
Turbo C++ editor.
```

If you make a mistake, you can use BACKSPACE to correct it. Your screen will now look like the one shown in Figure 3-1. Notice the position of the cursor and the values associated with the line and column display at the lower left of the editor window. Also, notice that now an asterisk is displayed to the left of the line and column indicators. The asterisk is displayed only after a change has been made to the file.

Because the Turbo C++ editor is a *screen editor,* you can use the arrow keys to move the cursor around the text at random. Also, when you click the mouse, the cursor moves to the position of the mouse pointer. At this time, use either the arrow keys or the mouse to position the cursor at the far left side of the line that

Figure 3-1.

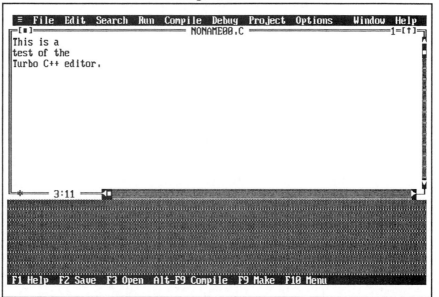

Editor screen with text entered

reads "test of the." Now type **very small** and press ENTER. As you do so, watch the way the existing line is moved to the right instead of being overwritten. This is what happens when the editor is in insert mode. If you had toggled the editor into overwrite mode, the original line would have been overwritten. Your screen will now look like Figure 3-2.

Deleting Characters, Words, and Lines

You can delete a single character in two ways: with the BACKSPACE key or with the DEL key. The BACKSPACE key deletes the character immediately to the left of the cursor while the DEL key deletes the character under the cursor.

Figure 3-2.

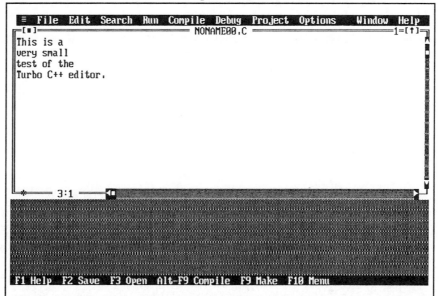

Editor screen after inserting a line

You can delete an entire word that is to the right of the cursor by typing CTRL-T. A word is any set of characters delimited by one of the following characters:

space $ / − + * ' ^ [ ] ( ) . ; , < >

You can remove an entire line by typing CTRL-Y. It does not matter where the cursor is positioned in the line—the entire line is deleted. You should try deleting a few lines and words at this time.

If you wish to delete from the current cursor position to the end of the line, type the sequence CTRL-Q Y.

Moving, Copying, and Deleting
Blocks of Text

The Turbo C++ editor allows you to manipulate a block of text. You can move or copy it to another location or delete it altogether. In order to do any of these things you must first define a block. A *block* can be as short as a single character or as large as your entire file. However, typically, a block is somewhere between these two extremes. You can define a block in two different ways: using the keyboard or using the mouse. To define a block using the keyboard, move the cursor to the start of the block and type the sequence CTRL-K B. Next, move the cursor to the end of the block and type the sequence CTRL-K K. The block that you have defined will be highlighted. To define a block using the mouse, first position the mouse pointer at the start of the block. Next, press and hold the left mouse button and move the mouse to the end of the block. Finally, release the button.

For example, move the cursor to the "t" at the start of the third line and type CTRL-K B. Next, move the cursor to the end of the last line and type CTRL-K K (or use the mouse). Your screen should look like Figure 3-3.

To move a block of text, place the cursor where you want the text to go and type the sequence CTRL-K V. This causes the previously defined block of text to be deleted from its current position and placed at the new location.

To copy a block, type the sequence CTRL-K C. For example, move the cursor to the top of the file and type CTRL-K C. Your screen will look like Figure 3-4. You should experiment with these commands at this time.

To delete the currently marked block, type the sequence CTRL-K Y. You can also execute this command by activating the **Edit** option on the main menu and then selecting the **Cut** entry. Either way you execute this command, the block you delete is automatically put into a special editor window called the *clipboard*.

Figure 3-3.

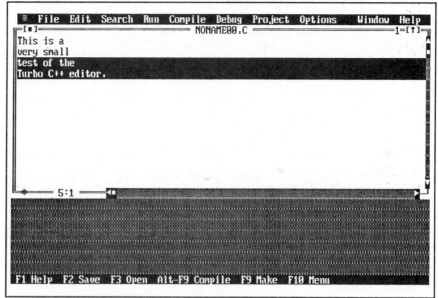

Editor screen after defining a block

Figure 3-4.

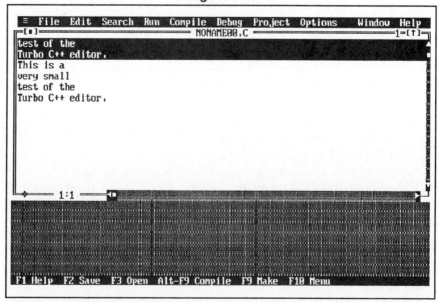

Editor screen after block move

You may mark a single word by positioning the cursor under the first character in the word and typing CTRL-K T.

To indent an entire block one character position use the command CTRL-K I. To unindent a block one character position use CTRL-K U.

Using the Clipboard

Using the **Edit** main menu options, you can make use of the clipboard to add greater flexibility to moving or copying text. Also, as you will see later on, using the clipboard you can easily move text between two editor windows.

In general, the clipboard is a temporary depository for fragments of text that have been copied from another file. To move text into the clipboard, you need to mark the region and then either delete that block or, using the **Edit** menu, select the **Copy** option. If you select **Copy**, the block is not deleted from the file, but it is still copied into the clipboard.

To retrieve a block of text from the clipboard, use the **Edit** menu **Paste** command. This causes the most recently deleted or copied block of text in the clipboard to be copied into the current editor window at the current cursor location.

You can see the contents of the clipboard by selecting the **Show clipboard** option on the **Edit** menu. This also activates the clipboard window, and you may select any part of the contents of the clipboard you desire.

If you wish to delete a block without having it copied to the clipboard, first select the block and execute the **Clear** option on the **Edit** menu. This removes the block, but does not copy it to the clipboard.

You can edit more than one file at a time by simply loading another file or selecting the **New** option in the **File** menu. This causes another editor window to be created. To copy text from one window to another, simply define the block you want in the source window, copy it to the clipboard, and then paste it into the target window.

One final point: When you activate the Help system and request information on a C++ feature, it is likely that a programming example will be included. If this is the case, you can automatically move the example code to the clipboard by selecting the **Copy example** option from the **Edit** menu.

More on Cursor Movement

The Turbo C++ editor has a number of special cursor commands. These commands are summarized in Table 3-1. You should experiment with these commands at this time. Of course, you may also move the cursor by positioning the mouse pointer at the desired location and clicking.

Find and Replace

To find a specific sequence of characters, use the CTRL-Q F command. You will then be prompted by the dialog window shown in Figure 3-5 for the string you wish to find. You can also specify various search options. The search options modify the way the search is conducted. The default setting causes the search to proceed from the current cursor position forward, with case sensitivity and substring matches allowed. Let's look at each of the search options at this time.

By default, the search for the string you enter is conducted from the current cursor location forward in the file (towards the end). You can change this so that the search proceeds in the opposite direction by selecting the **Backward** option. You can also have the search cover the entire file by selecting the **Entire scope** option.

Table 3-1.

Command	Action
CTRL-A	Moves to the start of the word that is to the left of the cursor
CTRL-S	Moves left one character
CTRL-D	Moves right one character
CTRL-F	Moves to the start of the word that is to the right of the cursor
CTRL-E	Moves the cursor up one line
CTRL-R	Moves the cursor up one full screen
CTRL-X	Moves the cursor down one line
CTRL-C	Moves the cursor down one full screen
CTRL-W	Scrolls the screen down
CTRL-Z	Scrolls the screen up
PGUP	Moves the cursor up one full screen
PGDN	Moves the cursor down one full screen
HOME	Moves the cursor to the start of the line
END	Moves the cursor to the end of the line
CTRL-Q E	Moves the cursor to the top of the screen
CTRL-Q X	Moves the cursor to the bottom of the screen
CTRL-Q R	Moves the cursor to the beginning of the file
CTRL-Q C	Moves the cursor to the end of the file
CTRL-PGUP	Moves the cursor to the beginning of the file
CTRL-PGDN	Moves the cursor to the end of the file
CTRL-HOME	Moves the cursor to the top of the screen
CTRL-END	Moves the cursor to the bottom of the screen

The Cursor Commands

By default, the search is case sensitive. This means that upper- and lowercase characters are treated as different characters. However, you can have upper- and lowercase treated as if they are the same. In this case an "a" will match an "A."

By default, if the string you enter is contained within another, larger string, this will produce a match. (This is called a *substring*

Figure 3-5.

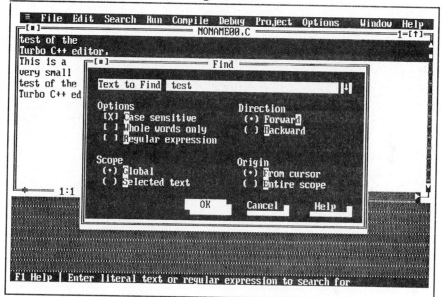

The Find dialog box

match.) For example, if you enter **is** for the search string, then the editor will find a match in the word "this." You can cause the search to match only whole words by checking the **Whole words only** box.

You can confine the search to a block by selecting the **Selected text** option.

If you check the **Regular Expression** box, then you can use the wildcard characters shown in Table 3-2 in your search string. Here are some examples:

Expression	*Matches*
h..lo	hello (and others)
^test	test (at start of line)
test$	test (at end of line)
[two]	t, w, or o
x*	x, xx, xxx, and so on

Table 3-2.

Character	Purpose
^	Matches the start of a line.
$	Matches the end of a line.
.	Matches any character.
*	Matches any number (including 0) of occurrences of the character it follows.
+	Matches any number (except 0) of occurrences of the character it follows.
[*string*]	Matches a single occurrence of any one character in *string*. You may specify a range using the hyphen. If the first character in the string is a ^, then the construct will match any characters except those in the string.
\	Causes the character it precedes to be treated literally and not as a wildcard.

The Regular Expression Wildcard Characters

Remember that to use regular expressions, you must check the **Regular expression** box in the **Find** dialog box.

You can repeat a search simply by typing CTRL-L. This is very convenient when you are looking for something specific in the file.

To activate the replace command, type CTRL-Q A. Its operation is identical to the find command except that it allows you to replace the string you are looking for with another. You will see the dialog box shown in Figure 3-6.

As you can see, the options available in the **Replace** dialog box are similar to those available with **Find**, with one addition. By default, the editor will ask you before making a change. You can turn off this feature by deselecting **Prompt on replace**.

You may enter control characters into the search string by first typing CTRL-P followed by the control character you want.

The **Find** and **Replace** options can also be activated using the **Search** main menu option.

Figure 3-6.

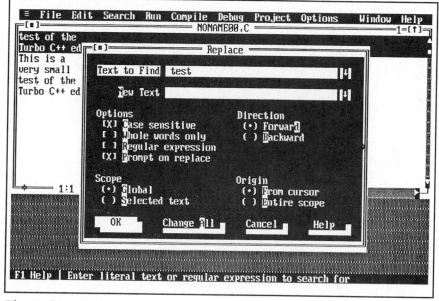

The Replace dialog box

Setting and Finding Place Markers

You can set up to four place markers in your file by typing CTRL-K
n, where *n* is the number of the place marker (0-3). After a marker
has been set, the command CTRL-Q *n,* where *n* is the marker
number, causes the cursor to go to that marker. Place markers are
especially convenient in large files.

Saving and Loading Your File

There are three ways to save your file. Two of them will save it to
a file that has the same name as that shown in the title of the editor

window. The third way allows you to save your file under a different name and then makes that the current name of your file. Let's look at how each works.

At this time exit the editor and return to the main menu by pressing F10. Select the **File** option. As you learned in Chapter 2, the **Save** option saves what is currently in the editor into a disk file by the name shown in the window title. If you have not specified a file to edit, then invoking this option will cause the file to be saved as NONAME00.C. While this does not hurt anything, you will probably want to use a different filename. To accommodate this, Turbo C++ will prompt you for a different filename. This prompt only occurs if NONAME*nn*.C is the name of the source file. Otherwise, the file is saved without further interaction.

If you wish to save the contents of the editor into a file with a name other than that shown on the editor status line, use the **Save as** option. (To access this option, **Full menus** must be On.) This allows you to enter the name of the file to which you wish to write the current contents of the editor. It also makes this the default filename. Select this option now. When prompted for the filename, enter **test**. This causes your file to be saved. You can also save your file from inside the editor by pressing the F2 key. This is the same as the **Save** option in the **File** menu.

To load a file you may either press F3 while inside the editor or select the **Open** option from the **File** menu. This causes a dialog box to be displayed, prompting for the name of the file you wish to load. There are two ways that you can specify the filename. First, you can type it in. Second, you can tab to the list of files shown in the dialog box and make a selection. By default, all files with the .C extension are displayed. If you have a mouse, you can double-click on the desired file and it will be loaded.

By default, when you save a file that already exists on disk, the old version of the file is not overwritten. Instead, it is kept as a backup file and its extension is changed to .BAK. (You can turn off automatic backup, as you will see later in this chapter.)

Understanding Auto-Indentation

As you most likely know, good programmers use indentation to help make the programs they write clearer and easier to understand. To assist in this practice, after you press ENTER, the Turbo C++ editor will automatically place the cursor at the same indentation level as the line that was previously entered, assuming that auto-indentation is on. You toggle this feature on and off by typing CTRL-O I. To see how auto-indentation works, enter the following few lines exactly as they are shown here:

```
This is an illustration
    of the auto-indentation
    mechanism
        of the Turbo C++
        editor.
```

As you enter the text, notice how Turbo C++ automatically maintains the last indentation level. You will find this feature quite handy when you are entering C++ source code.

You can turn off the auto-indentation feature by pressing CTRL-O I.

Moving Blocks of Text to and from Disk Files

It is possible to move a block of text into a disk file for later use. This is done by first defining a block and then typing CTRL-K W. After you have done this you will be prompted for the name of the file in which you wish to save the block. The original block of text is not removed from your program.

To read a block in, type the command CTRL-K R. You will be prompted for the filename. The contents of that file will be read in at the current cursor location.

These two commands are the most useful when you are moving text between two or more files, as is so often the case during program development.

Pair Matching

As you will see, there are several delimiters in C++ that work in pairs. For example, the { }, the [ ], and the ( ). In very long or complex programs, it is sometimes difficult to manually find the proper companion to a delimiter. It is possible to have the editor find the corresponding companion delimiter automatically.

The Turbo C++ editor will find the companion delimiter for the following delimiter pairs:

```
{ }
[ ]
( )
 <  >
/* */
" "
 '  '
```

To find the matching delimiter, place the cursor on the delimiter you wish to match and type CTRL-Q [for a forward match or CTRL-Q] for a backward match. The editor will move the cursor to the matching delimiter.

Some delimiters are nestable and some are not. The nestable delimiters are { }, [ ], ( ), < >, and sometimes the comment symbols (when the nested comments option is enabled). The editor will find the proper matching delimiter in accordance with C++ syntax. If for some reason the editor cannot find a proper match, the cursor will not be moved.

Miscellaneous Commands

You can abort any command that requests input by typing CTRL-U or ESC at the prompt or by clicking the mouse on a part of the screen that is outside the dialog box. For example, if you execute the **find** command and then change your mind, simply press ESC or click the mouse outside the box.

If you wish to enter a control character into the file, type CTRL-P followed by the control character you want. Control characters are displayed in either low intensity or reverse intensity depending on how your system is configured.

To undo changes made to a line before you have moved the cursor off that line, simply type CTRL-Q L. You can also undo changes to a line by selecting the **Restore line** option from the **Edit** menu. Remember that once the cursor has been moved off the line, all changes are final.

If you wish to go to the start of a block, enter CTRL-Q B. Typing CTRL-Q K takes you to the end of a block.

You print the file using the CTRL-K P command. This command prints the entire file if no block has been defined. Otherwise, it just prints the block.

One particularly useful command is CTRL-Q P, which puts the cursor back to its previous position. This is handy if you want to search for something and then return to where you were.

By default, when you press the TAB key, a tab character is entered into your file. However, using the command CTRL-O T causes an equivalent number of spaces to be inserted instead of a tab character. The CTRL-O T command is actually a toggle that lets you change between the two ways that tabs are processed.

By default, when you press the BACKSPACE key at the start of a new line, the cursor will automatically move to the left one indentation level each time it is pressed. You can toggle this feature using the CTRL-O U command. When it is off, the cursor will back up only one space each time the BACKSPACE key is pressed no matter how deeply indented it is.

Command Summary

Table 3-3 shows all the Turbo C++ editor commands.

Changing the Editor Defaults

You can change some aspects of the way the editor operates by selecting **Options** from the main menu and then selecting the **Environment** entry. Next, select the **Editor** item. (You will need to have **Full menus** turned on to do this.) You will see the dialog box shown in Figure 3-7.

The **Create backup files, Insert mode,** and **Autoindent mode** options are self-explanatory. If you turn the **Use tab character** option off, then the appropriate number of spaces will be substituted for the tab character. The **Optimal fill** option controls what characters Turbo C++ uses when it auto-indents—when on, it mixes spaces and tabs; when off, it uses spaces only. When **Backspace unindents** is on, then each time you press BACKSPACE on a blank line, the cursor backs up one indentation level. If the option is off, the cursor backs up one character each time BACKSPACE is pressed. When **Cursor through tabs** is on, when you move the

Table 3-3.

Action	Command
Cursor Commands	
Move left one character	LEFT ARROW or CTRL-S
Move right one character	RIGHT ARROW or CTRL-D
Move left one word	CTRL-A
Move right one word	CTRL-F
Move up one line	UP ARROW or CTRL-E
Move down one line	DOWN ARROW or CTRL-X
Scroll up	CTRL-W
Scroll down	CTRL-Z
Move up one page	PGUP or CTRL-R
Move down one page	PGDN or CTRL-C
Move to start of line	HOME or CTRL-Q S
Move to end of line	END or CTRL-Q D
Move to top of screen	CTRL-Q E
Move to bottom of screen	CTRL-Q X
Move to beginning of file	CTRL-Q R
Move to end of file	CTRL-Q C
Move to start of block	CTRL-Q B
Move to end of block	CTRL-Q K
Move to last cursor position	CTRL-Q P
Insert Commands	
Toggle insert mode	INS or CTRL-V
Insert a blank line	ENTER or CTRL-N
Delete Commands	
Delete entire line	CTRL-Y
Delete to end of line	CTRL-Q Y
Delete character on left	BACKSPACE
Delete character at cursor	DEL or CTRL-G
Delete word to the right	CTRL-T

Turbo C++ Editor Command Summary by Category

Table 3-3. *(continued)*

Action	Command
Block Commands	
Mark start of block	CTRL-K B
Mark end of block	CTRL-K K
Mark a word	CTRL-K T
Copy a block	CTRL-K C
Delete a block	CTRL-K Y
Hide or display a block	CTRL-K H
Move a block	CTRL-K V
Write a block to disk	CTRL-K R
Read a block from disk	CTRL-K W
Indent a block	CTRL-K I
Unindent a block	CTRL-K U
Print a block	CTRL-K P
Find Commands	
Find	CTRL-Q F
Find and replace	CTRL-Q A
Find a place marker	CTRL-Q (NUM)
Repeat find	CTRL-L
Pair Matching	
Match pair forward	CTRL-Q [
Match pair reverse	CTRL-Q]
Miscellaneous Commands	
Abort	CTRL-U or ESC
Toggle auto-indentation mode	CTRL-O I
Control character prefix	CTRL-P
Exit editor	F10
New file	F3

Turbo C++ Editor Command Summary by Category

Table 3-3. *(continued)*

Action	Command
Miscellaneous Commands	
Restore overwritten error message	CTRL-Q W
Save	F2
Set a place marker	CTRL-K (NUM)
Toggle tab mode	CTRL-O T
Undo	CTRL-Q L
Toggle backspace mode	CTRL-O U

Turbo C++ Editor Command Summary by Category

Figure 3-7.

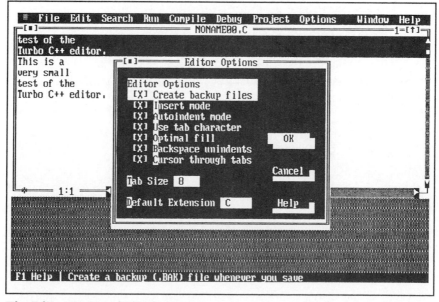

The Editor Options dialog box

cursor through a tab, it does not jump to the next tab position but moves through the tab one space at a time. When the option is off, the cursor jumps to the next tab position.

You can also change the tab size and the default filename extension.

Invoking Turbo C++ *with a Filename*

You can specify the name of the file you want to edit when you invoke Turbo C++. To do this, you simply type the name of the file after the "TC" on the command line. For example, typing **MYFILE** after "TC" will execute Turbo C++ and cause MYFILE.C to be loaded into the editor. The .C extension is added automatically by Turbo C++. If MYFILE.C does not exist, it is created. If, for some reason, you do not want to use an extension on the filename, put a period after the name. This causes Turbo C++ to not append the .C extension.

PART

II

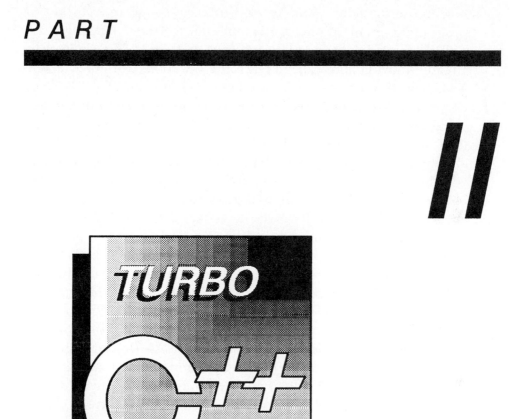

The C Language

Now that you have Turbo C++ installed on your computer, know how to use the editor, and know your way around the Turbo C++ programming environment, it is time to learn the C language.

This book is organized to address the needs of readers who already know C and want to learn the C++ object oriented extensions, and those readers who are new to both C and C++. Because C++ is a superset of C, you cannot program in C++ until you can program in C. Therefore, Part II of this book throroughly teaches the C language, and Part III discusses the C++ additions to C. If you already know C, skip to Part III at this time. If you don't know C, you should carefully work through Part II because you will need to be proficient in C in order to learn, use, and understand C++'s enhanced features.

Everything that you learn in Part II relates to both C and C++. However, those features that C++ has in common with C will be referred to as "C features." Only those features of C++ that are unique to C++ will be referred to as "C++ features." In this way, you will be able to easily identify the constructs specific to C++.

The version of C on which C++ is based is the one standardized by ANSI. Throughout this part of the book, the ANSI C standard will be referenced occasionally. The reason for this is that all ANSI standard features of C will be portable to practically any C or C++ programming environment. Any enhanced or extended features of Turbo C++ that are not part of the standard will be flagged as such so that you will know that a feature may not be portable.

For the programs presented in Part II of this book, you will need to use the .C, not .CPP, extension. This causes Turbo C++ to compile them as C, not C++ programs. The reason for this is that there are a few very minor differences between C and C++.

Before proceeding, you should know that the following notational conventions will be observed:

- Any word that is part of the Turbo C/C++ language will be printed in boldface when referred to in text.

- Any variable or function name used in a program will be printed in boldface when referred to in text.

- Descriptive words that are not part of the actual language but that are used to form a general description will be displayed in italics.

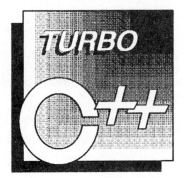

Some C
Essentials

When it comes to programming languages, the old adage "You can't learn it if you don't know it already" has never been more true. The trouble is that each element in a programming language does not exist in a void but rather in relationship to the other elements. To solve this problem, a number of simple sample programs are developed and discussed in this chapter without going into a lot of details. Also, a few essential aspects of C are presented. This chapter is designed for either the novice programmer or the programmer who has never used a structured language before. It will give you a rough idea of how C works.

Most of the material presented here will be examined more fully later, so if you already know a little about C, you may want to skip to Chapter 5 at this time.

Preparing the IDE

Before proceeding, you must change one option in the integrated development environment. As you will learn in this chapter, Turbo C++ issues two kinds of messages when it compiles your program: error messages and warning messages. You need to turn off one warning message. The reason for this is that C has so many features that it is simply not possible to present an overview of all of them in this chapter. In fact, some features require that you know quite a bit about C before you can understand why they are needed and how to use them. Although all the programs in this book are correct, those in this and the next few chapters will cause an annoying warning message to be displayed when you compile them, unless you turn it off. While this warning is useful to the experienced C programmer, it is not relevant to someone just learning C.

To turn off the warning message, follow this procedure. First, make sure that **Full menus** is on. Next, select the **Options** entry on the main menu and select the **Compiler** option. Then, choose the **Messages** option. Now, tab to the **Frequent Errors** box and select it. The first check box is called **Function should return a value**. If this box has an "X" in it (as it will by default), remove it by pressing SPACEBAR. If the box is already empty, do nothing. Finally, press the ESC key until you have backed out of all the menus.

NOTE   Be sure to keep this option off until you are told to turn it on in Chapter 9.

C Is Case Sensitive

It is important to know that C is *case sensitive*. This means that upper- and lowercase letters are treated as separate characters. For example, in some languages, the variable names **count**, **Count**, and **COUNT** are three ways of specifying the same variable. However, in C, these would be three different variables. So, when you enter the sample programs shown in this book, be very careful to use the proper case.

A Simple C Program

To begin, execute Turbo C++ and enter the following short program:

```
#include <stdio.h>

/* Sample program #1. */

main()
{
  int age;

  age = 39;

  printf("My age is %d\n", age);
}
```

Once you are done editing, press F10 to return to the main menu. To compile and run this program, select the **Run** main menu option and the **Run** submenu option (or, press CTRL-F9). Turbo C++ will then compile the program, link it with the necessary library functions (more on libraries shortly), and execute it.

As the compilation begins, Turbo C++ opens the *compiler/linker* window, which allows you to monitor the progress of the compilation. Your screen will look similar to that shown in Figure 4-1 during compilation. When the compilation is complete, the screen will clear and the line "My age is 39" followed by a carriage return-linefeed is briefly displayed. Immediately after the program terminates, the Turbo C integrated development environment is redisplayed. If you wish to examine the execution screen again, press ALT-F5 to toggle between the two screens.

Let's examine this program in detail.

A Closer Look

Take a closer look at each line in sample program #1. The first line,

```
#include <stdio.h>
```

Figure 4-1.

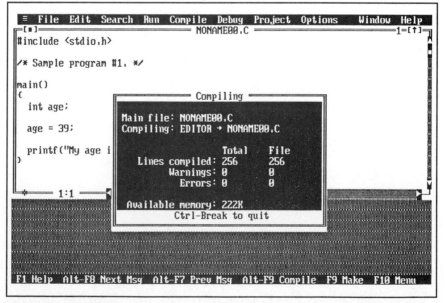

Turbo C compilation window

tells the compiler to include the file STDIO.H in the compilation. This file contains information needed by the program to ensure the correct operation of C's standard I/O library functions. Turbo C++ supplies a number of these types of files that are referred to as *header files*. Some programs will require more than one header file, so make sure that you include these lines in your program. We will discuss header files and the **#include** directive later in this book.

The second line,

```
/* Sample program #1. */
```

is a comment. In C, comments begin with the sequence /* and are terminated by */. Anything that is between the beginning and ending comment symbols is ignored by the compiler.

If you examine the sample program closely, you will notice that a blank line follows the comment line. In C, blank lines are permitted and have no effect on the program.

The line,

```
main()
```

specifies the name of a function. All C programs begin execution by calling the **main( )** function. You will learn more about functions a little later.

The next line consists of a single curly brace, which signifies the start of the **main( )** function.

The first line of code inside function **main( )** is

```
int age;
```

This line declares a variable called **age** and tells the compiler that it is an integer. In C, all variables must be declared before they are used. The declaration process involves the specification of the variable's name as well as its type. In this case, **age** is of type **int**, which is C's keyword for integer. Integers are whole numbers between −32,768 and 32,767.

The next line is

```
age = 39;
```

which is an assignment statement. It places the value 39 into the variable **age**. Notice that C uses a single equal sign for assignment. Also notice that this statement ends in a semicolon. All statements in C are terminated by a semicolon.

The next line, which outputs information to the screen, is

```
printf("My age is %d\n", age);
```

This statement is very important for two reasons. First, it is an example of a function call. Second, it illustrates the use of C's standard output function **printf( )**. This line of code consists of two parts: the function name, which is **printf( )**, and its two arguments: **"My age is %d\n"**, and **age**. Since this is a C statement, it ends in a semicolon.

In C, there are no built-in I/O routines. Instead, functions are provided by C's standard library to perform these (and other) activities. Your program simply calls the appropriate function when needed. (In fact, Turbo C++'s standard library contains many useful functions.) Programs you write can also contain functions that you create, in addition to the library functions. In either case, to call a function is quite easy: simply write its name and supply any arguments it may need. (An argument is a value passed to the function when it is called.)

The **printf( )** function works like this. The first argument is a quoted string (sometimes called the *control string*) that may contain either normal characters or format codes that begin with the percent sign. Normal characters are displayed as is on the screen in the order in which they are encountered. A format code informs **printf( )** that a non-character item is to be displayed. In this case, the **%d** means that an integer is to be output in decimal format. The value to be displayed is found in the second argument, in this case **age**. The **\n** is a special code that tells **printf( )** to issue a carriage return-linefeed sequence, called a *newline* in C terminology. To understand the relationship between the normal characters and the format codes, change the line to read

```
printf("My %d age is\n", age);
```

and rerun the program. The message now displayed is "My 39 age is." The point is that where the format command occurs in the string determines where the second argument to **printf( )** will be printed. As you will see shortly, **printf( )** is substantially more powerful than is illustrated by this example.

The last line of the program is a closing curly brace and it signals the end of the **main( )** function. When the end of the **main( )** function is reached, program execution is terminated.

Handling Errors

Using the editor, remove the semicolon that terminates the line "age = 39." Try to compile the program. As you would expect, errors are generated. They are displayed in the message window. Your screen will look like Figure 4-2. Notice that the error is highlighted in the message window and a block cursor is positioned at the point in the program where Turbo C++ detects the error. Remember, the compiler tries to make sense out of whatever you give it, so the point at which an error will be detected might be one line after it occurred because that is where Turbo C++ finally decided you made a mistake.

Figure 4-2.

```
≡  File  Edit  Search  Run  Compile  Debug  Project  Options    Window  Help
┌─────────────────────────── NONAME00.C ──────────────────────────1────┐
│#include <stdio.h>                                                     │
│                                                                       │
│/* Sample program #1. */                                              │
│                                                                       │
│main()                                                                 │
│{                                                                      │
│  int age;                                                             │
│                                                                       │
│  age = 39                                                             │
│                                                                       │
│  printf("My age is %d\n", age);                                      │
│}                                                                      │
│                                                                       │
│                                                                       │
│ ── 11:1 ──                                                            │
├─[■]═══════════════════════ Message ════════════════════════2═[↑]═─┤
│Compiling C:\TC\NONAME00.C:                                           ▲│
│Error C:\TC\NONAME00.C 11: Expression syntax in function main()       ││
│                                                                       ││
│                                                                       ││
│                                                                      ▼│
│◄─                                                                   ─►│
│ F1 Help  Space View source  ◄┘ Edit source  F10 Menu                 │
└───────────────────────────────────────────────────────────────────────┘
```

A compilation with errors

One of the nicest things about the Turbo C++ integrated environment is that you can interactively fix the errors in your program. By pressing ALT-F8 you can advance to the next error. Pressing ALT-F7 takes you to the previous error. Pressing ENTER activates the editor. You should fix your program at this time.

Errors Versus Warnings

C was designed to be a very forgiving language and to allow virtually anything that is syntactically correct to be compiled. However, some things, even though syntactically correct, are suspicious. When Turbo C++ encounters one of these situations, it prints a warning. You, as the programmer, then decide whether its suspicions are justified. As long as you are using Turbo C++'s default settings and turned off the one warning message discussed earlier, the programs in this book should not generate any warning errors. Sometimes spurious warning messages are generated as a side effect of a real error, but you will undoubtedly encounter several legitimate warnings as you continue to write C programs.

In addition to warning messages, there are options in Turbo C++ that cause additional information about your program to be displayed while it is being compiled. This information is also displayed in the form of a warning message even though there is technically nothing to warn you against. The option that you turned off at the start of this chapter falls into this category. The information that it reports about your program may be useful to you when you are an experienced C programmer, but it is not relevant to the programs that you are currently writing.

A Second Program

Although the first sample program illustrated some important aspects about C, it was fairly pointless. The second sample program does something that is useful: it converts from feet to meters. In doing so it also illustrates a second library function called **scanf( )**, which is used to read information entered by the user at the keyboard. Enter the following program into your computer now:

```
#include <stdio.h>

/* Sample program #2 - feet to meters. */

main()
{
  int feet;
```

```
    float meters;

    printf("Enter number of feet: ");

    scanf("%d", &feet);

    meters = feet * 0.3048; /* feet to meters conversion */

    printf("%d feet is %f meters\n", feet, meters);
}
```

Some important new things are introduced. First, two variables are declared: **feet** is an integer; and **meters** is of type **float**, which means that it can have a fractional component. This is called a *floating-point* number.

The library function **scanf( )** is used to read an integer entered at the keyboard. The **%d** in the first argument tells **scanf( )** to read an integer, and to place the results in the variable that follows. The **&** in front of **feet** is necessary for **scanf( )** to work properly, but you will have to take this on faith until you know more about how C works.

Next, the number of feet is converted to meters. Notice that even though **feet** is an integer, it may be divided by a floating-point number and assigned to a floating-point variable. Unlike many other modern languages, C allows different types of data to be mixed in an expression. As with virtually all other programming languages, the * signifies multiplication.

The conversion is displayed using a call to **printf( )**. As you can see, this time **printf( )** takes three arguments: the control string, and the variables **feet** and **meters**. The general rule for **printf( )** is that there are as many arguments following the control string as there are format codes in the control string. Since there are two format codes, two additional arguments are needed. These arguments are matched in order, from left to right, with the format commands. If you look closely, you will notice that a **%f** is used to print **meters**, not a **%d**. This is because **printf( )** must know precisely what type of data it is going to display. The **%f** means that a value of type **float** follows.

A Variation

One limitation to sample program #2 is that it can only convert whole numbers of feet into meters. A more flexible program would also be able to convert floating-point values into meters. This can be accomplished by changing the program as shown here:

```
#include <stdio.h>

/* Sample program #2, 2nd version - feet to meters. */

main()
{
  float feet, meters;   /* make feet a float */

  printf("Enter number of feet: ");

  scanf("%f", &feet);   /* read a float */

  meters = feet * 0.3048; /* feet to meters conversion */

  printf("%f feet is %f meters\n", feet, meters);
}
```

As you can see, the first thing that has been changed is that **feet** is now of type **float**. Notice that you can declare several variables of the same type by using a comma-separated list. Next, the **scanf( )** statement is called using a **%f** instead of a **%d** format code. This causes it to read a floating-point variable. (Do you notice the similarity between the **printf( )** and **scanf( )** format codes? They are the same.) Finally, the **printf( )** statement now needs a **%f** format code to display the **feet**.

A Quick Review

Before proceeding, let's review the most important things that you have learned.

- All C programs must have a **main( )** function—it is there that program execution begins.

- All variables must be declared before they are used.

- C supports a variety of data types, including integer and floating point.

- The **printf( )** function is used to output information to the screen.

- The **scanf( )** function reads information from the keyboard.

- Program execution stops when the end of **main( )** is encountered.

What Is a C Function?

The C language is based on the concept of building blocks. The building blocks are called *functions*. A C program is a collection of one or more functions. To write a program, you first create functions and then put them together.

In C, a function is a subroutine that contains one or more C statements and performs one or more tasks. In well-written C code, each function performs only one task. Each function has a name and a list of arguments that it will receive. In general, you can give a function whatever name you please, with the exception of **main**, which is reserved for the function that begins execution of your program. (Of course, no function can have the same name as a reserved word.)

When denoting functions, this book will use a notational convention that has become standard when writing about C. A function will have parentheses after the function name. For example, if a function's name is **max** then it will be written **max( )** when referred to in text. This notation will help you distinguish variable names from function names in this book.

You can create other functions in much the same way that you created the **main( )** function and call them from other parts of your program. For example, this program uses the function **hello( )** to print "hello" on the screen:

```
#include <stdio.h>

/* A simple program with two functions. */

main()
{
  hello(); /* call the hello function */
}

hello()
{
  printf("hello\n");
}
```

Functions with Arguments

A function argument is simply a value that is passed to the function at the time that it is called. You have already seen two functions that take arguments: **printf( )** and **scanf( )**. You can create functions that take arguments, too. For example, the function **sqr( )** in this program takes an integer argument and displays its square:

```
#include <stdio.h>

/* A program that uses a function with an argument. */

main()
{
  int num;

  num = 100;

  sqr(num);  /* call sqr() with num */
```

```
}

sqr(int x)   /* parameter declaration is inside parentheses */
{
  printf("%d squared is %d\n", x, x*x);
}
```

As you can see in the declaration of **sqr( )**, the variable **x** that will receive the value passed to **sqr( )** is declared inside the parentheses that follow the function name. (Functions that don't take arguments don't need any variables so the parentheses are empty.) When **sqr( )** is called, the value of **num**—in this case, 100—is passed to **x**. This causes the line "100 squared is 10000" to be displayed. You should enter this program to convince yourself that it does, indeed, operate as expected.

It is important to keep two terms straight. First, *argument* refers to the value that is used to call a function. The variable that receives the value of the arguments used in the function call is called a *formal parameter* of the function. In fact, functions that take arguments are called *parameterized functions*. The important thing is that the variable used as an argument in a function call has nothing to do with the formal parameter that receives its value.

Another simple example of a parameterized function is shown here. The function **mul( )** prints the product of its two integer arguments. Notice that the parameters to **mul( )** are declared using a comma-separated list.

```
#include <stdio.h>

/* Another example of function arguments. */

main()
{
  mul(10, 11);
}

mul(int a, int b)
{
  printf("%d", a*b);
}
```

REMEMBER   The type of an argument used to call a function must be the same type as the formal parameter receiving that argument. For example, you should not try to call **mul( )** with two floating-point arguments. (As you will learn, C provides for some automatic type conversions that allow some flexibility in this area, but it is best when beginning to always make sure that the type of the argument matches the type of the parameter.)

Functions Returning Values

Before leaving this discussion of functions it is necessary to lightly touch on function return values. Many of the C library functions that you will use return a value. In C, a function may return a value to the calling routine using the **return** keyword. To illustrate, the previous program that prints the product of two numbers can be rewritten like this. Notice that the return value is assigned to a variable by placing the function on the right side of an assignment statement.

```
#include <stdio.h>

/* A program that uses return. */

main()
{
  int answer;

  answer = mul(10, 11); /* assign return value */

  printf("The answer is %d\n", answer);
}

/* This function returns a value */
mul(int a, int b)
{
  return a*b;
}
```

In this example, **mul( )** returns the value of **a∗b** using the **return** statement. This value is then assigned to **answer**. That is, the value returned by the **return** statement becomes **mul( )**'s value in the calling routine.

 CAUTION   Just as there are different types of variables, there are different types of return values. Make sure that the variable receiving a function's return value is the same type as that returned by the function. The type returned by the **mul( )** routine is **int** by default. (Later, you will see how to return values of different types.)

It is possible to cause a function to return by using the **return** statement without any value attached to it, making the returned value undefined. Also, there can be more than one **return** in a function.

The General Form of a Function

The general form of a C function is shown here:

return-type function-name (parameter list)
{
   body of code
}

For functions without parameters, there will be no parameter list.

Two Simple Commands

In order to understand the examples in the next few chapters it is necessary to understand, in their simplest form, two C commands:

the **if** and the **for**. In later chapters these commands will be explored more thoroughly.

The if

The C **if** statement operates in much the same way as an IF statement operates in any other language. Its simplest form is

if(*condition*) *statement;*

where *condition* is an expression that evaluates to either true or false. In C, true is nonzero and false is zero. This fragment prints the phrase "10 is less than 11" on the screen.

```
if(10 < 11) printf("10 is less than 11");
```

The comparison operators are similar to those in other languages, such as < for less than and or >= for greater than or equal to. However, in C, the equality operator is ==. Therefore, this statement does not print the message "hello."

```
if(10==11) printf("hello"):
```

The for Loop

The **for** loop in C can operate much like the FOR loop in other languages, including Turbo Pascal and BASIC. Its simplest form is

for(*initialization, condition, increment*) *statement;*

where *initialization* is used to set the loop control variable to an initial value. *Condition* is an expression that is tested each time the loop repeats. As long as it is true (nonzero), the loop keeps running. The *increment* portion increments the loop control variable. For example, this program prints the numbers 1 through 100 on the screen:

```
#include <stdio.h>

/* A program that illustrates the for loop. */

main()
{
  int count;

  for(count=1; count<=100; count++) printf("%d ", count);
}
```

As you can see, **count** is initialized to 1. Each time the loop repeats, the condition **count< =100** is tested. If it is true, the **printf( )** statement is executed and **count** is increased by one. The two plus signs after **count** tell C to increment **count** by one each time through the loop. When **count** is greater than 100, the condition is false and the loop stops.

Blocks of Code

Because C is a structured language it supports the creation of blocks of code. A *code block* is a logically connected group of program statements that is treated as a unit. In C, a code block is created by placing a sequence of statements between opening and closing braces. In the example

```
if(x<10) {
  printf("too low, try again");
  scanf("%d", &x);
}
```

the two statements after the **if** and between the braces are both executed if **x** is less than 10. These two statements together with the braces represent a block of code. They are a logical unit: one of the statements cannot execute without the other also executing. In C, the target of most commands may be either a single statement or a code block. Not only do code blocks allow many algorithms to be implemented with greater clarity, elegance, and efficiency, but they also help the programmer to conceptualize the true nature of the routine.

Characters and Strings

Another very important data type in C is **char**, which stands for character. A character is a one-byte value that can be used to hold printable characters or integers in the range of 0 through 255. A character constant is enclosed between single quotes. For example, this program prints the letters "ABC" on the screen. Notice that a new **printf( )** format code is introduced, which prints a single character.

```
#include <stdio.h>

/* A simple example using characters. */

main()
{
  char ch;

  ch = 'A';
  printf("%c", ch);

  ch = 'B';
  printf("%c", ch);

  ch = 'C';
  printf("%c", ch);
}
```

Although it is possible to use **scanf( )** to read a single character from the keyboard, a more common way is to use Turbo C++'s library function **getche( )**. The **getche( )** function waits until a key is pressed and then returns the result. For example, this program will print "you pressed my magic key" if you type an **H**.

```
#include <stdio.h>
#include <conio.h>

main()
{
  char ch;

  ch = getche();  /* read one character from the keyboard */

  if(ch=='H') printf("you pressed my magic key\n");
}
```

This program also illustrates that characters can be used in **if** statements.

Strings

In C, a *string* is an array of characters terminated by a null. (In C, a null is essentially the same as a 0.) C does not have a string type, per se. Instead, you declare an array of characters and use the various string functions found in the library to manipulate them. Although the subject of arrays is discussed later in this book, here you will be shown a few basic principles.

In C, an array may have from one to several dimensions, but this chapter is only concerned with one-dimensional arrays. A one-dimensional array is a list of variables of the same type. You create such an array by placing the size of the array, enclosed between square brackets, after the array name. The following fragment declares an 80-element character array called **str**.

```
char str[80];
```

To reference a specific element, place the index between brackets after the array name. All arrays in C are indexed from zero. Therefore, **str[0]** is the first element, **str[1]** is the second element, and **str[79]** is the 80th and last element.

The single most important thing you should remember about arrays in C is that there is no bounds checking performed. This means that it is possible, if you are not careful, for your program to "run off the end" of an array. For now, the easiest way to prevent this is to always use an array that is large enough to hold what will be put into it. Remember that all strings end in a null. So your array must be at least one character larger than the largest string it is going to hold in order for the null terminator to fit. In C, a null is specified as the character constant '\0'. Therefore, in order for a character array to be large enough to hold the word "hello," it will need to be at least six characters long: five for the string and one for the null terminator, as shown here:

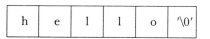

To read a string from the keyboard, first create a character array to hold the string and then use the library function **gets( )**. The **gets( )** function takes the name of the string as an argument and reads characters from the keyboard until the ENTER key is pressed. The ENTER is not stored but is replaced by the null terminator. The following program illustrates this principle:

```
#include <stdio.h>

/* A string example. */

main()
{
  char str[80];

  printf("enter your name: ");
```

```
  gets(str);

  printf("hello %s", str);
}
```

Notice that the format code **%s** is used to tell **printf( )** that a string should be printed.

printf( ): A Quick Review

Nearly every program example in Part II of this book that performs console output will use the **printf( )** function. You have already seen several examples in the preceding programs. Let's take a more formal look at it now.

The general form of **printf( )** is

printf("*control string*", *argument list*)

In the **printf( )** function, the control string contains either characters to be displayed on the screen, or format codes that specify how to display the rest of the arguments, or both. These are the format codes that you have learned so far:

Code	Meaning
%d	Display an integer in decimal format
%f	Display a float in decimal format
%c	Display a character
%s	Display a string

There are several other format codes that will be explained later.

Format control commands may be embedded anywhere in the control string. When you call **printf( )**, the control string is scanned. All regular characters are simply printed on the screen as is. When a format code is encountered, **printf( )** remembers it and uses it when printing the appropriate argument. Format codes and arguments are matched left to right. The number of format codes in the control string tells **printf( )** how many subsequent arguments to expect.

The following examples show the **printf( )** function in action:

```
printf("%s %d", "this is a string ", 100);
```

displays:

```
this is a string 100
```

```
printf("this is a string %d", 100);
```

displays:

```
this is a string 100
```

```
printf("number %d is decimal, %f is float.", 10, 110.789);
```

displays:

```
number 10 is decimal, 110.789 is float.
```

```
printf("%s", "HELLO\n");
```

displays:

```
HELLO
```

You *must* have the same number of arguments as you have format codes in the control string. If you don't, either you will get garbage on the screen or information won't be displayed.

scanf( ): A Quick Review

The **scanf( )** function is one of C's input functions. Although it can be used to read virtually any type of data entered at the keyboard, often you will use it to input integers or floating-point numbers. The general form of **scanf( )** is

scanf("*control string*", *argument list*);

For now, assume that the control string may only contain format codes. (In fact, until you study **scanf( )** in detail later, don't put anything in the control string other than the format codes or you will probably confuse it.) The two codes you will need are **%d** and **%f,** which tell **scanf( )** to read an integer and a floating-point number, respectively. The argument list must contain exactly the same number of arguments as there are format codes in the control string. Should this not be the case, various things could occur—including a program crash! The variables following the control string will contain the values you entered at the keyboard after the call to **scanf( )** returns.

The variables that will receive the values read from the keyboard must be preceded by an **&** in the argument list. It is too complicated to explain why this is necessary at this time except to say that it lets **scanf( )** place a value into the argument.

Semicolons, Braces, and Comments

You may have been wondering why so many statements are terminated with a semicolon. In C, the semicolon is a *statement terminator*. That is, each individual statement must be ended with a semicolon. It indicates the end of one logical entity. (For those of you who know Pascal, be careful. The semicolon in Pascal is a statement *separator;* in C it is a statement *terminator*).

In C, a *block* is a set of logically connected statements, which are inside opening and closing braces. If you consider a block as a group of statements, it makes sense that the block is not followed by a semicolon.

C does not recognize the end of the line as a terminator. This means there are no constraints on the position of statements. This makes it easier to group or separate statements for visual clarity, as shown by these two equivalent code fragments:

```
x = y;

y = y+1;

mul(x, y);
```

This is the same as

```
x = y;
y = y+1;
mul(x, y);
```

Comments in C may be placed anywhere in a program and are enclosed between two markers. The starting comment marker is **/*** and the ending comment marker is ***/**. In ANSI standard C comments cannot be nested. For example, the following comment within a comment will generate a compile time error:

```
/* this is /* an error */ */
```

Turbo C++ does have an option that allows nested comments but using it will render your code non-portable.

Indentation Practices

As you will have noticed from the previous examples, certain statements are indented. Since C does not care where you place statements relative to each other on a line you are free to format your programs to your choosing. However, over the years, a common and accepted indentation style has developed that allows for very readable programs. This book will follow that style and it is recommended that you do as well. Using this style, you indent one level after each opening brace and back up one level at each closing brace. There are certain statements that encourage some additional indenting, and these will be covered later.

Sometimes, in a particularly complex routine, the indentation is so great that the lines of code begin to wrap around. To avoid this, you can break a statement into two parts and put them on separate lines. For example, the following is perfectly valid:

```
count = 10 * unit /
       amount_left;
```

In general, you can break a line wherever you can place a space. You should break lines only when necessary, however, because it does tend to confuse anyone reading the code.

The C Library

The C library and library functions have been mentioned frequently in this chapter. All C compilers have a library that provides functions to perform the most commonly needed tasks. The designers of Turbo C++ have implemented a library that exceeds that defined in the ANSI standard for C. It contains most of the general-purpose functions that you will use. You should take a look at the section of the Turbo C++ user manual that describes these functions because they can save you the trouble of reinventing them. Throughout this book, library functions will be introduced as needed. Appendix A discusses the most important ones.

When you use a function that is not part of the program you wrote, the compiler "remembers" its name. When the linker takes over, it finds the missing function and adds it to your object code. The functions that are kept in the library are in *relocatable* format. This means that the memory addresses for the various machine code instructions have not been absolutely defined; instead, only offset information has been stored. When your program links with the functions in the standard library, these memory offsets are used to create the actual addresses used. There are several technical manuals and books that explain this process in detail. However, you do not need any further explanation of the actual relocation process in order to program in C.

Table 4-1.

auto	double	int	struct
break	else	long	switch
case	enum	register	typedef
char	extern	return	union
const	float	short	unsigned
continue	for	signed	void
default	goto	sizeof	volatile
do	if	static	while

The 32 Keywords as Defined by the ANSI C Standard

The C Keywords

C, like all other programming languages, consists of keywords and syntax rules that apply to each keyword. A keyword is essentially a command and, to a great extent, the keywords of a language define what can be done and how it will be done.

Turbo C++ supports the entire set of keywords specified by the ANSI C standard. These are listed in Table 4-1.

Turbo C++ has 16 additional keywords that are used to take better advantage of the memory organization of the 8088/8086 family of processors, and three that give support for interlanguage programming and interrupts. These extended keywords are shown in Table 4-2.

All C keywords are lowercase. As stated earlier, C is case sensitive; hence, **else** is a keyword, ELSE is not. A keyword may not be used for any other purpose in a Turbo C program. For example, it may not be used as the name of a variable.

Table 4-2.

asm	cdecl
_cs	_ds
_es	_export
far	huge
interrupt	_loadds
near	pascal
_regparam	_saveregs
_seg	_ss

The Extended Keywords

Review of Terms

Before continuing, you should review these terms:

- *Source code*   The text of a program that a user can read; commonly thought of as "the program."

- *Object code*   Translation of the source code of a program into machine code, which the computer can read and execute directly.

- *Linker*   A program that links separately compiled functions together into one program; used to combine the functions in the standard C library with the code that you wrote.

- *Library*   A collection of standard functions that may be used by your program. These functions include all I/O operations as well as other useful routines.

- *Compile time*   The events that occur while your program is being compiled. A common compile-time occurrence is a syntax error.

- *Run time*   The events that occur while your program is executing.

5

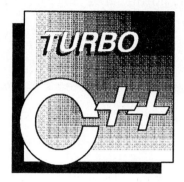

Variables, Constants, Operators, and Expressions

Variables and constants are manipulated by operators to form expressions. These are the underpinnings of the C language. Before you can go much further in your study, it is necessary to understand the concepts presented in this chapter. Unlike other computer languages, notably BASIC, which have a very simple (and limited) approach to variables, operators, and expressions, C gives much greater power and importance to these elements.

Although you might feel the desire to skip ahead to the meat of the language, you are urged not to do so because this chapter presents some very important principles.

Identifier Names

The C language defines the names that are used to reference variables, functions, labels, and various other user-defined objects as *identifiers*. An identifier in C can vary from one to several characters. The first character must be a letter or an underscore with subsequent characters being letters, numbers, or the underscore. Here are some examples of correct and incorrect identifier names:

Correct	*Incorrect*
count	1count
test23	hi!there
high_balance	high..balance

In Turbo C, the first 32 characters of an identifier name are significant. This means that if two variables have the first 32 characters in common and differ only on the 33rd, Turbo C will not be able to tell them apart. For example, these two identifiers,

this_is_a_very_long_name_used_as_an_example
this_is_a_very_long_name_used_as_an_example_too

will appear like this to Turbo C:

this_is_a_very_long_name_used_as

In Turbo C++, however, identifiers may be any length.

As you should remember, in C, upper- and lowercase characters are treated as different and distinct from one another. Hence, **count**, **Count**, and **COUNT** are three separate identifiers.

An identifier may not be the same as a keyword, and it should not have the same name as a function—a function you wrote or functions in the C library.

Data Types

As you saw in Chapter 4, all variables in C must be declared prior to their use. This is necessary because the compiler must know what type of data a variable is before it can properly compile any statement that uses it. In C there are five basic data types: character, integer, floating point, double floating point, and (somewhat surprisingly) valueless. The keywords used to declare variables of these types are **char**, **int**, **float**, **double**, and **void**, respectively. For Turbo C++ for the IBM PC, the size and range of each data type are shown in Table 5-1.

Table 5-1.

Type	Bit Width	Range
char	8	−128 to 127
int	16	−32768 to 32767
float	32	3.4E−38 to 3.4E+38
double	64	1.7E−308 to 1.7E+308
void	0	valueless

Size and Range of Turbo C++'s Basic Data Types

Variables of type **char** are used to hold 8-bit ASCII characters such as "A", "B", "C", or any other 8-bit quantity. Variables of type **int** can hold integer quantities that do not require a fractional component. Variables of this type are often used for controlling loops and conditional statements. Variables of the types **float** and **double** are employed when either a fractional component is required or when your application requires very large or very small numbers. The difference between a **float** and a **double** variable is the magnitude of the largest (and smallest) number that they can hold. As Table 5-1 shows, a **double** can store a number many times larger than a **float**. The purpose of the **void** type is discussed later in this book.

Type Modifiers

With the exception of type **void**, the basic data types may have various *modifiers* preceding them. A modifier is used to alter the meaning of the base type to more precisely fit the needs of various situations. A list of modifiers is shown here:

    signed
    unsigned
    long
    short

The modifiers **signed**, **unsigned**, **long**, and **short** may be applied to character and integer base types. However, **long** may also be applied to **double**. Table 5-2 shows all allowed combinations of the basic types and the type modifiers.

Although allowed, the use of **signed** for integers is redundant because the default integer declaration assumes a signed number.

The difference between signed and unsigned integers is in the way the high-order bit of the integer is interpreted. If a signed

Table 5-2.

Type	Bit Width	Range
char	8	−128 to 127
unsigned char	8	0 to 255
signed char	8	−128 to 127
int	16	−32768 to 32767
unsigned int	16	0 to 65535
signed int	16	−32768 to 32767
short int	16	−32768 to 32767
unsigned short int	16	0 to 65535
signed short int	16	−32768 to 32767
long int	32	−2147483648 to 2147483647
signed long int	32	−2147483648 to 2147483647
unsigned long int	32	0 to 4294967295
float	32	3.4E−38 to 3.4E+38
double	64	1.7E−308 to 1.7E+308
long double	80	3.4E−4932 to 1.1E+4932

All Possible Combinations of Turbo C++'s Basic Types and Modifiers

integer is specified, then the Turbo C compiler will generate code that assumes the high-order bit of an integer is to be used as a *sign flag*. If the sign flag is 0, then the number is positive; if it is 1, then the number is negative. Negative numbers are represented using the *two's complement* approach. In this method, all bits in the number (except the sign flag) are reversed and then one is added to this number. Finally, the sign flag is set to 1.

Signed integers are important for a great many algorithms, but they have only half the absolute magnitude of their unsigned brothers. For example, here is 32,767 in binary:

0 1 1 1 1 1 1 1   1 1 1 1 1 1 1 1

If the high-order bit was set to 1, the number would then be interpreted as −1 (assuming two's complement format). However, if you declared this to be an **unsigned int**, then when the high-order bit is set to 1, the number becomes 65,535.

To understand the difference between the way that signed and unsigned integers are interpreted, you should run this short program now:

```
#include <stdio.h>

/* Show the difference between signed and unsigned
   integers.
*/
main()
{
  int i;    /* a signed integer */
  unsigned int j; /* an unsigned integer */

  j = 60000;
  i = j;
  printf("%d %u", i, j);
}
```

When this program is run, the output is −5536 60000. The reason for this is that the bit pattern that represents 60000 as an unsigned integer is interpreted as −5536 by a signed integer. As you know, the **%d** tells **printf( )** to display an integer in decimal form. The **%u** is another format code that tells **printf( )** that an **unsigned int** is to be displayed.

C allows a shorthand notation for declaring **unsigned**, **short**, or **long** integers. You may simply use the word **unsigned**, **short**, or **long** without the **int**. The **int** is implied. For example,

```
unsigned x;
unsigned int y;
```

both declare unsigned integer variables.

Variables of type **char** may be used to hold values other than just the ASCII character set. A **char** variable can also be used as a "small" integer with the range −128 through 127, and can be used in place of an integer when the situation does not require larger numbers. For example, the following program uses a **char** variable to control the loop that prints the alphabet on the screen:

```
/* This program prints the alphabet. */

#include <stdio.h>

main()
{
  char letter;

  for(letter = 'A'; letter <= 'Z'; letter ++)
    printf("%c ", letter);
}
```

If the **for** loop seems weird to you, keep in mind that the character "A" is represented inside the computer as a number and that the values from A to Z are sequential in ascending order.

Declaring Variables

The general form of a variable-declaration statement is shown here:

  type variable_list;

Here, *type* must be a valid C data type and *variable_list* may consist of one or more identifier names with comma separators. Some declarations are shown here, for example:

```
int i, j, l;

short int si;

unsigned int ui;

double balance, profit, loss;
```

Unlike some other computer languages, in C, the name of a variable has nothing to do with its type.

Where Variables Are Declared

Where a variable is declared has a great effect on how that variable can be used by the other parts of your program. The rules that determine how a variable can be used, based upon where it has been declared, are called the *scope rules* of the language. A complete discussion of these rules and their ramifications will have to wait until you know a little bit more about C, but the basics will be covered here.

There are three places in a C program where variables can be declared. The first is outside of all functions, including the **main( )** function. This sort of variable is called *global* and may be used by any part of your program. The second place a variable may be declared is inside a function. Variables declared in this way are called *local* variables and may be used only by statements that are also in the same function. In essence, a local variable is known only to the code inside its function and unknown outside that function.

The last place that variables are declared is in the declaration of the formal parameters of a function. (If you recall from Chapter 4, the formal parameters are used to receive the arguments when that function is called.) Aside from performing the special service of receiving the information that is passed to a function, these parameters act like any other local variables. Figure 5-1 shows a short program that declares variables at each place and produces the following output:

```
..........the current sum is 0
..........the current sum is 1
..........the current sum is 3
..........the current sum is 6
```

```
.........the current sum is 10
.........the current sum is 15
.........the current sum is 21
.........the current sum is 28
.........the current sum is 36
.........the current sum is 45
```

As you can see, the global variable **sum** may be accessed by any function in the program. However, the local variable **count** in

Figure 5-1.

```
/* Sum the numbers 0 through 9. */
#include <stdio.h>
int sum;  ◄─────────────────────────── Global variable

main()
{
  int count ◄──────────────────────────── Local variable

  sum = 0; /* initialize */
  for(count=0; count<10; count++) {
    total(count);
    display();
  }
}

/* add to running total */
total(int x) ◄──────────────────────────── Formal parameter
{
  sum = x + sum;
}
display()

{         ┌─────────────────────────────── Local variable
  int count; /* this count is different from
              the one in main()
          */
  for(count=0; count<10; count++) printf(".");
  printf("the current sum is %d\n", sum);
}
```

Using global and local variables

main( ) cannot be directly accessed by **total( )** and must be passed as an argument. This is necessary because a local variable can only be used by code in the same function in which the variable is declared. Finally, note that the **count** in **display( )** is completely separate from the **count** in **main( )**. Again, because a local variable is known only to the function in which it is declared, C treats the **count** in **main( )** as a completely separate variable from the one in **display( )**.

There are two very important things about variables that you need to understand. First, no two global variables may have the same name. If they did, the compiler would not know which one to use. Trying to declare two global variables with the same name will cause an error message. Second, a local variable in one function may have the same name as variables in another function without conflict. The reason for this is that the code and data inside one function are completely separate from that in another function. Stated simply, the statements inside one function have no knowledge about the statements inside another function. Of course, no two variables within the same function can have the same name. After a few more chapters, once you know more about functions, these basic concepts will be expanded and elaborated.

Constants

In C, *constants* refer to fixed values that may not be altered by the program. For the most part, constants and their usage are so intuitive that they have been used in one form or another by all the preceding sample programs. However, the time has come to cover them formally.

Constants can be of any of the basic data types. The way each constant is represented depends upon its type. *Character constants* are enclosed between single quotes. For example, ′**a**′ and ′**%**′ are both character constants. *Integer constants* are specified as numbers without fractional components. For example, **10** and **−100** are integer constants. *Floating-point constants* require the use of the decimal point followed by the number's fractional component. For example, **11.123** is a floating-point constant. Some further examples are shown here:

Data Type	*Constant Examples*
char	'a' ' \n' '9'
int	1 123 21000 −234
long int	35000 −34
short int	10 −12 90
unsigned int	10000 987 40000
float	123.23 4.34e−3
double	123.23 12312333 −0.9876324

Hexadecimal and Octal Constants

As you probably know, in programming it is sometimes easier to use a number system based on 8 or 16 instead of 10. The number system based on 8 is called *octal* and it uses the digits 0 through 7. In octal the number 10 is the same as 8 in decimal. The base 16 number system is called *hexadecimal* and uses the digits 0 through 9 plus the letters A through F, which stand for 10, 11, 12, 13, 14, and 15. For example, the hexadecimal number 10 is 16 in decimal. Because of the frequency with which these two number systems are used, C allows you to specify integer constants in hexadecimal or octal instead of decimal if you prefer. A hexadecimal constant must begin with "0x" (a zero followed by an x), followed by the constant in hexadecimal form. An octal constant begins with a zero. Here are some examples:

```
hex = 0xFF;    /* 255 in decimal */

oct = 011;     /* 9 in decimal */
```

String Constants

C supports one other type of constant in addition to those of the predefined data types: the string. A *string* is a set of characters enclosed by double quotes. For example, **"this is a test"** is a string. You have seen examples of strings in some of the **printf( )** statements in the sample programs.

You must not confuse strings with characters. A single character constant is enclosed by single quotes, for example ′**a**′. However, ″**a**″ is a string containing only one letter.

Backslash Character Constants

Enclosing all character constants in single quotes works for most printing characters, but a few, such as the carriage return, are impossible to enter into a string from the keyboard. For this reason, C provides the special *backslash character constants*. These codes are shown in Table 5-3.

You use a backslash code in exactly the same way as you would any other character. For example:

```
ch = '\t';

printf("this is a test\n");
```

This code fragment first assigns a tab to **ch** and then prints "this is a test" on the screen followed by a new line. You will see more examples of the backslash codes a little later in this book.

Table 5-3.

Code	Meaning
\b	Backspace
\f	Form feed
\n	Newline
\r	Carriage return
\t	Horizontal tab
\"	Double quote
\'	Single quote character
\0	Null
\\	Backslash
\v	Vertical tab
\a	Bell (alert)
\N	Octal constant (where N is an octal constant)
\x$N$	Hexadecimal constant (where N is a hexadecimal constant)

Backslash Codes

Variable Initializations

You can give most variables in C a value when they are declared by placing an equal sign and a constant after the variable name. The general form of initialization is

type variable __ name = constant;

Some examples are

```
char ch = 'a';

int first = 0;

float balance = 123.23;
```

Global variables are initialized only at the start of the program. Local variables are initialized each time the function in which they are declared is entered. All global variables are initialized to zero if no other initializer is specified. Local variables that are not initialized will have unknown values before the first assignment is made to them.

The main advantage of initializing variables is that it reduces slightly the amount of code in the program. For a simple example of variable initialization, here is a reworked version of the running total program shown in Figure 5-1. This version allows you to enter a number, and then the program sums the numbers from 1 through the value entered.

```c
/* An example using variable initialization. */

#include <stdio.h>

main()
{
  int t;

  printf("enter a number: ");
  scanf("%d", &t);
  total(t);
}

total(int x)
{
  int sum=0, i, count;

  for(i=0; i<x; i++) {
    sum = sum + i;
    for(count=0; count<10; count++) printf(".");
    printf("the current sum is %d\n", sum);
  }
}
```

As you will learn in Part III, variable initialization takes on an expanded role in C++.

Operators

C is very rich in built-in operators. An *operator* is a symbol that tells the compiler to perform specific mathematical or logical manipulations. C has three general classes of operators: *arithmetic, relational and logical,* and *bitwise.* In addition, C has some special operators for particular tasks. In this chapter only the arithmetic, relational and logical, and assignment operators will be examined. The others will be discussed later.

Arithmetic Operators

Table 5-4 lists the C arithmetic operators. The operators +, −, *, and / all work the same way in C as they do in most other computer languages. These can be applied to any built-in data type allowed by C. When / is applied to an integer or character, any remainder will be truncated; for example, 10/3 will equal 3 in integer division.

Table 5-4.

Operator	Action
−	Subtraction, also unary minus
+	Addition
*	Multiplication
/	Division
%	Modulus division
− −	Decrement
+ +	Increment

Arithmetic Operators

The modulus division operator, %, yields the remainder of an integer division. However, as such, % cannot be used on type **float** or **double**. The following program calculates the quotient and remainder of an integer entered by the user:

```c
#include <stdio.h>

main()
{
  int x, y;

  printf("enter dividend and divisor: ");
  scanf("%d%d", &x, &y);

  printf("quotient %d\n", x/y);
  printf("remainder %d ", x%y);

}
```

The unary minus in effect multiplies its single operand by −1. That is, any number preceded by a minus sign switches its sign.

Increment and Decrement

C allows two very useful operators not generally found in other computer languages. These are the *increment* and *decrement* operators, + + and − −. The operation + + adds one to its operand, and − − subtracts one. Therefore, the following operations,

```c
x++;
x--;
```

are the same as

```c
x = x+1;
x = x-1;
```

Both the increment and decrement operators may either precede or follow the operand. For example,

```
x = x+1;
```

can be written as

```
++x;
```

or as

```
x++;
```

There is, however, a difference when they are used in an expression. When an increment or decrement operator precedes its operand, then C will perform the increment or decrement operation prior to using the operand's value. If the operator follows its operand, then C will use the operand's value before incrementing or decrementing it. Consider the following:

```
x = 10;
y = ++x;
```

In this case, **y** will be set to 11 because **x** is first incremented and then assigned to **y**. However, if the code had been written as

```
x=10;
y = x++;
```

y would have been set to 10 and then **x** incremented. In both cases, **x** is set to 11; the difference is *when* it happens. There are significant advantages in being able to control when the increment or decrement operation takes place, as you will see later in this book.

This is the precedence of the arithmetic operators:

highest	$++$ $--$
	$-$ (unary)
	$*$ / %
lowest	$+$ $-$

Operators on the same precedence level are evaluated by the compiler from left to right. Of course, parentheses may be used to alter the order of evaluation. Parentheses are treated by C in the same way they are by virtually all other computer languages: they force an operation, or set of operations, to a higher precedence level.

Relational and Logical Operators

In the terms *relational operator* and *logical operator, relational* refers to the relationships values can have with one another and *logical* refers to the ways these relationships can be connected. Key to the concepts of relational and logical operators is the idea of *true* and *false*. In C, true is any value other than zero. False is zero. Expressions that use relational or logical operators will return 0 for false and 1 for true. Table 5-5 shows the relational and logical operators.

The relational operators are used to determine the relationship of one quantity to another. They always return a 1 or a 0 depending upon the outcome of the test. The following program illustrates the outcome of each operation and displays the results of each operation as a 0 or a 1:

```
/* This program illustrates the relational operators. */

#include <stdio.h>

main()
{
  int i, j;

  printf("enter two numbers: ");
  scanf("%d%d", &i, &j);

  printf("%d == %d is %d\n", i, j, i==j);
  printf("%d != %d is %d\n", i, j, i!=j);
  printf("%d <= %d is %d\n", i, j, i<=j);
  printf("%d >= %d is %d\n", i, j, i>=j);
  printf("%d < %d is %d\n", i, j, i <j);
  printf("%d > %d is %d\n", i, j, i>j);

}
```

You should enter this program now and experiment with various combinations of numbers.

Table 5-5.

Relational Operators	
Operator	*Action*
>	Greater than
> =	Greater than or equal
<	Less than
< =	Less than or equal
= =	Equal
! =	Not equal
Logical Operators	
&&	AND
| |	OR
!	NOT

Relational and Logical Operators

The relational operators may be applied to any of the basic data types. For example, this fragment displays the message "greater than" because in the ASCII collating sequence, a 'B' is greater than an 'A'.

```
ch1 = 'A';
ch2 = 'B';
if(ch2 > ch1) printf("greater than");
```

Later in this book you will see many more uses of the relational operators.

The logical operators are used to support the basic logical operations of AND, OR, and NOT according to this truth table. The table uses 1 for true and 0 for false.

p	*q*	*p AND q*	*p OR q*	*NOT p*
0	0	0	0	1
0	1	0	1	1
1	1	1	1	0
1	0	0	1	0

The program shown here illustrates the operation of the logical operators:

```
/* This program illustrates the logical operators. */

#include <stdio.h>

main()
{
  int i, j;

  printf("enter two numbers (each being either 0 or 1): ");
  scanf("%d%d", &i, &j);

  printf("%d AND %d is %d\n", i, j, i && j);
  printf("%d OR %d is %d\n", i, j, i || j);
  printf("NOT %d is %d\n", i, !i);
}
```

You should enter this program and experiment with various combinations of true and false until you are comfortable with the operations.

Both the relational and logical operators are lower in precedence than the arithmetic operators. This means that an expression such as **10 > 1+12** is evaluated as if it were written **10 > (1+12)**. The result is, of course, false.

It is permissible to combine several operations together into one expression, as shown here:

```
10>5 && !(10<9) || 3<=4
```

This will evaluate as true.

The following table shows the relative precedence of the relational and logical operators:

highest	!
	> >= < <=
	== !=
	&&
lowest	||

As with arithmetic expressions, it is possible to use parentheses to alter the natural order of evaluation in a relational and/or logical expression. For example,

```
1 && !0 ||1
```

will be true because the **!** will be evaluated first making the AND true. However, when the same expression is parenthesized as shown here, the result is false:

```
1 && !(0 || 1)
```

Because (1 ¦¦ 0) evaluates to true, the NOT changes the result to false and thus causes the AND to be false.

Remember that all relational and logical expressions produce a result of either 0 or 1. Therefore, the following program is not only correct, but will also print the number 1 on the display:

```
#include <stdio.h>

main()
{
  int x;

  x = 100;
  printf("%d", x>10);
}
```

The relational and logical operators are used to support the program-control statements including all the loops as well as the **if** statement. For example, this program uses an **if** statement to print the even numbers between 1 and 100:

```
/* Print the even numbers between 1 and 100. */

#include <stdio.h>

main()
{
  int i;
  for(i=1; i<=100; i++)
    if(!(i%2)) printf("%d ",i);
}
```

In this example, the modulus operation will produce a zero (false) result when used on an even number. This result is then inverted by the NOT.

You will see many more examples of the relational and logical operators in following chapters.

The Assignment Operator

The assignment operator in C is the single equal sign. Unlike many other computer languages, C allows the assignment operator to be used in expressions that also involve relational or logical operators. For example, consider the **if** statement in this program:

```
#include <stdio.h>

main()
{
  int x, y, product;

  printf("enter two numbers: ");
  scanf("%d%d", &x, &y);

  if( (product=x*y) < 0 )
    printf("one number is negative\n");
  else
    printf("positive product is: %d", product);
}
```

Notice the expression in the **if**. First, **product** is assigned the value of **x*y**. Next, the parenthesized assignment expression is tested against zero. This code is perfectly valid. In fact, statements of this type are very common in professionally written C code. Let's take a close look at how and why it works.

In C, the assignment operator can be thought of as doing two things. First, it assigns the value of the right side to the variable on the left. However, when it is used as part of a larger expression, the assignment operator produces the value of the right side of the expression. Therefore the **(product = x*y)** part of the expression assigns **product** the value of **x*y** as well as returning that value. It is this value that is then tested against zero in the **if**. The parentheses are necessary because the assignment operator is lower in precedence than the relational operators.

Expressions

Operators, constants, and variables are the constituents of *expressions*. An expression in C is any valid combination of those pieces. Because most expressions tend to follow the general rules of algebra, they are often taken for granted. However, there are a few aspects of expressions that relate specifically to C and these will be discussed now.

Type Conversion in Expressions

When constants and variables of different types are mixed in an expression, they are converted to the same type. The C compiler will convert all operands "up" to the type of the largest operand. This is done on an operation-by-operation basis, as described in these type-conversion rules:

1. All **char**s and **short int**s are converted to **int**s. All **float**s are converted to **double**s.

2. For all operand pairs, if one of the operands is a **long double**, the other operand is converted to **long double**. If one of the operands is **double**, the other operand is converted to **double**. If one of the operands is **long**, the other operand is converted to **long**. If one of the operands is **unsigned**, the other is converted to **unsigned**.

Once these conversion rules have been applied, each pair of operands will be of the same type and the result of each operation will be the same as the type of both operands. Please note that rule 2 has several conditions that must be applied in sequence.

For example, consider the type conversions that occur in Figure 5-2. First, the character **ch** is converted to an integer and **float f** is converted to **double**. Then the outcome of **ch/i** is converted to a **double** because **f*d** is **double**. The final result is **double** because, by this time, both operands are **double**.

Figure 5-2.

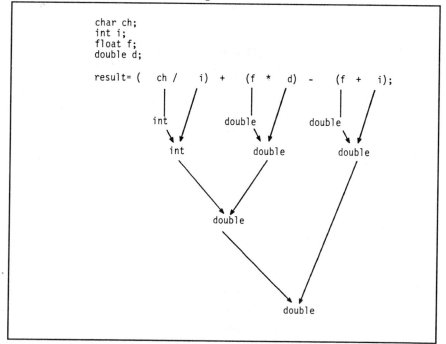

A type-conversion example

Casts

It is possible to force an expression to be of a specific type by using a construct called a *cast*. The general form of a cast is

(type) expression

where *type* is one of the standard C data types. For example, if **x** is an integer and you wish to make sure the expression **x/2** will evaluate to type **float**, to ensure a fractional component, you could write

```
(float) x / 2
```

Here, the cast (**float**) is associated with the **x**, which causes the 2 to be elevated to type **float** and the outcome to be **float**. However, be careful: If you write it as follows, no fractional component will be evaluated:

```
(float) (x /2)
```

In this case, an integer division is carried out and the result of that is elevated to **float**.

Casts are often considered operators. As an operator, a cast is unary and has the same precedence as any other unary operator.

There are times when a cast can be very useful. For example, suppose you wish to use an integer for loop control, yet perform some computation on it that requires a fractional part, as in this program:

```
#include <stdio.h>

main() /* print i and i/3 with fractions */
{
  int i;
```

```
   for(i=1; i<=100; ++i )
      printf("%d / 2 is: %f\n", i, (float) i/3);
}
```

Without the cast (**float**), only an integer division would have been performed; but the cast ensures that the fractional part of the answer will be displayed on the screen.

Spacing and Parentheses

You may place spaces in an expression at your discretion to make it more readable. For example, the following two expressions are the same:

```
x=645/(num_entry)-y*(3127/balance);

x = 645 / (num_entry) - y * (3127 / balance);
```

Use of redundant or additional parentheses will not cause errors or slow down the execution of the expression. You are encouraged to use parentheses to make clear the exact order of evaluation, both for yourself and for others who may have to understand your program later. For example, which of the following two expressions is easier to read?

```
x=y/3-34*temp-127;

x = (y/3) - (34*temp) - 127;
```

CHAPTER

6

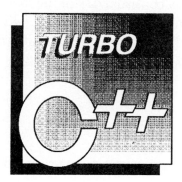

Program-Control Statements

In a sense, the program-control statements are the essence of any computer language because they govern the flow of program execution. The way they are implemented in many ways defines the personality of the language. C's program-control statements are both rich and powerful and help explain its popularity.

The program-control statements may be separated into three categories. The first consists of the conditional instructions **if** and

121

switch. The second are the loop-control statements **while, for,** and **do-while**. The final category is the unconditional branch instruction **goto**.

Remember that a statement may consist of one of the following: a single statement; a block of statements; or nothing, which is called an *empty statement*. In the descriptions presented here, the term *statement* is used to mean all of these possibilities.

The if Statement

Although you had a short introduction to the **if** statement in Chapter 4, it is now time to look at it in depth.

The general form of the **if** statement is

if(*condition*) *statement*;
else *statement*;

The **else** clause is optional. If *condition* evaluates to true (anything other than 0), the *statement* or block that forms the target of the **if** will be executed; otherwise, if it exists, the statement or block that is the target of the **else** will be executed. Remember that only the code associated with the **if** or the code associated with the **else** will execute, never both. Keep in mind that the target of both the **if** and the **else** may be single statements or blocks of statements.

To demonstrate the **if** in action, we will develop a simple program that performs number-base conversions. This program will be capable of displaying the following conversions:

- decimal to hexadecimal
- hexadecimal to decimal

- decimal to octal
- octal to decimal

The program will allow you to first select the type of conversion from a menu and then prompt you for the number to be converted. It will then display that number in the selected format. This makes a nice utility program.

The key to the program's conversion capabilities are two special **printf( )** and **scanf( )** format commands: **%x** and **%o**. When you use the **%x** format command with **printf( )**, you cause an integer to be displayed in hexadecimal format. If you use **%x** in a call to **scanf( )**, you cause **scanf( )** to input an integer using hexadecimal format. Similarly, the **%o** format code causes **printf( )** to output an integer in octal format and **scanf( )** to read an integer using octal format.

The conversion program uses a series of **if**s to determine which type of conversion to perform. Since the equality operation will match only one of the menu selections, only one conversion will execute each time the program is run. Note that in this program the target of each **if** is a block of code. The conversion program is shown in the following listing:

```
/* Number Base converter program #1.

          decimal --> hexadecimal
      hexadecimal --> decimal
          decimal --> octal
            octal --> decimal

*/

#include <stdio.h>

main()
{
  int choice;
  int value;

  printf("Convert:\n");
  printf("     1: decimal to hexadecimal\n");
```

```
printf("       2: hexadecimal to decimal\n");
printf("       3: decimal to octal\n");
printf("       4: octal to decimal\n");
printf("enter your choice: ");
scanf("%d", &choice);

if(choice==1) {
  printf("enter decimal value: ");
  scanf("%d", &value);
  printf("%d in hexadecimal is: %x", value, value);
}

if(choice==2) {
  printf("enter hexadecimal value: ");
  scanf("%x", &value);
  printf("%x in decimal is: %d", value, value);
}

if(choice==3) {
  printf("enter decimal value: ");
  scanf("%d", &value);
  printf("%d in octal is: %o", value, value);
}
if(choice==4) {
  printf("enter octal value: ");
  scanf("%o", &value);
  printf("%o in decimal is: %d", value, value);
}
}
```

Using the else Statement

You can associate an **else** with any **if**. If the conditional expression associated with the **if** is true, its target will be executed. If it is false, then the target of the **else** will be executed. The following program demonstrates this fundamental principle.

```
/* A simple if-else example. */

#include <stdio.h>

main()
{
```

```
int i;

printf("enter a number: ");
scanf("%d", &i);

if(i<0) printf("number is negative");
else printf("number is positive or zero");
}
```

For each integer you enter, the program tells you if it is negative.

The if-else-if Ladder

A common programming construct is the **if-else-if** *ladder*. The following example illustrates this construct:

if (*condition*)
  statement;
else if (*condition*)
  statement;
else if (*condition*)
  statement;
.
.
.
else
  statement;

The conditional expressions are evaluated from the top downward. As soon as a true condition is found, the statement associated with it is executed, and the rest of the ladder is bypassed. If none of the conditions are true, then the final **else** will be executed. The final **else** often acts as a *default condition;* that is, if all other conditional tests fail, then the last **else** statement is performed. If the final **else** is not present and all other conditions are false, then no action will take place.

You can use an **if-else-if** ladder to improve the number-base conversion program previously developed. In the original version, each **if** statement was evaluated in succession even if one of the earlier statements had succeeded. Although not of any great significance in this case, the redundant evaluation of all the **if**s is not very efficient or elegant in principle. The following program solves this problem. In this **if-else-if** ladder version, as soon as an **if** statement succeeds, the rest of the statements are bypassed.

```
/* Number Base converter program #2 — if-else-if ladder.
            decimal --> hexadecimal
        hexadecimal --> decimal
            decimal --> octal
              octal --> decimal

*/

#include <stdio.h>

main()
{
  int choice;
  int value;

  printf("Convert:\n");
  printf("      1: decimal to hexadecimal\n");
  printf("      2: hexadecimal to decimal\n");
  printf("      3: decimal to octal\n");
  printf("      4: octal to decimal\n");
  printf("enter your choice: ");
  scanf("%d", &choice);

  if(choice==1) {
    printf("enter decimal value: ");
    scanf("%d", &value);
    printf("%d in hexadecimal is: %x", value, value);
  }
  else if(choice==2) {
    printf("enter hexadecimal value: ");
    scanf("%x", &value);
    printf("%x in decimal is: %d", value, value);
```

```
  }
  else if(choice==3) {
    printf("enter decimal value: ");
    scanf("%d", &value);
    printf("%d in octal is: %o", value, value);
  }
  else if(choice==4) {
    printf("enter octal value: ");
    scanf("%o", &value);
    printf("%o in decimal is: %d", value, value);
  }
}
```

The Conditional Expression

Sometimes, newcomers to C are confused by the fact that any valid C expression can be used to control the **if** statement. That is, the type of expression need not be restricted to only those involving the relational and logical operators (as is the case in a language like BASIC). All that is required is that the expression evaluate to either a zero or nonzero value. For example, this program reads two integers from the keyboard and displays the quotient. In order to avoid a divide-by-zero error, an **if** statement, controlled by the second number, is used.

```
/* Divide the first number by the second. */

#include <stdio.h>

main()
{
  int a, b;

  printf("enter two numbers: ");
  scanf("%d%d", &a, &b);

  if(b) printf("%d\n", a/b);
  else printf("cannot divide by zero\n");
}
```

This approach works because if **b** is zero, then the condition controlling the **if** is false and the **else** executes. Otherwise, the condition is true (nonzero) and the division takes place. It is not necessary to write this **if** statement like this

```
if(b == 0) printf("%d\n", a/b);
```

because it is redundant.

Nested ifs

One of the most confusing aspects of **if** statements in any programming language are nested **if**s. A *nested* **if** is an **if** statement that is the object of either an **if** or an **else**. The reason that nested **if**s are so troublesome is that it can be difficult to know which **else** associates with which **if**. Consider this example:

```
if(x)
  if(y) printf("1");
  else printf("2");
```

To which **if** does the **else** refer? Fortunately, C provides a very simple rule for resolving this question. In C, the **else** is linked to the closest **if** within the same code block that does not already have an **else** statement associated with it. In this case, the **else** is associated with the **if(y)** statement. To make the **else** associate with the **if(x)** you must use braces to override its normal association, as shown here:

```
if(x) {
  if(y) printf("1");
}
else printf("2");
```

The **else** is now associated with the **if(x)** because it is no longer part of the **if(y)** code block.

The switch Statement

Although the **if-else-if** ladder can perform multiway tests, it is hardly elegant. The code can be very hard to follow and can confuse even its author at a later date. For these reasons, C has a built-in multiple-branch decision statement called **switch**. In the **switch**, a variable is successively tested against a list of integer or character constants. When a match is found, the statement or sequence associated with that constant is executed. The constants need not be in any special order. The general form of the **switch** statement is

```
switch(variable) {
    case constant1:
        statement sequence
        break;
    case constant2:
        statement sequence
        break;
    case constant3:
        statement sequence
        break;
        .
        .
        .
    default:
        statement sequence
}
```

where the **default** statement is executed if no matches are found. The **default** is optional and, if it is not present, no action takes place if all matches fail. When a match is found, the statements associated with that **case** are executed until the **break** is reached or, in the case of the **default** (or last **case** if no **default** is present), the end of the **switch** statement is encountered. (The switch statement is similar to BASIC's **ON-GOTO** statement and Pascal's **CASE** statement.)

There are three important things to know about the **switch** statement:

1. It differs from the **if** statement in that **switch** can only test for equality whereas the **if** conditional expression can be of any type.

2. No two **case** constants in the same **switch** can have identical values. Of course, a **switch** statement enclosed by an outer **switch** may have **case** constants that are the same.

3. A **switch** statement is more efficient than an **if-else-if** ladder.

Often, you will use **switch** to route a menu selection to its proper routine. Along this line, you can use one to make a further improvement to the number-base conversion program. The version shown here eliminates that rather ugly series of **if**s and substitutes a nice, clean **switch** statement in its place:

```
/* Number Base convertor program #3 using the switch statement.
            decimal --> hexadecimal
        hexadecimal --> decimal
            decimal --> octal
              octal --> decimal

*/

#include <stdio.h>

main()
{
```

```
int choice;
int value;

printf("Convert:\n");
printf("      1: decimal to hexadecimal\n");
printf("      2: hexadecimal to decimal\n");
printf("      3: decimal to octal\n");
printf("      4: octal to decimal\n");
printf("enter your choice: ");
scanf("%d", &choice);

switch(choice) {
  case 1:
    printf("enter decimal value: ");
    scanf("%d", &value);
    printf("%d in hexadecimal is: %x", value, value);
    break;
  case 2:
    printf("enter hexadecimal value: ");
    scanf("%x", &value);
    printf("%x in decimal is: %d", value, value);
    break;
  case 3:
    printf("enter decimal value: ");
    scanf("%d", &value);
    printf("%d in octal is: %o", value, value);
    break;
  case 4:
    printf("enter octal value: ");
    scanf("%o", &value);
    printf("%o in decimal is: %d", value, value);
    break;
  }
}
```

The default Statement

You can specify a statement sequence in the **switch** that will
execute if no matches are found by adding a **default** statement.
The **default** statement is a good way to tidy up any loose ends that
might be hanging around a **switch** statement. For example, in the
number-base conversion program, you can use a **default** state-

ment to inform the user that an invalid response was entered and to try again, as this fragment shows:

```
switch(choice) {
  case 1:
    printf("enter decimal value: ");
    scanf("%d", &value);
    printf("%d in hexadecimal is: %x", value, value);
    break;
  case 2:
    printf("enter hexadecimal value: ");
    scanf("%x", &value);
    printf("%x in decimal is: %d", value, value);
    break;
  case 3:
    printf("enter decimal value: ");
    scanf("%d", &value);
    printf("%d in octal is: %o", value, value);
    break;
  case 4:
    printf("enter octal value: ");
    scanf("%o", &value);
    printf("%o in decimal is: %d", value, value);
    break;
  default:
    printf("invalid selection, try again\n");
    break;
}
```

A Closer Look at the break Statement

Although **break** statements are generally needed inside a **switch**, syntactically, they are optional. They are used to terminate the statement sequence associated with each constant. However, if the **break** statement is omitted, execution will continue on into the next **case**'s statements until either a **break** or the end of the **switch** is reached. You can think of the **case**s as labels. Execution will start at the label that matches and continue until a **break** statement is found, or the **switch** ends. Pay special attention to the **switch** statement in this rather silly program:

```
/* A very silly program. */

#include <stdio.h>

main()
{
  int t;

  for(t=0; t<10; t++)
    switch(t) {
      case 1:
        printf("Now");
        break;
      case 2:
        printf(" is ");
      case 3:
        printf("the");
        printf(" time for all good men\n");
        break;
      case 5:
      case 6:
        printf("to ");
        break;
      case 7:
      case 8:
      case 9:
        printf(".");
  }

}
```

When run, the following output is produced:

```
Now is the time for all good men
the time for all good men
to to ...
```

This program also illustrates the fact that you can have empty **case** statements. This is helpful when several conditions use the same statement sequence. As you can probably guess, the ability for the **case**s to run together when no **break** is present enables very efficient programs to be written by avoiding the unwarranted duplication of code.

It is important to understand that the statements associated with each label are not code blocks but rather *statement sequences.* (Of course, the entire **switch** statement does define a block.) This technical distinction is not usually important except in certain special situations that will be discussed later in this book.

Nested switch Statements

It is possible to have a **switch** as part of the statement sequence of an outer **switch**. Even if the **case** constants of the inner and outer **switch** contain common values, no conflicts will arise. For example, the following code fragment is perfectly acceptable:

```
switch(x) {
  case 1:
    switch(y) {
      case 0: printf("divide by zero error");
              break;
      case 1: process(x, y);
    }
    break;
  case 2:
    .
    .
    .
```

As another example, the very simple database program shown next illustrates how you might use a nested **switch** statement. This program asks the user for the region and the first initial of the salesperson, and then displays the current sales figure for that person. Nested **switch**es are required because several of the salespeople have similar first initials. Notice that a new standard library function, **toupper( )**, is introduced. It returns the upper-case equivalent of its character argument. It is used in this program to allow the user to enter responses in either upper- or lowercase. (The complement of **toupper( )** is **tolower( )**, which converts uppercase characters to lowercase.) The header file required by **toupper( )** is CTYPE.H.

```c
/* A simple regional salesperson database. */

#include <stdio.h>
#include <conio.h>
#include <ctype.h>

main()
{
  char division, salesperson;

  printf("Divisions are: East, Midwest, and West\n");
  printf("Enter first letter of division: ");
  division = getche();
  division = toupper(division); /* make uppercase */
  printf("\n");
  switch(division) {
    case 'E':
      printf("Salespersons are: Ralph, Jerry, and Mary\n");
      printf("Enter the first letter of salesperson: ");
      salesperson = toupper(getche());
      printf("\n");

      switch(salesperson) {
        case 'R': printf("Sales: $%d\n", 10000);
          break;
        case 'J': printf("Sales: $%d\n", 12000);
          break;
        case 'M': printf("Sales: $%d\n", 14000);
          break;
      }
      break;

    case 'M':
      printf("Salespersons are: Ron, Linda, and Harry\n");
      printf("Enter the first letter of salesperson: ");
      salesperson = toupper(getche());
      printf("\n");

      switch(salesperson) {
        case 'R': printf("Sales: $%d\n", 10000);
          break;
        case 'L': printf("Sales: $%d\n", 9500);
          break;
```

```
      case 'H': printf("Sales: $%d\n", 13000);
        break;
    }
    break;

  case 'W':
    printf("Salespersons are: Tom, Jerry, and Rachel\n");
    printf("Enter the first letter of salesperson: ");
    salesperson = toupper(getche());
    printf("\n");

    switch(salesperson) {
      case 'R': printf("Sales: $%d\n", 5000);
        break;
      case 'J': printf("Sales: $%d\n", 9000);
        break;
      case 'T': printf("Sales: $%d\n", 14000);
        break;
    }
    break;
  }
}
```

To see how it works, select the Midwest region by typing **M**. This means that **case 'M'** is selected by the outer **switch** statement. To see Harry's sales total type **H**. This causes the value 13000 to be displayed.

Note that a **break** statement in a nested **switch** has no effect on the outer **switch**.

Loops

Loops allow a set of instructions to be repeated until a certain condition is reached. C supports the same type of loops as other modern, structured languages. The C loops are the **for**, the **while**, and the **do-while**. Each will be examined in turn.

The for Loop

Although the simple form of the **for** loop was introduced in Chapter 4, here you may be surprised to see just how powerful and flexible it is. First review what you have learned about it.

for Loop Basics

The general form of the **for** statement is

for(*initialization*; *condition*; *increment*) *statement*;

In its simplest form, the *initialization* is an assignment statement that is used to set the loop-control variable. The *condition* is usually a relational expression that determines when the loop will exit by testing the loop-control variable against some value. The *increment* usually defines how the loop-control variable will change each time the loop is repeated. These three major sections must be separated by semicolons. The **for** loop will continue to execute as long as the condition is true. Once the condition becomes false, program execution will resume at the statement following the **for**.

For a simple example, the following program prints the numbers 1 through 100 on the terminal:

```
#include <stdio.h>

main()
{
  int x;

  for(x=1; x<=100; x++) printf("%d ", x);
}
```

In this program, **x** is initially set to 1. Since **x** is less than 100, **printf( )** is called. After **printf( )** returns, **x** is increased by 1, and tested to see if it is still less than or equal to 100. This process repeats until **x** is greater than 100, at which point the loop terminates. In this example, **x** is the *loop-control variable,* which is changed and checked each time the loop repeats.

The **for** loop need not always run in a forward direction. A negative-running loop is created by decrementing rather than incrementing the loop-control variable. For example, this one prints the numbers 100 through 1 on the screen:

```
#include <stdio.h>

main()
{
  int x;

  for(x=100; x>0; x--) printf("%d ", x);
}
```

However, you are not restricted to incrementing or decrementing the loop-control variable. You may change the loop control variable any way you want. For example, this loop prints the numbers 0 through 100 by fives:

```
#include <stdio.h>

main()
{
  int x;

  for(x=0; x<=100; x=x+5) printf("%d ", x);
}
```

By using a code block, you can have **for** repeat multiple statements as shown in this example, which prints the square of the numbers 0 through 99:

```
#include <stdio.h>

main()
```

```
{
  int i;

  for(i=0; i<100; i++) {
    printf("this is i: %d", i);
    printf(" and i squared: %d\n", i*i);
  }
}
```

An important point about **for** loops is that the conditional test is always performed at the top of the loop. This means that the code inside the loop may not be executed at all if the condition is false to begin with. For example:

```
x = 10;

for(y=10; y!=x; ++y) printf("%d", y);

printf("%d", y);
```

This loop will never execute because **x** and **y** are in fact equal when the loop is entered. Because this causes the conditional expression to evaluate to false, neither the body of the loop nor the increment portion of the loop will be executed. Hence, **y** will still have the value 10 assigned to it, and the output will be only the number 10 printed once on the screen.

Variations of the for Loop

The foregoing discussion described the most common form of the **for** loop. However, several variations are allowed that increase its power, flexibility, and applicability to certain programming situations.

One of the most common variations is the use of two or more loop-control variables. Here is an example that uses both the variables **x** and **y** to control the loop:

```
#include <stdio.h>

main()
{
  int x,y;

  for(x=0, y=0; x+y<100; ++x, y++)
    printf("%d ", x+y);

}
```

This program prints the numbers from 0 to 98 by twos. Notice that commas are used to separate the initialization and increment statements. The comma is actually a C operator that means essentially "do this and this" and will be discussed more fully later in this book. Each time through the loop, both **x** and **y** are incremented and both **x** and **y** must be at the correct value for the loop to terminate.

The conditional expression does not necessarily have to involve testing the loop-control variable against some target value. In fact, the condition may be any valid C expression. This means that you can test for several possible terminating conditions. For example, this program helps drill children on addition. If the child tires and wants to stop, he or she types **N** when asked for more. Pay special attention to the condition portion of the **for** loop. The conditional expression causes the **for** to run up to 99 times or until the user answers no to the prompt.

```
/* Addition drill. */

#include <stdio.h>
#include <conio.h>

main()
{
  int i, j, answer;
  char done = ' ';

  for(i=1; i<100 && done!='N'; i++) {
    for(j=1; j<10; j++) {
      printf("what is %d + %d? ", i, j);
```

```
        scanf("%d", &answer);
        if(answer != i+j) printf("wrong\n");
        else printf("right\n");
    }
    printf("more? ");
    done = getche();
    printf("\n");
  }
}
```

Another interesting variation of the **for** loop is possible because, in actuality, each of the three sections of the **for** statement may consist of any valid C expression. They need not actually have anything to do with what the section is used for in the standard case. With this in mind, consider the following example:

```
/* An unusual use of the for loop. */
#include <stdio.h>

main()
{
  int t;

  for(prompt(); t=readnum(); prompt())
    sqrnum(t);
}

prompt()
{
  printf("enter an integer: ");
}

readnum()
{
  int t;

  scanf("%d", &t);
  return t;
}
sqrnum(int num)
{
  printf("%d\n", num*num);
}
```

This program first displays a prompt and then waits for input. When a number is entered, its square is displayed and you are again prompted for input. This continues until a 0 is entered. If you look closely at the **for** loop in **main( )**, you will see that each part of the **for** is comprised of function calls that prompt the user and read a number from the keyboard. If the number entered is zero, the loop terminates because the conditional expression will be false; otherwise, the number is squared. Thus, in this **for** loop the initialization and increment portions are used in a nontraditional but completely valid sense. You should enter this program and try modifying it to behave in different ways.

Another interesting trait of the **for** loop is that pieces of the loop definition need not be there. In fact, there need not be an expression present for any of the sections—the expressions are optional. For example, this loop will run until the number 10 is entered:

```
for(x=0; x!=10; ) scanf("%d", &x);
```

Notice that the increment portion of the **for** definition is blank. This means that each time the loop repeats, **x** is tested to see if it equals 10, but **x** is not changed in any way. However, if you type **10** at the keyboard, the loop condition becomes false and the loop terminates.

The Infinite Loop

One of the most interesting uses of the **for** loop is the creation of the infinite loop. None of the three expressions that form the **for** loop are required, so it is possible to make an endless loop by leaving the conditional expression empty, as shown in this example:

```
for(;;) printf(" this loop will run forever.\n");
```

Breaking Out of a
for Loop

The **for(;;)** construct does not necessarily create an infinite loop because of a new application of C's **break** statement. When encountered anywhere inside the body of a loop, a **break** causes immediate termination. Program control picks up at the code following the loop, as shown here:

```
for(;;) {
  ch = getche();   /* get a character */
  if(x=='A') break;  /* exit the loop */
}

printf("you typed an A");
```

This loop will run until an **A** is typed at the keyboard. The **break** statement will be examined more closely later in this chapter.

Using for Loops with
No Bodies

A statement, as defined by C syntax, may be empty. This means that the body of the **for** (or any other loop for that matter) may also be empty. This fact can be used to improve the efficiency of certain algorithms as well as to create time-delay loops. This is how to create a time delay using **for**:

```
for(t=0; t<SOME_VALUE; t++) ;
```

The while Loop

The second loop available in C is the **while**. The general form is

while(*condition*) *statement*;

where *statement,* as stated earlier, can be an empty statement, a single statement, or a block of statements that is to be repeated. The *condition* may be any valid expression. The loop iterates while the *condition* is true. When the *condition* becomes false, program control passes to the line following the loop code.

The following example shows a keyboard-input routine that simply loops until the character **A** is pressed:

```
wait_for_char()
{
  char ch;

  ch = '\0';  /* initialize ch */
  while(ch!='A')  ch = getche();
}
```

First, **ch** is initialized to null. As a local variable, its value is not known when **wait_for_char( )** is executed. The **while** loop then begins by checking to see if **ch** is not equal to **A**. Because **ch** was initialized to null beforehand, the test is true and the loop begins. Each time a key is pressed on the keyboard, the test is tried again. Once an **A** is pressed, the condition becomes false because **ch** equals **A**, and the loop terminates.

As with **for** loops, **while** loops check the test condition at the top of the loop, which means that the loop code may not execute at all. This is why **ch** had to be initialized in the foregoing example to prevent it from accidentally containing **A**. Because the conditional test is performed at the top of the loop, the **while** is good for situations in which you may not want the loop to execute. This eliminates the need for a separate conditional test before the loop.

For example, the function **center( )** in the program that follows uses a **while** loop to output the correct number of spaces to center a line of text on an 80-column screen. If **len** is equal to zero, as it would be if the line to be centered was 80 characters long, the loop will not execute. This program uses another library function called **strlen( )**, which returns the length of its string argument. It uses the header file STRING.H.

```
/* A program that centers text on the screen. */

#include <stdio.h>
#include <string.h>

main()
{
  char str[255];
  int len;

  printf("enter a string: ");
  gets(str);

  center(strlen(str));
  printf(str);
}

/* Compute and output proper number of spaces to
   center a string of len length.
*/
center(int len)
{
  len = (80-len)/2;

  while(len>0) {
    printf(" ");
    len--;
  }
}
```

Where several separate conditions terminate a **while** loop, it is common to use a single variable as the conditional expression, with the value of this variable being set at various points throughout the loop. For example:

```
func1()
{
  int working;

  working = 1;   /* i.e., true */

  while(working) {
    working = process1();
    if(working)
      working = process2();
    if(working)
      working = process3();
  }
}
```

Here, any of the three routines may return false and cause the loop to exit.

There need not be any statements at all in the body of the **while** loop. For example,

```
while((ch=getche()) != 'A') ;
```

will simply loop until the character **A** is typed at the keyboard. If you feel a bit uncomfortable with the assignment inside the **while** conditional expression, remember that the equal sign is really just an operator that evaluates to the value of the right-hand operand.

The do-while Loop

Unlike the **for** and **while** loops, which test the loop condition at the top of the loop, the **do-while** loop checks its condition at the bottom of the loop. This means that a **do-while** loop will always execute at least once. The general form of the **do-while** loop is

```
do {

  statement;

} while(condition);
```

Although the braces are not necessary when only one statement is present, they are usually used to improve readability and avoid confusion (to the programmer, not the compiler) with the **while**.

This program uses a **do-while** loop to read numbers from the keyboard until one is less than 100:

```
#include <stdio.h>

main()
{
  int num;

  do {
    scanf("%d", &num);
  } while(num>100);
}
```

Perhaps the most common use of the **do-while** loop is in a menu-selection routine. Because you will always want a menu-selection routine to execute at least once, the **do-while** loop is an obvious choice. By testing for a valid response at the bottom of the loop, you can re-prompt the user until a valid response is entered. The following fragment shows how to add a **do-while** loop onto the menu for the number-base conversion program:

```
/* make sure that the user specifies a valid option */
do {
  printf("Convert:\n");
  printf("          1: decimal to hexadecimal\n");
  printf("          2: hexadecimal to decimal\n");
  printf("          3: decimal to octal\n");
  printf("          4: octal to decimal\n");
  printf("enter your choice: ");
  scanf("%d", &choice);
} while(choice<1 || choice>4);
```

After the options have been displayed, the program will loop until a valid option is selected.

Nested Loops

When one loop is inside of another, the inner loop is said to be *nested*. Nested loops provide the means of solving some interesting programming problems. For example, this short program displays the first four integer powers of the numbers 1 through 9:

```
/* Display a table of the first four powers of the
   numbers 1 to 9.
*/

#include <stdio.h>

main()
{
  int i, j, k, temp;

  printf("      i      i^2      i^3      i^4\n");
  for(i=1; i<10; i++) {  /* outer loop */
    for(j=1; j<5; j++) {   /* 1st level of nesting */
      temp = 1;
      for(k=0; k<j; k++) /* innermost loop */
        temp = temp*i;
      printf("%9d", temp);
    }
    printf("\n");
  }
}
```

When this program is run it produces the results shown in Figure 6-1. Notice that the numbers in the column all line up. This is due to the use of a *minimum-field-width specifier* in the **printf( )** statement that prints the numbers. If a number is placed between the percent sign and the "d", it tells **printf( )** to add spaces as necessary up to the width specified. In this way you can make the numbers in the columns line up.

Figure 6-1.

```
        i       i^2      i^3      i^4
        1        1        1        1
        2        4        8       16
        3        9       27       81
        4       16       64      256
        5       ?5      125      625
        6       36      216     1296
        7       49      343     2401
        8       64      512     4096
        9       81      729     6561
```

Output from the powers program

It is sometimes important to determine how many iterations an inner loop executes. This number is determined by multiplying the number of times the outer loop iterates by the number of times the inner loop repeats each time it is executed. In the power example, the outer loop repeats nine times and the second loop four times each time it is executed; thus, the second loop actually iterates 36 times. The innermost loop executes an average of two times, so its total number of iterations is 72.

As a last example of nested loops, a final improvement to the number-base conversion program using nested loops is shown here. The outer loop causes the program to run until the user tells it to stop. The inner loop ensures that the user enters a valid menu selection. Now, instead of simply converting one number per run, the program repeats until the user tells it to stop. This allows several numbers to be converted without having to restart the program each time.

```
/* Number Base converter program: Final version using
   nested while loops.

            decimal --> hexadecimal
        hexadecimal --> decimal
            decimal --> octal
              octal --> decimal
```

```
*/

#include <stdio.h>

main()
{
  int choice;
  int value;

  /* repeat until user says to quit */
  do {
    /* make sure that the user specifies a valid option */
    do {
      printf("Convert:\n");
      printf("        1: decimal to hexadecimal\n");
      printf("        2: hexadecimal to decimal\n");
      printf("        3: decimal to octal\n");
      printf("        4: octal to decimal\n");
      printf("        5: quit\n");
      printf("enter your choice: ");
      scanf("%d", &choice);
    } while(choice<1 || choice>5);

    switch(choice) {
      case 1:
        printf("enter decimal value: ");
        scanf("%d", &value);
        printf("%d in hexadecimal is: %x", value, value);
        break;
      case 2:
        printf("enter hexadecimal value: ");
        scanf("%x", &value);
        printf("%x in decimal is: %d", value, value);
        break;
      case 3:
        printf("enter decimal value: ");
        scanf("%d", &value);
        printf("%d in octal is: %o", value, value);
        break;
      case 4:
        printf("enter octal value: ");
        scanf("%o", &value);
        printf("%o in decimal is: %d", value, value);
        break;
    }
    printf("\n");
  } while(choice!=5);
}
```

Loop Breaking

The **break** statement has two uses. The first is to terminate a **case** in the **switch** statement. This use is covered in the section on the **switch** presented earlier in this chapter. The second is to force immediate termination of a loop, bypassing the normal loop conditional test. This use is examined here.

When the **break** statement is encountered inside a loop, the loop is immediately terminated and program control resumes at the next statement following the loop. For example:

```
#include <stdio.h>

main()
{
  int t;

  for(t=0; t<100; t++) {
    printf("%d ", t);
    if(t==10) break;
  }
}
```

This will print the numbers 0 through 10 on the screen and then terminate because the **break** will cause immediate exit from the loop, overriding the conditional test **t < 100** built into the loop.

The **break** is especially useful when an external event controls a loop, as illustrated by this simple program that tests your sense of time. It asks you to wait five seconds between the time you start and the time you end the program. To begin, execute the program. When you think five seconds are up, strike any key. If your sense of time is accurate, you win. (But no cheating with a watch!)

```
/* How's your internal timer? */

#include <stdio.h>
```

```
#include <time.h>
#include <conio.h>

main()
{
  long tm;

  printf("This program tests your sense of time!\n");
  printf("When ready, press return, wait five seconds\n"),
  printf("and strike any key: ");
  getche();
  printf("\n");

  tm = time(0);
  for(;;)
    if(kbhit()) break;
  if(time(0)-tm==5) printf("You win!!!");
  else printf("Your timing is off");
}
```

This program uses Turbo C's **time( )** function to read the current system time, in seconds. The **time( )** function needs the header file TIME.H for its proper operation. Because the number of seconds exceeds that which can be held by an integer, a **long int** variable is required. (The zero used as an argument to **time( )** causes the time to be returned by the function. Do not use any other values as arguments until you understand pointers—the subject of a later chapter.) Another new library function, **kbhit( )**, is introduced in this program. It checks to see if a key has been struck on the keyboard. If one has, it returns true; otherwise, it returns false. Its header file is CONIO.H.

It is important to realize that a **break** will cause an exit from only the innermost loop. For example, consider this fragment:

```
for(t=0; t<100; ++t) {
  count=1;
  for(;;) {
    printf("%d ", count);
    count++;
    if(count==10) break;
  }
}
```

It will print the numbers 1 through 10 on the screen a hundred times. Each time the **break** is encountered, control is passed back to the outer **for** loop.

A **break** used in a **switch** statement will affect only that **switch** and not any loop the **switch** happens to be in.

The continue Statement

The **continue** statement works in a somewhat similiar way to the **break** statement. But instead of forcing termination, **continue** forces the next iteration of the loop to take place, skipping any code in between. For example, the following program will display only even numbers:

```
#include <stdio.h>

main()
{
  int x;

  for(x=0; x<100; x++) {
    if(x%2) continue;
    printf("%d ", x);
  }
}
```

Each time an odd number is generated, the **if** statement executes because an odd number modulus 2 is always equal to 1, which is true. Thus, an odd number causes **continue** to execute and the next iteration to occur, bypassing the **printf( )** statement.

In **while** and **do-while** loops, a **continue** statement will cause control to go directly to the conditional test and then continue the looping process. In the case of the **for**, first the increment part of the loop is performed, next the conditional test is executed, and finally the loop continues.

As you can see in the following example, **continue** can also be used to expedite the termination of a loop by forcing the conditional test to be performed as soon as some terminating condition is encountered. Consider this program, which acts like a simple code machine:

```
/* A simple code machine. */
#include <stdio.h>
#include <conio.h>

main()
{
  printf("Enter the letters you want coded.\n");
  printf("Type a $ when you are done.\n");

  code();
}

/* code the letters */
code()
{
  char done, ch;

  done = 0;
  while(!done) {
    ch = getch();
    if(ch=='$') {
     done = 1;
     continue;
   }
    printf("%c", ch+1);  /* shift the alphabet one
                            position */
  }
}
```

You could use this function to code a message by shifting all characters one letter higher; for example, an **a** would become a **b**. The function will terminate when a **$** is read. No further iterations will occur because the conditional test, brought into effect by **continue**, will find **done** to be true and will cause the loop to exit.

Labels and goto

Although **goto** fell out of favor some years ago, it has recently managed to polish its tarnished image a bit. This book will not make a judgement as to its validity as a form of program control. It should be stated, however, that there are no programming situations that require its use—it is not a necessary item to make the language complete. Rather, it is a convenience, which, if used wisely, can be of benefit in certain programming situations. As such, **goto** is not used in this book outside of this section. (In a language like C, which has a rich set of control structures and allows additional control using **break** and **continue**, there is little need for it.) The chief concern most programmers have about **goto** is its tendency to confuse a program and render it nearly unreadable. However, there are times when the use of **goto** will actually clarify program flow rather than confuse it.

The **goto** requires a *label* for operation. A label is a valid C identifier followed by a colon. Furthermore, the label must be in the same function as the **goto** that uses it. For example, a loop from 1 to 100 could be written using a **goto** and a label, as shown here:

```
x = 1;

loop1:
  x++;
  if(x < 100) goto loop1;
```

One good use for **goto** is when exiting from a deeply nested routine. For example, consider the following code fragment:

```
for(...) {
  for(...) {
    while(...) {
```

```
    if(...) goto stop;
       .
       .
       .
  }
 }
}

stop:
  printf("error in program\n");
```

Eliminating the **goto** would force a number of additional tests to be performed. A simple **break** statement would not work here because it would exit from only the innermost loop. If you substituted checks at each loop, the code would then look like the following:

```
done = 0;
for(...) {
  for(...) {
    while(...) {
      if(...) {
        done = 1;
        break;
      }
       .
       .
       .
    }
    if(done) break;
  }
  if(done) break;
}
```

You should use **goto** sparingly, if at all. But if the code would be much more difficult to read without it, or if execution speed of the code is critical, then by all means use **goto**.

Now that your study of the program-control statements is complete, it is time to move on to arrays and strings.

7

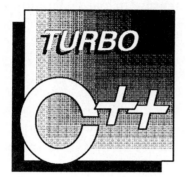

Arrays and Strings

An *array* is a collection of variables of the same type that are referenced by a common name. In C, all arrays consist of contiguous memory locations. The lowest address corresponds to the first element, and the highest address to the last element. Arrays may have from one to several dimensions. A specific element in an array is accessed by an *index*.

The array that you will most often use is the *character array*. Because there is no built-in string data type in C, arrays of characters are used. As you will see, this approach to strings allows greater power and flexibility than are available in languages that use a special string type.

One-Dimensional Arrays

The general form of a single-dimension array declaration is

type var_name[size];

Here, *type* declares the base type of the array. The *base type* determines the data type of each element that comprises the array and *size* defines how many elements the array will hold. For example, the following declares an integer array named **sample** that is ten elements long:

```
int sample[10];
```

In C, all arrays have zero as the index of their first element. Therefore, this declares an integer array that has ten elements, **sample[0]** through **sample[9]**. The following program loads an integer array with the numbers 0 through 9:

```
main()
{
  int x[10];  /* this reserves 10 integer elements */
  int t;

  for(t=0; t<10; ++t) x[t]=t;
}
```

For a one-dimensional array, the total size of the array in bytes is computed as shown here:

*Total bytes = size of base type * number of elements*

Arrays are very common in programming because they let you easily deal with a large number of related variables. For example, the use of arrays makes it easy to compute the average of a list of numbers, as shown in the following program. It reads ten integers entered by the user and then displays the average.

```
/* Find the average of ten numbers. */

#include <stdio.h>

main()
{
  int sample[10], i, avg;

  for(i=0; i<10; i++) {
    printf("enter number %d: ", i);
    scanf("%d", &sample[i]);
  }

  avg = 0;

  /* now, add up the numbers */
  for(i=0; i<10; i++) avg = avg+sample[i];
  printf("The average is %d\n", avg/10);
}
```

No Bounds Checking

C performs no bounds checking on arrays: nothing stops you from overrunning the end of an array. If this happens during an assignment operation you will be assigning values to some other variable's data, or even to a piece of the program's code. Put differently, an array of size **N** may be indexed beyond **N** without causing any compile or run-time error messages even though doing so will probably cause your program to crash. As the programmer, it is your job to ensure that all arrays are large enough to hold what the program will put in them and to provide bounds checking when it is needed. For example, this program will compile and run even though the array **crash** is being overrun. (*Do not try this example; it will crash your system!*)

```
/* An incorrect program.  Do Not Execute! */

main()
{
  int crash[10], i;

  for(i=0; i<100; i++) crash[i]=i;
}
```

In this case, the loop will still iterate 100 times, even though **crash** is only ten elements long. This causes important information to be overwritten, resulting in a program failure.

You might be wondering why the C language does not provide boundary checks on arrays. The answer is that C was designed to replace assembly language coding in most situations. Towards this end, virtually no error checking is included because it slows the execution of a program (often dramatically). Instead, C expects you, the programmer, to be responsible enough to prevent array overruns in the first place.

One-Dimensional Arrays Are Lists

One-dimensional arrays are essentially lists of information of the same type. For example, after running this program,

```
char str[7];

main()
{
  int i;

  for(i=0; i<7; i++) str[i] = 'A'+i;
}
```

str looks like this:

str[0]	str[1]	str[2]	str[3]	str[4]	str[5]	str[6]
A	B	C	D	E	F	G

Strings

By far the most common use for one-dimensional arrays is to create character strings. In C, a *string* is defined as consisting of a character array that is terminated by a *null*. A null is specified using '\0' and is zero. Because of the null terminator, it is necessary to declare character arrays to be one character longer than the largest string that they are to hold. For example, if you wish to declare an array **str** that can hold a 10-character string, you write

```
char str[11];
```

This makes room for the null at the end of the string.

As you saw in Chapter 5, although C does not have a string data type, it still allows string constants. A *string constant* is a list of characters enclosed by double quotation marks. For example:

"hello there" "this is a test"

It is not necessary to manually add the null onto the end of string constants—the compiler does that for you automatically. This means that the string "Turbo" will appear in memory like this:

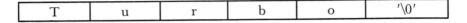

T	u	r	b	o	'\0'

Reading a String From the Keyboard

The easiest way to input a string from the keyboard is with the **gets( )** library function. The general form of a **gets( )** call is

gets(*array-name*);

To read a string, call **gets( )** with the name of the array, without any index, as its argument. Upon return from **gets( )** the array will hold the string input at the keyboard. The **gets( )** function will continue to read characters until you enter a carriage return. The header file used by **gets( )** is STDIO.H.

For example, this program simply repeats the string that you typed at the keyboard:

```
/* A simple string example. */

#include <stdio.h>

main()
{
  char str[80];

  printf("enter a string: ");
  gets(str); /* read a string from the keyboard */

  printf("%s", str);
}
```

Notice that **str** can be used as an argument to **printf( )**. Notice also that the array name without an index is used. For reasons that will be clear after you have read a few more chapters, the name of a character array, without an index, that holds a string can be used any place that a string constant can be used.

Keep in mind that **gets( )** does not perform any bounds checking on the array that calls it. Therefore, if the user enters a string longer than the size of the array, **gets( )** will write past the end of the array.

Some String Library Functions

C supports a wide range of string-manipulation functions. The most common are

    strcpy( )
    strcat( )
    strlen( )
    strcmp( )

The string functions all use the same header file: STRING.H. Let's take a look at these functions now:

The strcpy( ) Function   A call to **strcpy( )** takes this general form:

    strcpy(*to, from*);

The **strcpy( )** function is used to copy the contents of the string *from* into *to*. Remember that the array forming *to* must be large enough to hold the string contained in *from*. If it is not, the array will be overrun—possibly damaging your program.

The **strcpy( )** function does return a value, but you won't be able to understand its meaning until you have read the next chapter, so you can ignore it for the moment.

The following program will copy "hello" into string **str**:

```
#include <stdio.h>
#include <string.h>

main()
{

  char str[80];

  strcpy(str, "hello");
  printf("%s", str);
}
```

The strcat( ) Function   A call to **strcat( )** takes this form:

strcat(*s1*, *s2*);

The **strcat( )** function appends *s2* to *s1; s2* is unchanged. Both strings must be null terminated and the result is null terminated. For example, this program will print "hello there" on the screen:

```
#include <stdio.h>
#include <string.h>

main()
{

  char s1[20], s2[10];

  strcpy(s1, "hello");

  strcpy(s2, " there");

  strcat(s1, s2);

  printf("%s", s1);

}
```

Like **strcpy( )**, **strcat( )** returns a value, but you must wait until the next chapter in order to understand its meaning.

The strcmp( ) Function A call to **strcmp( )** takes this general form:

strcmp(*s1*, *s2*);

The **strcmp( )** function compares two strings and returns 0 if they are equal. If *s1* is lexicographically greater (greater in terms of dictionary order) than *s2*, then a positive number is returned; if it is less than *s2,* a negative number is returned.

The following function can be used as a password-verification routine:

```
/* Return true if password accepted; false otherwise. */
password()
{

  char s[80];

  printf("enter password: ");

  gets(s);

  if(strcmp(s, "password")) {  /* strings different */
    printf("invalid password\n");
    return 0;
  }

  /* strings compared the same */
  return 1;

}
```

The key to using **strcmp( )** is that it returns false when the strings match. Therefore, you will need to use the NOT operator if you wish something to occur when the strings are equal. For example, this program continues to request input until you type the word **quit**:

```
#include <stdio.h>
#include <string.h>

main()
{
```

```
char s[80];

for(;;) {
  printf("Enter a string: ");
  gets(s);
  if(!strcmp("quit", s)) break;
}
}
```

The strlen( ) Function   The general form of a call to **strlen( )** is

strlen(*s*);

where *s* is a string.

The **strlen( )** function returns the length of *s*.

The following will print the length of the string you enter at the keyboard:

```
#include <stdio.h>
#include <string.h>

main()
{
  char str[80];

  printf("enter a string: ");

  gets(str);

  printf("%d", strlen(str));

}
```

For example, if you entered the string "hi there", this program would display "8". The null terminator is not counted by **strlen( )**.

The next program prints the string entered at the keyboard in reverse. For example, "hello" will print as "olleh". Remember that strings are simply character arrays; thus, each character may be referenced individually.

```
/* Print a string backwards. */
#include <stdio.h>
#include <string.h>

main()
{
  char str[80];
  int i;

  printf("enter a string: ");
  gets(str);

  for(i=strlen(str)-1; i>=0; i--) printf("%c", str[i]);
}
```

As a final example, the following program illustrates the use of several string functions:

```
#include <stdio.h>
#include <string.h>

main()
{
  char s1[80], s2[80];

  printf("enter two strings: ");

  gets(s1); gets(s2);

  printf("lengths: %d %d\n", strlen(s1), strlen(s2));

  if(!strcmp(s1, s2)) printf("The strings are equal\n");

  strcat(s1, s2);
  printf("%s\n", s1);
}
```

If this program is run and the strings "hello" and "hello" are entered, then the output will be

```
lengths: 5 5
The strings are equal
hellohello
```

It is important to remember that **strcmp( )** returns false if the strings are equal, so be sure to use the ! to reverse the condition, as shown in this example, if you are testing for equality.

Using the Null Terminator

The fact that all strings are null terminated can often be put to good use to simplify various operations on strings. For example, look at how little code is required to make every character in a string uppercase:

```
/* Convert a string to uppercase. */
#include <stdio.h>
#include <string.h>
#include <ctype.h>

main()
{
  char str[80];
  int i;

  strcpy(str, "this is a test");

  for(i=0; str[i]; i++) str[i] = toupper(str[i]);

  printf("%s", str);
}
```

This program will print "THIS IS A TEST". It uses the library function **toupper( )**, which returns the uppercase equivalent of its character argument, to convert each character in the string. It uses the header file CTYPE.H. Notice that the test condition of the **for** loop is simply the array indexed by the control variable. The reason this works is because a true value is any nonzero value. Therefore, the loop runs until it encounters the null terminator, which is zero. Since the null terminator marks the end of the string, the loop stops precisely where it is supposed to. As you progress, you will see many examples that use the null terminator in a similar fashion.

A printf( ) Variation

Up to now, to display the string held in a character array using **printf( )**, this basic format was used:

printf("%s", *array-name*);

However, remember that the first argument to **printf( )** is a string, and that all characters that are not format commands are printed. Therefore, if you wish to print only one string, you can used this form:

printf(*array-name*);

For example, this program prints "Hello Tom" on the screen:

```c
#include <stdio.h>
#include <string.h>

main()
{
  char str[80];

  strcpy(str, "Hello Tom");

  printf(str);
}
```

Two-Dimensional Arrays

C allows multidimensional arrays. The simplest form of the multidimensional array is the *two-dimensional array*. A two-dimensional array is, in essence, a list of one-dimensional arrays. To declare a two-dimensional integer array **twod** of size 10,20 you would write

```
int twod[10][20];
```

Pay careful attention to the declaration: unlike most other computer languages, which use commas to separate the array dimensions, C places each dimension in its own set of brackets.

Similarly, to access point 3,5 of array **twod**, you would use **twod[3][5]**. In the following example, a two-dimensional array is loaded with the numbers 1 through 12:

```
main()
{
  int t,i, num[3][4];

  for(t=0; t<3; ++t)
    for(i=0; i<4; ++i)
      num[t][i] = (t*4)+i+1;
}
```

In this example, **num[0][0]** will have the value 1, **num[0][1]** the value 2, **num[0][2]** the value 3, and so on. The value of **num[2][3]** will be 12.

Two-dimensional arrays are stored in a row-column matrix, where the first index indicates the row and the second indicates the column. This means that the rightmost index changes faster than the leftmost when accessing the elements in the array in the order they are actually stored in memory. See Figure 7-1 for a

Figure 7-1.

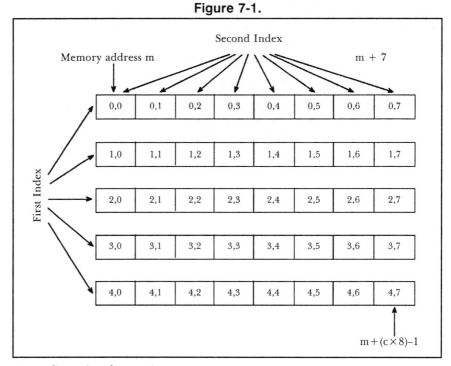

A two-dimensional array in memory

graphic representation of a two-dimensional array in memory. In essence, the first (leftmost) index can be thought of as a pointer to the correct row.

You should remember that storage for all global array elements is allocated at compile time. This means that the memory that holds a global array is needed the entire time your program executes.

In the case of a two-dimensional array, the following formula will find the number of bytes of memory:

*bytes = row * column * size of data type*

Therefore, an integer array with dimensions 10,5 would have

$$10 \times 5 \times 2$$

or 100 bytes allocated.

It is very common to use two-dimensional arrays to process tables of information. For example, the following fragment could be used to print the batting averages for a baseball team:

```
#define PLAYERS 9
#define ATBATS   100

int battingavg[PLAYERS][ATBATS];

    .
    .
    .

display_averages()
{
  int i, j;
  int hits;

  for(i=0; i<PLAYERS; i++) {
    for(j=0, hits=0; j<ATBATS; j++)
      hits = hits + battingavg[i][j];
    printf("Player %d hit %f\n", i+1,
            (float) hits/(float) ATBATS);
  }
}
```

At the end of this chapter you will see another example of two-dimensional arrays in action.

Arrays of Strings

It is not uncommon in programming to use an array of strings. For example, the input processor to a database may verify user commands against a string array of valid commands. To create an array of strings, a two-dimensional character array is used with the size of the left index determining the number of strings and the size of the right index specifying the maximum length of each string. For example, this declares an array of 30 strings, each having a maximum length of 80 characters:

```
char str_array[30][80];
```

To access an individual string is quite easy: you simply specify only the left index. For example, this statement calls **gets( )** with the third string in **str_array**:

```
gets(str_array[2]);
```

This is functionally equivalent to

```
gets(&str_array[2][0]);
```

but the previous form is much more common in professionally written C code. (The "&" is required in the second form, for reasons that will become clear in the next chapter.)

To help you better understand how string arrays work, study the following short program that accepts lines of text entered at the keyboard and redisplays them when a blank line is entered.

```
/* Enter and display strings. */
#include <stdio.h>

main()
{
  register int t, i;
  char text[100][80];

  for(t=0; t<100; t++) {
    printf("%d: ", t);
    gets(text[t]);
    if(!text[t][0]) break; /* quit on blank line */
  }

  /* redisplay the strings */
  for(i=0; i<t; i++)
    printf("%s\n", text[i]);
}
```

This program inputs lines of text until a blank line is entered, then redisplays each line.

Multidimensional Arrays

C allows arrays with more than two dimensions. The general form of a multidimensional array declaration is

type name[*size1*][*size2*] . . . [*sizeN*];

For example, this creates a $4 \times 10 \times 3$ integer array:

```
int threed[4][10][3];
```

Arrays of three or more dimensions are not often used because of the amount of memory required to hold them. Storage for global array elements is allocated permanently during the execution of your program. For example, a four-dimensional character array with dimensions 10,6,9,4 would require

$$10 \times 6 \times 9 \times 4$$

or 2,160 bytes.

If the array were two-byte integers, 4320 bytes would be needed. If the array were **double** (8 bytes long), then 34,560 bytes would be required. The storage required increases exponentially with the number of dimensions. A program with arrays of more than three or four dimensions may find itself quickly out of memory!

Array Initialization

C allows the initialization of arrays. The general form of array initialization is similar to that of other variables, as shown here:

type-specifier array__name[size1] . . . [sizeN] = { *value-list* };

The *value-list* is a comma-separated list of constants that are type compatible with the base type of the array. The first constant will be placed in the first position of the array, the second constant in the second position, and so on. Notice that a semicolon follows the **}**. In the following example, a 10-element integer array is initialized with the numbers 1 through 10:

```
int i[10] = {1, 2, 3, 4, 5, 6, 7, 8, 9, 10};
```

This means that **i[0]** will have the value 1 and **i[9]** will have the value 10.

Character arrays that will hold strings allow a shorthand initialization that takes this form:

char *array__name[size]* = *"string"*;

For example, this code fragment initializes **str** to the phrase **hello**:

```
char str[6] = "hello";
```

This is the same as writing

```
char str[6] = {'h', 'e', 'l', 'l', 'o', '\0'};
```

Because strings in C must end with a null, make sure that the array you declare is long enough to include it. This is why **str** is six characters long even though "hello" is only five. When the string constant is used, the compiler will automatically supply the null terminator.

Multidimensional arrays are initialized in the same way as one-dimensional ones. For example, the following initializes **sqrs** with the numbers 1 through 10 and their squares:

```
int sqrs[10][2] = {
  1, 1,
  2, 4,
  3, 9,
  4, 16,
  5, 25,
  6, 36,
  7, 49,
  8, 64,
  9, 81,
  10, 100
};
```

Unsized Array Initializations

Imagine that you are using array initialization to build a table of error messages, as shown here:

```
char e1[14] = "invalid input\n";
char e2[23] = "selection out-of-range\n";
char e3[21] = "authorization denied\n";
```

As you might guess, it is very tedious to manually count the characters in each message to determine the correct array dimension. It is possible to let C automatically dimension the arrays in this example through the use of *unsized arrays.* If, in an array initialization statement, the size of the array is not specified, then the compiler will automatically create an array big enough to hold all the initializers present.

Using this approach, the message table becomes

```
char e1[] = "invalid input\n";
char e2[] = "selection out-of-range\n";
char e3[] = "authorization denied\n";
```

Besides being less tedious, the unsized array initialization method allows you to change any of the messages without fear of accidentally miscounting.

Unsized array initializations are not restricted to only one-dimensional arrays. For multidimensioned arrays, you must specify all but the leftmost dimensions in order to allow C to properly index the array. In this way, you can build tables of varying lengths with the compiler automatically allocating enough storage for them. For example, the declaration of **sqrs** as an unsized array is shown here:

```
int sqrs[][2] = {
   1, 1,
   2, 4,
   3, 9,
   4, 16,
   5, 25,
   6, 36,
   7, 49,
   8, 64,
   9, 81,
  10, 100
};
```

The advantage to this declaration over the sized version is that the table may be lengthened or shortened without changing the array dimensions.

A Sub Hunt Game

Two-dimensional arrays are commonly used to simulate board game matrices, such as those found in chess and checkers. While it is beyond the scope of this book to present a chess or checkers program, a simple sub hunt game will be developed.

In the sub hunt game the computer controls a submarine and you control a battleship. The object of the game is for one vessel to destroy the other. However, both ships have limited radar capabilities. The only way the submarine can find the battleship is to be directly under it. For the battleship to find the submarine, it must be directly above it. The winner is determined by who finds whom first, with the submarine and the battleship alternating moves at random about the "ocean."

The "ocean" is a small playing field that is just a 3×3-inch square. Both the submarine and the battleship treat this as an X,Y coordinate plane, with 0,0 being the upper-left corner. A two-dimensional array called **matrix** is used to hold the game board and each element in it is initialized to hold a space, which denotes an unused element. The use of a space to indicate a free element simplifies the function used to display the matrix, as you will see.

The **main( )** function and the global variables are shown here:

```
/* Battleship VS. Submarine - A Simple Computer Game. */

#include <stdio.h>
#include <stdlib.h>
#include <time.h> /* needed by randomize( ) */

char matrix[3][3] = {
          ' ', ' ', ' ',
          ' ', ' ', ' ',
          ' ', ' ', ' '
};

int compX, compY, playerX, playerY;
```

```
main()
{
  /* randomize the random number generator */
  randomize();

  compX = compY = playerX = playerY = 0;
  for(;;) {
    if(sub_tries()) {
      printf("Submarine wins!\n");
      break;
    }
    if(player_tries()) {
      printf("Battleship (you) win!\n");
      break;
    }
    display_board();
  }
  display_board();
}
```

The **randomize( )** function is used to randomize C's random-number generator, which is used to generate the computer's move, as you will soon see.

The first function you need is the one that creates the computer's move. The computer (submarine) generates its moves using C's random-number generator **rand( )**, which returns a random number between 0 and 32,767. (Both **rand( )** and **randomize( )** use the header file STDLIB.H. The **randomize( )** function also requires the header file TIME.H.) A random value is generated for both the X and Y coordinates each time the computer is called upon to generate a move. These values are then used in a modulus operation to provide a number between 0 and 2. Finally, the computer checks to see if it has found (and by definition destroyed) the battleship. If the move it generated has the same coordinates as the current location of the battleship, the submarine wins. If the computer wins, the function returns true; otherwise, it returns false. The **sub_tries( )** function is shown here:

```
/* Generate  the  computer's  next  move  using  the  random
number
   generator.
*/
sub_tries()
{
  matrix[compX][compY] = ' ';

  compX = rand() % 3;
  compY = rand() % 3;

  if(matrix[compX][compY] == 'B')
    return 1; /* submarine won the fight */
  else {
    matrix[compX][compY] = 'S';
    return 0; /* it missed */
  }
}
```

The battleship gets its next move from the player. The function prompts the user for new coordinates and then sees whether it has found the submarine or not. If it has, the player wins and the function returns true. Otherwise, the function returns false. The **player_tries( )** function is shown here:

```
/* Get the player's next move. */
player_tries()
{
  matrix[playerX][playerY] = ' ';

  do {
    printf("Enter new coordinates (X,Y): ");
    scanf("%d%d", &playerX, &playerY);
  } while(playerX < 0 ¦¦ playerX > 2  ¦¦  playerY<0 ¦¦
        playerY > 2);

  if(matrix[playerX][playerY] == 'S')
    return 1; /* battleship won the fight */
  else {
    matrix[playerX][playerY] = 'B';
    return 0; /* it missed */
  }
}
```

After each series of moves the game board is displayed. The **display_board( )** function accomplishes this. An unused cell is blank. The one that holds the last position of the submarine will contain an **S** and the one that holds the battleship will contain a **B**.

```
/* Display the playing board. */
display_board()
{
  printf("\n");

  printf("%c | %c | %c\n", matrix[0][0],
         matrix[0][1], matrix[0][2]);
  printf("---|----|---\n");
  printf("%c | %c | %c\n", matrix[1][0],
         matrix[1][1], matrix[1][2]);
  printf("---|----|---\n");
  printf("%c | %c | %c\n", matrix[2][0],
         matrix[2][1], matrix[2][2]);
}
```

The entire sub hunt program is shown here. You should enter this program now and experiment with it. With a little thought you should be able to make it play a better game.

```
/* Battleship VS. Submarine - A Simple Computer Game. */

#include <stdio.h>
#include <stdlib.h>
#include <time.h> /* needed by randomize() */

char matrix[3][3] = {
        ' ', ' ', ' ',
        ' ', ' ', ' ',
        ' ', ' ', ' '
};

int compX, compY, playerX, playerY;

main()
{
  /* randomize the random number generator */
  randomize();

  compX = compY = playerX = playerY = 0;
  for(;;) {
    if(sub_tries()) {
      printf("Submarine wins!\n");
```

```
      break;
    }
    if(player_tries()) {
      printf("Battleship (you) win!\n");
      break;
    }
    display_board();
} display_board();

/* Generate the computer's next move using the random
   number generator.
*/
sub_tries()
{
   matrix[compX][compY] = ' ';

   compX = rand() % 3;
   compY = rand() % 3;

   if(matrix[compX][compY] == 'B')
     return 1; /* submarine won the fight */
   else {
     matrix[compX][compY] = 'S';
     return 0; /* it missed */
   }
}

/* Get the player's next move. */
player_tries()
{

   matrix[playerX][playerY] = ' ';
   do {
     printf("Enter new coordinates (X,Y): ");
     scanf("%d%d", &playerX, &playerY);
   } while(playerX < 0 || playerX > 2 || playerY<0 ||
           playerY > 2);

   if(matrix[playerX][playerY] == 'S')
     return 1; /* battleship won the fight */
   else {
     matrix[playerX][playerY] = 'B';
     return 0; /* it missed */
   }
}
```

```
/* Display the playing board. */
display_board()
{
  printf("\n");

  printf("%c ¦ %c ¦ %c\n", matrix[0][0],
         matrix[0][1], matrix[0][2]);
  printf("--- ¦ ---- ¦ ---\n");
  printf("%c ¦ %c ¦ %c\n", matrix[1][0],
         matrix[1][1], matrix[1][2]);
  printf("--- ¦ ---- ¦ ---\n");
  printf("%c ¦ %c ¦ %c\n", matrix[2][0],
         matrix[2][1], matrix[2][2]);
}
```

Now that arrays are behind you, it is time to move on to one of C's most important features: pointers.

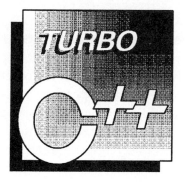

Pointers

The understanding and correct use of pointers is critical to the creation of most successful C programs. The reason for this is threefold. First, pointers provide the means by which functions can modify their calling arguments. Second, they are used to support C's dynamic allocation routines. Third, they can be substituted for arrays in many situations—providing increased efficiency. Also, many C++ features rely heavily upon pointers, so a thorough understanding of pointers is very important.

In addition to being one of C's strongest features, pointers are also its most dangerous. For example, *uninitialized* or *wild pointers* can cause a system crash. Perhaps worse, it is easy to accidentally use pointers incorrectly, which causes bugs that are difficult to find.

Because of both their importance and potential for abuse, this chapter examines the subject of pointers in detail.

Pointers Are Addresses

A *pointer* is a variable that holds a memory address of another object. Most commonly, this address is the location of another variable in memory, although it could be the address of a port or special-purpose RAM, such as a video buffer. If one variable contains the address of another variable, then the first one is said to *point* to the second. This situation is illustrated in Figure 8-1.

Figure 8-1.

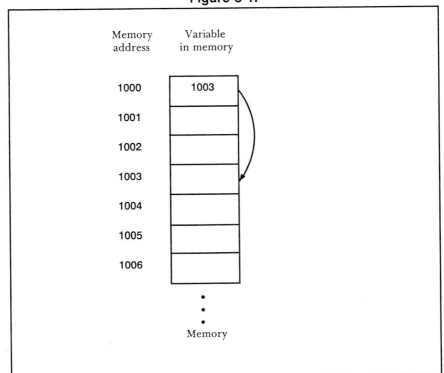

One variable that points to another

Pointer Variables

If a variable is going to hold a pointer, then it must be declared as such. A *pointer declaration* consists of a base type, an *, and the variable name. The general form for declaring a pointer variable is

 type **var-name*;

where *type* may be any valid C type and *var-name* is the name of the pointer variable. The *base type* of the pointer defines what type of variables the pointer can point to. For example, these statements declare one character pointer and two integer pointers.

```
char *p;

int *temp, *start;
```

The Pointer Operators

There are two special pointer operators: **&** and *. The **&** is a unary operator that returns the memory address of its operand. (A unary operator requires only one operand.) For example,

```
count_addr = &count;
```

places into **count_addr** the memory address of the variable **count**. This address is the computer's internal location of the variable. It has nothing to do with the *value* of **count**. The operation of the **&** can be remembered as returning the "the address of" the variable it precedes. Therefore, the assignment just given could be stated as "**count_addr** receives the address of **count**."

To better understand this assignment, assume the variable **count** is located at address 2000. Then, after the assignment, **count_addr** will have the value 2000.

The second operator is ***** and is the complement of the **&**. It is a unary operator that returns the *value of the variable located at the address that follows*. For example, if **count_addr** contains the memory address of the variable **count**, then

```
val = *count_addr;
```

will place the value of **count** into **val**. If **count** originally had the value 100, then **val** will have the value 100 because that is the value stored at location 2000, which is the memory address that was assigned to **count_value**. The operation of the ***** can be remembered as "at address." In this case, then, the statement could be read as "**val** receives the value at address **count_addr**."

Unfortunately, the multiplication sign and the "at address" sign are the same. This fact sometimes confuses newcomers to the C language. These operators have no relationship to each other. Both **&** and ***** have a higher precedence than all other arithmetic operators, except the unary minus, with which they are equal.

Here is a program that uses these operators to print the number 100 on the screen:

```
#include <stdio.h>

main()
{
   int *count_addr, count, val;

   count = 100;
```

```
   count_addr = &count;  /* get count's address */
   val = *count_addr;  /* get the value at that address */
   printf("%d", val);  /* displays 100 */
}
```

The Base Type Is Important

In the preceding discussion, you saw that it was possible to assign **val** the value of **count** indirectly through a pointer to **count**. At this point you may have thought of this important question: How does the compiler know how many bytes to copy into **val** from the address pointed to by **count_addr**? More generally, how does the compiler transfer the proper number of bytes for any assignment using a pointer? The answer is that the base type of the pointer determines the type of data that the compiler assumes the pointer is pointing to. In this case, because **count_addr** is an integer pointer, 2 bytes of information are copied into **val** from the address pointed to by **count_addr**. If it had been a **double** pointer, then 8 bytes would have been copied.

You must make sure that your pointer variables always point to the correct type of data. For example, when you declare a pointer to be of type **int**, the compiler assumes that any address it holds will point to an integer variable. Because C allows you to assign *any* address to a pointer variable, the following incorrect code fragment will compile, although Turbo C++ does report a warning message:

```
#include <stdio.h>

/* This program will not work correctly. */
main()
{
   float x=10.1, y;
```

```
int  *p;

p = &x;
y = *p;
printf("%f", y);
}
```

This will *not* assign the value of **x** to **y**. Because **p** is declared to be an integer pointer, only 2 bytes of information will be transferred to **y**, not the 4 that normally make up a floating-point number.

Pointer Expressions

In general, expressions involving pointers conform to the same rules as any other C expressions. In this section, a few special aspects of pointer expressions will be examined.

Pointer Assignments

As with any variable, a pointer may be used on the right side of an assignment statement to assign its value to another pointer. For example:

```
#include <stdio.h>

main()
{
  int x;
  int *p1, *p2;

  x = 101;

  p1 = &x;
  p2 = p1;
```

```
/* print the hexadecimal value of the
    address of x - - not x's value! */
printf("at location %p ", p2);

/* now print x's value */
printf("is the value %d\n", *p2);
}
```

The address, in hexadecimal, of **x** is displayed by using another of **printf( )**'s format codes. The **%p** specifies that a pointer address is to be displayed using hexadecimal notation.

Pointer Arithmetic

There are only two arithmetic operations that may be used on pointers: addition and subtraction. To understand what occurs in pointer arithmetic, let **p1** be a pointer to an integer with a current value of 2000. After the expression

```
p1++;
```

p1's contents will be 2002, not 2001. Each time **p1** is incremented, it will point to the *next integer*. The same is true of decrements. For example,

```
p1--;
```

will cause **p1** to have the value 1998, assuming that it was previously 2000.

Each time that a pointer is incremented, it will point to the memory location of the next element of its base type. Each time it is decremented it will point to the location of the previous element. In the case of pointers to characters, this will appear to be "normal" arithmetic. However, all other pointers will increase or decrease by the length of the data type they point to. For example, assuming one-byte characters and two-byte integers, when a character pointer is incremented, its value increases by one; however, when an integer pointer is incremented its value increases by two. Figure 8-2 illustrates this concept.

You are not limited to only increments and decrements, however. You may add or subtract integers to or from pointers. The expression

```
p1 = p1 + 9;
```

will make **p1** point to the ninth element of **p1**'s base type beyond the one it is currently pointing to.

Figure 8-2.

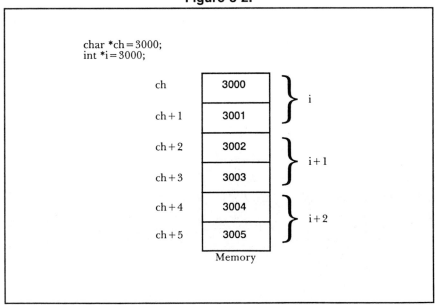

The relation of pointer arithmetic to the base type of the pointer

You may subtract one pointer from another. If both pointers point to different elements of the same array, then the result of the subtraction is the same as subtracting the indices of the elements pointed to.

Aside from addition and subtraction of a pointer and an integer and subtraction of one pointer from another, no other arithmetic operations may be performed on pointers. Specifically, you may not:

- multiply or divide pointers
- add two pointers
- apply the bitwise shift and mask operators to pointers
- add or subtract type **float** or **double** to or from pointers

Pointer Comparisons

It is possible to compare two pointers in a relational expression. For instance, given two pointers **p** and **q**, the following statement is perfectly valid:

```
if(p<q) printf("p points to lower memory than q\n");
```

Generally, pointer comparisons should only be used when two or more pointers are pointing to a common object.

Pointers and Arrays

There is a close relationship between pointers and arrays. Consider this fragment:

```
char str[80], *p1;

p1 = str;
```

Here, **p1** has been set to the address of the first array element in **str**. In C, an array name without an index is the address to the start of the array. In essence, it is a pointer to the array. The same result—a pointer to the first element of the array **str**—can also be generated like this:

```
p1=&str[0];
```

However, this is considered poor form by most C programmers.

If you wished to access the fifth element in **str** you could write

```
str[4]
```

or

```
*(p1+4)
```

Both statements would return the fifth element.

 REMEMBER   Arrays start at zero, so a 4 is used to index **str**. You would also add four to the pointer **p1** to get the fifth element, because **p1** currently points to the first element of **str**.

In essence, C allows two methods of accessing array elements. This is important because pointer arithmetic can be faster than array indexing. Since speed is often a consideration in programming, the use of pointers to access array elements is very common in C programs.

To see an example of how pointers can be used in place of array indexing, consider these two programs—one with array indexing and one with pointers—that display the contents of a string in lowercase.

```
#include <stdio.h>
#include <ctype.h>
```

```
/* array version */
main()
{
  char str[80];
  int i;

  printf("enter a string in uppercase: ");
  gets(str);

  printf("here's the string in lowercase: ");

  for(i=0; str[i]; i++) printf("%c", tolower(str[i]));
}


#include <stdio.h>
#include <ctype.h>

/* pointer version */
main()
{
  char str[80], *p;

  printf("enter a string in uppercase: ");
  gets(str);

  printf("here's the string in lowercase: ");

  p = str;  /* get the address of str */
  while(*p) printf("%c", tolower(*p++));
}
```

The array version is slower than the pointer version because it takes longer to index an array than it does to use the * operator.

Sometimes, novice C programmers make the mistake of thinking that they should never use array indexing because pointers are much more efficient. But this is not the case. If the array is going to be accessed in strictly ascending or descending order, then pointers are faster and easier to use. However, if the array is going to be accessed randomly, then array indexing can be better because it will generally be as fast as evaluating a complex pointer expression and is easier to code and understand. Also, when you use array indexing, you are letting the compiler do some of the work for you.

Indexing a Pointer

In C, it is possible to index a pointer as if it were an array. This further points out the close relationship between pointers and arrays. For example, this fragment is perfectly valid and prints the numbers 1 through 5 on the screen:

```
/* Indexing a pointer like an array. */

#include <stdio.h>

main()
{
  int i[5] = {1, 2, 3, 4, 5};
  int *p, t;

  p = i;

  for(t=0; t<5; t++) printf("%d ", p[t]);
}
```

In C, the statement **p[t]** is identical to **(p+t)**.

Pointers and Strings

Since an array name without an index is a pointer to the first element of that array, what is really happening when you use the string functions discussed in the previous chapter is that only a pointer to the strings is passed to the functions, not the actual string itself. To see how this works, here is one way **strlen( )** could be written:

```
strlen(char *s)
{
  int i=0;
```

```
while(*s) {
  i++;
  s++;
}
return i;
}
```

Remember that all strings in C are terminated by a null, which is a false value. Therefore, a statement such as

```
while(*s)
```

is true until the end of the string is reached. Here, **strlen( )** will return 0 if called with a zero-length string. Otherwise, it returns the length of the string.

At this point you are probably wondering how **strlen( )** can be called with a string constant as an argument. For example, you may wonder how the following fragment works.

```
printf("length of TEST is %d", strlen("TEST"));
```

The answer is that when a string constant is used, only a pointer to it is passed to **strlen( )**. The actual string is stored automatically by Turbo C++.

More generally, when a string constant is used in any type of expression, it is treated as a pointer to the first character in the string. For example, this program is perfectly valid and prints the phrase "this program works" on the screen:

```
#include <stdio.h>

main()
{
  char *s;

  s = "this program works";
```

```
  printf(s);
}
```

The characters that make up a string constant are stored in a special *string table* maintained by Turbo C++. Your program uses only a pointer to that table.

Getting the Address of an Array Element

So far, the examples have been concerned with assigning the address of the start of an array to a pointer. However, it is possible to assign the address of a specific element of an array—by applying the **&** to an indexed array. For example, this fragment places the address of the third element of **x** into **p**:

```
p = &x[2];
```

One place that this practice is especially useful is in finding a substring. For example, this program will print the remainder of a string, that is entered at the keyboard, from the point where the first space is found:

```
#include <stdio.h>

/* Display the string left after the first space
   is encountered. */
main()
{
  char s[80];
  char *p;
  int i;

  printf("enter a string: ");
```

```
gets(s);

/* find first space or end of string */
for(i=0; s[i] && s[i]!=' '; i++) ;

p = &s[i];

printf(p);
}
```

This works because **p** will be pointing to either a space or a null (if no spaces are contained in the string). If it is a space, then the remainder of the string will be printed. If it is a null, then **printf( )** prints nothing. For example, if "hi there" is entered, then "there" is displayed.

Arrays of Pointers

Pointers may be arrayed as you would any other data types. The declaration for an **int** pointer array of size 10 is

```
int *x[10];
```

To assign the address of an integer variable called **var** to the third element of the pointer array, you would write

```
x[2] = &var;
```

To find the value of **var**, you would write

```
*x[2]
```

A common use of pointer arrays is to hold pointers to error messages. You can create a function that will output a message, given its code number, as shown in **serror( )** here:

```
char *err[] = {
  "cannot open file\n",
  "read error\n",
  "write error\n",
  "media failure\n"
};

serror(int num)
{
  printf("%s",err[num]);
}
```

As you can see, **printf( )** is called inside **serror( )** with a character pointer, which points to one of the various error messages indexed by the error number passed to the function. For example, if **num** is passed a 2, then the message **write error** is displayed.

Another interesting application for initialized arrays of character pointers uses C's **system( )** function, which lets your program send a command to the operating system. A call to **system( )** takes this general form:

system(*"command"*);

where *command* is the operating-system command to be executed. For example, assuming a DOS environment, this statement causes the default directory to be displayed:

```
system("DIR");
```

The program that follows implements a very tiny menu-driven

user interface that can execute four DOS commands: DIR, CHKDSK, TIME, and DATE.

```
/* A very simple menu-driven DOS user interface. */
#include <stdio.h>
#include <stdlib.h>
#include <conio.h>

main()
{
  /* create an array of strings */
  char *command[] = {
    "DIR",
    "CHKDSK",
    "TIME",
    "DATE"
  };
  char ch;

  for(;;) {
    do {
      printf("1: directory\n");
      printf("2: check the disk\n");
      printf("3: set time\n");
      printf("4: set date\n");
      printf("5: quit\n");
      printf("\nselection: ");
      ch = getche();
      printf("\n");
    } while((ch<'1') || (ch>'5'));
    if(ch=='5') break; /* end */

    /* execute the specified command */
    system(command[ch-'1']);
  }
}
```

You might find it interesting to expand this program to allow the user access to more DOS commands. For example, you could add the COPY command and, when it is chosen, prompt the user for the source and target filenames. The COPY command and the filenames could then be concatenated to form the string that is passed to DOS.

An Interesting Example Using Arrays and Pointers

To further illustrate the interconnectedness between arrays and pointers, a very simple English-to-German translation program will be developed. The program supports a very small table of English words along with their German equivalents, using a two-dimensional array of strings. It lets you enter an English sentence, and it outputs a very rough German approximation. (The German language is gender-sensitive, which is ignored by this program. Also, no verb conjugations are performed.)

The first thing you need is the English-German table shown here, although you are free to expand it if you wish.

```
char trans[][20] = {
  "is", "ist",
  "this", "das",
  "not", "nicht",
  "a", "ein",
  "book", "Buch",
  "apple", "Apfel",
  "I", "Ich",
  "bread", "Brot",
  "drive", "fahren",
  "to", "zu",
  "buy", "kaufen",
  "", "",
};
```

Each English word is paired with its German equivalent. Note that the longest word must not exceed 19 characters.

The **main( )** function of the translation program is shown here along with the necessary global variables:

```
char input[80];
char word[80];
char *p;
```

```
main()
{
  int loc;

  printf("Enter English sentence: ");
  gets(input);
  p = input;   /* give p the address of the array input */
  printf("Rough German translation: ");

  get_word();    /* get the first word */

  /* This is the main loop.  It reads a word at a time
     from the input array and translates each word
     into German.
  */
  do {
    /* find the index of the English word in trans */
    loc = lookup(word);

    /* printf the German if a match is found */
    if(loc!=-1) printf("%s ", trans[loc+1]);
    else printf("<unknown> ");

    get_word();  /* get next word */
  } while(*word);  /* repeat until a null string is returned */
}
```

The program operates like this: First, the user is prompted for an English sentence. This sentence is read in the **input** string. The pointer **p** is then assigned the address of the start of **input**. This pointer is used by **get_word( )** to read one word at a time from the **input** string. Each word is put into the **word** array. The main loop then looks up each word, using **lookup( )**, which returns the index of the English word or −1 if the word is not in the table. By adding one to this index, the German equivalent is found.

The **lookup( )** function is shown here:

```
/* This function returns the location of a match
   between the string pointed to by s and the trans
   array.
*/
lookup(char *s)
```

```
{
  int i;

  for(i=0; *trans[i]; i++)
    if(!strcmp(trans[i], s)) break;

  if(*trans[i]) return i;
  else return -1;
}
```

You call **lookup( )** with a pointer to the English word and **lookup( )** returns its index if it is in the table and −1 if it is not found.

The **get_word( )** function is shown in the following. As far as this function is concerned, words are delimited only by spaces or by the null terminator.

```
/* This function will read the next word from the input
   array.  Each word is assumed to be separated by a space
   or the null terminator. No other punctuation is allowed.
   The word returned will be a null length string when the
   end of the input string is reached.
*/
get_word()
{
  char *q;

  /* reload address of word each time function is called */
  q = word;

  /* get the next word */
  while(*p && *p!=' ') {
    *q = *p;
    p++;
    q++;
  }
  if(*p==' ') p++;
  *q = '\0';   /* null terminate each word */
}
```

Upon return from **get_word( )**, the global variable **word** will contain either the next English word in the sentence or a null.

The entire translation program is shown here:

```
/* A (very) simple English to German Translator. */

#include <stdio.h>
#include <string.h>

char trans[][20] = {
  "is", "ist",
  "this", "das",
  "not", "nicht",
  "a", "ein",
  "book", "Buch",
  "apple", "Apfel",
  "I", "Ich",
  "bread", "Brot",
  "drive", "fahren",
  "to", "zu",
  "buy", "kaufen",
  "", ""
};

char input[80];
char word[80];
char *p;

main()
{
  int loc;

  printf("Enter English sentence: ");
  gets(input);
  p = input;   /* give p the address of the array input */
  printf("Rough German translation: ");

  get_word();    /* get the first word */

  /* This is the main loop.  It reads a word at a time
     from the input array and translates each word
     into German.
  */
  do {
    /* find the index of the English word in trans */
    loc = lookup(word);

    /* printf the German if a match is found */
    if(loc!=-1) printf("%s ", trans[loc+1]);
```

```
      else printf("<unknown> ");

      get_word();  /* get next word */
   } while(*word); /* repeat until a null string returned */
}

/* This function returns the location of a match
   between the string pointed to by s and the trans
   array.
*/
lookup(char *s)
{
  int i;

  for(i=0; *trans[i]; i++)
    if(!strcmp(trans[i], s)) break;

  if(*trans[i]) return i;
  else return -1;
}

/* This function will read the next word from the input
   array.  Each word is assumed to be separated by a space
   or the null terminator. No other punctuation is allowed.
   The word returned will be a null length string when the
   end of the input string is reached.
*/
get_word()
{
  char *q;

  /* reload address of word each time function is called */
  q = word;

  /* get the next word */
  while(*p && *p!=' ') {
    *q = *p;
    p++;
    q++;
  }
  if(*p==' ') p++;
  *q = '\0';  /* null terminate each word */
}
```

As an example translation, if you enter "I drive to buy a book" the program responds with "Ich fahren zu kaufen ein Buch." This is not grammatically correct German, but at least it's in the ballpark.

You should study the interplay between the pointers and arrays in this program. One point to keep firmly in mind is that **trans[0]** is the same as a pointer to the first entry in the table, **trans[1]** is the same as a pointer to the second entry, and so on. In addition, the **trans** array is actually an array of pointers to the strings shown in its declaration. The strings themselves are stored in Turbo C++'s string table.

Pointers to Pointers

The concept of arrays of pointers is straightforward because the indexes keep the meaning clear. However, pointers to pointers can be very confusing.

A pointer to a pointer is a form of *multiple indirection,* or a chain of pointers. As you can see in Figure 8-3, in the case of a normal pointer, the value of the pointer is the address of the variable that contains the value desired. In the case of a pointer to a pointer,

Figure 8-3.

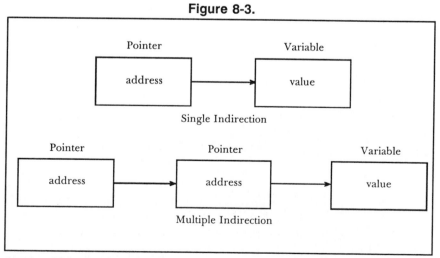

Single and multiple indirection

the first pointer contains the address of the second pointer, which points to the variable, which contains the value desired.

Multiple indirection can be carried on to whatever extent desired, but there are few cases where more than a pointer to a pointer is needed, or indeed, wise to use. Excessive indirection is difficult to follow and prone to conceptual errors. (Do not confuse multiple indirection with *linked lists,* which are used in databases and the like.)

A variable that is a pointer to a pointer must be declared as such. This is done by placing an additional asterisk in front of its name. For example, this declaration tells the compiler that **newbalance** is a pointer to a pointer of type **float**:

```
float **newbalance;
```

It is important to understand that **newbalance** is not a pointer to a floating-point number but rather a pointer to a **float** pointer.

In order to access the target value indirectly pointed to by a pointer to a pointer, the asterisk operator must be applied twice, as is shown in this short example:

```
#include <stdio.h>

main()
{
  int x, *p, **q;

  x = 10;
  p = &x;
  q = &p;

  printf("%d", **q); /* print the value of x */
}
```

Here, **p** is declared as a pointer to an integer and **q** as a pointer to a pointer to an integer. The call to **printf( )** will print the number 10 on the screen.

Initializing Pointers

After a pointer is declared, but before it has been assigned a value, it will contain an unknown value. If you try to use the pointer prior to giving it a value, you will probably crash not only your program, but even your operating system—a very nasty type of error!

By convention, a pointer that is pointing nowhere should be given the value null, to signify that it points to nothing. However, just because a pointer has a null value does not make it "safe." If you use a null pointer on the left side of an assignment statement, you will still run the risk of crashing your program and the operating system.

Because a null pointer is assumed to be unused, you can use it to make many of your pointer routines easier to code and more efficient. For example, you can use a null pointer to mark the end of a pointer array. If this is done, then a routine that accesses that array will know that it has reached the end when the null value is encountered. This type of approach is illustrated by the **for** loop shown here:

```
/* Look up a name assuming last element of p
   is null. */

for(t=0; p[t]; ++t)
   if(!strcmp(p[t],name)) break;
```

The loop will run until either a match is found or a null pointer is encountered. Because the end of the array is marked with a null, the condition controlling the loop will fail when it is reached.

It is very common practice in professionally written C programs to initialize strings. You saw two examples earlier in this chapter in the section on pointer arrays. Another variation on this theme is the following type of string declaration:

```
char *p="hello world\n";
```

As you can see, the pointer **p** is not an array. The reason this sort of initialization works has to do with how C handles string constants. As mentioned, Turbo C++ creates a string table that is used internally by the compiler to store the string constants used by the program. Therefore, this declaration statement places the address of the string "hello world", as stored in the string table, into the pointer **p**. Throughout the program **p** can be used like any other string. For example, the following program is perfectly valid:

```
#include <stdio.h>
#include <string.h>

char *p="hello world";

main()
{
  register int t;

  /* print the string forward and backwards */
  printf(p);
  for(t=strlen(p)-1; t>-1; t--) printf("%c", p[t]);
}
```

However, your program should not make assignments to the string table through **p**, because the table may become corrupted.

Problems with Pointers

Nothing will get you into more trouble than a "wild" pointer! Pointers are a mixed blessing. They give you tremendous power and are necessary for many programs, but when a pointer accidentally contains a wrong value, it can be the most difficult bug to track down.

An erroneous pointer bug is difficult to find because the pointer itself is not the problem; the problem is that each time you perform an operation using it, you are reading or writing to some unknown piece of memory. If you read from it, the worst that can happen is that you get garbage. However, if you write to it, you will be writing over other pieces of your code or data. This may not show up until later in the execution of your program and may lead you to look for the bug in the wrong place. There may be little or no evidence to suggest that the pointer is the problem. This type of bug has caused programmers to lose sleep, time and time again.

Because pointer errors are such nightmares, you should do your best to never generate one! A few of the more common errors are discussed here, beginning with the classic example of a pointer error: the *uninitialized pointer*. Consider the following:

```
/* This program is wrong.  Do Not Execute. */
main()
{
  int x, *p;

  x = 10;
  *p = x;
}
```

This program assigns the value 10 to some unknown memory location. The pointer **p** has never been given a value; therefore it contains a garbage value. Although Turbo C++ will issue a warning message for the error in this example, the same sort of problem arises when a pointer is simply pointing to the wrong place. For example, you might accidently assign the pointer the wrong address. This type of problem often goes unnoticed when your program is very small because the odds are **p** will contain a "safe" address—one that is not in your code, data area, or oper-ating system. However, as your program grows, the probability of **p** pointing to something vital increases. Eventually, your program stops working. To avoid this sort of trouble, always make sure that a pointer is pointing at something valid before it is used.

A second common error is caused by a simple misunderstand-ing of how to use a pointer. Consider the following:

```
#include <stdio.h>

/* This program is wrong.  Do Not Execute. */
main()
{
  int x, *p;

  x = 10;
  p = x;
  printf("%d", *p);

}
```

The call to **printf( )** will not print the value of **x**, which is 10, onto the screen. It will print some unknown value. The reason is that the assignment

```
p = x;
```

is wrong. That statement has assigned the value 10 to the pointer **p**, which is supposed to contain an address, not a value. To make the program correct, you should write:

```
p = &x;
```

In this simple example, Turbo C++ will warn you about the error in the program. However, not all errors of this general type may be caught by the compiler.

Do not avoid using pointers just because when handled incorrectly they can cause some very tricky bugs. You should be careful and make sure that you know where each pointer is pointing before using it.

Now that you have a basic understanding of pointers, you are ready to unlock the power of C++'s functions.

9

Functions: A Closer Look

Functions are the building blocks of C. Except for a brief overview presented in Chapter 4, you have been using functions in a more or less intuitive way. In this chapter you will study functions in detail, learning such things as how to make a function modify its arguments, how to return different types of data, and how to use function prototypes. Also examined are the scope rules and lifetime of variables, how to make recursive functions, and some special properties of the **main( )** function.

The General Form of a Function

The general form of a function is

type-specifier function __ name(parameter declarations)
{
   body of the function
}

The type specifier specifies the type of value that the function will return using the **return** statement. It may be any valid type. If no type is specified, then, by default, the function is assumed to return an integer result. The programs you have been using prior to this point have made use of this fact. (Later in this chapter you will learn how to return different types.) The parameter declaration list is a comma-separated list of variable types and names that will receive the values of the arguments when the function is called. A function may be without parameters, in which case the parameter list will be empty. However, even if there are no parameters, the parentheses are still required.

It is important to understand one thing about a function's parameter declaration list. Unlike variable declarations in which many variables can be declared to be of a common type using a comma-separated list of variable names, all function parameters must include both the type and variable name. That is, the parameter declaration list for a function takes this general form:

f(*type varname1, type varname2, . . . , type varnameN*)

For example, this is a correct parameter declaration:

```
f(int x, int y, float z)
```

However, the following is incorrect because each parameter must include its own type:

```
f(int x, y, float z)
```

The return Statement

Although the **return** statement was introduced in Chapter 4 as a means of returning a value from a function, it will be examined more fully here.

The **return** statement has two important uses. First, it will cause an immediate exit from the current function. That is, the **return** will cause program execution to return to the calling code as soon as it is encountered. Second, it may be used to return a value. Both of these uses are examined here.

Returning from a Function

There are two ways that a function terminates execution and returns to the caller. The first way is when the last statement in the function has executed and, conceptually, the function's ending } is encountered. (Of course, the curly brace is not actually present in the object code, but you can think of it in this way.)

For example, this function simply prints a string backwards on the display:

```
void pr_reverse(char *s)
{
  register int t;
  for(t=strlen(s)-1; t>-1; t--) printf("%c", s[t]);
}
```

Once the string has been displayed, there is nothing left for the function to do, so it returns to the place it was called from.

The second way a function can return is through the use of the **return** statement. The **return** statement can be used without any value associated with it. For example, the following function will print the outcome of one number raised to a positive integer power. If the exponent is negative, the **return** statement causes the function to terminate before the final curly brace is reached but no value is returned.

```
void power(int base, int exp)
{
  int i;

  if(exp<0) return; /* can't do negative exponents */

  i = 1;

  for( ; exp; exp--) i = base * i;
  printf("The answer is: %d: ", i);
}
```

Returning a Value

To return a value from a function, you must follow the **return** statement with the value to be returned. For example, this function returns the maximum value of its two arguments:

```
max(int a, int b)
{
  int temp;

  if(a>b) temp = a;
  else temp = b;

  return temp;
}
```

Notice that the function returns an integer value. This is the default return type of a function if no other type is explicitly specified in the function's definition.

It is possible for a function to contain two or more **return** statements. More than one **return** is often used to simplify and make more efficient some algorithm. For example, the **max( )** function is better written as shown here:

```
max(int a, int b)
{
  if(a>b) return a;
  else return b;
}
```

Another example of a function that uses two **return** statements is the **find_substr( )** function, shown here. It returns either the starting index of a substring within a string, or −1 if no match is found. Without the use of the second **return** statement, a temporary variable and extra code would need to be used.

```
find_substr(char *sub, char *str)
{
  register int t;
  char *p, *p2;

  for(t=0; str[t]; t++) {  /* get starting point */
    p = &str[t];
    p2 = sub;
    while(*p2 && *p2==*p) { /* while equal advance */
      p++;                  /* through the string */
      p2++;
    }
```

```
    if(!*p2) return t;    /* if at the end of sub then match */
                          /* has been found */
  }
  return -1;
}
```

If this function is called with the substring containing "ere" and the main string containing "Hi there," then the function will return the value 5.

Even though you have just seen two examples where the use of more than one **return** statement leads to simpler and more efficient functions, it must be stated that having too many **return**s can destructure a function and cause its meaning to be confused. The best advice is to use multiple **return**s only when they contribute significantly to the performance of the function.

All functions, except those declared to be of type **void**, return a value. (Functions declared as **void** will be discussed in the next section.) This value is explicitly specified by the **return** statement, or unknown if no **return** statement is specified. This means that a function may be used as an operand in any valid C expression. Therefore, each of the following expressions is valid in C and C++:

```
x = abs(y);

if(max(x,y) > 100) printf("greater");

for(ch=getchar(); isdigit(ch);) ... ;
```

However, a function cannot be the target of an assignment. A statement such as,

```
swap(x, y) = 100;    /* incorrect statement */
```

is wrong. Turbo C++ will flag it as an error and will not compile a program that contains such a statement.

Although all functions not of type **void** have return values, when you write programs your functions generally will be of three types. The first is simply computational. It is specifically designed to perform operations on its arguments and return a value based on that operation—in essence it is a "pure" function. Examples of this sort of function are the library functions **sqrt( )** and **sin( )**, which return a number's square root and sine, respectively.

The second type of function manipulates information and returns a value that simply indicates the success or failure of that manipulation. An example is **fwrite( )**, which is used to write information to a disk file. If the write operation is successful, **fwrite( )** returns the number of items you requested to be written; any other value indicates an error has occurred. (You will learn about file I/O in the next chapter.)

The last type of function has no explicit return value. In essence, the function is strictly procedural and produces no value. For murky, historical reasons, many times functions that really don't produce an interesting result will return something anyway. For example, **printf( )** returns the number of characters written; yet it would be very unusual to find a program that actually checked this. Therefore, although all functions (except those of type **void**) return values, you don't necessarily have to use them for anything. A very common question concerning function return values is, "Don't I have to assign this value to some variable since a value is being returned?" The answer is no. If there is no assignment specified, then the return value is simply discarded. Consider the following program that uses **mul( )**:

```
#include <stdio.h>

main()
{
  int x, y, z;

  x = 10;   y = 20;
  z = mul(x, y);              /* 1 */
  printf("%d", mul(x, y));    /* 2 */
  mul(x, y);                  /* 3 */
}

mul(int a, int b)
```

```
{
  return a*b;
}
```

In line 1, the return value of **mul( )** is assigned to **z**. In line 2, the return value is not actually assigned, but it is used by the **printf( )** function. Finally, in line 3, the return value is lost because it is neither assigned to another variable nor used as part of an expression.

Functions Returning Noninteger Values

When the type of a function is not explicitly declared, it automatically defaults to **int**. For many functions this default is fine. However, when it is necessary to return a different data type it requires a two-step process. First, the function must be given an explicit type specifier; second, the compiler must be told the type of the function before the first call is made to it. It is only in this way that Turbo C++ can generate correct code for functions returning noninteger values.

Functions may be declared to return any valid C data type. The method of declaration is similar to that of variables: the type specifier precedes the function name. The type specifier tells the compiler what type of data the function is to return. This information is critical if the program is going to run correctly because different data types have different sizes and internal representations.

Before a function returning a noninteger type can be used, its type must be made known to the rest of the program. The reason for this is easy to understand. In C++, unless directed to the contrary, a function is assumed to return an integer value. If your program calls a function that returns a different type prior to that function's declaration, the compiler will mistakenly generate the wrong code for the function call. The best way to inform the compiler about the return type of a function is to use a *function prototype* and this approach is discussed next.

Using Function Prototypes

The function prototype is one of the most important new concepts you will learn about in this chapter. A function prototype performs two special tasks. First, it identifies the return type of the function so that the compiler can generate the correct code for the type of data the function returns. Second, it specifies the type and number of arguments used by the function. It takes this general form:

type func-name(parameter list);

The prototype normally goes near the top of the program, or in a header file, and must be included before any call is made to the function.

Function prototypes are not part of the original K&R C but were added by the ANSI standards committee. They enable C to provide strong type checking, similar to that provided by languages such as Turbo Pascal, in addition to telling the compiler about the return type of the function. When prototypes are used, they allow the compiler to find and report any illegal type conversions between the type of arguments used to call a function and the type definition of its parameters. Prototypes also allow Turbo C++ to report when a function is called with too few or too many arguments. These other aspects of prototypes will be looked at later in this chapter. In this section, you will see how to use a function prototype to return a noninteger data type.

For an introductory example of a function returning a noninteger type, here is a program that uses a function called **sum( )**, which returns a **double** value that is the sum of its two **double** arguments:

```c
#include <stdio.h>

double sum(double a, double b);   /* prototype the function */

main()
{
  double first, second;

  first = 1023.23;
  second = 990.9;
  printf("%f", sum(first, second));
}

double sum(double a, double b) /* return a float */
{
  return a+b;
}
```

The prototype tells the compiler that **sum( )** will return a double floating-point data type. This allows the compiler to correctly generate code for calls to **sum( )**. If you remove the prototype from this program, it will generate incorrect results.

For a somewhat more practical example, here is a program that computes the area of a circle given its radius:

```c
#include <stdlib.h>

float area(float radius);   /* prototype */

main()
{
  float r;

  printf("Enter radius: ");
  scanf("%f", &r);
  printf("Area is: %f\n", area(r));
}
```

```
float area(float radius)
{
  return 3.1416 * radius * 2;
}
```

Here, the **area( )** function returns a **float** value, so the compiler must be told of this prior to the function call.

The key point to understand about returning data of types other than integer is that the compiler needs to know the return type in advance. The best way to accomplish this is by using a function prototype. Now that you have learned about prototypes, this book will use them in all subsequent examples and your code should, in general, include prototypes, even when the function is simply returning an integer.

Returning Pointers

Although functions that return pointers are handled exactly the same as any other type of function, a few important concepts need to be discussed.

As you know, pointers are *neither* integers nor unsigned integers. They are the memory addresses of a certain type of data. The reason for this distinction lies in the fact that when pointer arithmetic is performed, it is relative to the base type. That is, if an integer pointer is incremented, it will contain a value that is 2 greater than its previous value. More generally, each time a pointer is incremented, the pointer will point to the next data item of its type. Since each data type may be of different length, the compiler must know what type of data the pointer is pointing to in order to make it point to the next data item. Therefore, a function that returns a pointer must be declared as such.

For example, here is a function that returns a pointer into a string at the place where a character match is found:

```
/* Return a pointer to the first character
   in s that matches c. */

char *match(char c, char *s)
{
  int count;

  count = 0;

  /* look for match or null terminator */
  while(c!=s[count] && s[count]!='\0') count++;

  /* if match, return pointer to location;
     otherwise return a null pointer
  */
  if(s[count]) return(&s[count]);
  else return (char *) '\0';
}
```

The function **match( )** will attempt to return a pointer to the place in a string where the first match with **c** is found. If no match is found, a pointer to the null terminator will be returned. A short program that uses **match( )** is shown here:

```
#include <stdio.h>
#include <conio.h>

char *match(char c, char *s);

main()
{
  char s[80], *p, ch;

  printf("enter a string and a character: ");
  gets(s);
  ch = getche();
  p = match(ch, s);
  if(p)  /* there is a match */
    printf("%s ", p);
  else
    printf("no match found");
}
```

This program reads a string and then a character. If the character is in the string, then the program prints the string from the point of the match. Otherwise, it prints "no match found." For example, if you enter **"hi there"** as the string and **t** as the character, the program will respond with "there."

Functions of Type void

When a function does not return any value, it can be declared as **void**. Doing so prevents its use in any expression and helps head off accidental misuse. For example, the function **print‗vertical( )** prints its string argument vertically down the side of the screen. Since it returns no value, it is declared as **void**.

```
void print_vertical(char *str)
{
  while(*str)
    printf("%c\n", *str++);
}
```

You must include a prototype for **print‗vertical( )** in any program that uses it. If you don't, Turbo C++ will assume that it is returning an integer. Thus, when the compiler actually reaches the function, it will declare a type mismatch. This program shows a proper example:

```
#include <stdio.h>

void print_vertical(char *str);

main()
{
  print_vertical("hello");
}

void print_vertical(char *str)
{
  while(*str)
    printf("%c\n", *str++);
}
```

In the past, functions that did not return values were simply allowed to default to type **int**. However, you should declare all functions not returning values as **void** because it is good practice. From this point on, the examples in this book will use **void** where needed.

More on Prototypes

In this section, we will examine some other aspects of the function prototype.

Argument Mismatches

Aside from telling the compiler about the return type of a function, a prototype also prevents that function from being called with an incorrect type or number of arguments. Although C will automatically convert the type of an argument into the type of parameter that is receiving it, some type conversions are simply illegal. If a function is prototyped, any illegal type conversion will be found and an error message will be issued. For example, the following program will cause an error because there is an attempt to call **sqr_it( )** with an integer argument instead of the integer pointer required. (It is illegal to transform an integer into a pointer.)

```
/* This program uses a function prototype to
   enforce strong type checking.
*/

int sqr_it(int *i); /* prototype */
```

```
main()
{
  int x;

  x = 10;
  sqr_it(x);   /* type mismatch */
}

sqr_it(int *i)

{
  *i = *i * *i;
}
```

As another example, this program will not compile because **sqr _ it( )** is called with the wrong number of arguments:

```
/* This program shows how a function must
   be called with the proper number of arguments.
*/

int sqr_it(int *i); /* prototype */

main()
{
  int x;

  x = 10;
  sqr_it(&x, 10);   /* wrong number of arguments */
}

sqr_it(int *i)

{
  *i = *i * *i;
}
```

Aside from telling the compiler about a function's return data type, use of function prototypes helps you trap bugs before they occur by preventing a function from being called with invalid arguments. Prototypes also help verify that your program is working correctly by not allowing functions to be called with the wrong number of arguments.

Header Files: A Closer Look

Early in this book, you were told about the standard header files. However, you were only told that they contained information needed by certain library functions. While this partial explanation is true, it does not tell the whole story. Turbo C++'s header files contain two main things: certain definitions used by the functions and the prototypes for the standard functions related to the header file. For example, the reason that STDIO.H has been included in almost all programs in this book is that it contains the prototype for the **printf( )** function. By including the appropriate header file for each library function used in your programs, it is possible for the compiler to catch any accidental errors you may make when using them. Further, it is a good idea to get into the habit of including all appropriate header files because this is required in a C++ program.

You should be aware of the fact that you can let Turbo C++ warn you when a function prototype has not been included for any function in your program. To do this in the integrated environment, use the **Options** main menu entry. If you are using the command line compiler, use the **−wpro** option.

Prototyping Functions That Have No Parameters

As you know, a function prototype tells the compiler about the type of data returned by a function as well as the type and number of parameters used by the function. However, since prototypes were not part of the original version of C, a special case is created when you need to prototype a function that takes no parameters. The reason for this is that the ANSI C standard stipulates that when no parameters are included in a function's prototype, no information whatsoever is being specified about the type or number of the function's parameters. This meaning is necessary in order to ensure that old-style C programs can be compiled by modern compilers, such as Turbo C++. However, what if you specifically want to tell Turbo C++ that a function actually takes no parameters? The answer is that you use the keyword **void** inside the parameters list. For example, examine this short program:

```c
#include <stdio.h>

void myname(void);

main()
{
  myname();
}

void myname(void)
{
  printf("Herb");
}
```

In this program, the prototype to **myname( )** explicitly tells the compiler that **myname( )** takes no arguments. Since the parameter list of the function must agree with its prototype, the **void** must also be included in the declaration of **myname( )**. With this prototype, Turbo C++ will not compile a call to **myname( )** that looks like this:

```c
myname("Herb");
```

However, if the **void** is left out of the parameter list specification, no error will be reported.

From this point forward in the book, whenever a function takes no arguments it will be explicitly declared as having a **void** parameter list. Although not necessary, for the sake of consistency, the **main( )** function will also be declared as **main(void)** when it has no parameters.

About Old C Programs

Prototypes were added to C by the advent of the ANSI C standard. Prior to the standard, it was not possible to fully prototype a function. Only the function's return value could be specified, but nothing about its parameters could be declared. Thus, the compiler was able to generate the proper code for return values. However, because nothing was specified about the function's parameters, functions could be called with the incorrect type or number of arguments without any complaint from the compiler. Because the ANSI C standard needed to be downwardly compatible with the old K&R de facto standard, it specified that this partial prototype is still legal. This way, old programs can be compiled using Turbo C++. However, for new programs, you should always use a full prototype. The old form discussed here cannot be used in a C++ program.

A partial prototype statement has the general form

type __ specifier function __ name( );

Even if the function takes arguments, none are listed in its type declaration. Using this partial approach, the **sum( )** program from earlier in this chapter would look like this:

```
#include <stdio.h>

double sum();  /* partial prototype */
```

```
main(void)
{
  double first, second;

  first = 1023.23;
  second = 990.9;
  printf("%f", sum(first, second));
}

double sum(double a, double b) /* return a float */
{
  return a+b;
}
```

The reason that it is important for you to know about partial prototypes is that there are a great many existing books and articles containing old-style C code. Don't be concerned if you only find partial prototypes in these programs; Turbo C will be able to correctly compile the programs as they stand. If you want to use some old code in a C++ program, you will need to convert any partial prototypes into full prototypes.

Scope Rules of Functions

The *scope rules* of a language are the rules that govern whether a piece of code knows about, or has access to, another piece of code or data. This subject was touched upon lightly in Chapter 4; now it will be examined more closely.

In C, each function is a discrete block of code. A function's code is private to that function and cannot be accessed by any statement in any other function except through a call to that function. (It is not possible, for instance, to use **goto** to jump into the middle of another function.) The code that comprises the body of a function is hidden from the rest of the program and, unless it uses global variables or data, it can neither affect nor be affected by other parts of the program except as specified by your program. Stated another way, the code and data that are defined within one function cannot interact with the code or data defined in another function, unless explicitly specified, because the two functions have a different scope.

There are three types of variables: *local variables, formal parameters,* and *global variables.* The scope rules govern how each of these may be accessed by other parts of your program and establish their lifetimes. The following discussions look more closely at the scope rules.

Local Variables

As you know, variables that are declared inside a function are called *local variables*. However, C supports a broader concept of the local variable than you have previously seen. A variable may be declared inside any block of code and be local to it. In reality, variables local to a function are simply a special case of the more general concept. Local variables may be referenced only by statements that are inside the block in which the variables are declared. Stated another way, local variables are not known outside their own code block; their scope is limited to the block within which they are declared. You should remember that a block of code is begun when an opening curly brace is encountered, and terminated when the matching closing curly brace is found.

One of the most important things to understand about local variables is that they exist only while the block of code in which they are declared is executing. That is, a local variable is created upon entry into its block and destroyed upon exit.

The most common code block in which local variables are declared is the function. For example, consider the following two functions:

```
void func1(void)
{
  int x;

  x = 10;
}

void func2(void)
{
  int x;

  x = -199;
}
```

The integer variable **x** was declared twice, once in **func1( )** and once in **func2( )**. The **x** in **func1( )** has no bearing on, or relationship to, the **x** in **func2( )**. The reason for this is that each **x** is only known to the code that is within the same block as the variable's declaration.

To demonstrate this fact, try this short program:

```
#include <stdio.h>

void f(void);

main(void)
{
  int x;

  x = 10;

  printf("x in main is %d\n", x);
  f();
  printf("x in main is still %d\n", x);
}

void f(void)
{
  int x;

  x = 100;

  printf("the x in f() is %d\n", x);
}
```

The C language contains the keyword **auto**, which can be used to declare local variables. However, since all nonglobal variables are, by default, assumed to be **auto**, it is virtually never used. Hence, you will not see it used in any of the examples in this book.

It is common practice to declare all variables needed within a function at the start of that function's code block. This is done mostly to make it easy for anyone reading the code to know what variables are used. However, it is not necessary to do this because local variables may be declared at the start of any block of code. To understand how this works, consider the following function:

```c
void f(void)
{
  char ch;

  printf("continue (y/n)? :");
  ch = getche();

  /* enter this block only if answer is yes */
  if(ch == 'y') {
    char s[80];  /* this is created only upon
                       entry into this block */
    printf("enter name:");
    gets(s);
    process_it(s);  /* do something */
  }
}
```

Here, the local variable **s** will be created upon entry into the **if** code block and destroyed upon exit. Furthermore, **s** is known only within the **if** block and may not be referenced elsewhere —even in other parts of the function that contains it.

Because local variables are created and destroyed with each entry and exit from the block in which they are declared, their content is lost once the block is left. This is especially important to remember in terms of a function call. When a function is called, its local variables are created, and upon its return, they are destroyed. This means that local variables cannot retain their values between calls. (There is an exception to this, which will be explained later.)

Unless otherwise specified, storage for local variables is on the stack. The fact that the stack is a dynamic and changing region of memory explains why local variables cannot, in general, hold their values between function calls.

Formal Parameters

As you know, if a function is to use arguments, then it must declare variables that will accept the values of those arguments. Aside from receiving the function's input parameters, they behave like any other local variables inside the function. These variables are called the *formal parameters* of the functions.

REMEMBER   You must make sure that the formal parameters you declare are of the same type as the arguments you will use to call the function. Also, even though these variables perform the special task of receiving the value of the arguments passed to the function, they can be used like any other local variable.

Global Variables

Unlike local variables, *global variables* are known throughout the entire program and may be used by any piece of code. In essence, their scope is global to the program. Also, they will hold their value during the entire execution of the program. Global variables are created by declaring them outside of any function. They may be accessed by any expression regardless of what function that expression is in.

In the following program, you can see that the variable **count** has been declared outside of all functions. Its declaration was before the **main( )** function. However, it could have been placed anywhere, as long as it was not in a function, prior to its first use. Common practice dictates that it is best to declare global variables at the top of the program.

```
#include <stdio.h>
int count;   /* count is global  */

void func1(void), func2(void);

main(void)
{
  count = 100;
  func1();
}

void func1(void)
{
  func2();
  printf("count is %d", count); /* will print 100 */
}

void func2(void)
{
  int count;

  for(count=1; count<10; count++)
    printf(".");
}
```

Looking closely at this program, it should be clear that although neither **main( )** nor **func1( )** has declared the variable **count**, both may use it. However, **func2( )** has declared a local variable called **count**. When **func2( )** references **count**, it will be referencing only its local variable, not the global one. It is very important to remember that if a global variable and a local variable have the same name, all references to that variable name inside the function where the local variable is declared will refer to that local variable and will have no effect on the global variable. This can be a convenient benefit, but forgetting it can cause your program to act very strangely, even though it "looks" correct.

Storage for global variables is in a fixed region of memory set aside for this purpose by Turbo C++. Global variables are very helpful when the same data is used in many functions in your program. You should avoid using unnecessary global variables, however, for three reasons:

- They take up memory the entire time your program is executing, not just when they are needed.

- Using a global where a local variable will do makes a function less general because it relies on something that must be defined outside itself.

- Using a large number of global variables can lead to program errors because of unknown, and unwanted, side effects.

This last reason is evidenced in BASIC, where all variables are global. A major problem in developing large programs is accidentally changing a variable's value because it was used elsewhere in the program. This can also happen in C if you use too many global variables in your programs.

One of the principal points of a structured language is the compartmentalization of code and data. In C, compartmentalization is achieved through the use of functions and local variables. For example, here are two ways to write **mul( )** — a simple function that computes the product of two integers:

General   *Specific*

```
                      int x,y;
mul(int x, int y)     mul()
  {                     {
     return(x*y);          return(x*y);
  }                     }
```

Both functions will return the product of the variables **x** and **y**. However, the generalized, or *parameterized,* version can be used to return the product of *any* two numbers, whereas the specific version can be used to find only the product of the global variables **x** and **y**.

A Final Scope Example

The various scopes of view in a short program are graphically depicted in Figure 9-1. In the figure, code contained in an inner scope has knowledge of the outer scopes but the opposite is not true. The code in outer scopes has no effect on or knowledge of that in inner scopes.

You should be able to understand the various scopes in this example if you study the figure closely. You may want to experiment a little to see how various changes affect the program.

Function Parameters and Arguments: A Closer Look

This section will take a closer look at how C handles function parameters and arguments.

Call by Value, Call by Reference

In general, subroutines can be passed arguments in one of two ways. The first is called *call by value.* This method copies the *value* of an argument into the formal parameter of the subroutine.

Therefore, changes made to the parameters of the subroutine have no effect on the variables used to call it.

Figure 9-1.

```
/* SCOPE: A program with various scopes */
#include <stdio.h>
#include <string.h>

int count; /* global to entire program */

void play(char *p);

main(void)
{
  char str[80];   /* local to main() */

  printf("enter a string: ");
  gets(str);
  play(str);
}

void play(char *p) /* p is local to play */
{

  if(!strcmp(p, "add")) {
    int a, b;  /* local to if block inside play */
    printf("enter two integers: ");
    scanf("%d%d", &a, &b);
    printf("%d\n", a+b);
  }

  /* int a, b not known here */
  else if (!strcmp(p, "beep")) printf("%c", 7);
}
```

The scopes of the SCOPE program

Call by reference is the second way a subroutine can have arguments passed to it. In this method, the *address* of an argument is copied into the parameter. Inside the subroutine, the address is used to access the actual argument used in the call. This means that changes made to the parameter will affect the variable used to call the routine.

C uses call by value to pass arguments. This means, in general, that you cannot alter the variables used to call the function. (You will find out later in this chapter how to "force" a call by reference by using pointers to allow changes to the calling variables.) Consider the following function:

```c
#include <stdio.h>

sqr(int x);

main(void)
{
  int t=10;

  printf("%d %d", sqr(t), t);
}

sqr(int x)
{
  x = x*x;
  return(x);
}
```

In this example, the value of the argument to **sqr( )**, 10, is copied into the parameter **x**. When the assignment **x = x*x** takes place, the only thing modified is the local variable **x**. The variable **t**, used to call **sqr( )**, will still have the value 10. Hence, the output will be 100 10.

 REMEMBER   It is a copy of the value of the argument that is passed into that function. What occurs inside the function will have no effect on the variable used in the call.

Creating a Call by Reference

Even though C's parameter-passing convention is call by value, it is possible to create a call by reference by passing a pointer to the argument. Since this will cause the address of the argument to be passed to the function, it will then be possible to change the value of the argument outside the function.

Pointers are passed to functions just like any other value. Of course, it is necessary to declare the parameters as pointer types. For example, consider the function **swap( )**, which exchanges the value of its two integer arguments, shown here:

```
void swap(int *x, int *y)
{
  int temp;

  temp = *x;   /* save the value at address x */
  *x = *y;     /* put y into x */
  *y = temp;   /* put x into y */
}
```

The * operator is used to access the variable pointed to by its operand. Hence, the contents of the variables used to call the function will be swapped.

It is important to remember that **swap( )** (or any other function that uses pointer parameters) must be called with the *addresses of the arguments*. This program shows the correct way to call **swap( )**:

```
#include <stdio.h>

void swap(int *x, int *y);

main(void)
{
  int x, y;

  x = 10;
  y = 20;
```

```
   printf("initial values of x and y: %d %d \n", x, y);
   swap(&x, &y);
   printf("swapped values of x and y: %d %d \n", x, y);
}
```

In this example, the variable **x** is assigned the value 10 and **y** the value 20. Then **swap( )** is called with the addresses of **x** and **y**. The unary operator **&** is used to produce the addresses of the variables. Therefore, the addresses of **x** and **y**, not their values, are passed into the function **swap( )**.

At this point you should be able to understand why you had to put the **&** in front of the arguments to **scanf( )** that were to receive values. In actuality, you were passing their addresses so that the calling variable could be modified.

As you will see in Part III, C++ contains a feature that makes generating a call by reference easier and more elegant.

Calling Functions with Arrays

When an array is used as an argument to a function, only the address of the array is passed, not a copy of the entire array. When you call a function with an array name, a pointer to the first element in the array is passed into the function. (Remember, in C, an array name without any index is a pointer to the first element in the array.) This means that the parameter declaration must be of a compatible pointer type. There are three ways to declare a parameter that is to receive an array pointer. First, it may be declared as an array of the same type and size as that used to call the function, as shown here:

```
#include <stdio.h>

void display(int num[10]);
```

```
main(void)   /* print some numbers */
{
  int t[10],i;

  for(i=0; i<10; ++i) t[i]=i;
  display(t);
}

void display(int num[10])
{
  int i;

  for(i=0; i<10; i++) printf("%d ", num[i]);
}
```

Even though the parameter **num** is declared to be an integer array of 10 elements, the C compiler will automatically convert it to an integer pointer. This is necessary because no parameter can actually receive an entire array. Since only a pointer to the array will be passed, a pointer parameter must be there to receive it.

A second way to declare an array parameter is to specify it as an unsized array, as shown here:

```
void display(int num[])
{
  int i;

  for(i=0; i<10; i++) printf("%d ", num[i]);
}
```

Here, **num** is declared to be an integer array of unknown size. Since C provides no array boundary checks, the actual size of the array is irrelevant to the parameter (but not to the program, of course). This method of declaration also actually defines **num** as an integer pointer.

The final way that **num** can be declared, and the most common form in professionally written C programs, is as a pointer, as shown here:

```
void display(int *num)
{
  int i;
```

```
  for(i=0; i<10; i++) printf("%d ",num[i]);
}
```

This is allowed because any pointer may be indexed using [] as if it were an array.

Recognize that all three methods of declaring an array parameter yield the same result: a pointer.

On the other hand, an array *element* used as an argument is treated like any other simple variable. For example, the same program just examined could have been written without passing the entire array, as shown here:

```
#include <stdio.h>

void display(int num);

main(void) /* print some numbers */
{
  int t[10],i;

  for(i=0; i<10; ++i) t[i]=i;
  for(i=0; i<10; i++) display(t[i]);
}

void display(int num)
{
  printf("%d ", num);
}
```

As you can see, the parameter to **display( )** is of type **int**. It is not relevant that **display( )** is called using an array element, because only that one value of the array is used.

It is important to understand that when an array is used as a function argument, its address is passed to a function. This is an exception to C's call-by-value parameter-passing convention. This means that the code inside the function will be operating on, and potentially altering, the actual contents of the array used to call the function. For example, consider the function **print_upper( )**, which prints its string argument in uppercase.

```
/* Print a string in uppercase. */
#include <stdio.h>
#include <ctype.h>

void print_upper(char *string);

main(void)
{
  char s[80];

  printf("enter a string: ");
  gets(s);
  print_upper(s);
  printf("\noriginal string is altered: %s", s);
}

void print_upper(char *string)
{
  register int t;

  for(t=0; string[t]; ++t)  {
    string[t] = toupper(string[t]);
    printf("%c", string[t]);
  }
}
```

After the call to **print_upper( )**, the contents of array **s** in **main( )** will be changed to uppercase. If this is not what you want to happen, you could write the program like this:

```
/* Print string as uppercase. */
#include <stdio.h>
#include <ctype.h>

void print_upper(char *string);

main(void)
{
  char s[80];

  printf("enter a string: ");
  gets(s);
  print_upper(s);
  printf("\noriginal string is unchanged: %s", s);
}
```

```
void print_upper(char *string)
{
  register int t;

  for(t=0; string[t]; ++t)
    printf("%c", toupper(string[t]));
}
```

In this version, the contents of array **s** remain unchanged because its values are not altered.

A classic example of passing arrays into functions is found in the standard library function **strcat( )**. Although the **strcat( )** in the standard library is somewhat different, the function shown here will give you an idea of how it works. To avoid confusion with the standard function, this one is called **hsstrcat( )**. (In case you don't remember, **strcat( )** concatenates two strings together. **strcat( )** also returns a pointer to the first string, so that is why 1 is returned—although its value is seldom used.)

```
/* Demonstrate hsstrcat() */

#include <stdio.h>

char *hsstrcat(char *s1, char *s2);

main(void)
{
  char s1[80], s2[80];

  printf("Enter two strings: ");
  gets(s1);
  gets(s2);

  hsstrcat(s1, s2);

  printf("concatenated: %s", s1);
}

char *hsstrcat(char *s1, char *s2)
{
  char *temp;

  temp = s1;
  /* first, find the end of s1 */
```

```
while(*s1) s1++;

/* add s2 */
while(*s2) {
  *s1 = *s2;
  s1++;
  s2++;
}
*s1 = '\0';   /* add the null terminator */
return temp;
}
```

The **hsstrcat( )** function must be called with two character arrays, which by definition are character pointers. Upon entry, **hsstrcat( )** finds the end of the first string. Next it adds the second string onto the end of the first. Finally, it null-terminates the first string.

argc, argv, and env—Arguments to main( )

Sometimes it is very useful to pass information into a program when you run it. The general method is to pass information into the **main( )** function through the use of *command-line arguments*. A command-line argument is the information that follows the program's name on the command line of the operating system. For example, you can compile programs from the command line by typing

> tcc *program_name*

where *program_name* is the program you wish compiled. The name of the program is passed into the Turbo C++ compiler as an argument.

There are three special built-in arguments to **main( )**. The first two, **argc** and **argv**, are used to receive command-line arguments. The third is **env** and it is used to access the DOS environmental parameters active at the time the program begins execution. These are the only arguments that **main( )** can have. Let's look at them more closely.

The **argc** parameter will hold the number of arguments on the command line and is an integer. It will always be at least 1 because the name of the program qualifies as the first argument. The **argv** parameter is a pointer to an array of character pointers. That is, **argv** is a pointer to an array of strings. Each element in this array points to a command-line argument. All command-line arguments are strings — any numbers will have to be converted by the program into the proper format. The following short program will print "hello" followed by your name on the screen if you type it directly after the program name:

```
#include <stdio.h>
#include <process.h>

main(int argc, char *argv[])   /* name program */
{
  if(argc!=2) {
    printf("You forgot to type your name\n");
    exit(0);
  }
  printf("Hello %s", argv[1]);
}
```

If you titled this program NAME and your name was Tom, then to run the program you would type **name Tom**. The output from the program would be "Hello Tom." For example, if you were logged into drive A and running DOS, you would see

```
A>NAME Tom
Hello Tom
A>
```

after running NAME.

Each command-line argument must be separated by a space or a tab. Commas, semicolons, and the like are not considered separators. For example,

```
one, two, and three
```

is made up of four strings, while

```
one,two,and three
```

is two strings—commas are not legal separators.

If you need to pass a command-line argument that contains spaces, you must place it between quotes. For example, this will be treated as a single command-line argument:

```
"this is one argument"
```

It is important that you declare **argv** properly. A common method is

```
char *argv[];
```

The empty brackets indicate that it is an array of undetermined length. You can now access the individual arguments by indexing **argv**. For example, **argv[0]** will point to the first string, which is always the program's name; **argv[1]** will point to the first argument, and so on. (In versions of DOS before 3.0, **argv[0]** was blank.)

An interesting and useful program using command-line arguments is shown next. It executes a series of DOS commands entered at the command line. It accomplishes this using the **system( )** library function. This function passes whatever string it is called with to the operating system. Assuming that the string contains a valid operating system command, that command is executed, and then the program resumes.

```
/* COMLINE: a program that executes whatever DOS
   commands are specified on the command line.
*/
#include <stdio.h>
#include <stdlib.h>

main(int argc, char *argv[])
{
  int i;

  for(i=1; i<argc; i++)
    system(argv[i]);
}
```

Assuming that you call this program COMLINE, the following command line causes the DOS commands VER, CHKDSK, and DIR *.C to be executed in that sequence.

C>COMLINE VER CHKDSK "DIR *.C"

You will be surprised by how many uses you will find for this program.

To access an individual character in one of the command strings, you add a second index to **argv**. For example, this program will display on the screen all the arguments with which it was called, a character at a time:

```
/* The program prints all command line arguments it is
   called with. */
#include <stdio.h>

main(int argc, char *argv[])
{
  int t, i;

  for(t=0; t<argc; ++t) {
    i = 0;
    while(argv[t][i]) {
      printf("%c", argv[t][i]);
      ++i;
    }
    printf(" ");
  }
}
```

Remember, the first index accesses the string and the second index accesses that character of the string.

Usually, you will use **argc** and **argv** to get initial commands into your program. In Turbo C++, you can have as many command-line arguments as the operating system will allow. In DOS, you are limited to one 128-character line. You normally use these arguments to indicate a filename or an option. Using command-line arguments will give your program a very professional appearance and facilitate the program's use in batch files.

The **env** parameter is declared the same as the **argv** parameter. It is a pointer to an array of strings that contain environmental settings. The last string in the array is null, which marks the end. This program prints all current environmental strings:

```
#include <stdio.h>

main(int argc, char *argv[], char *env[])
{
  int i;

  for(i=0; env[i]; i++) printf("%s\n", env[i]);
}
```

Notice that you must declare both the **argc** and **argv** parameters even if they are not used because the parameter declarations are position dependent. It is perfectly valid to leave off the **env** declaration if it is not used.

One final point: As mentioned earlier in this chapter, when no arguments to **main( )** are used, it is common to declare **main( )**'s argument list as **void**.

Returning Values from main( )

Although none of the programs you have seen so far do so, it is possible to return an integer value from **main( )**. This value is passed back to the calling process, which is usually the operating system. You can return a value from **main( )** using the **return** statement just like you do with any other function. For DOS and OS/2, a return value of 0 indicates the successful termination of a program. Any other value indicates that the program terminated because of some error.

To see how this works, you can improve the COMLINE program from the preceding section so that it returns an error code to the operating system if one of the commands fails. To accomplish this, you take advantage of another feature of the Turbo C++ **system( )** function. This function will return 0 if the operation was successful and −1 otherwise.

```
/* COMLINE: a program that executes whatever DOS
   commands are specified on the command line.

   Return error code to the operating system if
   an operation fails.
*/
#include <stdio.h>
#include <stdlib.h>

main(int argc, char *argv[])
{
  int i;

  for(i=1; i<argc; i++) {
    if(system(argv[i])) {
      printf("%s failed\n", argv[i]);
      return -1; /* failure code */
    }
  }
  return 0;  /* return success code */
}
```

Some programmers like to specifically declare **main( )** as **void** if it does not return a value, using a statement like this:

```
void main(void)
```

However, this is not necessary and this practice will not be followed in this book. Another approach is to always return a value from **main( )**. Now that you know about returning values from **main( )**, all subsequent programs in this book will do this.

 NOTE Now that returning values from **main( )** and function prototypes have been covered, you should turn on the warning message that you turned off in Chapter 4. This message will be displayed any time a function that isn't declared with a return type of **void** doesn't return a value.

Recursion

In C and C++, functions may call themselves. A function is *recursive* if a statement in the body of the function calls itself. Sometimes called *circular definition,* recursion is the process of defining something in terms of itself.

Examples of recursion abound. A recursive way to define an unsigned integer number is as the digits 0, 1, 2, 3, 4, 5, 6, 7, 8, 9 plus or minus another integer number. For example, the number 15 is the number 7 plus the number 8; 21 is 9 plus 12; and 12 is 9 plus 3.

For a computer language to be recursive, a function must be able to call itself. The classic example of recursion is shown in the function **factr( )**, which computes the factorial of an integer. The factorial of a number N is the product of all the whole numbers between 1 and N. For example, 3 factorial is $1 \times 2 \times 3$, or 6. Both **factr( )** and its iterative equivalent are shown here:

```
factr(int n)   /* recursive */
{
  int answer;
```

```
  if(n==1) return(1);
  answer = factr(n-1)*n;
  return(answer);
}

fact(int n)     /* non-recursive */
{
  int t, answer;

  answer = 1;
  for(t=1; t<=n; t++) answer = answer*(t);
  return(answer);
}
```

The operation of the nonrecursive version of **fact( )** should be clear. It uses a loop starting at 1 and ending at the target value and progressively multiplies each number by the moving product.

The operation of the recursive **factr( )** is a little more complex. When **factr( )** is called with an argument of 1, the function returns 1; otherwise, it returns the product of **factr(n−1)*n**. To evaluate this expression, **factr( )** is called with **n−1**. This happens until **n** equals 1 and the calls to the function begin returning.

Computing the factorial of 2, the first call to **factr( )** will cause a second call to be made with the argument of 1. This call will return 1, which is then multiplied by 2 (the original **n** value). The answer is then 2. You might find it interesting to insert **printf( )** statements into **factr( )**, which will show at what level each call is and what the intermediate answers are.

When a function calls itself, new local variables and parameters are allocated storage on the stack and the function code is executed with these new variables from the start. A recursive call does not make a new copy of the function. Only the arguments and variables are new. As each recursive call returns, the old local variables and parameters are removed from the stack and execution resumes at the point of the function call inside the function. Recursive functions could be said to telescope out and back.

Most recursive routines do not significantly reduce code size or variable storage. Also, the recursive versions of most routines may execute a bit more slowly than the iterative equivalents because of the added overhead of the function calls; but this will not be noticeable in most cases. Many recursive calls to a function could cause a stack overrun, but this is unlikely. Because storage for function parameters and local variables is on the stack and each new call creates a new copy of these variables, it is possible that the stack could overrun your program and cause a crash. However, you probably will not have to worry about this unless a recursive function runs wild.

The main advantage to recursive functions is that they can be used to create clearer and simpler versions of several algorithms than their iterative brothers. For example, the QuickSort sorting algorithm is quite difficult to implement in an iterative way. Also, some problems, especially AI-related ones, seem to lend themselves to recursive solutions. Finally, some people seem to think recursively more easily than iteratively.

When writing recursive functions, you must have an **if** statement somewhere to force the function to return without the recursive call being executed. If you don't do this, once you call the function, it will never return. This is a very common error when writing recursive functions. Use **printf( )** and **getchar( )** liberally during development so that you can watch what is going on and abort execution if you see that you have made a mistake.

Here is another example of a recursive function. The function is called **siren( )** and it uses the Turbo C++ **sound( )** and **nosound( )** functions to create an ascending siren sound. The **sound( )** function is called with an integer argument that becomes the frequency of the sound produced by the computer's speaker. The sound continues until your program calls **nosound( )**, which takes no arguments. The **siren( )** function calls itself until the frequency is less than 100. At that point the recursive calls begin to unravel and the siren sound is produced.

```
/* This program sounds a siren. */
#include <stdio.h>
#include <dos.h>
int siren(int freq);
```

```
main(void)
{
  siren(1000);
  return 0;
}

siren(int freq)
{
  int i;

  if(freq>100)
    siren(freq-100);

  /* turn on sound */
  sound(freq);

  /* delay just a bit */
  for(i=0; i<10000; i++) ;
  nosound(); /* turn off sound */
}
```

Classic Versus Modern Function Parameter Declarations

When C was first invented, a different function parameter declaration method was used. This older method is sometimes called the *classic* form. The declaration approach used so far in this book is called the *modern* form. Turbo C++ supports both forms. (However, the ANSI C standard strongly *recommends* the modern form.) The reason that it is important for you to know the classic form is because there are literally millions of lines of C code in existence that use it. Also, many programs published in books and magazines use this form because it will work with all compilers —even old ones. Let's see how the classic form differs from the modern one.

The classic function parameter declaration consists of two parts: a parameter list, which goes inside the parentheses that follow the function name; and the actual parameter declarations, which go between the closing parenthesis and the function's opening curly brace. The general form of the classic parameter definition is shown here:

> *type func_name(parm1, parm2,. . .parmN)*
> *type parm1;*
> *type parm2;*
>   .
>   .
>   .
> *type parmN;*
> *{*
>   *function code*
> *}*

For example, the modern declaration

```
float f(int a, int b, char ch)
{
  .
  .
  .
 }
```

will look like this in its classic form:

```
float f(a, b, ch)
int a, b;
char ch;
{
  .
  .
  .
 }
```

Notice that in classic form, more than one parameter can be in the list after the type name.

Keep in mind that there are some very subtle reasons why the modern form is a little better than the classic form, so this is why it is used in this book. However, if you see a program that uses the classic form, remember that Turbo C++ can compile it with no trouble whatsoever—although the use of the classic function declaration in a C++ program will cause a warning message to be displayed, which can become annoying.

Implementation Issues

There are a few important things to remember when you create functions, which affect their efficiency and usability. These issues are the subject of this section.

Parameters and General-Purpose Functions

A general-purpose function is one that will be used in a variety of situations, perhaps by many different programmers. Typically, you should not base general-purpose functions on global data. It is best if all of the information a function needs is passed to it by its parameters.

Besides making your functions general purpose, parameters keep your code readable and less susceptible to bugs that result from side effects.

Efficiency

Functions are the building blocks of C and crucial to the creation of all but the most trivial programs. Let nothing said in this section be construed to be otherwise. However, in certain specialized applications, you may need to eliminate a function and replace it with *in-line code* instead. In-line code is the equivalent of a function's statements used without a call to that function. In-line code is used instead of function calls only when execution time is critical.

There are two reasons why in-line code is faster than a function call. First, a call instruction takes time to execute. Second, if there are arguments to pass, these have to be placed on the stack, which also takes time. For almost all applications, this very slight increase in execution time is of no significance. But it could be very important in time-critical tasks. Each function call uses time that would be saved if the code in the function were placed in line. For example, following are two versions of a program that prints the square of the numbers from 1 to 10. The in-line version will run faster than the other because the function call takes time.

In Line

```
#include <stdio.h>

main(void)
{
   int x;

   for(x=1; x<11; ++x)
   printf("%d", x*x);
   return 0;
}
```

Function Call

```
#include <stdio.h>
 int sqr(int a);

main(void)
{
   int x;

   for(x=1; x<11; ++x)
   printf("%d", sqr(x));
   return 0;
}

sqr(int a)
{
   return a*a;
}
```

Now that you have seen the power of Turbo C++ functions, it is time to delve into its I/O system.

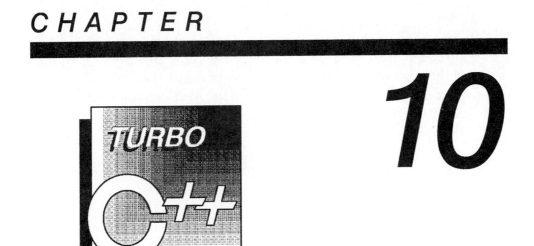

Input, Output, and Disk Files

Input and output in C are accomplished through the use of library functions; there are no C keywords that perform I/O operations. The ANSI standard, which is followed by Turbo C++, defines one complete set of I/O functions. However, the old UNIX standard contains two distinct systems of routines that handle I/O operations. The first method, defined by both the ANSI standard and UNIX C is called the *ANSI file system* (sometimes the terms *formatted* or *buffered* are used instead). The second is the *UNIX-like* file system (sometimes called either *unformatted* or *unbuffered*) and is defined only under the UNIX de-facto standard.

The ANSI standard does not define the UNIX-like file system. This is justified by several arguments, including the fact that the two file systems are largely redundant. However, because both file systems are currently in widespread use, Turbo C++ supports both approaches. Hence, this chapter will cover both, but the greatest emphasis will be placed on the ANSI standard I/O system. This is because use of the UNIX-like system, which is not defined by the ANSI standard, is expected to decline. Thus, new code should be written using the ANSI I/O functions.

It is the purpose of this chapter to present an overview of I/O in C and to illustrate the way in which the core functions of each file system work together. Keep in mind that the C library contains a very rich and diverse assortment of I/O routines — more than can be covered here. You will want to study your user manual to see what else is available.

NOTE Although C++ supports the I/O functions discussed in this chapter, it also provides its own object oriented method of performing I/O. However, there are three reasons why you need to learn about C I/O. First, many of the concepts implicit to the C I/O system are shared by the C++ approach. Second, there are thousands (maybe millions) of C programs in existence. These will not be converted to C++ programs overnight. Instead, they will migrate towards C++ over several years, with C++ features added a little at a time. Therefore, you will almost certainly encounter the I/O functions discussed in this chapter, and it is important that you understand what they do. (This will be especially true if you are given the task of converting a C program into a C++ program.) Third, the C I/O system is very rich and you might find that some operations are more easily performed using C-like functions.

Before beginning your exploration of C's I/O system, you need to learn about two special compiler directives and some terminology.

Two Preprocessor Directives

It is possible to include various instructions to the C compiler in the source code of a C program. These are called *preprocessor directives* and, although not actually part of the C language, they expand the scope of the C programming environment. All preprocessor directives begin with a # sign. Although most of the preprocessor directives will be covered later, two of them are needed for you to use C's file system.

#define

The **#define** directive is used to define an identifier and a string that will be substituted for the identifier each time it is encountered in the source file. The identifier is called the *macro name* and the replacement process is called *macro substitution*. The general form of the directive is

#define *identifier token-sequence*

Notice that there is no semicolon in this statement. A *token-sequence* is any sequence of characters. The characters need not be enclosed by quotation marks. There may be any number of spaces between the identifier and the token-sequence, but once the sequence begins, it is terminated only by a newline.

For example, if you wished to use the word TRUE for the value 1 and the word FALSE for the value 0, then you would declare the following two macro **#define**s:

```
#define TRUE 1
#define FALSE 0
```

This will cause the compiler to substitute a 1 or a 0 each time the name TRUE or FALSE is encountered in your source file. For example, the following will print "0 1 2" on the screen:

```
printf("%d %d %d",FALSE, TRUE, TRUE+1);
```

Once a macro name has been defined, it may be used as part of the definition of other macro names. For example, this code defines the names **ONE**, **TWO**, and **THREE** to their respective values:

```
#define ONE     1
#define TWO     ONE+ONE
#define THREE   ONE+TWO
```

It is important to understand that macro substitution is simply the replacing of an identifier with its associated string. Therefore, if you wish to define a standard error message you might write something like this:

```
#define E_MS "standard error on input\n"

    .
    .
    .

printf(E_MS);
```

The compiler will actually substitute the string "standard error on input\n" when the identifier **E_MS** is encountered. To the compiler, the **printf( )** statement will actually appear to be

```
printf("standard error on input\n");
```

No text substitutions will occur if the identifier occurs within a string. For example,

```
#define XYZ this is a test
     .
     .
     .
printf("XYZ");
```

will not print "this is a test," but rather "XYZ."

A common usage of **#define** is to define the size of something, such as an array dimension, that might change over the evolution of a program. In the following simple program, the macro **MAX_SIZE** is used to dimension an integer array as well as to control the loop condition of the **for** loop that initializes it:

```
#include <stdio.h>

#define MAX_SIZE 16

unsigned int  pwrs_of_two[MAX_SIZE];

/* Display powers of 2. */
main(void)
{
  int i;

  pwrs_of_two[0] = 1; /* start the sequence */

  for(i=1; i<MAX_SIZE; i++)
     pwrs_of_two[i] = pwrs_of_two[i-1] * 2;

  printf("The first 16 powers of 2: \n");
  for(i=0; i<MAX_SIZE; i++)
    printf("%u ", pwrs_of_two[i]);

  return 0;
}
```

The reason that **#define** is introduced in this chapter is that the header files used by the I/O system contain various defined constants that you will be using.

#include

Until now, you have used the **#include** directive without formal explanation. Now it is time for a closer look at this important command.

The **#include** preprocessor directive instructs the compiler to include another source file with the one that has the **#include** directive in it. The source file to be read in must be enclosed between double quotes or angle brackets. For example, the directives,

```
#include "TEST"
#include <TEST>
```

both instruct the compiler to read and compile the file called TEST.

It is valid for included files to have **#include** directives in them. These are referred to as *nested includes*.

If explicit pathnames are specified as part of the filename identifier, then only those directories will be searched for the included file. Otherwise, if the filename is enclosed in quotes, the current working directory is searched first. If the file is not found, then any directories specified on the command line using the **−I** compiler option are searched. Finally, if the file has still not been found, the standard directories, as defined by the implementation, are searched.

If no explicit pathnames are specified and the filename is enclosed by angle brackets, the file is first searched for in the directories specified in the compiler command line **−I** option. If the file is not found, then the standard directories are searched. At no time is the current working directory searched.

If you have installed Turbo C++ in accordance with Borland's instructions, then you will want to use angle brackets—the method used in the examples in this book.

Streams and Files

Before beginning a discussion of C's I/O system it is important to understand the difference between the terms *stream* and *file*. The C I/O system supplies a consistent interface to the C programmer independent of the actual device being accessed. That is, the C I/O system provides a level of abstraction between the programmer and the device being used. This abstraction is called a *stream* and the actual device is called a *file*. It is important to understand how they interact.

Streams

The ANSI C file system is designed to work with a wide variety of devices including terminals, disk drives, and tape drives. Even though each device is very different, the ANSI C file system transforms each into a logical device called a stream. All streams are similar in their behavior. Because streams are largely independent of devices, the same functions that write to a disk file can also write to the console. There are two types of streams: text and binary.

Text Streams

A *text stream* is a sequence of characters. In a text stream, certain character translations may occur as required by the host environment. For example, a newline may be converted to a carriage return-linefeed pair, which is what Turbo C++ does. Therefore, there may not be a one-to-one relationship between the characters that are written (or read) and those in the external device. Also, because of possible translations, the number of characters written (or read) may not be the same as that found in the external device.

Binary Streams

A *binary stream* is a sequence of bytes that has a one-to-one correspondence to that found in the external device. That is, no character translations will occur. Also, the number of bytes written (or read) will be the same as the number found in the external device. However, a binary stream may be padded with null bytes so that it fills a sector on a disk.

Files

In C, a file is a logical concept that may be applied to everything from disk files to terminals. A stream is associated with a specific file by performing an open operation. Once a file is open, then information may be exchanged between it and your program.

Not all files have the same capabilities. For example, a disk file can support random access while a tape drive cannot. This illustrates an important point about the C I/O system: all streams are the same but all files are not.

If the file can support random access (sometimes referred to as *position requests*), then opening that file also initializes the *file position indicator* to the start of the file. As each character is read from or written to the file, the position indicator is incremented, thus ensuring progression through the file.

A file is disassociated from a specific stream through a close operation. On streams opened for output, closing a stream causes the contents, if any, of its associated buffer to be written to the external device. This process is generally referred to as *flushing* the stream and it guarantees that no information is accidentally left in the disk buffer. All files are closed automatically when your program terminates normally.

Each stream that is associated with a file has a file control structure of type **FILE**. This structure is defined in the header STDIO.H. You must not make modifications to this file control structure. (You will learn about structures in the next chapter, but briefly, a structure is simply a group of variables accessed under one name. This is similar to a RECORD in Turbo Pascal. At any rate, you do not need to know anything about structures to use the I/O routines.)

Conceptual Versus Actual

In light of the foregoing discussion, the following summarizes the way the C I/O system operates. As far as the programmer is concerned, all I/O takes place through streams, which are sequences of characters. Furthermore, all streams are the same. The file system links a stream to a file. In the language of C programmers, a file is any external device capable of I/O. Because different devices have differing capabilities, all files are not the same. However, these differences as they relate to the programmer are minimized by the C I/O system because it converts the raw information coming from the device into a stream (and vice versa). Aside from the limitation that only certain types of files support random access, the programmer need not worry about the actual physical device and is free to concentrate on the logical device called the stream.

If this approach seems confusing or strange, you need to see it in the context of languages like BASIC or FORTRAN, in which each device supported by the implementation has its own completely separate file system. In C's approach, the programmer need only think in terms of streams and use only one file system to accomplish all I/O operations.

Console I/O

Console I/O refers to operations that occur at the keyboard and screen of your computer. Generally, console I/O is performed using a special case of the ANSI file system (plus a few special Turbo C++ functions that support better interaction between the computer and the user). Because input and output to the console is such a common affair, a subsystem of the ANSI file system was created that deals exclusively with console I/O. Technically, these functions will direct their operations to the standard input and standard output of the system. In many operating systems, including DOS, it is possible to redirect the console I/O to other devices. However, for simplicity of discussion it is assumed that the console will be the device used since it is the most common. Later you will learn how these functions are connected with other file system functions.

Reading and Writing Characters

The simplest of the console I/O functions are **getche( )**, which reads a character from the keyboard, and **putchar( )**, which prints a character to the screen. The **getche( )** function waits until a key is pressed and then returns its value. The key pressed is also echoed to the screen automatically. The **putchar( )** function will write its character argument to the screen at the current cursor position. The prototypes for **getche( )** and **putchar( )** are shown here:

    int getche(void);

    int putchar(int *c*);

Don't be disturbed by the fact that **getche( )** returns an integer; the low-order byte contains the character. Also, even though **putchar( )** is declared as using an integer parameter, only the low-order byte is actually output to the screen. The header file for **getche( )** is in CONIO.H and the header file for **putchar( )** is in STDIO.H.

The following program inputs characters from the keyboard and prints them in reverse case. That is, uppercase prints as lowercase, and lowercase prints as uppercase. The program halts when a period is typed. The header file CTYPE.H is required by the **islower( )** library function, which returns true if its argument is lowercase and false if it is not.

```
#include <stdio.h>
#include <conio.h>
#include <ctype.h>

main(void)  /* case switcher */
{
  char ch;

  printf("enter chars, enter a period to stop\n");
  do {
    ch = getche();
    if(islower(ch)) putchar(toupper(ch));
    else putchar(tolower(ch));
  } while (ch!='.'); /* use a period to stop*/
  return 0;
}
```

There are two important variations on **getche( )**. The first is **getchar( )**, which is the original, UNIX-based character input function. The trouble with **getchar( )** is that it buffers input until a carriage return is entered. The reason for this is that the original UNIX systems line-buffered terminal input—that is, you had to hit a carriage return for anything you had just typed to actually be sent to the computer. The effect of this is that there are one or more characters waiting in the input queue after **getchar( )** returns. This is quite annoying in today's interactive environments and its use is not recommended. It is supported by Turbo C++ to ensure portability with UNIX-based programs and because it is defined by the ANSI C standard. You may want to play with it a little to better understand its effect. The **getchar( )** function uses the STDIO.H header file.

A second, more useful, variation on **getche( )** is **getch( )**, which operates precisely like **getche( )** except that the character you type is not echoed to the screen. It uses the CONIO.H header.

 NOTE   Neither **getche( )** nor **getch( )** is defined by the ANSI standard. However, they are provided with Turbo C++ (and most other PC-based C and C++ compilers) because of the trouble with **getchar( )**.

Reading and Writing Strings

On the next step up, in terms of complexity and power, are the functions **gets( )** and **puts( )**. They enable you to read and write strings of characters at the console.

The **gets( )** function reads a string of characters entered at the keyboard and places them at the address pointed to by its character pointer argument. You may type characters at the keyboard until you strike a carriage return. The carriage return does not become part of the string; instead a null terminator is placed at the end and **gets( )** returns. In fact, it is impossible to use **gets( )** to return a carriage return (**getchar( )** can do so, though).

Typing mistakes can be corrected by using the \ prior to striking ENTER. The prototype for **gets( )** is

```
char *gets(char *s);
```

where *s* is a character array that receives the characters input by the user. Its prototype is found in STDIO.H. The following program reads a string into the array **str** and prints its length:

```
#include <stdio.h>
#include <string.h>

main(void)
{
  char str[80];

  gets(str);
  printf("length is %d", strlen(str));
  return 0;
}
```

The **gets( )** function returns a pointer to **s**.

The **puts( )** function writes its string argument to the screen followed by a newline. Its prototype is

```
int puts(char *s);
```

It recognizes the same backslash codes as **printf( )**, such as "\t" for tab. A call to **puts( )** requires far less overhead than the same call to **printf( )** because **puts( )** can only output a string of characters —it cannot output numbers or do format conversions. Therefore, **puts( )** takes up less space and runs faster than **printf( )**. Hence, the **puts( )** function is often used when it is important to have highly optimized code. The **puts( )** function returns a non-negative value if successful, **EOF** otherwise. The following statement writes "hello" on the screen.

```
puts("hello");
```

The **puts( )** function uses the STDIO.H header file.

The simplest functions that perform console I/O operations are summarized in Table 10-1.

Formatted Console I/O

In addition to the simple console I/O functions just described, the C standard library contains two functions that perform formatted input and output on built-in data types: **printf( )** and **scanf( )**. The term *formatted* refers to the fact that these functions can read and write data in various formats that are under your control. The **printf( )** function is used to write data to the console; **scanf( )**, its complement, reads data from the keyboard. Both **printf( )** and **scanf( )** can operate on any of the built-in data types, including characters, strings, and numbers. Although you have been using these functions since the start of this book, they will be examined in detail here.

Table 10-1.

Function	Operation
getchar( )	Reads a character from the keyboard; waits for carriage return
getche( )	Reads a character with echo; does not wait for carriage return
getch( )	Reads a character without echo; does not wait for carriage return
putchar( )	Writes a character to the screen
gets( )	Reads a string from the keyboard
puts( )	Writes a string to the screen

Functions that Perform Console I/O Operations

printf( )

The prototype for **printf( )** is

  int printf(char *control_string, . . .);

The prototype for **printf( )** is in STDIO.H. Notice the three periods at the end of **printf( )**'s prototype. When a function can take a variable number of arguments, then its prototype uses the three periods to specify this.

   The control string consists of two types of items. The first type is made up of characters that will be printed on the screen. The second type contains format commands that define the way the arguments are displayed. A format command begins with a percent sign and is followed by the format code. The format commands are shown in Table 10-2. There must be exactly the same number of arguments as there are format commands, and the format commands and the arguments are matched in order. For example, the **printf( )** call,

```
printf("Hi %c %d %s", 'c', 10, "there!");
```

displays: "Hi c 10 there!".

   The format commands may have modifiers that specify the field width, the number of decimal places, and a left justification flag. An integer placed between the % sign and the format command acts as a *minimum field width specifier*. This pads the output with blanks or zeros to ensure that it is at least a certain minimum length. If the string or number is greater than that minimum, it will be printed in full even if the minimum is overrun. The default padding is done with spaces. If you wish to pad with zeros, place a 0 before the field width specifier. For example, **%05d** will pad a number of fewer than five digits with zeros so that its total length is five.

Table 10-2.

Command	Format
%c	A single character
%d	Decimal
%i	Decimal
%e	Scientific notation (using lowercase e)
%E	Scientific notation (using uppercase E)
%f	Decimal floating point
%g	Uses **%e** or **%f**, whichever is shorter
%G	Same as **%g**, except that an uppercase E is used if the **%e** format is selected
%o	Octal
%s	String of characters
%u	Unsigned decimal
%x	Hexadecimal (using lowercase letters)
%X	Hexadecimal (using uppercase letters)
%%	Prints a % sign
%p	Displays a pointer
%n	The associated argument is a pointer to an integer into which is placed the number of characters written so far

printf( ) Format Commands

To specify the number of decimal places printed for a floating-point number, place a decimal point after the field width specifier followed by the number of decimal places you wish to display. For example, **%10.4f** will display a number at least ten characters wide with four decimal places. When this is applied to strings or integers, the number following the period specifies the maximum field length. For example, **%5.7s** will display a string that will be at least five characters long and will not exceed seven. If the string is longer than the maximum field width, the string will be truncated.

By default, all output is *right-justified:* if the field width is larger than the data printed, the data will be placed on the right edge of the field. You can force the information to be left-justified by placing a minus sign directly after the %. For example, **%−10.2f** will left-justify a floating-point number with two decimal places in a 10-character field.

There are two format command modifiers that allow **printf( )** to display **short** and **long** integers. These modifiers may be applied to the **d, i, o, u,** and **x** type specifiers. The l modifier tells **printf( )** that a **long** data type follows. For example, **%ld** means that a **long int** is to be displayed. The **h** modifier instructs **printf( )** to display a **short int**. Therefore, **%hu** indicates that the data is of type **short unsigned int**.

The **l** modifier may also prefix the floating-point commands of **e, f,** and **g** to indicate that a **double** follows. The **L** modifier specifies a **long double**.

With **printf( )**, you can output virtually any format of data you desire. Figure 10-1 shows some examples.

scanf( )

The general-purpose console input routine is **scanf( )**. It can read all the built-in data types and automatically convert numbers into the proper internal format. It is much like the reverse of **printf( )**. The general form of **scanf( )** is

```
int scanf(char *control_string, . . .);
```

The prototype for **scanf( )** is in STDIO.H. The control string consists of three classifications of characters:

- format specifiers
- white-space characters
- nonwhite-space characters

Figure 10-1.

printf( ) Statement	*Output*
("%-5.2f",123.234)	¦123.23¦
("%5.2f",3.234)	¦ 3.23¦
("%10s","hello")	¦ hello¦
("%-10s","hello")	¦hello ¦
("%5.7s","123456789")	¦1234567¦

Some **printf( )** *examples*

The input format specifiers are preceded by a **%** sign and tell **scanf( )** what type of data is to be read next. These codes are listed in Table 10-3. For example, **%s** reads a string while **%d** reads an integer.

Table 10-3.

Code	*Meaning*
%c	Read a single character
%d	Read a decimal integer
%i	Read a decimal integer
%e	Read a floating-point number
%f	Read a floating-point number
%h	Read a short integer
%o	Read an octal number
%s	Read a string
%x	Read a hexadecimal number
%p	Read a pointer
%n	Receive an integer value equal to the number of characters read so far

scanf( ) *Format Codes*

A white-space character in the control string causes **scanf( )** to skip over one or more white-space characters in the input stream. A white-space character is either a space, a tab, or a newline. In essence, one white-space character in the control string will cause **scanf( )** to read, but not store, any number (including zero) of white-space characters up to the first nonwhite-space character.

A nonwhite-space character causes **scanf( )** to read and discard a matching character. For example, *"%d,%d"* causes **scanf( )** to first read an integer, then read and discard a comma, and finally read another integer. If the specified character is not found, **scanf( )** will terminate.

All the variables used to receive values through **scanf( )** must be passed by their addresses. This means that all arguments must be pointers to the variables used as arguments. If you remember, this is C's way of creating a call by reference and it allows a function to alter the contents of an argument. For example, to read an integer into the variable **count**, you would use the following **scanf( )** call:

```
scanf("%d", &count);
```

Strings will be read into character arrays, and the array name, without any index, is the address of the first element of the array. So, to read a string into the character array **address**, you would use the following:

```
scanf("%s", address);
```

In this case, **address** is already a pointer and need not be preceded by the **&** operator.

The input data items must be separated by spaces, tabs, or newlines. Punctuation such as commas, semicolons, and the like do not count as separators. This means that,

```
scanf("%d%d", &r, &c);'
```

will accept an input of **10 20**, but will fail with **10,20**. As in **printf( )**, the **scanf( )** format codes are matched in order with the variables receiving input in the argument list.

An * placed after the % and before the format code will read data of the specified type but suppress its assignment. Thus,

```
scanf("%d%*c%d", &x, &y);
```

given the input **10/20** will place the value 10 into **x**, discard the division sign, and give **y** the value 20.

The format commands can specify a maximum field length modifier. This is an integer number placed between the % and the format command code that limits the number of characters read for any field. For example, to read no more than 20 characters into **str**, you would write

```
scanf("%20s", str);
```

If the input stream is greater than 20 characters, then a subsequent call to input begins where this call leaves off. For example, if you entered

```
ABCDEFGHIJKLMNOPQRSTUVWXYZ
```

as the response to the **scanf( )** call in this example, only the first 20 characters up to the "T" are placed into **str** because of the maximum size specifier. This means that the remaining characters, "UVWXYZ," are not used. If another **scanf( )** call is made, such as

```
scanf("%s", str);
```

then "UVWXYZ" are placed into **str**. Input for a field may terminate before the maximum field length is reached if a white-space character is encountered. In this case, **scanf( )** moves on to the next field.

Although spaces, tabs, and newlines are used as field separators, when reading a single character, these are read like any other character. For example, with an input stream of "x y,"

```
scanf("%c%c%c", &a, &b, &c);
```

will return with the character "x" in **a**, a space in **b**, and the character "y" in **c**.

 CAUTION If you have any other characters in the control string — including spaces, tabs, and newlines — those characters will be used to match and discard characters from the input stream. Any character that matches is discarded. For example, given the input stream **10t20**,

```
scanf("%st%s", &x, &y);
```

will place 10 into **x** and 20 into **y**. The "t" is discarded because of the "t" in the control string. For another example,

```
scanf("%s ", name);
```

will *not* return until you type a character *after* you type a white-space character. This is because the space after the **%s** has instructed **scanf( )** to read and discard spaces, tabs, and newline characters.

You may not use **scanf( )** to display a prompting message. Therefore, all prompts must be done explicitly prior to the **scanf( )** call.

The **scanf( )** function also includes a very powerful feature called a *scanset*. A scanset defines a list of characters that will be matched by **scanf( )**. The **scanf( )** function will continue to read characters so long as they are in the scanset. As soon as a character is input that does not match any in the scanset, **scanf( )** moves on to the next (if any) format specifier. A scanset is defined by putting a list of the characters you want to scan for inside square brackets. The beginning square bracket must be prefixed by a percent sign. For example, this scanset tells **scanf( )** to read only the digits 0 through 9:

```
%[1234567890]
```

The argument corresponding to the scanset must be a pointer to a character array. Upon return from **scanf( )**, the array will contain a null-terminated string comprised of the characters read. To see how this works, try this program:

```
#include <stdio.h>

main(void)
{
  char s1[80], s2[80];

  scanf("%[1234567890]%s", s1, s2);
  printf("\n%s¦¦%s", s1, s2);
  return 0;
}
```

Try this program using the input,

   "123456789abcdefg987654"

followed by a carriage return. The program will then display

```
123456789¦¦abcdefg987654
```

Because the "a" is not part of the scanset, **scanf( )** stops reading characters into **s1** when it is encountered and the remaining characters are put into **s2**.

You can specify a range inside a scanset by using a hyphen. For example, this tells **scanf( )** to accept the characters A through Z:

```
%[A-Z]
```

You can specify more than one range within a scanset. For example, this program reads digits and letters. It also illustrates that you can use the maximum field specifier with a scanset.

```c
#include <stdio.h>

main(void)
{
  char str[80];

  printf("Enter digits and letters: ");
  scanf("%78[a-z0-9]", str);
  printf("\n%s", str);
  return 0;
}
```

You can specify an inverted set if the first character in the set is a ^. When the ^ is present, it instructs **scanf( )** to accept any character that *is not* defined by the scanset.

One important point to remember is that the scanset is case-sensitive. Therefore, if you want to scan for both upper- and lowercase letters you must specify them individually.

The ANSI I/O System

The ANSI I/O system is comprised of several interrelated functions. The most common are shown in Table 10-4. These functions require that the header file STDIO.H be included in any program in which they are used.

The File Pointer

The common thread that ties the ANSI C I/O system together is the *file pointer*. A file pointer is a pointer to information that

Table 10-4.

Function	Operation
fopen( )	Opens a stream
fclose( )	Closes a stream
putc( )	Writes a character to a stream
getc( )	Reads a character from a stream
fseek( )	Seeks to the specified byte in a stream
fprintf( )	Is to a stream what **printf( )** is to the console
fscanf( )	Is to a stream what **scanf( )** is to the console
feof( )	Returns true if the end of the file is reached
ferror( )	Returns true if an error has occurred
fread( )	Reads a block of data from a stream
fwrite( )	Writes a block of data to a stream
rewind( )	Resets the file position locator to the beginning of the file
remove( )	Erases a file

The Most Common ANSI File System Functions

defines various things about the file, including its name, status, and current position. In essence, the file pointer identifies a specific disk file and is used by the stream associated with it to direct the operation of the ANSI C I/O functions. A file pointer is a pointer variable of type **FILE**, which is defined in STDIO.H. In order to read or write files, your program will need to use file pointers. To obtain a file pointer variable, use a statement like the following:

```
FILE *fp;
```

Opening a File

The **fopen( )** function serves two purposes. First, it opens a stream for use and it links a file with that stream. Second, it returns the file pointer associated with that file. Most often, and for the rest of this discussion, the file is a disk file. The **fopen( )** function has this prototype:

FILE *fopen(char *filename*, char *mode*);

where *mode* is a string containing the desired open status. The filename must be a string of characters that comprise a valid filename for the operating system and may include a path specification.

The legal values for *mode* are shown in Table 10-5. If you do not specify a "t" for text or a "b" for binary, then the file is opened according to the value in Turbo C++'s global variable **_fmode**. This variable will be set to either **O_TEXT** for text mode or **O_BINARY** for binary mode. It is **O_TEXT** by default. The macros **O_BINARY** and **O_TEXT** are found in FCNTL.II. This book assumes that **_fmode** is in its default setting.

As stated, **fopen( )** returns a file pointer. Your program should never alter the value of this pointer. If an error occurs when trying to open the file, **fopen( )** returns a null.

As Table 10-5 shows, a file may be opened in either text or binary mode. In text mode, carriage return-linefeed sequences are translated to newline characters on input. On output, the reverse occurs: newlines are translated to carriage return-linefeeds. No such translations occur on binary files.

If you wished to open a file for writing with the name **test**, then you would write

```
FILE *fp;

fp = fopen("test", "w");
```

Table 10-5.

Mode	Meaning
"r"	Open a file for reading
"w"	Create a file for writing
"a"	Append to a file
"rb"	Open a binary file for reading
"wb"	Create a binary file for writing
"ab"	Append to a binary file
"r+"	Open a file for read/write
"w+"	Create a file for read/write
"a+"	Append or create a file for read/write
"r+b"	Open a binary file for read/write
"w+b"	Create a binary file for read/write
"a+b"	Append or create a binary file for read/write
"rt"	Open a text file for reading
"wt"	Create a text file for writing
"at"	Append to a text file
"r+t"	Open a text file for read/write
"w+t"	Create a text file for read/write
"a+t"	Append or create a text file for read/write

The Legal Values for Mode

However, you will usually see it written like this:

```
FILE *fp;

if ((fp = fopen("test","w"))==NULL) {
  puts("cannot open file\n");
  exit(1);
}
```

The macro **NULL** is defined in STDIO.H. This method detects any error in opening a file, such as a write-protected or a full disk, before attempting to write to it. A null is used because no file pointer will ever have that value. Also introduced by this fragment is another library function: **exit( )**. A call to **exit( )** causes immediate termination of the program, no matter what function **exit( )** is called from. It has this prototype (found in STDLIB.H):

> void exit(int *val*);

The value of *val* is returned to the operating system. As you learned in the previous chapter, by convention, a return value of 0 signifies successful termination. Any other value indicates that the program terminated because of some problem.

If you use **fopen( )** to open a file for writing, then any preexisting file by that name will be erased and a new file started. If no file by that name exists, then one will be created. If you want to add to the end of the file, then you must use mode "a". Opening a file for read operations requires that the file exists. If it does not, an error will be returned. Finally, if a file is opened for read/write operations it will not be erased if it exists; however, if it does not exist it will be created.

Writing a Character

The **putc( )** function is used to write characters to a stream that was previously opened for writing by the **fopen( )** function. The function is declared as

> int putc(int *ch*, FILE **fp*);

where *fp* is the file pointer returned by **fopen( )** and *ch* is the character to be output. The file pointer tells **putc( )** which disk file to write to. For historical reasons, *ch* is formally called an **int** but only the low-order byte is used.

If a **putc( )** operation is a success then it will return the character written. Upon failure, an **EOF** is returned. **EOF** is a macro defined in STDIO.H that stands for end-of-file.

Reading a Character

The **getc( )** function is used to read characters from a stream opened in read mode by **fopen( )**. The function is declared as

```
int getc(FILE *fp);
```

where *fp* is a file pointer of type **FILE** returned by **fopen( )**. For historical reasons, **getc( )** returns an integer, but the high-order byte is zero.

The **getc( )** function will return an **EOF** mark when the end of the file has been reached or an error has occurred. Therefore, to read a text file until the end-of-file mark is read, you could use the following code:

```
ch = getc(fp);

while(ch!=EOF) {
  ch = getc(fp);
}
```

Using feof( )

The ANSI file system can also operate on binary data. When a file is opened for binary input, it is possible that an integer value equal to the **EOF** mark may be read. This would cause the previous routine to indicate an end-of-file condition even though the physical end of the file had not been reached. To solve this problem, ANSI C includes the function **feof( )**, which is used to determine the end of the file when reading binary data. The **feof( )** function has this prototype:

   int feof(FILE *fp*);

Its prototype is in STDIO.H. It returns true if the end of the file has been reached; otherwise, zero is returned. Therefore, the following routine reads a binary file until the end of the file is encountered.

```
while(!feof(fp)) ch = getc(fp);
```

Of course, this same method may be applied to text files as well as binary files.

Closing a File

The **fclose( )** function is used to close a stream that was opened by a call to **fopen( )**. It writes any data still remaining in the disk buffer to the file and does a formal operating-system-level close on the file. Failure to close a stream invites all kinds of trouble, including lost data, destroyed files, and possible intermittent errors in your program. An **fclose( )** also frees the file control block associated with the stream and makes it available for reuse. As you probably know, there is an operating system limit to the number of open files you may have at any one time, so it may be necessary to close one file before opening another.

   The **fclose( )** function is declared as

   int fclose(FILE *fp*);

where *fp* is the file pointer returned by the call to **fopen( )**. A return value of zero signifies a successful close operation; any other value indicates an error. You can use the standard function **ferror( )** (discussed next) to determine and report any problems. Generally, the only time **fclose( )** will fail is when a diskette has been prematurely removed from the drive or if there is no more space on the diskette.

ferror( ) and rewind( )

The **ferror( )** function is used to determine if a file operation has produced an error. If a file is opened in text mode and an error in reading or writing occurs, **EOF** is returned. You use **ferror( )** to determine which event happened. The function **ferror( )** has the prototype

    int ferror(FILE *fp);

where *fp* is a valid file pointer. It returns true if an error has occurred during the last file operation; it returns false otherwise. Because each file operation sets the error condition, **ferror( )** should be called immediately after each file operation; otherwise, an error may be lost. The prototype for **ferror( )** is in STDIO.H.

    The **rewind( )** function will reset the file position locator to the beginning of the file specified as its argument. Its prototype is

    void rewind(FILE *fp);

where *fp* is a valid file pointer. The prototype for **rewind( )** is in STDIO.H.

Using fopen( ), getc( ), putc( ), and fclose( )

The functions **fopen( )**, **getc( )**, **putc( )**, and **fclose( )** comprise the minimal set of file routines. A simple example of using **putc( )**, **fopen( )**, and **fclose( )** is the program **ktod** below. It reads characters from the keyboard and writes them to a disk file until a dollar sign is typed. The filename is specified from the command line. For example, if you call this program **ktod**, then typing **ktod test** will allow you to enter lines of text into the file called **test**.

```
/* ktod: A key to disk program. */

#include <stdio.h>
#include <stdlib.h>

main(int argc, char *argv[])
{
  FILE *fp;
  char ch;

  if(argc!=2) {
    printf("You forgot to enter the filename\n");
    exit(1);
  }

  if((fp=fopen(argv[1], "w"))==NULL) {
    printf("cannot open file\n");
    exit(1);
  }

  do {
    ch = getchar();
    if(EOF==putc(ch, fp)) {
      printf("File Error");
      break;
    }
  } while (ch!='$');

  fclose(fp);
  return 0;
}
```

The complementary program **dtos**, shown next, will read any ASCII file and display the contents on the screen.

```
/* dtos: A program that reads files and displays them
           on the screen.
*/

#include <stdio.h>
#include <stdlib.h>

main(int argc, char *argv[])
{
  FILE *fp;
  char ch;

  if(argc!=2) {
    printf("You forgot to enter the filename\n");
    exit(1);
  }

  if((fp=fopen(argv[1], "r"))==NULL) {
    printf("cannot open file\n");
    exit(1);
  }

  ch = getc(fp);    /* read one character */

  while (ch!=EOF) {
    putchar(ch);   /* print on screen */
    ch = getc(fp);
  }
  if(ferror(fp)) printf("File Error");

  fclose(fp);
  return 0;
}
```

The following program will copy a file of any type. Notice that the files are opened in binary mode and that **feof( )** is used to check for the end of the file.

```
/* Copy a file. */

#include <stdio.h>
#include <stdlib.h>
```

```
main(int argc, char *argv[])
{
  FILE *in, *out;
  char ch;

  if(argc!=3) {
    printf("You forgot to enter a filename\n");
    exit(1);
  }

  if((in=fopen(argv[1], "rb"))==NULL) {
    printf("cannot open source file\n");
    exit(1);
  }
  if((out=fopen(argv[2], "wb")) == NULL) {
    printf("cannot open destination file\n");
    exit(1);
  }

  /* this code actually copies the file */
  while(!feof(in)) {
    ch = getc(in);
    if(ferror(in)) {
      printf("Error reading file");
      break;
    }
    putc(ch, out);
    if(ferror(out)) {
      printf("Error writing file");
      break;
    }
  }

  fclose(in);
  fclose(out);
  return 0;
}
```

Using getw( ) and putw( )

In addition to **getc( )** and **putc( )**, Turbo C++ supports two additional buffered I/O functions: **putw( )** and **getw( )**. These functions are not defined by the ANSI C standard. They are used to read and write integers to and from a disk file. These functions work exactly the same as **putc( )** and **getc( )** except that instead of reading or writing a single character, they read or write an integer. They have the following prototypes:

```
int putw(int i, FILE *fp);
int getw(FILE *fp);
```

The following code fragment will write an integer to the disk file pointed to by *fp*:

```
putw(100, fp);
```

The prototypes for **getw( )** and **putw( )** are in STDIO.H.

fgets( ) and fputs( )

ANSI C's I/O system includes two functions that can read and write strings from streams: **fgets( )** and **fputs( )**. Their prototypes are shown here:

```
char *fputs(char *str, FILE *fp);
char *fgets(char *str, int length, FILE *fp);
```

The function **fputs( )** works exactly like **puts( )** except that it writes the string to the specified stream. The **fgets( )** function reads a string from the specified stream until either a newline character is read or *length −1* characters have been read. If a newline is read, it will be part of the string (unlike **gets( )**). The resultant string will be null terminated.

The prototypes for **fgets( )** and **fputs( )** are in STDIO.H.

fread( ) and fwrite( )

The ANSI I/O system provides two functions, called **fread( )** and **fwrite( )**, that allow the reading and writing of blocks of data. Their prototypes are shown here:

> unsigned fread(void *buffer*, int *num _ bytes*,
> int *count*, FILE *fp*);
> ; unsigned fwrite(void *buffer*, int *num _ bytes*,
> int *count*, FILE *fp*);

In the case of **fread( )**, *buffer* is a pointer to a region of memory that will receive the data read from the file. For **fwrite( )**, *buffer* is a pointer to the information that will be written to the file. The number of bytes to be read or written is specified by *num _ bytes*. The argument *count* determines how many items (each being *num _ bytes* in length) will be read or written. Finally, *fp* is a file pointer to a previously opened stream. Both functions have their prototypes defined in STDIO.H.

The **fread( )** function returns the number of items read, which can be less than *count* if the end of the file is reached or an error occurs. The **fwrite( )** function returns the number of items written. This value will equal *count* unless an error occurs.

As long as the file has been opened for binary data, **fread( )** and **fwrite( )** can read and write any type of information. For example, this program writes a **float** to a disk file:

```
/* Write a floating point number to a disk file. */
#include <stdio.h>
#include <stdlib.h>

main(void)
{
  FILE *fp;
  float f=12.23;
```

```
    if((fp=fopen("test","wb"))==NULL) {
      printf("cannot open file\n");
      exit(1);
    }

    if(fwrite(&f, sizeof(float), 1, fp)!=1)
      printf("File Error");

    fclose(fp);
    return 0;
}
```

As this program illustrates, the buffer can be, and often is, simply a variable. This program also introduces another C operator: **sizeof**. The **sizeof** compile-time operator returns the size, in bytes, of the variable or data type it precedes. Although it would have been possible to look up the size of a **float** and use this value, using **sizeof** ensures that this program will work correctly even if, at some later date, the size of a **float** changes. You will learn more about **sizeof** later in this book.

One of the most useful applications of **fread( )** and **fwrite( )** involves reading and writing arrays (or, as you will see later, structures). For example, this fragment writes the contents of the floating-point array **sample** to the file **sample** using a single **fwrite( )** statement:

```
#include <stdio.h>
#include <stdlib.h>

main(void)
{
  FILE *fp;
  float sample[100];
  int i;

  if((fp=fopen("sample","wb"))==NULL) {
    printf("cannot open file\n");
    exit(1);
  }

  for(i=0; i<100; i++) sample[i] = (float) i;

  /* this saves the entire array in one step */
  if(fwrite(sample, sizeof(sample), 1, fp)!=1)
    printf("File Error");
```

```
    fclose(fp);
    return 0;
}
```

Notice how **sizeof** is used to determine the size of **sample**.

   The next program uses **fread( )** to read the information written by the previous program. It displays the numbers on the screen for verification.

```
#include <stdio.h>
#include <stdlib.h>

main(void)
{
  FILE *fp;
  float sample[100];
  int i;

  if((fp=fopen("sample","rb"))==NULL) {
    printf("cannot open file\n");
    exit(1);
  }

  /* this reads the entire array in one step */
  if(fread(sample, sizeof(sample), 1, fp)!=1)
    printf("File Error");

  for(i=0; i<100; i++) printf("%f ", sample[i]);

  fclose(fp);
  return 0;
}
```

   Later in this book you will see several other, more complex examples of how these functions can be used.

fseek( ) and Random Access I/O

You can perform random read and write operations using the ANSI C I/O system with the help of **fseek( )**, which sets the file position locator. Its prototype type is shown here:

int fseek(FILE *fp*, long *numbytes*, int *origin*);

Here, *fp* is a file pointer returned by a call to **fopen( )**; *numbytes,* a long integer, is the number of bytes from *origin* to make the current position; and *origin* is one of the following macros defined in STDIO.H:

Origin	*Macro Name*	*Actual Value*
Beginning of file	SEEK _ SET	0
Current position	SEEK _ CUR	1
End of file	SEEK _ END	2

Therefore, to seek *numbytes* from the start of the file, *origin* should be **SEEK _ SET**. To seek from the current position use **SEEK _ CUR**; from the end of the file, use **SEEK _ END**.

The following fragment reads the 235th byte in a file that is called **test**.

```
   .
   .
   .

FILE *fp;
char ch;

if((fp=fopen("test", "rb"))==NULL) {
  printf("cannot open file\n");
  exit(1);
}

fseek(fp, 234, 0);
ch = getc(fp);    /* read one character */
                  /* at 235th position */
   .
   .
   .
```

A return value of zero means that **fseek( )** succeeded. A nonzero value indicates failure.

A more interesting example is the **DUMP** program shown here, which uses **fseek( )** to let you examine the contents in both ASCII and hexadecimal of any file you choose. You can look at the file in 128-byte sectors, moving about in the file in either direction. The output displayed is similar in style to the format used by DEBUG when given the "D" (dump memory) command. You exit the program by typing −1 when prompted for the sector. Notice the use of **fread( )** to read the file. At the end of the file, it is likely that less than **SIZE** number of bytes will be read, so the number returned by **fread( )** is passed to **display( )**. (Remember that **fread( )** returns the number of items actually read.) Enter this program into your computer. You should study it until you are certain how it works.

```c
/* DUMP: A simple disk look utility using fseek */
#include <stdio.h>
#include <ctype.h>    /* needed by isprint() library
                         function */
#include <stdlib.h>   /* needed by exit() */

#define SIZE 128

char buf[SIZE];
void display(int numread);

main(int argc, char *argv[])
{
  FILE *fp;
  int sector, numread;

  /* if incorrect number of args, then error */
  if(argc!=2) {
    printf("usage: dump filename\n");
    exit(1);
  }

  if((fp=fopen(argv[1], "rb"))==NULL) {
    printf("cannot open file\n");
    exit(1);
  }

  for(;;) {
    printf("enter sector (-1 to quit): ");
```

```
      scanf("%ld", &sector);
      if(sector<0) break;
      if(fseek(fp, sector*SIZE, SEEK_SET)) {
        printf("seek error\n");
      }
      if((numread=fread(buf, 1, SIZE, fp)) != SIZE) {
        printf("EOF reached\n");
      }

      display(numread);
   }
   return 0;
}

/* display  the file */
void display(int numread)
{
  int i, j;

  for(i=0; i<=numread/16; i++) {
    for(j=0; j<16; j++) printf("%3X", buf[i*16+j]);
    printf("   ");
    for(j=0; j<16; j++) {
      if(isprint(buf[i*16+j])) printf("%c", buf[i*16+j]);
      else printf(".");
    }
    printf("\n");
  }
}
```

Notice that a new library function called **isprint( )** is used to determine which characters are printing characters and which are not. The **isprint( )** function returns true if the character is printable and false otherwise. It requires the use of the header file CTYPE.H, which is included near the top of the program. An example output with **DUMP** used on itself is displayed in Figure 10-2.

The Standard Streams

Whenever a program starts execution, five streams are opened automatically. The first three are standard input (**stdin**), standard

Figure 10-2.

```
enter sector (-1 to quit): 0
  D   A  2F  2A  20  44  55  4D  50  3A  20  41  20  73  69  6D    ../* DUMP: A sim
 70  6C  65  20  64  69  73  6B  20  6C  6F  6F  6B  20  75  74    ple disk look ut
 69  6C  69  74  79  20  75  73  69  6E  67  20  66  73  65  65    ility using fsee
 6B  20  2A  2F   D   A  23  69  6E  63  6C  75  64  65  20  3C    k */..#include <
 73  74  64  69  6F  2E  68  3E   D   A  23  69  6E  63  6C  75    stdio.h>..#inclu
 64  65  20  3C  63  74  79  70  65  2E  68  3E  20  20  20  2F    de <ctype.h>    /
 2A  20  6E  65  65  64  65  64  20  62  79  20  69  73  70  72    * needed by ispr
 69  6E  74  28  29  29  20  6C  69  62  72  61  72  79   D   A    int()) library..
  0   0   0   0   0   0   0   0   0   0   0   0   0   0   0   0    ................
enter sector (-1 to quit): 1
  9   9   9  66  75  6E  63  74  69  6F  6E  20  2A  2F   D   A    ...function */..
 23  69  6E  63  6C  75  64  65  20  3C  73  74  64  6C  69  62    #include <stdlib
 2E  68  3E  20  20  2F  2A  20  6E  65  65  64  65  64  20  62    .h>   /* needed b
 79  20  65  78  69  74  28  29  20  2A  2F   D   A   D   A  23    y exit() */....#
 64  65  66  69  6E  65  20  53  49  5A  45  20  31  32  38   D    define SIZE 128.
  A   D   A  63  68  61  72  20  62  75  66  5B  53  49  5A  45    ...char buf[SIZE
 5D  3B   D   A  76  6F  69  64  20  64  69  73  70  6C  61  79    ];..void display
 28  69  6E  74  20  6E  75  6D  72  65  61  64  29  3B   D   A    (int numread);..
  0   0   0   0   0   0   0   0   0   0   0   0   0   0   0   0    ................
enter sector (-1 to quit):
```

*Sample output from the **DUMP** program*

output (**stdout**), and standard error (**stderr**). Normally, these refer to the console but they may be redirected by the operating system to some other stream device. Because these are file pointers they may be used by the ANSI I/O system to perform I/O operations on the console. For example, **putchar( )** could be defined as

```
putchar(char c)
{
  putc(c, stdout);
}
```

You may use **stdin**, **stdout**, and **stderr** as file pointers in any function that uses a variable of type **FILE ***.

The console I/O functions **getchar( )**, **putchar( )**, **printf( )**, and **scanf( )** actually perform their I/O operations using **stdin** and

stdout. Since DOS allows redirected I/O using the > and < command-line operators, these functions can also read and write disk files. For example, compile this program (called **IOTEST**):

```
#include <stdio.h>

main(void)
{
  printf("Hello there");
  return 0;
}
```

Now, execute it as shown here:

```
C>IOTEST > OUT
```

As you will see, nothing is displayed on the screen. However, if you list the contents of **OUT**, you will see that the message has been written to it.

You should keep in mind that **stdin**, **stdout**, and **stderr** are not variables but constants, and as such they cannot be altered. Also, just as these file pointers are created automatically at the start of your program, they are closed automatically at the end; you should not try to close them.

In addition to the three standard streams, Turbo C++ also automatically opens the streams **stdprn** and **stdaux**. They are associated with the printer and the auxiliary ports respectively.

fprintf( ) and fscanf( )

In addition to the basic I/O functions just discussed, the ANSI C I/O system includes **fprintf( )** and **fscanf( )**. These functions behave exactly like **printf( )** and **scanf( )** except that they operate with disk files. The prototypes of **fprintf( )** and **fscanf( )** are

```
int fprintf(FILE *fp, char *control_string, . . .);
int fscanf(FILE *fp, char *control_string, . . .);
```

where *fp* is a file pointer returned by a call to **fopen( )**. Except for directing their output to the file defined by *fp*, they operate exactly like **printf( )** and **scanf( )**, respectively.

To illustrate how useful these functions can be, the following program maintains a simple telephone directory in a disk file. You may enter names and numbers or you can look up a number given a name.

```c
/* A simple telephone directory. */

#include <stdio.h>
#include <conio.h>
#include <string.h>
#include <stdlib.h>
#include <ctype.h>

void add_num(void), lookup(void);
int menu(void);

main(void)  /* fscanf - fprintf example */
{
  char choice;

  do {
    choice = menu();
    switch(choice) {
      case 'a': add_num();
        break;
      case 'l': lookup();
        break;
    }
  } while (choice!='q');
  return 0;
}

/* Display menu and get request. */
menu(void)
{
  char ch;
```

```
  do {
    printf("(A)dd, (L)ookup, or (Q)uit: ");
    ch = tolower(getche());
    printf("\n");
  } while(ch != 'q' && ch != 'a' && ch != 'l');

  return ch;
}

/* Add a name and number to the directory. */
void add_num(void)
{
  FILE *fp;
  char name[80];
  int a_code, exchg, num;

  /* open it for append */
  if((fp=fopen("phone","a"))==NULL) {
    printf("cannot open directory file\n");
    exit(1);
  }

  printf("enter name and number: ");
  fscanf(stdin, "%s%d%d%d", name, &a_code, &exchg, &num);
  fscanf(stdin, "%*c"); /* remove CR from input stream */

  /* write to file */
  fprintf(fp,"%s %d %d %d\n", name, a_code, exchg, num);

  fclose(fp);
}

/* Find a number given a name. */
void lookup(void)
{
  FILE *fp;
  char name[80], name2[80];
  int a_code, exchg, num;

  /* open it for read */
  if((fp=fopen("phone","r"))==NULL) {
    printf("cannot open directory file\n");
    exit(1);
  }

  printf("name? ");
  gets(name);
  /* look for number */
  while(!feof(fp)) {
```

```
      fscanf(fp, "%s%d%d%d", name2, &a_code, &exchg, &num);
      if(!strcmp(name, name2)) {
        printf("%s: (%d) %d-%d\n", name, a_code, exchg, num);
        break;
      }
    }
    fclose(fp);
}
```

This program allows you to add a number to the phone directory and to look up a number. It first displays a short menu. When you add a number, the **add_num( )** function is called. When you look up a number, **lookup( )** is called. You should enter this program and run it at this time. When entering numbers, be sure to separate the name, area code, prefix, and number by spaces. For example, this is a correct entry:

```
Alex 213 555 1234
```

After you have entered a couple of names and numbers, examine the file **phone**. As you should expect, it appears just the way it would if the information had been displayed on the screen using **printf( )**.

 CAUTION   Although **fprintf( )** and **fscanf( )** often are the easiest way to write and read assorted data to disk files, they are not always the most efficient. Because formatted ASCII data is being written just as it would appear on the screen, instead of in binary, extra overhead is incurred with each call. So, if speed or file size is a concern, you should probably use **fread( )** and **fwrite( )**.

Erasing Files

The **remove( )** function erases the specified file. Its prototype is

> int remove(char *filename);

It returns zero upon success; nonzero if it fails.

The UNIX-Like File Routines

Because C was originally developed under the UNIX operating system, a second disk file I/O system was created. It uses functions that are separate from the ANSI file system functions. These are the low-level UNIX-like disk I/O functions and are shown in Table 10-6. These functions all require that the header file IO.H be included near the beginning of any program that uses them.

The reason the disk I/O subsystem comprised of these functions is sometimes called the *unbuffered I/O system* is because you, as the programmer, must provide and maintain *all* disk buffers — the routines will not do it for you. Unlike the functions **getc( )** and **putc( )**, which write and read characters from or to a stream of data, the functions **read( )** and **write( )** will read or write one complete buffer of information with each call. (This is similar to **fread( )** and **fwrite( ).**)

As stated at the beginning of this chapter, the UNIX-like file system is not defined by the ANSI standard. This implies that programs that use it will have portability problems at some point

Table 10-6.

Function	Operation
read( )	Reads a buffer of data
write( )	Writes a buffer of data
open( )	Opens a disk file
close( )	Closes a disk file
lseek( )	Seeks to the specified byte in a file
unlink( )	Removes a file from the directory

The UNIX-Like I/O Functions

in the future. It is therefore expected that the use of the UNIX-like file system will diminish over the next few years. However, at the time of this writing a great many existing C programs use it, and it is supported by virtually all existing C compilers. Hence, it is included in this chapter.

 NOTE The prototypes and related information necessary to the use of the UNIX-like file system are found in the header file IO.H.

open( ), creat( ), and close( )

Unlike the ANSI I/O system, the UNIX-like system does not use file pointers of type **FILE**, but rather file descriptors called *handles* of type **int**. To open a file using the UNIX-like file system, use the **open( )** function. The prototype for **open( )** is

   int open(char *filename*, int *mode*, int *access*);

where *filename* is any valid filename and *mode* is one of the following macros defined in FCNTL.H.

Macro Name	Meaning	Actual Value
O _ RDONLY	Read-only	1
O _ WRONLY	Write-only	2
O _ RDWR	Read/write	4

Turbo C++ also allows some options to be added to these basic modes. Consult your manual for these options.

The *access* parameter only relates to UNIX environments and is included for compatibility. Turbo C++ also defines a DOS-specific version called **_open( )** that is declared as

   int _open(char *filename*, int *mode*);

thus bypassing the *access* parameter altogether. In the examples in this chapter, *access* will be set to zero.

A successful call to **open( )** returns a non-negative integer called the *file descriptor*. A return value of −1 means that the file cannot be opened. The file descriptor is required by the other UNIX-like file system functions. A file descriptor is fundamentally different from the file pointer used by the ANSI I/O system.

You will usually see the call to **open( )** like this:

```
if((fd=open(filename, mode, 0)) == -1)  {
   printf("cannot open file\n");
   exit(1);
}
```

If the file specified in the **open( )** statement does not appear on the disk, the operation will fail. It will not create the file.

The prototype for **close( )** is

int close(int *fd*);

If **close( )** returns a −1, it was unable to close the file. This could occur if the diskette was removed from the drive, for example.

A call to **close( )** releases the file descriptor so that it can be reused for another file. There is always some limit to the number of open files that may exist simultaneously, so you should close a file when it is no longer needed. More importantly, a close operation forces any information in the internal disk buffers of the operating system to be written to disk. Failure to close a file can lead to loss of data.

You will use **creat( )** to create a new file for write operations. The prototype for **creat( )** is

int creat(char **filename*, int *access*);

where *filename* is any valid filename. The *access* argument is used to specify access modes and to mark the file as being either binary or text. Because **creat( )**'s use of *access* relates to the UNIX environment, Turbo C++ provides a special MS-DOS version called **_ creat( )**, which takes a file attribute byte for *access* instead. In DOS, each file has an attribute byte associated with it that specifies various bits of information. Table 10-7 shows how this attribute byte is organized.

The values in the table are additive. That is, if you wished to create a read-only hidden file, you would use the value 3 (1 + 2) for *access*. Generally, to create a standard file, *access* will be 0.

read( ) and write( )

Once a file has been opened for writing it may be accessed by **write( )**. The prototype for **write( )** is

int write(int *fd*, void **buf*, unsigned *size*);

Table 10-7.

Bit	Value	Meaning
0	1	Read-only file
1	2	Hidden file
2	4	System file
3	8	Volume label name
4	16	Subdirectory name
5	32	Archive
6	64	Unused
7	128	Unused

The Organization of the DOS Attribute Byte

Each time a call to **write( )** is executed, *size* characters are written to the disk file specified by *fd* from the buffer pointed to by *buf*. It will return the number of bytes written after a successful write operation. Upon failure, a −1 is returned.

The function **read( )** is the complement of **write( )**. Its prototype is

$$\text{int read(int } fd, \text{ void } *buf, \text{ unsigned } size);$$

where *fd*, *buf,* and *size* are the same as for **write( )** except that **read( )** will place the data read into the buffer pointed to by *buf*. If **read( )** is successful, it returns the number of characters actually read. It will return 0 upon the physical end-of-file, and −1 if errors occur.

The program shown here illustrates some aspects of the UNIX-like I/O system. It will read lines of text from the keyboard and write them to a disk file. After they are written, the program will read them back.

```
/* Read and write using UNIX-like I/O. */

#include <fcntl.h>
#include <io.h>
#include <stdio.h>
#include <stdlib.h>
#include <string.h>

int input(char *buf, int fd1);
void display(char *buf, int fd2);

#define BUF_SIZE  128

main(void)
{
  char buf[BUF_SIZE];
  int fd1, fd2;

  if((fd1=_creat("test",  O_WRONLY ))==-1) { /* open */
    printf("cannot open file\n");
    exit(1);
  }
```

```
    /* read some text */
    input(buf, fd1);

    /* now close file and read back */
    close(fd1);

    if((fd2=open("test", 0, O_RDONLY))==-1) { /* open */
      printf("cannot open file\n");
      exit(1);
    }

    /* display text */
    display(buf, fd2);
    close(fd2);
    return 0;
}

/* Read some lines of text from the keyboard. */
input(char *buf, int fd1)
{
  register int t;

  printf("enter text, to stop enter 'quit' on a new line\n");
  do {
    for(t=0; t<BUF_SIZE; t++) buf[t]='\0';
    printf(": ");
    gets(buf); /* input chars from keyboard */
    if(write(fd1, buf, BUF_SIZE)!=BUF_SIZE) {
      printf("error on write\n");
      exit(1);
    }
  } while (strcmp(buf, "quit"));
}

/* Display the text. */
void display(char *buf, int fd2)
{
  for(;;) {
    if(read(fd2, buf, BUF_SIZE)==0) return;
    printf("%s\n",buf);
  }
}
```

unlink( )

If you wish to remove a file from the directory, you can use
unlink( ). Although **unlink( )** is considered part of the UNIX-like

I/O system, it will remove any file from the directory. The prototype of **unlink( )** is

```
int   unlink(char *filename);
```

Here, *filename* is a character pointer to any valid filename. **Unlink( )** will return an error (usually −1) if it was unable to erase the file. This could happen if the file was not present on the diskette to begin with, or if the diskette was write-protected.

Random Access Files and lseek( )

Random access file I/O under the UNIX-like I/O system is supported through calls to **lseek( )**. Its prototype is

```
long   lseek(int fd, long numbytes, int origin);
```

where *fd* is a file descriptor returned by a **creat( )** or **open( )** call. The *numbytes* must be a **long int**. The *origin* parameter must be one of the following macros.

Origin	Macro Name	Actual Value
Beginning of file	SEEK_SET	0
Current position	SEEK_CUR	1
End of file	SEEK_END	2

Therefore, to seek *numbytes* from the start of the file, *origin* should be **SEEK_SET**. To seek from the current position, use **SEEK_CUR**; and from the end of the file, use **SEEK_END**.

The **lseek( )** function returns *numbytes* on success. Therefore, **lseek( )** will be returning a **long** integer. Upon failure, a −1 is returned.

For an example using **lseek( )**, the **DUMP** program developed earlier is reworked using the UNIX-like I/O system. It not only shows the operation of **lseek( )** but illustrates many of the UNIX-like I/O functions.

```c
#include <stdio.h>
#include <fcntl.h>
#include <io.h>
#include <ctype.h>
#include <stdlib.h>

#define SIZE    128

char buf[SIZE];
void display(int num);

main(int argc, char *argv[])   /* read buffers */
{
  char s[10];
  int fd, sector, numread;
  long pos;

  if(argc!=2) {
    printf("You forgot to enter the filename.");
    exit(1);
  }

  if((fd=open(argv[1], O_RDONLY, 0))==-1) { /* open */
    printf("cannot open file\n");
    exit(1);
  }

  for(;;) {
    printf("\n\nbuffer: ");
    gets(s);

    sector = atoi(s); /* get the sector to read */
    if(sector<0) break;

    pos = (long) (sector*SIZE);
    if(lseek(fd, pos, SEEK_SET)!=pos)
      printf("seek error\n");
```

```
      numread = read(fd, buf, SIZE);
      if(numread==-1) {
        printf("File Error");
        break;
      }

      display(numread);
    }
    close(fd);
    return 0;
}

void display(int numread)
{
  int i, j;

  for(i=0; i<=numread/16; i++) {
    for(j=0; j<16; j++) printf("%3X", buf[i*16+j]);
    printf("   ");
    for(j=0; j<16; j++) {
      if(isprint(buf[i*16+j])) printf("%c", buf[i*16+j]);
      else printf(".");
    }
    printf("\n");
  }
}
```

CHAPTER

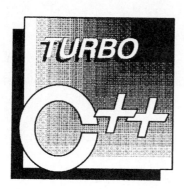

11

Advanced Data Types

Up to now, this book has used only the five basic data types. Although these are sufficient for many programming situations, they cannot satisfy all the demands of the serious programmer. Toward this end, C allows various *type modifiers* to be applied to the basic types. You have already seen two type modifiers: **long** and **short**. In addition to these, Turbo C++ supplies four more categories of modifiers:

- access modifiers
- storage modifiers
- Turbo C++ specific function type modifiers
- Turbo C++ specific memory model modifiers

The type modifier precedes the basic type that it modifies in the declaration statement. That is, the general form of a variable declaration is expanded to look like this:

type-modifier type-specifier variable-list;

The subject of memory models, segments, and overrides is complex and beyond the scope of this book. Therefore, the memory model modifiers **near**, **far**, and **huge** will not be discussed here. (However, these modifiers are discussed in Appendix D.) The other modifiers will be examined in turn.

In addition to the type modifiers, this chapter looks at a special type of pointer: the function pointer.

Access Modifiers

C has two type modifiers that are used to control the ways in which variables may be accessed or modified. These modifiers are called **const** and **volatile**. They are also commonly referred to as *type qualifiers*.

const

Variables declared with the **const** modifier may not be changed during execution by your program. You may give them an initial value, however. For example,

```
const float version =  3.20;
```

creates a **float** variable called **version** that may not be modified by your program. It can, however, be used in other types of expressions. A **const** variable will receive its value either from an explicit initialization or by some hardware-dependent means. Applying the **const** modifier to a variable's declaration ensures that the variable will not be modified by other parts of your program.

Variables of type **const** have one very important use — they can protect the arguments to a function from being modified by that function. That is, when a pointer is passed to a function, it is possible for that function to modify the actual variable pointed to by the pointer. However, if the pointer is specified as **const** in the parameter declaration, it will not be possible for the function code to modify what it points to. For example, the **code( )** function in this short program shifts each letter in a message by one. Therefore an "A" becomes a "B," and so forth. The use of **const** in the parameter declaration ensures that the code inside the function cannot modify the object pointed to by the parameter.

```
#include <stdio.h>

void code(const char *str);

main(void)
{
  code("this is a test");
  return 0;
}

void code(const char *str)
{
  while(*str) printf("%c", (*str++)+1);
}
```

If, for some reason, you write **code( )** in such a way that the argument to it will be modified, it will not compile correctly. For example, if you write **code( )** in this way,

```
/* this is wrong */
void code(const char *str)
{
```

```
  while(*str) {
    *str = *str + 1;
    printf("%c", *str++);
  }
}
```

you will see the following compiler error message.

```
Cannot modify a const object in function code
```

The second use for **const** is to provide verification that your program does not, in fact, modify a variable. Remember that a variable of type **const** can be modified by something outside your program. For example, a hardware device may set its value. However, by declaring a variable as **const** you can prove that any changes to that variable occur because of external events.

volatile

The modifier **volatile** is used to tell the compiler that a variable's value may be changed in ways not explicitly specified by the program. For example, a global variable's address may be passed to the clock routine of the operating system and used to hold the real time of the system. In this situation the contents of the variable are altered without any explicit assignment statements in the program. The reason the external alteration of a variable may be important is that Turbo C++ will automatically optimize certain expressions by making the assumption that the content of a variable is unchanged if it does not occur on the left side of an assignment statement. For example, assume that **clock** is being updated every tenth second by the computer's clock mechanism. If it is not declared as **volatile** then the following statements will not work properly.

```
int clock, timer;
    .
    .
    .
timer = clock;
/* do something */
printf("elapsed time is %d\n", clock-timer);
```

Because **clock** is not altered by the program and it is not declared as **volatile**, Turbo C++ may optimize the code in such a way that the value of **clock** is not reexamined in the **printf( )** statement. However, if you declare **clock** as

```
volatile int clock;
```

no such optimization will take place and **clock**'s value will be examined each time it is referenced.

Although it seems strange at first thought, it is possible to use **const** and **volatile** together. For example, if 0x30 is assumed to be the value of a port that is changed only by external conditions, then the following declaration would be precisely what you would want to prevent any possibility of accidental side effects:

```
const volatile unsigned char *port=0x30;
```

Storage Class Specifiers

There are four storage class specifiers supported by C:

> auto
> extern
> static
> register

These are used to tell the compiler how the variable that follows should be stored. The storage specifier precedes the rest of the variable declaration. Its general form is

storage-class-specifier type-specifier variable-list;

Each specifier will be examined in turn.

auto

The **auto** specifier is used to declare local variables. However, it is rarely (if ever) used because local variables are **auto** by default. It is extremely rare to see this keyword used in a program.

extern

All the programs that you have been working with so far have been quite small—so small, in fact, that many fit within the 25 lines of the screen. However, in real programming tasks, programs tend to be much larger. Even though Turbo C++ is extremely fast at compiling, as the file grows the compilation time will eventually get long enough to be annoying. When this happens, you should break your program into two or more separate files. That way, small changes to one file do not require that the entire program be recompiled, which means substantial time savings in large projects.

C contains the **extern** keyword, which helps support the multiple file approach. Although the subject of multiple files and separate compilation is covered in Appendix B, we will take a very quick look at it here as it relates to **extern**.

Because C allows separately compiled modules of a large program to be linked together in order to speed up compilation and aid in the management of large projects, there must be some way of telling all the files about the global variables required by the program. Your program can have only one copy of each global variable. If you try to declare two global variables with the same name inside the same file, the compiler simply selects one and uses it. (In C++, however, declaring two global variables using the same name is an error.) If you try to declare the global variables needed by your program in each file of a multiple file program, you will have trouble. Although the compiler does not issue any error messages at compile time, you are actually trying to create two (or more) copies of each variable. This will be found by the linker when it attempts to link your modules together. The linker will issue a warning message because it will not know which variable to use. The solution is to declare all of your globals in one file and to use **extern** declarations in the other file as shown in Figure 11-1.

Figure 11-1.

```
File 1                  File 2

int x, y;               extern int x, y;
char ch;                extern char ch;
main(void)              func22(void)
{                       {
    .                       x = y/10;
    .                   }
    .
}                       func23(void)
                        {
func1(void)                 y = 10;
{                       }
  x = 123;
}
```

Using global variables in separately compiled modules

In file 2, the global variable list is copied from file 1 and the **extern** specifier is added to the declarations. The **extern** specifier tells the compiler that the following variable types and names have already been declared elsewhere. In other words, **extern** lets the compiler know what the types and names are for these global variables without actually creating storage for them again. When the linker links the two modules together, all references to the external variables are resolved.

When you access a global variable inside a function that is in the same file as the declaration for the global variable, you may elect to declare it using **extern**, although you don't have to. (Frankly, it is rare to see it done.) This program fragment shows the use of this option:

```
int first, last;  /* global definition of first
                      and last */

main(void)
{
  extern int first;  /* optional use of the
                        extern declaration */
  .
  .
  .
}
```

Although **extern** variable declarations can occur inside the same file as the global declaration, they are not necessary. If the compiler comes across a variable that has not been declared, it will see if it matches any of the global variables. If it does, then it will assume that it is the variable being referenced.

static Variables

Variables of type **static** are permanent variables within either their own function or the file. They differ from global variables because they are not known outside their function or file, but they do maintain their values between calls. This feature can make them very useful when you write generalized functions and function libraries, which may be used by other programmers. Because **static** has different effects when used on local variables than it does on global ones, they will be examined separately.

static Local Variables

When the **static** modifier is applied to a local variable, it causes the compiler to create permanent storage for it in much the same way that it does for a global variable. The key difference between a **static** local variable and a global variable is that the **static** local variable remains known only to the block in which it is declared. In simple terms, a **static** local variable is a local variable that retains its value between function calls.

It is very important to the creation of stand-alone functions that **static** local variables are available because there are several types of routines that must preserve a value between calls. If **static** variables were not allowed then globals would have to be used —opening the door to possible side effects. A good example of a function that would require such a variable is a number series generator that produces a new number based on the last one. It would be possible for you to declare a global variable to hold the generated value. However, each time the function was used in a program, you would have to remember to declare that global variable and make sure that it did not conflict with any other global variables already declared, which would be a major drawback. The better solution is to declare the variable that holds the generated number to be **static**, as in this program:

```
#include <stdio.h>

int series(void);
main(void)
```

```
{
  int i;

  for(i=0; i<10; i++)
    printf("%d ", series());
  return 0;
}

series(void)
{
  static int series_num;

  series_num=series_num + 23;
  return(series_num);
}
```

In this example, the variable **series_num** stays in existence between function calls, instead of coming and going as a normal local variable would. This means that each call to **series( )** can produce a new member of the series based on the last number without declaring **series _num** globally.

You may have noticed something unusual about the function **series( )** as it stands in the example. The static variable **series_num** is never given an initial value. This means that it will be zero the first time because Turbo C++ initializes **static** local variables to zero. While this is acceptable for some applications, most series generators will need a well-defined starting point. To do this requires that **series_num** be initialized prior to the first call to **series( )**, which can easily be done only if **series _num** is a global variable. However, avoiding the need to make **series_num** global was the entire point of making it **static** to begin with. This leads to the second use of **static**.

static Global Variables

When the specifier **static** is applied to a global variable it instructs the compiler to create a global variable that is known only to the *file* in which the **static** global variable is declared. This means that even though the variable is global, other routines in other files may have no knowledge of it or alter its contents directly; thus, it is not subject to side effects. Therefore, for the few situations where a local **static** cannot do the job, you can create a small file that contains only the functions that need the global **static** variable, separately compile that file, and use it without fear of side effects.

To see how a global **static** can be used, the series generator example from the previous section is recoded so that a starting seed value can be used to initialize the series through a call to a second function called **series_start( )**. The entire file containing **series( )**, **series_start( )**, and **series_num** is shown here:

```
/* this must all be in one file - preferably by itself */

static int series_num;

series(void)
{
   series_num = series_num+23;
   return(series_num);
}

/* initialize series_num */
void series_start(int seed)
{
   series_num=seed;
}
```

Calling **series_start( )** with some known integer value initializes the series generator. After that, calls to **series( )** will generate the next element in the series.

Remember that the names of local **static** variables are known only to the block of code in which they are declared, and the names of global **static** variables are known only to the file in which they reside. This means that if you place the **series( )** and **series_start( )** functions in a library, you can use the functions, but you cannot reference the variable **series_num**. It is hidden from the rest of the code in your program. In fact, you may even declare and use another variable called **series_num** in your program (in another file, of course) and not confuse anything. In essence, the **static** modifier allows variables to exist that are known only to the functions that need them, thereby controlling and limiting the possibility of side effects.

Variables of type **static** enable you, the programmer, to hide portions of your program from other portions. This can be a tremendous advantage when you are trying to manage a very large and complex program. The **static** storage specifier lets you create very general functions that you can save in libraries for later use.

register Variables

Another important type modifier found in C is called **register** and is traditionally applied only to variables of type **int** and **char**. In the original version of C, the **register** specifier requests the compiler to keep the value of variables declared with this modifier in the register of the CPU rather than in memory, where variables are normally stored. This means that operations on **register** variables can occur much faster than operations on variables stored in memory because no memory access is required to determine or modify their values. (A memory access takes much longer than a register access.) However, the ANSI C standard has expanded the meaning of **register**. Now, **register** can be applied to any type of data and the compiler will attempt to make access to any variable modified by **register** as fast as possible. However, as is the case with Turbo C++, when applied to variables of type **char** or **int**, generally this still means putting them in a register of the CPU.

The **register** specifier can only be applied to local variables and to the formal parameters in a function. Hence, global **register** variables are not allowed.

It is important to understand that the **register** modifier is simply a *request* to the compiler; it is not a *command*. The compiler is free to ignore it. The reason for this is simple: there are a limited number of registers or other fast-access memory locations. At some point these will be exhausted and any subsequent **register** variables will have to be treated as normal variables. For Turbo C++, there may be two variables actually held in CPU registers within any function. You don't have to worry about declaring too many **register** variables, though, because Turbo C++ will automatically make **register** variables into nonregister variables when the limit is reached.

The fact that access to **register** variables can be very fast makes **register** variables ideal for loop control. Here is an example that uses a **register** variable of type **int** to control a loop. This function computes the result of m^e for integers:

```
int_pwr(int m, register int e)
{
  register int temp;

  temp = 1;

  for( ;e ;e--) temp = temp * m;
  return temp;
}
```

In this example, both **e** and **temp** are declared to be **register** variables because both are used within the loop. In general practice, **register** variables are used where they will do the most good, which implies that they be used in places where many references will be made to the same variable.

To see the difference **register** variables make, the following program measures the execution time of two **for** loops that differ only in the type of variable that controls them. This program uses the **time( )** function found in Turbo C++'s standard library.

```
/* This program shows the difference a register
   variable can make to the speed of program
   execution.
*/
#include <stdio.h>
#include <time.h>
```

```
unsigned int i;   /* non-register */
unsigned int delay;

main(void)
{
  register unsigned int j;
  long t;

  t = time('\0');
  for(delay=0; delay<10; delay++)
    for(i=0; i<64000; i++);
  printf("time for non-register loop: %ld\n", time('\0')-t);

  t = time('\0');
  for(delay=0; delay<10; delay++)
    for(j=0; j<64000; j++) ;
  printf("time for register loop: %ld", time('\0')-t);

  return 0;
}
```

When you run this program, you will find that the register-controlled loop executes in about half the time of the non-register-controlled loop.

One last point: Turbo C++ will automatically make the first two local character or integer variables into **register** types as an optimization. This is why **i** is global.

Type Conversion in Assignments

Type conversion refers to the situation in which variables of one type are mixed with variables of another type. When this occurs in an assignment statement, the *type conversion rule* is very easy: the value of the right side (expression side) of the assignment is converted to the type of the left side (target variable), as illustrated by this example:

```
#include <stdio.h>

int  x;
char ch;
float  f;

main(void)
{
  x = 1000;
  ch = x;      /* 1 */
  printf("%d ", ch);

  f = 100.23;
  x = f;       /* 2 */
  printf("%d ", x);

  ch = 'a';
  f = ch;      /* 3 */
  printf("%f ", f);

  x = 100;
  f = x;       /* 4 */
  printf("%f ", f);

  return 0;
}
```

In line 1, the left high-order bits of the integer variable **x** are lopped off, leaving **ch** with the lower 8 bits. If **x** is between 256 and 0 to begin with, then **ch** and **x** will have identical values. Otherwise, the value of **ch** will reflect only the lower-order bits of **x**. In line 2, **x** will receive the nonfractional part of **f**. In line 3, **f** receives the 8-bit integer value stored in **ch** except in the floating-point format. This also happens in line 4, except that **f** will receive an integer value converted into floating-point format. This program outputs

−24 100 97.00 100.00.

When you are converting from integers to characters and long integers to integers, the basic rule is that the appropriate amount of high-order bits will be removed. This means that 8 bits will be lost when going from an integer to a character and 16 bits will be lost when going from a long integer to an integer.

Table 11-1 summarizes these assignment type conversions. You must remember one important point: The conversion of an **int** to a **float**, or a **float** to **double** and so on, will not add any precision or accuracy. These kinds of conversions will change only the form in which the value is represented.

To use Table 11-1 to make a conversion not directly shown, simply convert one type at a time until you finish. For example, to convert from a **double** to an **int**, first convert from a **double** to **float** and then from a **float** to an **int**.

Table 11-1.

To	*From*	*Possible Information Loss*
char	unsigned char	If value > 127 then target will be negative
char	short int	High-order 8 bits
char	int	High-order 8 bits
char	long int	High-order 24 bits
short int	int	No change; short and int are the same in Turbo C++
short int	long int	High-order 16 bits
int	long int	High-order 16 bits
int	float	Fractional part and possibly more
float	double	Precision; result rounded
double	long double	Precision; result rounded

The Outcome of Common Type Conversions in Turbo C++

Function Type Modifiers

Turbo C++ defines three type modifiers that may be applied only to functions. They are **pascal**, **cdecl**, and **interrupt**. These modifiers are not defined in the ANSI standard, but they are provided by Turbo C++ in order to take the best possible advantage of the PC programming environment.

pascal

The **pascal** type modifier tells the compiler to use a Pascal-like parameter-passing convention for the function's arguments rather than Turbo C++'s normal method. This allows for two possibilities. First, you can create functions written in Turbo C++ to be used by other compilers. Second, you can use a Pascal compiler's library routines by declaring them at the top of your C program as being of type **pascal**.

For example, this version of the **int_pwr( )** function can be compiled for use by a Pascal compiler:

```
/* compile for Pascal compilers */
pascal int_pwr(int m, register int e)
{
  register int temp;

  temp = 1;

  for( ; e; e--) temp = temp * m;
  return temp;
}
```

If you wish to compile all the functions in a file to be of type **pascal**, you can do so without use of the **pascal** type modifier by using the **Option** main menu selection. Next, select **Compiler** and finally, select **Code Generation**. You can now set the calling convention to Pascal. This tells Turbo C++ to treat all functions as if they were for use with a Pascal compiler.

cdecl

The **cdecl** keyword is the opposite of **pascal** because it tells Turbo C++ to compile a function so that its parameters are passed in a way that is compatible with other C functions. It has application only when the compiler has been set to compile using the Pascal calling convention and you have a few files that you do not want compiled in the **pascal** format.

interrupt

The **interrupt** modifier tells Turbo C++ that the function it modifies will be used as an interrupt handler. This causes all CPU registers to be preserved each time the function is entered and the function to exit with an IRET (return from interrupt) instruction. The development and installation of interrupt handlers is beyond the scope of this book, but the interested reader is directed to my book *Born to Code in C* [Berkeley, Ca.: Osborne/McGraw-Hill, 1989] for coverage of interrupt functions as they relate to the creation of Terminate and Stay-Resident (TSR) programs.

Pointers to Functions

A particularly confusing yet powerful feature of C is the *function pointer*. A function pointer is, in a way, a new type of data. Even though a function is not a variable, it still has a physical location in memory that can be assigned to a pointer. The address assigned to the pointer is the entry point of the function. This pointer can then be used in place of the function's name. It also allows functions to be passed as arguments to other functions.

To understand how function pointers work, you must understand a little about how a function is compiled and called in Turbo C++. First, as each function is compiled, source code is transformed into object code and an entry point is established. When a call is made to a function while your program is running, a machine language "call" is made to this entry point. Therefore, a pointer to a function actually contains the memory address of the entry point of the function.

The address of a function is obtained by using the function's name without any parentheses or arguments. (This is similar to the way an array's address is obtained when only the array name, without indices, is used.) For example, consider this program, paying very close attention to the declarations:

```
#include <stdio.h>
#include <string.h>

void check(char *a, char *b, int (*cmp)());

main(void)
{
  char s1[80], s2[80];
  int (*p)();

  p = strcmp;  /* assign pointer to function */

  printf("enter the first string: ");
  gets(s1);
  printf("enter the second string: ");
  gets(s2);

  check(s1, s2, p);

  return 0;
}
void check(char *a, char *b, int (*cmp)())
```

```
{
  printf("testing for equality\n");
  if(!(*cmp) (a, b)) printf("equal");
  else printf("not equal");
}
```

As shown in the program, a function pointer is declared using this statement:

```
int (*p)();
```

When the function **check( )** is called, two character pointers and one function pointer are passed as parameters. Inside the function **check( )**, the arguments are declared as character pointers and a function pointer. Notice how the function pointer is declared. You must use a similar method when declaring other function pointers, except that the return type of the function may be different. You may also specify the function's parameter types if you want. The parentheses around the ***cmp** are necessary for the compiler to interpret this statement correctly. Without the parentheses around ***cmp** the compiler would be confused.

Once inside **check( )**, you can see how the **strcmp( )** function is called. The statement

```
(*cmp) (a,b)
```

performs the call to the function, in this case **strcmp( )**, which is pointed to by **cmp** with the arguments **a** and **b**. Again, the parentheses around ***cmp** are necessary. This also represents the general form of using a function pointer to call the function it points to.

Note that it is possible to call **check( )** using **strcmp** directly, as shown here:

```
check(s1, s2, strcmp);
```

This eliminates the need for an additional pointer variable.

You may be asking yourself why anyone would want to write a program in this way. Obviously, in this example, nothing is gained and significant confusion is introduced. However, there are several good uses for function pointers. One such use is to create a *generic* function, which can be used to perform the same type of operation on different data types. You can get the flavor of this type of usage by studying the expanded version of the previous example. In this program, **check( )** can be made to check for either alphabetical equality or numeric equality, simply by calling it with a different comparison function:

```c
#include <ctype.h>
#include <string.h>
#include <stdio.h>
#include <stdlib.h>

void check(char *a, char *b, int (*cmp)());
int numcmp(char *a, char *b);

main(void)
{
  char s1[80], s2[80];

  gets(s1);
  gets(s2);

  if(tolower(*s1) <= 'z' && tolower(*s1) >= 'a')
     check(s1, s2, strcmp);
  else
     check(s1, s2, numcmp);

  return 0;
}

void check(char *a, char *b, int(*cmp)() )
{
  printf("testing for equality\n");
  if(!(*cmp) (a,b)) printf("equal");
  else printf("not equal");
}

numcmp(char *a, char *b)
{
  if(atoi(a)==atoi(b)) return 0;
  else return 1;
}
```

Dynamic Allocation

Before leaving the subject of advanced data types, it is necessary to discuss C's dynamic allocation system, which allows the dynamic creation of variables during your program's execution.

There are two primary ways in which a C program can store information in the main memory of the computer. The first uses global and local variables that are defined by the C language. In the case of global variables, the storage is fixed throughout the run time of your program. For local variables, storage is allocated from the stack space. In either case, they require the programmer to know, in advance, the amount of storage needed for every situation. The second way information can be stored is through the use of C's dynamic allocation system. In this method (using the default small memory model), storage for information is allocated from the free memory area that lies between your program and its permanent storage area and the stack.

Figure 11-2 shows conceptually how a C program appears in memory. The stack grows downward as it is used, so the amount of memory needed by it is determined by how your program is designed. For example, a program with many recursive functions will make much greater demands on stack memory than one that does not have recursive functions. (Remember that because local variables are stored on the stack, each recursive call to a function requires additional stack space.) The memory required for the program and global data is fixed during the execution of the program. Memory to satisfy a dynamic allocation request is taken from the free memory area. As you might guess, it is possible, under fairly extreme cases, for free memory to become exhausted.

 NOTE   This section discusses C's approach to dynamic allocation. Although these functions are supported by C++, C++ also defines another method of dynamic allocation. However, it is very likely

Figure 11-2.

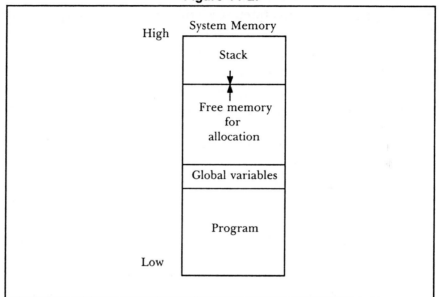

A conceptual view of a C program's memory usage

that you will encounter the C-like dynamic allocation functions, so it is important that you know what they do.

Allocating and Freeing Memory

The core of C's allocation system are the functions **malloc( )** and **free( )**. (Actually, Turbo C++ has several other dynamic allocation functions that add flexibility, but these two are the most important.) They work together using the free memory region to establish and maintain a list of available storage. The **malloc( )** function allocates memory and the **free( )** function releases it. That is, each time a **malloc( )** memory request is made, a portion of the remaining free memory is allocated. Each time a **free( )** memory release call is made, memory is returned to the system. Any program that uses these functions should include the header file STDLIB.H. (In C++, you *must* include all appropriate header files.)

The **malloc( )** function has this prototype:

void *malloc(unsigned *number_of_bytes*);

It returns a pointer of type **void**, which means that you can assign it to any type of pointer. After a successful call, **malloc( )** will return a pointer to the first byte of the region of memory allocated from the heap. If there is not enough available memory to satisfy the **malloc( )** request, an allocation failure occurs and **malloc( )** returns a null. You can use **sizeof** to determine the exact number of bytes needed for each type of data. In this way you can make your programs portable to a variety of systems.

The **free( )** function is the opposite of **malloc( )** in that it returns previously allocated memory to the system. Once the memory has been freed, it may be reused by a subsequent call to **malloc( )**. The function **free( )** has this prototype:

void free(void *p*);

The only really important thing to remember is that you must *never* call **free( )** with an invalid argument because the free list would be destroyed.

The following short program allocates enough storage for 40 integers, prints their values, and then releases the memory back to the system.

```
#include <stdio.h>
#include <stdlib.h>  /* needed by malloc() and free() */

main(void)  /* short allocation example */
{
  int *p, t;

  p = malloc(40*sizeof(int));
  if(!p) /* make sure it's a valid pointer */
    printf("out of memory\n");
  else {
    for(t=0; t<40; ++t) *(p+t) = t;
    for(t=0; t<40; ++t) printf("%d ",*(p+t));
    free(p);
  }

  return 0;
}
```

 REMEMBER   Before using the pointer returned by **malloc( )**, always make sure that your allocation request succeeds by testing the return value against zero. Do not try to use a pointer of value zero because it will most likely crash your system.

Dynamic allocation is very good when you don't know in advance how many items of data you will be dealing with. Although meaningful examples of dynamic allocation tend to be fairly long and complex, the following example gives you the flavor of its use. It first asks the user how many numbers are to be averaged. It then allocates an array large enough to hold them, inputs the numbers, averages them, and finally frees the array.

```
/* This program averages an arbitrary number of integers. */
#include <stdlib.h>
#include <stdio.h>

main(void)
{
  int *p;
  int num, i, avg;

  printf("enter number of integers to average: ");
  scanf("%d", &num);
```

```
/* allocate space */
if((p = malloc(sizeof(int)*num))==NULL) {
  printf("allocation error");
  exit(1);
}

for(i=0; i<num; i++) {
  printf("%d: ", i+1);
  scanf("%d",&p[i]);
}

avg = 0;
for(i=0; i<num; i++) avg = avg + p[i];

printf("average is: %d", avg/num);

free(p);

return 0;
}
```

As you will see in Part III of this book, although C++ supports **malloc( )** and **free( )**, it also provides its own alternative approach to dynamic allocation.

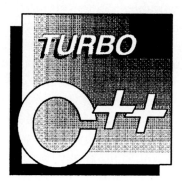

12

User-Defined Data Types

C allows you to create five different kinds of custom data types. The first is the *structure*, which is a grouping of variables under one name. It is sometimes called a *conglomerate* or *aggregate* data type. The second user-defined type is the *bit-field*, which is a type of structure that allows easy access to the bits within a word. The third is the *union*, which enables the same piece of memory to be defined as two or more different types of variables. A fourth custom data type is the *enumeration*, which is a list of symbols. The fifth user-defined type is created through the use of **typedef** and it creates a new name for an existing type. This chapter explores these user-defined types.

Structures

In C, a *structure* is a collection of variables that is referenced under one name, providing a convenient means of keeping related information together. A *structure declaration* forms a template that may be used to create structure variables. The variables that comprise the structure are called *structure elements* or *structure members*. (Structures in C are the equivalent of records in Pascal.)

Generally, all the elements in the structure will be logically related to each other. For example, the name and address information found in a mailing list would normally be represented in a structure. The following code fragment declares a structure template that defines the name and address fields of such a structure. The keyword **struct** tells the compiler that a structure template is being defined.

```
struct addr {
  char name[30];
  char street[40];
  char city[20];
  char state[3];
  unsigned long int zip;
};
```

Notice that the declaration is terminated by a semicolon. This is because a structure declaration is a statement. Also, the structure tag **addr** identifies this particular data structure and is its type specifier.

At this point in the code, *no variable has actually been declared.* Only the form of the data has been defined. To declare an actual variable with this structure, you would write

```
struct addr addr_info;
```

This will declare a structure variable of type **addr** called **addr-_info**. When you declare a structure, you are, in essence, defining a complex variable type made up of the structure elements. It is not until you declare a variable of that type that one actually exists.

C will automatically allocate sufficient memory to accommodate all the variables that comprise a structure variable. Figure 12-1 shows how **addr_info** would appear in memory.

You may also declare one or more variables at the same time that you declare a structure. For example:

```
struct addr {
  char name[30];
  char street[40];
  char city[20];
  char state[3];
  unsigned long int zip;
} addr_info, binfo, cinfo;
```

This will define a structure type called **addr** and declare variables **addr_info**, **binfo**, and **cinfo** of that type.

Figure 12-1.

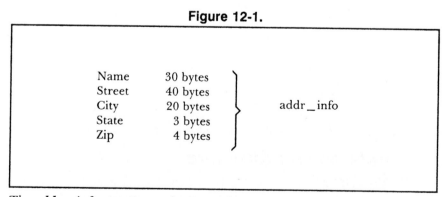

Name	30 bytes	
Street	40 bytes	
City	20 bytes	addr_info
State	3 bytes	
Zip	4 bytes	

*The **addr_ info** structure as it appears in memory*

If you only need one structure variable, then the structure tag is not needed. That means that

```
struct  {
  char name[30];
  char street[40];
  char city[20];
  char state[3];
  unsigned long int zip;
} addr_info;
```

declares one variable named **addr_info** as defined by the structure preceding it.

The general form of a structure declaration is

> struct *struct-type-name* {
>   *type element_name1;*
>
>   *type element_name2;*
>
>   *type element_name3;*
>   .
>   .
>   .
>   *type element_nameN;*
> } *structure_variables;*

where either the structure type name or the structure variables may be omitted, but not both.

Referencing Structure Members

Individual structure members are referenced through the use of the member-selection operator: the period. (The member selection operator is often referred to as the *dot operator*.) For example, the following code will assign the zip code 12345 to the **zip** field of the structure variable **addr_info** declared earlier:

```
addr_info.zip = 12345;
```

The structure variable name followed by a period and the element name will reference that individual structure element. All structure elements are accessed in the same way. The general form is

structure _ varname.element _ name

Therefore, to print the zip code to the screen, you could write

```
printf("%lu", addr_info.zip);
```

This will print the zip code contained in the **zip** variable of the structure variable **addr_info**.

In the same fashion, the character array **addr_info.name** can be used in a call to **gets( )** as shown here:

```
gets(addr_info.name);
```

This will pass a character pointer to the start of element **name**.

If you wished to access the individual elements of **addr_info.name**, you could index **name**. For example, you could print the contents of **addr_info.name** one character at a time by using this code:

```
register int t;
for(t=0; addr_info.name[t]; ++t) putchar(addr_info.name[t]);
```

Arrays of Structures

Perhaps the most common use of structures is in *arrays of structures*. To declare an array of structures, you must first define a structure and then declare an array variable of that type. For example, to declare a 100-element array of structures of type **addr** (defined earlier), you would write

```
struct addr addr_info[100];
```

This creates 100 sets of variables that are organized as defined in the structure **addr**.

To access a specific structure, the structure name is indexed. For example, to print the zip code of structure 3, you would write

```
printf("%lu", addr_info[2].zip);
```

Like all array variables, arrays of structures begin their indexing at zero.

A Mailing List Example

To help illustrate how structures and arrays of structures are used, a simple mailing list program will be developed that uses an array of structures to hold the address information. The functions in this program interact with structures and their elements to illustrate structure usage.

In this example, the information that will be stored includes

```
name
street
city, state, zip
```

To define the basic data structure, **addr**, that will hold this information, you would write

```
struct addr {
  char name[30];
  char street[40];
  char city[20];
  char state[3];
  char zip[10];
} addr_info[SIZE];
```

Notice that this structure uses a string to hold the zip code instead of an unsigned integer. This approach accommodates postal codes with letters as well as numbers, as used by Canada and other countries. The array **addr_ info** contains **SIZE** structures of type **addr**, where **SIZE** may be defined to suit the specific need.

The first function needed for the program is **main( )**, which is shown here:

```
main(void)
{
  char choice;

  init_list();

  for(;;) {
    choice = menu();
    switch(choice) {
      case 'e': enter();
        break;
      case 'd': display();
        break;
      case 's': save();
        break;
      case 'l': load();
        break;
      case 'q': return 0;
    }
  }
}
```

First, the function **init_list( )** prepares the structure array for use by putting a null character into the first byte of the name field of each structure in the array. The program assumes that a structure variable is not in use if the name field is empty. The **init_list( )** function is written as shown here:

```
/* Initialize the addr_info array. */
void init_list(void)
{
  register int t;

  for(t=0; t<SIZE; t++) *addr_info[t].name = '\0';
  /* a zero length name signifies empty */
}
```

The **menu( )** function will display the options and return the user's selection:

```
/* Get a menu selection. */
menu(void)
{
  char ch;

  do {
    printf("(E)nter\n");
    printf("(D)isplay\n");
    printf("(L)oad\n");
    printf("(S)ave\n");
    printf("(Q)uit\n\n");
    printf("choose one: ");
    ch = getche();
    printf("\n");
  } while(!strchr("edlsq", tolower(ch)));
  return tolower(ch);
}
```

This function makes use of another of Turbo C++'s library functions: **strchr( )**, which has this prototype:

char *strchr(char *str, char ch);

This function searches the string pointed to by *str* for an occurrence of the character found in *ch*. If the character is found, a pointer to that character is returned. This is by definition a true value. However, if no match is found, a null is returned, which is by definition false. It is used in this program to see whether the user entered a valid selection.

The **enter( )** function prompts the user for input and places the information entered into the first free structure. If the array is full, then the message "list full" is printed on the screen.

```c
/* Enter names into list. */
void enter(void)
{
  register int i;

  /* look for an unused structure in the array */
  for(i=0; i<SIZE;i++)
    if(!*addr_info[i].name) break;

  /* i will equal SIZE only when no free structures
     are found.
  */
  if(i==SIZE) {
    printf("list full\n");
    return;
  }

  /* input the info */
  printf("name: ");
  gets(addr_info[i].name);

  printf("street: ");
  gets(addr_info[i].street);

  printf("city: ");
  gets(addr_info[i].city);

  printf("state: ");
  gets(addr_info[i].state);

  printf("zip: ");
  gets(addr_info[i].zip);
}
```

The routines **save( )** and **load( )** shown here are used to save and load the mailing list database. Notice how little code is contained in each routine because of the power of the **fread( )** and **fwrite( )** functions.

```c
/* Save the list. */
void save(void)
{
  FILE  *fp;
  register int i;

  if((fp=fopen("maillist","wb"))==NULL) {
    printf("cannot open file\n");
    return;
  }

  for(i=0; i<SIZE; i++)
    if(*addr_info[i].name)
      if(fwrite(&addr_info[i], sizeof(struct addr), 1, fp)!=1)
        printf("file write error\n");
  fclose(fp);
}

/* Load the file. */
void load(void)
{
  FILE  *fp;
  register int i;

  if((fp=fopen("maillist","rb"))==NULL) {
    printf("cannot open file\n");
    return;
  }

  init_list();
  for(i=0; i<SIZE; i++)
    if(fread(&addr_info[i], sizeof(struct addr), 1, fp)!=1) {
      if(feof(fp)) {
        fclose(fp);
        return;
      }
      printf("file read error\n");
    }
}
```

Both routines confirm a successful file operation by checking the return value of **fread( )** or **fwrite( )**. Also, **load( )** must explicitly check for the end of the file through the use of **feof( )**, because **fread( )** returns the same value whether the end of the file has been reached or an error has occurred.

The final function the program needs is **display( )**. It prints the entire mailing list on the screen:

```
/* Display the address list. */
void display(void)
{
  register int t;

  for(t=0; t<SIZE; t++) {
    if(*addr_info[t].name) {
      printf("%s\n", addr_info[t].name);
      printf("%s\n", addr_info[t].street);
      printf("%s\n", addr_info[t].city);
      printf("%s\n", addr_info[t].state);
      printf("%s\n\n", addr_info[t].zip);
    }
  }
}
```

The complete listing for the mailing list program is shown here. If you have any doubts about your understanding of structures, you should enter this program into your computer and study its execution, making changes and watching their effect. Furthermore, you should try adding functions that search the list, remove an address from the list, and send the list to the printer.

```
/* A simple mailing list that uses an array
   of structures. */

#include <conio.h>
#include <stdio.h>
#include <ctype.h>
#include <string.h>
#include <stdlib.h>

#define SIZE 100

struct addr {
  char name[40];
```

```
      char street[40];
      char city[30];
      char state[3];
      char zip[10];
} addr_info[SIZE];

void enter(void), init_list(void), display(void);
void save(void), load(void);
int menu(void);

main(void)
{
  char choice;

  init_list();

  for(;;) {
    choice = menu();
    switch(choice) {
      case 'e': enter();
        break;
      case 'd': display();
        break;
      case 's': save();
        break;
      case 'l': load();
        break;
      case 'q': return 0;
    }
  }
}

/* Initialize the addr_info array. */
void init_list(void)
{
  register int t;

  for(t=0; t<SIZE; t++) *addr_info[t].name = '\0';
  /* a zero length name signifies empty */
}

/* Get a menu selection. */
menu(void)
{
  char ch;

  do {
    printf("(E)nter\n");
    printf("(D)isplay\n");
    printf("(L)oad\n");
```

```
      printf("(S)ave\n");
      printf("(Q)uit\n\n");
      printf("choose one: ");
      ch = getche();
      printf("\n");
  } while(!strchr("edlsq", tolower(ch)));
  return tolower(ch);
}

/* Input names into the list */
void enter(void)
{
  register int i;

  /* find the first free structure */
  for(i=0; i<SIZE; i++)
    if(!*addr_info[i].name) break;

  /* i will equal SIZE if the list is full */
  if(i==SIZE) {
    printf("list full\n");
    return;
  }

  /* enter the information */
  printf("name: ");
  gets(addr_info[i].name);

  printf("street: ");
  gets(addr_info[i].street);

  printf("city: ");
  gets(addr_info[i].city);

  printf("state: ");
  gets(addr_info[i].state);

  printf("zip: ");
  gets(addr_info[i].zip);
}

/* Display the list. */
void display(void)
{
  register int t;

  for(t=0; t<SIZE; t++) {
    if(*addr_info[t].name) {
      printf("%s\n", addr_info[t].name);
      printf("%s\n", addr_info[t].street);
```

```
              printf("%s\n", addr_info[t].city);
              printf("%s\n", addr_info[t].state);
              printf("%s\n\n", addr_info[t].zip);
      }
   }
}

/* Save the list. */
void save(void)
{
  FILE  *fp;
  register int i;

  if((fp=fopen("maillist","wb"))==NULL) {
    printf("cannot open file\n");
    return;
  }

  for(i=0; i<SIZE; i++)
    if(*addr_info[i].name)
      if(fwrite(&addr_info[i], sizeof(struct addr), 1, fp)!=1)
    printf("file write error\n");
  fclose(fp);
}

/* Load the file. */
void load(void)
{
  FILE  *fp;
  register int i;

  if((fp=fopen("maillist","rb"))==NULL) {
    printf("cannot open file\n");
    return;
  }

  init_list();
  for(i=0; i<SIZE; i++)
     if(fread(&addr_info[i], sizeof(struct addr), 1, fp)!=1) {
       if(feof(fp)) {
          fclose(fp);
          return;
       }
     printf("file read error\n");
     }
}
```

Assigning Structures

If two structure variables are of the same type, you can then assign one to the other. In this case, all the elements of the structure on the left side of the assignment will receive the values of their corresponding elements from the structure on the right. For example, this program assigns the value of **one** to **two** and displays the result, 10 98.6.

```c
#include <stdio.h>

main(void)
{
  struct sample {
    int i;
    double d;
  } one, two;

  one.i = 10;
  one.d = 98.6;

  two = one;   /* assign one struct to another */

  printf("%d %lf", two.i, two.d);
  return 0;
}
```

REMEMBER   You cannot assign one structure to another if they are of different types—even if they share certain elements.

Passing Structures to Functions

So far, all structures and arrays of structures used in the examples have been assumed to be either global or defined within the function that uses them. In this section, special consideration will be given to passing structures and their elements to functions.

Passing Structure Elements to Functions

When you pass an element of a structure variable to a function, you are actually passing the value of that element to the function. Therefore, you are passing a simple variable. (Unless, of course, that element is complex, such as an array of characters.) For example, consider this structure:

```
struct {
  char x;
  int y;
  float z;
  char s[10];
} sample;
```

Here are examples of each element being passed to a function:

```
func(sample.x);   /* passes character value of x */

func2(sample.y); /* passes integer value of y */

func3(sample.z); /* passes float value of z */

func4(sample.s); /* passes address of string s */

func(sample.s[2]); /* passes character value of s[2] */
```

However, if you wished to pass the address of an individual structure element to achieve call-by-reference parameter passing, you would place the **&** operator before the variable name. For example, to pass the addresses of the elements in the structure variable **sample**, you would write this:

```
func(&sample.x);    /* passes address of character x */

func2(&sample.y);  /* passes address of integer y */

func3(&sample.z);  /* passes address of float z*/

func4(sample.s);   /* passes address of string s */

func(&sample.s[2]); /* passes address of character s[2] */
```

Notice that the **&** operator precedes the structure variable name, not the individual element name. Note also that the string element **s** already signifies an address so that no **&** is required.

Passing Entire Structures to Functions

When a structure is used as an argument to a function, the entire structure is passed using the standard call-by-value method. This, of course, means that any changes made to the contents of the structure inside the function to which it is passed do not affect the structure used as an argument.

The most important consideration to keep in mind when using a structure as a parameter is that the type of the argument must match the type of the parameter. For example, this program declares both the argument **arg** and the parameter **parm** to be of the same type of structure:

```
#include <stdio.h>

/* define a structure type */
struct sample {
  int a, b;
  char ch;
} ;

void f1(struct sample parm);
```

```
main(void)
{
  struct sample arg;  /* declare arg */

  arg.a = 1000;

  f1(arg);
  return 0;
}

void f1(struct sample parm)
{
  printf("%d", parm.a);
}
```

This program will, as you can easily see, print the number 1000 on the screen.

As this program example shows, it is best to define a structure type globally and then use its name to declare structure variables and parameters as needed. This helps ensure that the arguments and the parameters match. Also, it establishes in the mind of any third party reading your program the fact that **parm** and **arg** are the same type.

Pointers to Structures

C allows pointers to structures in the same way that it allows pointers to any other type of variable. However, there are some special aspects to structure pointers that you must be aware of.

Declaring a Structure Pointer

Structure pointers are declared by placing the * in front of a structure variable's name. For example, assuming the previously defined structure **addr**, the following declares **addr_pointer** to be a pointer to data of that type:

```
struct addr *addr_pointer;
```

Using Structure Pointers

There are several uses for structure pointers. One is to achieve a call-by-reference call to a function. Another is to create linked lists and other dynamic data structures using Turbo C++'s allocation system. This chapter will only be concerned with the first use; the second use is covered in my book *Turbo C/C++: The Complete Reference* [Berkeley, Ca.: Osborne/McGraw-Hill, 1990].

There is one major drawback to passing all but the simplest structures to functions: the overhead needed to push (and pop) all the structure elements onto the stack. In simple structures with few elements this overhead is not too important, but if several elements are used, or if some of the elements are arrays, then runtime performance may degrade to unacceptable levels. The solution to this problem is to pass only a pointer to the structure.

When a pointer to a structure is passed to a function, only the address of the structure is pushed (and popped) on the stack. This means that a very fast function call can be executed. Also, because the function will be referencing the actual structure and not a copy, it will be able to modify the contents of the elements of the structure used in the call.

To find the address of a structure variable, the **&** operator is placed before the structure variable's name. For example, given the fragment

```
struct bal {
  float balance;
  char name[80];
} person;

struct bal *p;  /* declare a structure pointer */
```

then

```
p = &person;
```

places the address of **person** into the pointer **p**. To access the **balance** element you could write

```
(*p).balance
```

You will seldom, if ever, see references made to a structure member with explicit use of the * operator, as shown in the preceding example. Because accessing a structure member via a pointer to that structure is so common, a special operator is defined by C to perform this task. It is the −>, which most C programmers call the *arrow* operator. It is formed by using the minus sign followed by a greater-than sign. The arrow is used in place of the dot operator when accessing a structure element using a pointer to the structure variable. For example, the previous statement is usually written like this:

```
p->person
```

To see how a structure pointer can be used, examine this simple program that prints the hours, minutes, and seconds on your screen using a software delay timer:

```c
/* Display a software timer. */

#include <stdio.h>
#include <conio.h>

struct time_struct {
  int hours;
  int minutes;
  int seconds;
} ;
void update(struct time_struct *t);
```

```
void display(struct time_struct *t);
void delay(void);

main()
{
  struct time_struct time;

  time.hours=0;
  time.minutes=0;
  time.seconds=0;

  for( ; !kbhit(); ) {
    update(&time);
    display(&time);
  }
  return 0;
}

void update(struct time_struct *t)
{
  t->seconds++;
  if(t->seconds==60) {
    t->seconds = 0;
    t->minutes++;
  }
  if(t->minutes==60) {
    t->minutes = 0;
    t->hours++;
  }
  if(t->hours==24) t->hours=0;
  delay();
}

void display(struct time_struct *t)
{
  printf("%d:", t->hours);
  printf("%d:", t->minutes);
  printf("%d\n", t->seconds);
}

void delay(void)
{
  long int t;
  for(t=1; t<128000; ++t) ;
}
```

The timing of this program is adjusted by varying the loop count in **delay( )**.

As you can see, a global structure called **time_struct** is defined but no variable is declared. Inside **main( )**, the structure **time** is declared and initialized to 00:00:00. This means that **time** is known directly only to the **main( )** function.

The two functions—**update( )**, which changes the time, and **display( )**, which prints the time—are passed the address of **time**. In both functions, the argument is declared to be of structure type **time_struct**. This is necessary so that the compiler will know how to reference the structure elements.

The actual referencing of each structure element is through the use of a pointer. For example, if you wanted to set the hours back to zero when 24:00:00 was reached you would write

```
if(t->hours==24) t->hours = 0;
```

This line of code tells the compiler to take the address of **t** (which is **time** in **main( )**) and assign zero to its element called **hours**.

REMEMBER Use the dot operator to access structure elements when operating on the structure itself. When you have a pointer to a structure, then the arrow operator should be used. Also remember that you have to pass the address of the structure to a function using the **&** operator.

While on the subject of time and structures, let's explore some of C's time and date functions. The functions that deal with the system time and date require the header TIME.H for their prototypes. Also included in this header are two defined types. The type **time_t** is capable of representing the system time and date as a long integer. This is referred to as the *calendar time*. The structure type **tm** holds the date and time broken down into its elements. The **tm** structure is defined as shown here:

```
struct tm {
  int tm_sec;  /* seconds, 0-59 */
  int tm_min;  /* minutes, 0-59 */
  int tm_hour; /* hours, 0-23 */
```

```
    int tm_mday; /* day of the month, 1-31 */
    int tm_mon;  /* months since Jan, 0-11 */
    int tm_year; /* years from 1900 */
    int tm_wday; /* days since Sunday, 0-6 */
    int tm_yday; /* days since Jan 1, 0-365 */
    int tm_isdst /* Daylight Savings Time indicator */
}
```

The value of **tm_isdst** will be positive if Daylight Savings Time is in effect, 0 if it is not in effect, and negative if there is no information available. This form of the time and date is called the *broken-down time*.

The foundation for C's time and date functions is **time( )**, which has this prototype:

time _ t time(time _ t *time)

The **time( )** function returns the number of seconds that have elapsed since January 1, 1970. It can be called either with a null pointer or with a pointer to a variable of type **time_t**. If the latter is used, then the argument will also be assigned the calendar time.

To convert the calendar time into broken-down time, use **localtime( )**, which has this prototype:

struct tm *localtime(time _ t *time)

The **localtime( )** function returns a pointer to the broken-down form of *time* in the form of a **tm** structure. The time is represented in local time. The *time* value is generally obtained through a call to **time( )**.

The structure used by **localtime( )** to hold the broken-down time is statically allocated and is overwritten each time the function is called. If you wish to save the contents of the structure, it is necessary to copy it elsewhere.

Although your programs can use the broken-down form of the time and date, the easiest way to generate a time and date string is to use **asctime( )**, whose prototype is shown here:

char *asctime(struct tm *ptr);

The **asctime( )** function returns a pointer to a string, which is the conversion of the information stored in the structure pointed to by *ptr* into the following form:

day month date hours:minutes:seconds year\n\0

The structure pointer passed to **asctime( )** is the one obtained from **localtime( )**.

Like **localtime( )**, the buffer used by **asctime( )** to hold the formatted output string is a statically allocated character array and is overwritten each time the function is called. Therefore, if you wish to save the contents of the string, it is necessary to copy it elsewhere.

The following program uses the time functions just described to print the system time and date on the screen:

```
/* This program displays the current system time. */

#include <stdio.h>
#include <time.h>

main(void)
{
  struct tm *ptr;
  time_t lt;

  lt = time('\0');

  ptr = localtime(&lt);
  printf(asctime(ptr));

  return 0;
}
```

Turbo C++ contains several other time and date functions. Refer to the *Turbo C++ Library Reference* for descriptions of the other functions.

Arrays and Structures Within Structures

Structure members may be of any valid C data type, including arrays and structures. You have already seen one example of an array member: the character array used in **addr_info**.

A structure element that is an array is treated as you might expect from the earlier examples. For example, consider this structure:

```
struct x {
  int a[10][10]; /* 10 x 10 array of ints */
  float b;
} y;
```

To reference integer 3,7 in **a** of structure **y**, you would write

```
y.a[3][7]
```

When a structure is an element of another structure, it is called a *nested* structure. For example, the structure variable element **address** is nested inside **emp** in this example:

```
struct emp {
  struct addr address;
  float wage;
} worker;
```

Here, **addr** is the structure defined previously and structure **emp** has been defined as having two elements. The first element is the structure of type **addr** that will contain an employee's address. The second is **wage**, which holds the employee's wage. The following code fragment will assign the zip code 98765 to the **zip** field of **address** of **worker**:

```
worker.address.zip = 98765;
```

As you can see, the elements of each structure are referenced from left to right from the outermost to the innermost.

Bit-Fields

Unlike most other languages, C has a built-in method to access one or more bits within a byte or word. This can be useful for a number of reasons: first, if storage is limited you can store several *Boolean* (true/false) variables in one byte; second, certain device interfaces transmit information encoded into bits within one byte; and third, certain encryption routines need to access the bits within a byte.

One method C uses to access bits is based on the structure called the *bit-field*. (In the next chapter you will learn a second way to access individual bits.) A bit-field is really just a special type of structure member that defines how long, in bits, each element is to be. The general form of a bit-field declaration is as follows:

```
struct struc-type-name {
    type name1 : length;
    type name2 : length;
    .
    .
    .
    type nameN : length;
}
```

A bit-field must be declared as **int**, **unsigned**, or **signed**. Bit-fields of length 1 should be declared as **unsigned** because a single bit cannot have a sign.

int biosequip(void)

The prototype for **biosequip( )** is found in BIOS.H.

The **biosequip( )** function returns a list of the equipment installed in the computer as a 16-bit value encoded as shown here:

Bit	*Equipment*
0	must boot from the floppy drive
1	80x87 math coprocessor installed
2, 3	motherboard RAM size
	0 0: 16k
	0 1: 32k
	1 0: 48k
	1 1: 64k
4, 5	Initial video mode
	0 0: unused
	0 1: 40x25 BW, color adapter
	1 0: 80x25 BW, color adapter
	1 1: 80x25, monochrome adapter
6, 7	number of floppy drives
	0 0: one
	0 1: two
	1 0: three
	1 1: four
8	DMA chip installed
9, 10, 11	number of serial ports
	0 0: zero
	0 0 1: one
	0 0: two
	0 1 1: three
	1 0 0: four
	1 0 1: five
	1 1 0: six
	1 1 1: seven

Bit	Equipment
12	game adapter installed
13	serial printer installed (PCjr only)
14, 15	number of printers
	0 0: zero
	0 1: one
	10:two
	1 1: three

This can be represented as a bit-field using this structure:

```
struct equip {
  unsigned floppy_boot: 1;
  unsigned has8087:     1;
  unsigned mother_ram:  2;
  unsigned video_mode:  2;
  unsigned floppies:    2;
  unsigned dma:         1;
  unsigned ports:       3;
  unsigned game_adpter: 1;
  unsigned unused:      1;
  unsigned num_printers:2;
} eq;
```

The following program uses this bit-field to display the number of floppy disk drives and the number of serial ports.

```
#include <stdio.h>
#include <bios.h>

main(void)
{
  struct equip {
    unsigned floppy_boot: 1;
    unsigned has8087:     1;
    unsigned mother_ram:  2;
    unsigned video_mode:  2;
    unsigned floppies:    2;
    unsigned dma:         1;
    unsigned ports:       3;
    unsigned game_adpter: 1;
    unsigned unused:      1;
    unsigned num_printers:2;
  } eq;
```

```
    int *i;

    i = (int *) &eq;

    *i = biosequip();

    printf("%d floppies\n", eq.floppies+1);

    printf("%d ports\n", eq.ports+1);

    return 0;
}
```

The integer pointer **i** is assigned the address of **eq**, and the return value of **biosequip( )** is assigned to **eq** via this pointer. This is necessary because C will not allow an integer to be cast into a structure. However, in the next section, you will see a better solution to this problem.

As you can see from this example, each bit-field is accessed using the dot operator. However, if the structure is referenced through a pointer, you must use the **->** operator.

You do not have to name each bit-field. This makes it easy to reach the bit you want, passing up unused ones. For example, the **unused** field could be left unnamed, as shown here:

```
struct equip {
  unsigned floppy_boot: 1;
  unsigned has8087:     1;
  unsigned mother_ram:  2;
  unsigned video_mode:  2;
  unsigned floppies:    2;
  unsigned dma:         1;
  unsigned ports:       3;
  unsigned game_adpter: 1;
  unsigned :            1;
  unsigned num_printers:2;
} eq;
```

Bit-field variables have certain restrictions. You cannot take the address of a bit-field variable. Bit-field variables cannot be arrayed. You cannot overlap integer boundaries. Whether the fields will run from right to left or from left to right varies among different types of CPUs; this implies that any code that uses bit-fields may have some machine dependencies.

It is valid to mix normal structure members with bit-field elements. For example:

```
struct emp {
  struct addr address;
  float pay;
  unsigned lay_off:1;   /* lay off or active */
  unsigned hourly:1;    /* hourly pay or wage */
  unsigned deductions:3; /* IRS deductions */
};
```

This structure defines an employee record that uses only one byte to hold three pieces of information: the employee's status, whether the employee is salaried, and the number of deductions. Without the use of the bit-field, this information would have taken three bytes.

The next section presents a program that uses a bit-field to display the ASCII character codes in binary.

Unions

In C, a **union** is a memory location that is used by several different variables of different types. The **union** declaration is similar to that of a structure, as shown in this example:

```
union u_type {
  int i;
  char ch;
} ;
```

As with structures, this declaration does not declare any variables. You may declare a variable either by placing its name at the end of the declaration, or by using a separate declaration statement. To declare a **union** variable **cnvt** of type **u_type** using the declaration just given, you would write

```
union u_type cnvt;
```

In **cnvt**, both integer **i** and character **ch** share the same memory location. (Of course, **i** occupies two bytes and **ch** uses only one.) Figure 12-2 shows how **i** and **ch** share the same address.

When a **union** variable is declared, the compiler will automatically create a variable large enough to hold the largest variable type in the **union**.

To access a **union** element you use the same syntax that you use for structures: the dot and arrow operators. If you are operating on the **union** directly, then use the dot operator. If the **union** variable is accessed through a pointer, use the arrow

Figure 12-2.

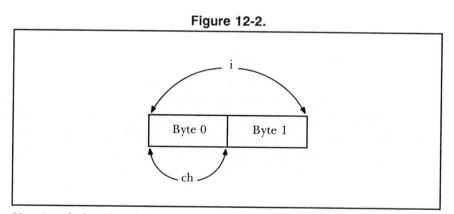

*How **i** and **ch** utilize the **union cnvt***

operator. For example, to assign the integer 10 to element **i** of **cnvt**, you would write

```
cnvt.i = 10;
```

Unions are used frequently when type conversions are needed because they let you look at a region of memory in more than one way. For example, the library function **putw( )** will write the binary representation of an integer to a disk file. Although there are many ways to code this function, the one shown here uses a **union**. First, a **union** is created that is comprised of one integer and a two-byte character array:

```
union pw {
  int i;
  char ch[2];
};
```

Now, **putw( )** can be written using this **union**:

```
void putw(union pw word, FILE *fp)  /* putw with union */
{
  putc(word->ch[0], fp); /* write first half */
  putc(word->ch[1], fp); /* write second half */
}
```

Although called with an integer, **putw( )** can still use the standard function **putc( )** to write an integer to a disk file.

The following program combines unions with bit-fields to display the ASCII code, in binary, generated when you press a key. The **union** allows **getche( )** to assign the value of the key to a character variable while the bit-field is used to display the individual bits. You should study this program to make sure that you fully understand its operation. (Be aware, however, that the implementation of this program is only to illustrate how unions can be used to look at the same piece of memory in two radically different ways. There are much more efficient ways to write the **decode( )** function that achieve the same results.)

```c
/* Display the ASCII code in binary for characters. */

#include <stdio.h>
#include <conio.h>

/* a bit-field that will be decoded */
struct byte {
  int a : 1;
  int b : 1;
  int c : 1;
  int d : 1;
  int e : 1;
  int f : 1;
  int g : 1;
  int h : 1;
};

union bits {
  char ch;
  struct byte bit;
} ascii ;

void decode(union bits b);

main(void)
{
  do {
    ascii.ch = getche();
    printf(": ");
    decode(ascii);
  } while(ascii.ch!='q'); /* quit if q typed */

  return 0;
}
```

```
/* Display the bit pattern for each character. */
void decode(union bits b)
{
  if(b.bit.h) printf("1 ");
    else printf("0 ");
  if(b.bit.g) printf("1 ");
    else printf("0 ");
  if(b.bit.f) printf("1 ");
    else printf("0 ");
  if(b.bit.e) printf("1 ");
    else printf("0 ");
  if(b.bit.d) printf("1 ");
    else printf("0 ");
  if(b.bit.c) printf("1 ");
    else printf("0 ");
  if(b.bit.b) printf("1 ");
    else printf("0 ");
  if(b.bit.a) printf("1 ");
    else printf("0 ");
  printf("\n");
}
```

Figure 12-3 shows a sample run.

To finish this section, let's see how a **union** can provide a means of loading an integer into a bit-field. As you will recall from the previous section, C will not allow an integer to be assigned to a bit-field structure directly. However, this program creates a **union** that contains an integer and a bit-field. When **biosequip( )** returns the equipment list encoded as an integer, it is assigned to the integer. However, the program is free to use the bit-field when reporting the results.

```
/* Display the number of floppies and ports. */
#include <bios.h>
#include <stdio.h>

main(void)
{
  struct equip {
    unsigned floppy_boot: 1;
    unsigned has8087:     1;
    unsigned mother_ram:  2;
    unsigned video_mode:  2;
    unsigned floppies:    2;
    unsigned dma:         1;
```

```
    unsigned ports:        3;
    unsigned game_adpter:  1;
    unsigned unused:       1;
    unsigned num_printers:2;
} ;

union {
 struct equip eq;
 unsigned i;
} eq_union;

eq_union.i = biosequip();

printf("%d floppies\n", eq_union.eq.floppies+1);

printf("%d ports\n", eq_union.eq.ports+1);

return 0;
}
```

Figure 12-3.

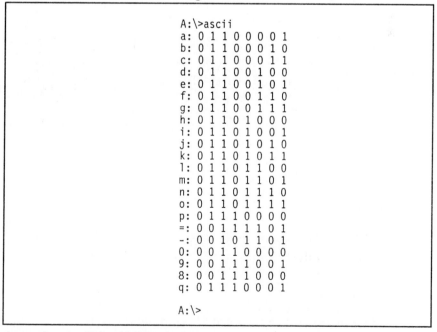

A sample run of the ASCII program

Enumerations

An *enumeration* is a set of named integer constants and it specifies all the legal values that a variable of that type may have. Enumerations are not uncommon in everyday life. For example, an enumeration of the coins used in the United States is

penny, nickel, dime, quarter, half-dollar, dollar

Enumerations are defined much like structures with the keyword **enum** used to signal the start of an enumeration type. The general form is shown here:

enum *enum-type-name* { *enumeration list* } *variable-list*;

The enumeration list is a comma-separated list of names that represents the values a variable of the enumeration type may have. Both the enumeration type name and the variable list are optional. As with structures, the enumeration type name is used to declare variables of its type. The following fragment defines an enumeration called **coin** and declares **money** to be of that type:

```
enum coin { penny, nickel, dime, quarter,
          half_dollar, dollar};

enum coin money;
```

Given these declarations, the following types of statements are perfectly valid:

```
money = dime;

if(money==quarter) printf("is a quarter\n");
```

The key point to understand about an enumeration is that each of the symbols stands for an integer value. As such, they may be used in any integer expression. Unless initialized otherwise, the value of the first enumeration symbol is zero, the value of the second symbol is 1, and so forth. Therefore,

```
printf("%d %d", penny, dime);
```

displays 0 2 on the screen.

It is possible to specify the value of one or more of the symbols by using an initializer. This is done by following the symbol with an equal sign and an integer value. Whenever an initializer is used, symbols that appear after it are assigned values greater than the previous initialization value. For example, the following assigns the value of 100 to **quarter**:

```
enum coin { penny, nickel, dime, quarter=100,
            half_dollar, dollar};
```

Now, the values of these symbols are as follows:

penny	0
nickel	1
dime	2
quarter	100
half_dollar	101
dollar	102

One common, but erroneous, assumption that is made about enumerations is that the symbols can be input and output directly. This is not the case. For example, the following code fragment will not perform as desired.

```
/* this will not work */

money = dollar;

printf("%s", money);
```

 REMEMBER   The symbol **dollar** is simply a name for an integer; it is not a string. For the same reason, it is not possible to use this code to achieve the desired results.

```
/* this code is wrong */

gets(s);

strcpy(money, s);
```

That is, a string that contains the name of a symbol is not automatically converted to that symbol.

Actually, to create code to input and output enumeration symbols is quite tedious (unless you are willing to settle for their integer values). For example, the following code is needed to display, in words, the kind of coin that **money** contains:

```
switch(money) {
  case penny: printf("penny");
        break;
  case nickel: printf("nickel");
        break;
  case dime: printf("dime");
        break;
  case quarter: printf("quarter");
        break;
  case half_dollar: printf("half_dollar");
        break;
  case dollar: printf("dollar");
}
```

Sometimes it is possible to declare an array of strings and use the enumeration value as an index in order to translate an enumeration value into its corresponding string. For example, this code will also output the proper string:

```
char name[][20]={
  "penny",
  "nickel",
  "dime",
  "quarter",
  "half_dollar",
  "dollar"
};
  .
  .
  .
printf("%s", name[money]);
```

This will only work, of course, if no symbol initializations are used because the string array must be indexed starting at zero. For example, this program prints the names of the coins:

```
#include <stdio.h>

enum coin { penny, nickel, dime, quarter,
            half_dollar, dollar};

enum coin money;

char name[][20]={
  "penny",
  "nickel",
  "dime",
  "quarter",
  "half_dollar",
  "dollar"
};

main(void)
{
  enum coin money;

  for(money=penny; money<=dollar; money++)
    printf("%s ", name[money]);

  return 0;
}
```

Given the fact that enumeration values must be converted manually to their English string values for console I/O, they find their greatest use in routines that do not make such conversions. It is common to see an enumeration used to define a compiler's symbol table, for example, which does not require interaction with users.

Using sizeof to Ensure Portability

Although you have been introduced to **sizeof** briefly in preceding chapters, it is time to take a closer look at it. You have seen that structures, unions, and enumerations can be used to create variables of varying sizes, and that the actual size of these variables may change from machine to machine. The **sizeof** unary operator is used to compute the size of any variable or type and can help eliminate machine-dependent code from your programs.

The **sizeof** operator takes the two forms shown here:

sizeof *var-name*
sizeof (*type-name*)

When computing the size of a specific variable, you don't need to enclose the variable's name within parentheses (although it is not wrong to do so). However, when computing the size of a type, it must be enclosed within parentheses. For example, both of the lines in this fragment display the size of an **int**:

```
int i;

printf("%d", sizeof i);
printf("%d", sizeof (int));
```

Turbo C++ has the following sizes for data types:

Type	*Size in Bytes*
char	1
int	2
long int	4
float	4
double	8
long double	10

Therefore, the code shown here will print the numbers 1, 2, and 8 on the screen.

```
char ch;
int i;
double f;

printf("%d", sizeof ch);

printf("%d",sizeof i);

printf("%d",sizeof f);
```

sizeof is a *compile-time* operator; all the information necessary to compute the size of any variable is known at compile time. For example, consider this:

```
union x {
   char ch;
   int i;
   float f;
} tom;
```

The **sizeof tom** will be 4 because the largest member of the **union** is a **float**. At run time, it does not matter what the **union tom** is *actually* holding; all that matters is the size of the largest variable it can hold. This is because the **union** must be as large as its largest element.

typedef

C allows you to explicitly define new data type names using the **typedef** keyword. You are not actually *creating* a new data type, but rather defining a new name for an existing type. This process can help make machine-dependent programs more portable; only the **typedef** statements have to be changed. It also can aid in documenting your code by allowing descriptive names for the standard data types. The general form of the **typedef** statement is

typedef *type name*;

where *type* is any allowable data type and *name* is the new name for this type. The new name you define is in addition to, not a replacement for, the existing type name.

For example, you could create a new name for **float** using

```
typedef float balance;
```

This statement tells the compiler to recognize **balance** as another name for **float**. Next, you could create a **float** variable using **balance**:

```
balance over_due;
```

Here, **over_due** is a floating-point variable of type **balance**, which is another word for **float**.

You can use **typedef** to create names for more complex types, too. For example:

```
typedef struct client_type {
  float due;
  int over_due;
  char name[40];
} client;
```

```
client clist[NUM_CLIENTS]; /* define array of
                              structures of type client */
```

In this example, **client** is not a variable of type **client_type** but rather another name for **struct client_type**.

Using **typedef** can help make your code easier to read and easier to port to another computer. But remember that you are not creating any new data types.

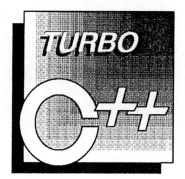

13

Advanced Operators

Earlier you learned about the more commonplace C operators. Unlike most languages, C contains several special operators that greatly increase its power and flexibility—especially for system level programming. It is these operators that you will study in this chapter.

Bitwise Operators

Unlike most other languages, C supports a complete arsenal of bitwise operators. Since C was designed to take the place of assembly language for most programming tasks, it was important that it had the ablilty to support all (or at least many) operations that can be done in assembler. *Bitwise operations* refer to the testing, setting, or shifting of the actual bits in a byte or word, which correspond to C's **char**, **int**, and **long** data types. Bitwise operations may not be used on type **float**, **double**, **long double**, **void**, or other more complex types. Table 13-1 lists the operators.

The bitwise AND, OR, and one's complement (NOT) are governed by the same truth table as their logical equivalents except that they work on a bit-by-bit level. The exclusive OR ˆ has the truth table shown here:

p	q	p ˆ q
0	0	0
1	0	1
1	1	0
0	1	1

As the table indicates, the outcome of an XOR is true only if exactly one of the operands is true; it is false otherwise.

Bitwise operations most often find application in device drivers, modem programs, disk file routines, printer routines, and the

Table 13-1.

Operator	Action
&	AND
¦	OR
^	Exclusive OR (XOR)
~	One's complement (NOT)
>>	Shift right
<<	Shift left

The Bitwise Operators

like because they can be used to mask off certain bits, such as parity. (The parity bit is used to confirm that the rest of the bits in the byte are unchanged. It is usually the high-order bit in each byte.)

In terms of its most common usage, you can think of the bitwise AND as a way to turn bits off. That is, any bit that is 0 in either operand will cause the corresponding bit in the variable to be set to 0. For example, the following function reads a character from the modem port using the library function **bioscom( )** and resets the parity bit to zero. The **bioscom( )** function is used to access the asynchronous serial ports on an IBM PC or compatible.

```
char get_char_from_modem(void)
{
  char ch;

  ch = bioscom(2, 0, 0); /* get a character from
                                  COM1 */
  return ch & 127;
}
```

Parity is indicated by the eighth bit, which is set to zero by ANDing it with a byte that has bits 1 through 7 set to 1 and bit 8 set to 0 (127 in decimal). The expression **ch & 127** means to AND together the bits in **ch** with the bits that make up the number 127. The net result is that the eighth bit of **ch** will be set to 0. In the following example, assume that **ch** has received the character "A" and has the parity bit set:

> parity bit
> ↓
>
> 1 1 0 0 0 0 0 1   **ch** containing an "A"
>   with parity set
>
>   0 1 1 1 1 1 1 1   127 in binary
>
> & _____   do bitwise AND
>
>   0 1 0 0 0 0 0 1   "A" without parity

The bitwise OR, as the reverse of AND, can be used to turn bits on. Any bit that is set to 1 in either operand will cause the corresponding bit in the variable to be set to 1. For example, this is **128 | 3**.

```
1 0 0 0 0 0 0 0        128 in binary

0 0 0 0 0 0 1 1        3 in binary

|  _____       bitwise OR

1 0 0 0 0 0 1 1        result
```

An exclusive OR, usually abbreviated XOR, will set a bit on if—and only if—the bits being compared are different. For example, this is **127 ^ 120**.

```
0 1 1 1 1 1 1 1        127 in binary

0 1 1 1 1 0 0 0        120 in binary

^  _____       bitwise XOR

0 0 0 0 0 1 1 1        result
```

In general, bitwise ANDs, ORs, and XORs apply their operations directly to each bit in the variable individually. For this reason and others, bitwise operations are not usually used in conditional statements the way the relational and logical operators are. For example if X equals 7, then **X && 8** evaluates to true (1), whereas **X & 8** evaluates to false (0).

REMEMBER   *Relational and logical operators always produce a result that is either 0 or 1, whereas the similar bitwise operations may produce any arbitrary value in accordance with the specific operation. In other*

words, bitwise operations may have values other than 0 or 1, while the logical operators will always evaluate to 0 or 1.

The AND operator is also useful when you want to check if a bit is on or off. For example, this statement checks to see if bit 4 in **status** is sct.

```
if(status & 8) printf("bit 4 is on");
```

The reason that 8 is used is that in binary it is represented as 0000 1000. That is, the number 8 translated into binary has only the fourth bit on. Hence, the **if** statement can only succeed when bit 4 of **status** is also on. An interesting use of this procedure is the **disp_binary( )** function shown here. It displays, in binary format, the bit pattern of its argument. You will use it later in this chapter to watch the effects of other bitwise operations.

```
/* display the bits within a byte */
void disp_binary(int i)
{
  register int t;

  for(t=128; t>0; t = t/2)
    if(i & t) printf("1 ");
    else printf("0 ");
  printf("\n");
}
```

The **disp_binary( )** function works by successively testing each bit in the byte, using the bitwise AND, to determine if it is on or off. If it is on, the digit "1" is displayed; otherwise, "0" is displayed. In the previous chapter a bit-field was used to decode and display a binary value. The code shown here is a better alternative because it is faster and smaller.

The shift operators, >> and <<, move all bits in an integral value to the right or left as specified. The general form of the shift right statement is *value > > number of bit positions*

and the shift left statement is

value < < number of bit positions

As bits are shifted off one end, zeros are brought in the other end. Remember that a shift is *not* a rotate. That is, the bits shifted off one end *do not* come back around to the other. The bits shifted off are lost, and zeros are brought in.

Bit shift operations can be very useful in decoding external device input, like D/A converters, and reading status information. The bitwise shift operators can also be used to perform very fast multiplication and division of integers. A shift left will effectively multiply a number by 2 and a shift right will divide it by 2, as shown in Figure 13-1.

Figure 13-1.

				x as each statement executes								value of x
unsigned char x;												
	x	=	7;	0	0	0	0	0	1	1	1	7
x	=	x	< < 1;	0	0	0	0	1	1	1	0	14
x	=	x	< < 3;	0	1	1	1	0	0	0	0	112
x	=	x	< < 2;	1	1	0	0	0	0	0	0	192
x	=	x	> > 1;	0	1	1	0	0	0	0	0	96
x	=	x	> > 2;	0	0	0	1	1	0	0	0	24

Each left shift multiplies by 2. Information has been lost after **x << 2** because a bit was shifted off the end.

Each right shift divides by 2. Subsequent divisions will not bring back any lost bits.

Example of multiplication and division with shift operators

The following program graphically shows the effect of the shift operators:

```
/* Example of bitshifting. */

#include <stdio.h>

void disp_binary(int i);

main(void)
{
  int i=1, t;

  for(t=0; t<8; t++) {
    disp_binary(i);
    i = i << 1;
  }

  printf("\n");

  for(t=0; t<8; t++) {
    i = i >> 1;
    disp_binary(i);
  }
  return 0;
}

/* Display the bits within a byte. */
void disp_binary(int i)
{
  register int t;

  for(t=128; t>0; t=t/2)
    if(i & t) printf("1 ");
    else printf("0 ");
  printf("\n");
}
```

It produces the following output:

```
0 0 0 0 0 0 0 1
0 0 0 0 0 0 1 0
0 0 0 0 0 1 0 0
0 0 0 0 1 0 0 0
0 0 0 1 0 0 0 0
0 0 1 0 0 0 0 0
0 1 0 0 0 0 0 0
1 0 0 0 0 0 0 0
```

```
1 0 0 0 0 0 0 0
0 1 0 0 0 0 0 0
0 0 1 0 0 0 0 0
0 0 0 1 0 0 0 0
0 0 0 0 1 0 0 0
0 0 0 0 0 1 0 0
0 0 0 0 0 0 1 0
0 0 0 0 0 0 0 1
```

Although C does not contain a rotate operator, it is easy to create a function to perform this task. A rotate is similar to a left-shift operation except that the bits that are shifted off one end are shifted onto the other end. For example, 1010 rotated left once is 0101. One way to perform a rotate requires the use of a **union** of two different types of data. The first type is a two-element array of the type of data you wish to rotate. The second is a type that is larger than the data you will be rotating. In this example, a bytewise left rotation is done. Hence, the following **union** is used:

```
union rotate {
  char ch[2];
  unsigned int i;
} rot;
```

The function that actually performs the rotation is shown here:

```
/* Rotate a byte. */
void rotate_it(union rotate *rot)
{
  rot->ch[1] = 0;   /* clear the high-order byte */

  rot->i = rot->i << 1;   /* shift once to the left */

  /* see if a bit has been shifted out of ch[0] */
  if(rot->ch[1]) rot->i = rot->i | 1;   /* OR it back in */
}
```

The function first clears the high-order byte of the integer **i** so that if a bit is shifted in, it can be detected. By applying the left-shift operator to the entire integer, a bit that leaves the byte **ch[0]** will not be lost but will be moved into **ch[1]**. If a bit is shifted out, it is ORed into the lower-order bit of **ch[0]**. A program that uses this function is shown here:

```
/* Do a rotation. */
#include <stdio.h>

union rotate {
  char ch[2];
  unsigned int i;
} rot;

void disp_binary(int i);
void rotate_it(union rotate *rot);

main(void)
{
  register int t;

  rot.ch[0] = 101;

  for(t=0; t<7; t++) {
    disp_binary(rot.i);
    rotate_it(&rot);
  }
  return 0;
}

/* Rotate a byte. */
void rotate_it(union rotate *rot)
{
  rot->ch[1] = 0;   /* clear the high-order byte */

  rot->i = rot-> i << 1;   /* shift once to the left */

  /* see if a bit has been shifted out of ch[0] */
  if(rot->ch[1]) rot->i = rot->i | 1;   /* OR it back in */
}

/* display the bits within a byte */
void disp_binary(int i)
{
  register int t;

  for(t=128; t>0; t=t/2)
    if(i & t) printf("1 ");
```

```
    else printf("0 ");
  printf("\n");
}
```

This program produces this output by rotating the original byte
seven times:

```
0 1 1 0 0 1 0 1
1 1 0 0 1 0 1 0
1 0 0 1 0 1 0 1
0 0 1 0 1 0 1 1
0 1 0 1 0 1 1 0
1 0 1 0 1 1 0 0
0 1 0 1 1 0 0 1
```

The one's complement operator, ~, will reverse the state of
each bit in the specified variable. That is, all ones are set to 0, and
all zeros are set to 1. An interesting use for the one's complement
operator is to view the extended character set. The character set
shown on the keyboard represents only a part of the entire
character set supported by the computer. The following program
uses the one's complement operator to reverse the bits in the
characters you type. These reversed bit patterns correspond to
much of the extended character set. For example, when you type
a lowercase "d," the cents sign is displayed. You will be surprised
by how many different characters are available.

```
/* A window into the PC's extended character set. */
#include <stdio.h>
#include <conio.h>

main(void)
{
  char ch;

  do {
    ch = getch();
    printf("%c", ~ch);
  } while(ch!='q');
```

```
    return 0;
}
```

The bitwise operators are used often in cipher routines. If you wished to make a disk file appear unreadable, you could perform some bitwise manipulations on it. One of the simplest methods is to complement each byte by using one's complement to reverse each bit in the byte, as shown here:

original byte   0 0 1 0 1 1 0 0

after 1st complement   1 1 0 1 0 0 1 1   } same

after 2nd complement 0 0 1 0 1 1 0 0

Notice that a sequence of two complements in a row will always produce the original number. Hence, the first complement would represent the coded version of that byte. The second complement would decode it to its original value.

You could use the **encode( )** function shown here to encode a character. To decode a previously coded character, you simply use **encode( )** a second time:

```
char encode(char ch)  /* a simple cipher function */
{
    return(~ch); /* complement it */
}
```

The ? Operator

The **?** operator can be used to replace **if/else** statements of this general form:

```
if(condition)
    expression
else
    expression
```

The key restriction is that the target of both the **if** and the **else** must be a single expression—not another C statement.

The **?** is called a *ternary operator* because it requires three operands and takes the general form,

$$Exp1 \; ? \; Exp2 \; : \; Exp3$$

where *Exp1*, *Exp2*, and *Exp3* are expressions. Notice the use and placement of the colon.

The value of a **?** expression is determined like this. *Exp1* is evaluated. If it is true, then *Exp2* is evaluated and becomes the value of the entire **?** expression. If *Exp1* is false, then *Exp3* is evaluated and its value becomes the value of the expression. For example, consider

```
x = 10;

y = x>9 ? 100 : 200;
```

In this example, **y** will be assigned the value 100. If **x** was less than 9, **y** would have received the value 200. The same code written using the **if/else** statement would be

```
x = 10;

if(x>9) y = 100;
else y = 200;
```

However, the use of the **?** operator to replace **if/else** statements is not restricted only to assignments. To see how its use can be expanded, it is important to remember that all functions (except those declared as **void**) may return a value. Hence, it is permissible to use one or more function calls in a C expression. When the function's name is encountered, the function is, of course, executed so that its return value may be determined. Therefore, it is possible to execute one or more function calls using the **?** operator by placing them in the expressions that form the operands.

For example:

```c
#include <stdio.h>

int f2(void);
int f1(int n);

main(void)
{
  int t;

  printf(": ");
  scanf("%d",&t);

  /* print proper message */
  t ? f1(t)+f2() : printf("zero entered");
  return 0;
}

int f1(int n)
{
  printf("%d ",n);
}

int f2(void)
{
  printf("entered");
}
```

In this simple example, if you enter a zero, then the **printf( )** function will be called and the "zero entered" message will appear. If you enter any other number, then both **f1( )** and **f2( )** will be executed. It is important to note that the value of the **?** expression is discarded in this example. It is not necessary to assign it to anything. However, notice that even though the functions **f1( )** and **f2( )** do not return values, they are declared to be of type **int**. This is necessary because a **void** function cannot be used in any type of expression, even one in which the return value is discarded. This is an example of C's flexibility.

Here's one final example of the **?** operator in action. It is used to prevent a divide-by-zero error.

```
/* This program uses the ? operator to prevent
   a division by zero. */

#include <stdio.h>
int div_zero(void);

main(void)
{
  int i, j, result;

  printf("Enter dividend and divisor: ");
  scanf("%d%d", &i, &j);

  /* this statement prevents a divide by zero error */
  result = j ? i/j : div_zero();

  printf("Result: %d", result);
  return 0;
}

div_zero(void)
{
  printf("cannot divide by zero\n");
  return 0;
}
```

C Shorthand

C has a special shorthand that simplifies the coding of a certain type of assignment statement. For example,

```
x = x+10;
```

can be written in C shorthand as

```
x += 10;
```

The operator pair **+=** tells the compiler to assign to **x** the value of **x** plus 10.

This shorthand will work for all the binary operators in C (that is, those that require two operands). The general form of the shorthand is

var op = *expression*;

For another example,

```
x = x-100;
```

is the same as

```
x -= 100;
```

You will see shorthand notation used widely in professionally written C programs and you should become familiar with it.

The Comma Operator

The comma operator is used to string together several expressions. The left side of the comma operator will always be evaluated as **void**. This means that the expression on the right side will become the value of the total comma-separated expression. For example,

```
x = (y=3, y+1);
```

first assigns **y** the value 3 and then assigns **x** the value 4. The parentheses are necessary because the comma operator has a lower precedence than the assignment operator.

Essentially, the comma's effect is to cause a sequence of operations to be performed. When it is used on the right side of an assignment statement, the value assigned is the value of the last expression of the comma-separated list. For example:

```
y = 20;

x = (y=y-5, 30/y);
```

After execution, **x** will have the value 2 because **y**'s original value of 20 is reduced by 5; then that value is divided into 30, yielding 2 as the result.

You can think of the comma operator as having the same meaning as the word "and" in English as it is used in the phrase "do this and this and this."

Square Brackets and Parentheses

In C, parentheses and square brackets are considered operators. Parentheses do the expected job of increasing the precedence of the operations inside of them. Square brackets perform array indexing and have already been discussed. It is interesting to note that not all other computer languages consider parentheses and the array indexing symbols to be operators.

Figure 13-2.

Highest	( ) [ ] –>.
	!˜ ++ -- - (type) * & sizeof
	* / %
	+ −
	<< >>
	< <= > >=
	= = !=
	&
	^
	¦
	&&
	¦ ¦
	?
	= += −= *= /=
Lowest	,

Precedence of C operators

Precedence Summary

Figure 13-2 lists the precedence of all C operators. All operators, except the unary operators and the **?** operator, associate from left to right. The unary operators, *****, **&**, **−** and the **?** operator associate from right to left.

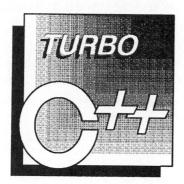

14

Screen Control Functions

Without a doubt, the development of successful programs in today's interactive environment demands full mastery over the screen. This chapter introduces several of Turbo C++'s screen control functions. Keep in mind that Turbo C++'s screen handling subsystems contain a large number of functions—many more than can be looked at in this chapter—so be sure to consult your user manual.

The Turbo C++ screen control package is broken down into two pieces: text mode screen control and graphics mode screen control. The text mode functions manage the screen's appearance when the video adapter is in a text mode and the graphics functions use the screen when the computer is in a graphics display mode. Although they are conceptually related, these two subsystems are actually entirely separate. This chapter begins with a look at several of the common text mode functions and concludes by examining the graphics subsystem.

 NOTE   The text and graphics screen functions described in this chapter were first developed for Turbo C version 1.5. Since they are not unique to Turbo C++, they are discussed as part of the C language. However, they are fully applicable to either the Turbo C or Turbo C++ environment.

The Basic Text Mode Functions

Before exploring some of the most important text mode screen control and manipulation functions, there are a couple of points to remember. First, all of Turbo C++'s text mode functions require the header CONIO.H to be present in any program that uses them. Second, the text mode functions expect the screen to be in a text, not a graphics, mode. Since this is the default mode of most PCs' operation, this should be no trouble. Shortly, you will learn to set the video mode to your liking.

Text Windows

Most of the routines in the Turbo C text mode subsystem operate on a *window,* not on the screen. Fortunately, the default window is the entire screen so you don't need to worry about creating any special windows in order to use the text and graphics routines. However, it is important to understand the basic concept of windows in order to get the most from the Turbo C++ screen functions.

A window is a rectangular portal that your program uses to send messages to the user. A window may be as large as the entire screen or as small as just a few characters. In sophisticated software it is not uncommon for the screen to have several windows at one time—one for each separate task performed by the program.

Turbo C++ lets you define the location and dimensions of a window. After you define a window, routines that manipulate text affect only the window you have defined—not the entire screen. For example, the **clrscr( )** function clears the active window, not the entire screen (unless, of course, the active window is the entire screen, as it is by default). In addition, all position coordinates are relative to the active window instead of the screen.

One of the most important aspects of windows is that Turbo C++ automatically prevents output from spilling past the boundaries of a window. If some output would go past a boundary, only the part that will fit is displayed and the rest is *wrapped* around to the next line.

For text windows, the coordinates of the upper-left corner are 1,1. The text mode screen functions that use coordinates apply them relative to the active window—not to the screen. Therefore, if you have two windows, the upper-left corner of either is considered location 1,1 when it is active.

For the moment, let's not worry about creating any windows and simply use the default window, which is the entire screen.

Clearing the Window

One of the most common screen handling functions you are likely to need is the one that clears the window of all text. This function is called **clrscr( )** and its prototype is

> void clrscr(void);

 REMEMBER   Even though this function seems to be the abbreviation of *clear screen,* it actually clears only the active window.

Positioning the Cursor

After clearing the window, the second most common screen control function is **gotoxy( )**, which positions the cursor. It has this prototype:

> void gotoxy(int *x,* int *y*);

Here, *x* and *y* specify, relative to the active window, the X,Y coordinate to which the cursor is positioned. If either coordinate is out of range, no action is taken. However, keep in mind that an out-of-range condition is not considered an error.

To see **clrscr( )** and **gotoxy( )** in action, try this short program. It prints the sentence "Text Screen Functions are Fun!" across the full height of the screen one vertical column at a time.

```
/* Demonstrate clrscr() and gotoxy(). */

#include <conio.h>
#include <stdio.h>
#include <string.h>

char mess[] = "Text Screen Functions are Fun!";

main(void)
{
  register int x, y;
  char *p;

  clrscr();

  p = mess;
  for(x=1; x<=strlen(mess); x++) {
```

```
      for(y=1; y<=12; y++) {
        gotoxy(x, y);
        printf("%c", *p);
        gotoxy(x, 25-y);
        printf("%c", *p);
      }
      p++;
    }
    getch();
    gotoxy(1, 25);

    return 0;
}
```

Clearing to End-of-Line

If your program requires user input, the **clreol( )** function will be very useful. It clears, from left to right, a line from the current cursor position to the end of the window. Its prototype is

      void clreol(void);

You can use this function along with **gotoxy( )** to construct a function that displays a prompting message at the specified coordinates after it has cleared the line. Using a function like **prompt( )**, shown in this program, is an easy way to keep your screen free of leftover messages.

```
#include <conio.h>
#include <stdio.h>

void prompt(char *s, int x, int y);

main(void)
{
  clrscr();
  prompt("this is a prompt", 1, 10);
  getch();
  prompt("this is too", 1, 10);
  getch();
```

```
   return 0;
}

void prompt(char *s, int x, int y)
{
  gotoxy(x, y);
  clreol();
  printf(s);
}
```

Deleting and Inserting Lines

Sometimes you will find yourself with a screen full of text and will want to remove (not simply erase) one or more lines, moving up the lines of text below the one removed. Alternatively, sometimes you will want to create a blank line where you need it on a screen full of text. To solve these problems, use the companion functions **delline( )** and **insline( )**. Their prototypes are shown here:

    void delline(void);

    void insline(void);

A call to **delline( )** causes the line the cursor is on to be deleted and all lines below that line to be moved up. A call to **insline( )** causes a new, blank line to be inserted just below the line that currently holds the cursor, and all lines below it to be moved down one line.

The following program illustrates **delline( )** by first filling the screen full of lines. The first line consists of "A"s, the second of "B"s, and so on. It then removes every other line.

```
#include <conio.h>
#include <stdio.h>
```

```
main(void)
{
  int x, y;

  clrscr();

  /* fill the screen with some lines */
  for(y=1; y<25; y++)
    for(x=1; x<80; x++) {
      gotoxy(x, y);
      printf("%c", (y-1)+'A');
    }

  /* delete every other line */
  for(y=2; y<26; y+=2) {
    gotoxy(1, y);
    delline();
  }

  return 0;
}
```

A small variation to this program uses **insline( )** to insert a blank
line at the same location as the deleted line. To see the effect of
this, modify the deletion loop as shown here:

```
/* delete every other line and insert a blank one */
for(y=2; y<26; y+=2) {
  gotoxy(1, y);
  delline();
  insline();
}
```

Creating Windows

So far, the examples have used the default window. However, you
can create windows of any size and at any location, provided they
fit on the screen, by using the **window( )** function. Its prototype is
shown here:

void window(int *left*, int *top*, int *right*, int *bottom*);

If any coordinate is invalid, **window( )** takes no action. Once a call to **window( )** has been successfully completed, all references to location coordinates are interpreted relative to the window, not the screen. For example, this fragment of code creates a window and writes a line of text at location 2,3 inside that window:

```
printf("at screen location 2, 3");
window(10, 10, 60, 15);
gotoxy(2, 3);
printf("at window location 2, 3");
```

The action of this fragment is illustrated in Figure 14-1.

 NOTE   It is important to understand that coordinates used to call **window( )** are screen absolute — not relative to the currently active window. This means that multiple windows do not need to be

Figure 14-1.

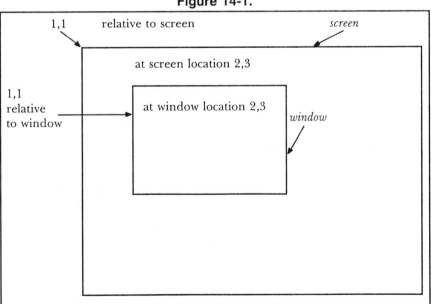

An illustration of relative coordinates inside a window

Figure 14-2.

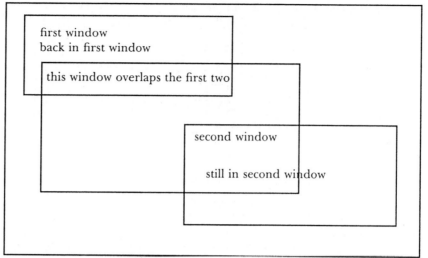

first window
back in first window

this window overlaps the first two

second window

still in second window

The output of the text window demonstration program

nested. Also, one window may overlap another window.

The following program first draws a border around the screen (for perspective), and then creates two separate windows with borders. The position of the text inside each window is specified by **gotoxy( )** statements, which are relative to each window. Finally, a third window is created, which overlaps the other two. The output from this program is shown in Figure 14-2.

```
/* A text window demonstration program */
#include <conio.h>
#include <stdio.h>

void border(int, int, int, int);

main(void)
{
  clrscr();

  /* draw a border around the screen for perspective */
  border(1, 1, 79, 25);
```

```
/* create first window */
window(3, 2, 40, 9);
border(3, 2, 40, 9);
gotoxy(3, 2);
printf("first window");

/* create a second window */
window(30, 10, 60, 18);
border(30, 10, 60, 18);
gotoxy(3, 2);
printf("second window");
gotoxy(5, 4);
printf("still in second window");

/* go back to first window */
window(3, 2, 40, 9);
gotoxy(3, 3);
printf("back in first window");
getch();

/* demonstrate overlapping windows */
window(5, 5, 50, 15);
border(5, 5, 50, 15);
gotoxy(2, 2);
printf("this window overlaps the first two");

getch();

return 0;
}

/* Draws a border around a text window. */
void border(int startx, int starty, int endx, int endy)
{
  register int i;

  gotoxy(1, 1);
  for(i=0; i<=endx-startx; i++)
    putch('*');

  gotoxy(1, endy-starty);
  for(i=0; i<=endx-startx; i++)
    putch('*');

  for(i=2; i<endy-starty; i++) {
    gotoxy(1, i);
    putch('*');
    gotoxy(endx-startx+1, i);
```

```
    putch('*');
  }
}
```

Some Window I/O Functions

Because C's normal output functions, such as **printf( )**, are not designed for use in a window-oriented screen environment, some functions that recognize windows are included in Turbo C++'s library. When you are using the default window, which is the entire screen, it does not matter significantly whether you use the window-based I/O functions or the standard functions. However, if you are using a smaller window, then you will want to use the window-oriented functions because they automatically prevent text from being written outside the active window. When using a window I/O function, text automatically wraps at the edge of the window. The new or modified text I/O functions are shown in Table 14-1.

The **cprintf( )** function operates exactly like **printf( )** except that it recognizes the window system. The **cputs( )** function corresponds to **puts( )** in like fashion. It differs from **puts( )** only

Table 14-1.

Function	Purpose
cprintf( )	Writes formatted output to the active window
cputs( )	Writes a string to the active window
putch( )	Outputs a character to the active window
getche( )	Inputs a character from the active window
cgets( )	Inputs a string from the active window

The Text I/O Functions for Use with Windows

in the fact that it recognizes windows. Unlike the standard I/O functions, such as **printf( )**, these functions automatically prevent output that is too big to fit in the active window from spilling over to another part of the screen. The same is true for **putch( )**. It will not allow a character to be written outside the current window. The function **getche( )** will not receive input outside the active window. Finally, **cgets( )** recognizes windows and does not allow user-entered text to exceed a window boundary.

To see the difference between a window I/O function and a standard function, try the following program and observe its results. As suggested by the program, the line output by **cprintf( )** wraps at the edge of the window; the one displayed by **printf( )** does not.

```
/* Demonstration cprintf(). */
#include <conio.h>
#include <stdio.h>

void border(int, int, int, int);

main(void)
{
  clrscr();

  /* create a window */
  window(3, 2, 20, 9);
  border(3, 2, 20, 9);
  gotoxy(2, 2);
  cprintf("This will wrap around at the edge of the window");
  printf("This will not wrap at the edge of the window");

  getch();

  return 0;
}

/* Draws a border around a text window. */
void border(int startx, int starty, int endx, int endy)
{
  register int i;

  gotoxy(1, 1);
  for(i=0; i<=endx-startx; i++)
```

```
    putch('*');

  gotoxy(1, endy-starty);
  for(i=0; i<=endx-startx; i++)
    putch('*');

  for(i=2; i<endy-starty; i++) {
    gotoxy(1, i);
    putch('*');
    gotoxy(endx-startx+1, i);
    putch('*');
  }
}
```

One other thing to understand about these basic I/O functions is that they are not redirectable. That is, C's standard I/O functions allow output to be redirected to or from a disk file or auxiliary device. This is not the case with the window-based text screen functions.

Text Modes

Up to this point, the default video mode of the computer, which is almost always 80 columns by 25 rows, has been used. However, there are actually five different text modes to choose from. If your computer has a graphics adapter, then you can choose between 40-column and 80-column modes as well as color or black and white. You can use the **textmode( )** function to change the video mode. Its prototype is

    void textmode(int *mode*);

The argument *mode* must be one of the values shown in Table 14-2. You may use either the integer value or the macro name. (The macros are defined in CONIO.H.)

Table 14-2.

Macro Name	Integer Equivalent	Description
BW40	0	40-column black and white
C40	1	40-column color
BW80	2	80-column black and white
C80	3	80-column color
MONO	7	80-column monochrome
LASTMODE	-1	Previous mode

The Text Video Modes

The main reason that you will want to include the **textmode( )** function in your programs is to ensure that the video mode currently used by the computer is the mode required by your program.

If your program sets the video mode, it should restore it to its original state before exiting. To do this, call **textmode( )** using **LASTMODE** as the argument. This automatically restores the video mode to what it was before your program changed it.

Outputting Text in Color

If you have a color monitor and a color graphics video adapter, you can display text in different colors. You can specify both the color of the text and the color of the background. Keep one fact firmly in mind, however: only the special window I/O functions can be used to display text in the specified colors. Functions such as **printf( )** will not work.

The **textcolor( )** function changes the color of subsequent text to that specified. It can also be used to cause the text to blink. The prototype of **textcolor( )** is

void textcolor(int *color*);

The argument *color* may have the values 0 through 15 with each corresponding to a different color. However, in CONIO.H macro names have been defined for each of these colors and are easier to remember. These macros and their integer equivalents are shown in Table 14-3.

Table 14-3.

Macro	*Integer Equivalent*
BLACK	0
BLUE	1
GREEN	2
CYAN	3
RED	4
MAGENTA	5
BROWN	6
LIGHTGRAY	7
DARKGRAY	8
LIGHTBLUE	9
LIGHTGREEN	10
LIGHTCYAN	11
LIGHTRED	12
LIGHTMAGENTA	13
YELLOW	14
WHITE	15
BLINK	128

The Color Macros and Integer Equivalents for Text

It is important to understand that a change to the color of the text affects only subsequent write operations; it does not change any text currently displayed on the screen.

To cause text to blink you must OR the value 128 (BLINK) with the color you desire. For example, this fragment causes subsequent text output to be green and blinking.

```
textcolor(GREEN | BLINK);
```

The function **textbackground( )** is used to set the background color of a text screen. As with **textcolor( )**, a call to **textbackground( )** affects only the background color of subsequent write operations. Its prototype is shown here:

void textbackground(int *color*);

The value for *color* must be in the range 0 through 6. This means that only the first seven colors shown in Table 14-3 can be used for the background.

The following program demonstrates the text color functions by displaying all combinations of foreground and background colors:

```
/* This program demonstrates color text. */

#include <conio.h>

main(void)
{
  register int fg, bg;

  textmode(C80);

  for(fg=BLUE; fg<=WHITE; fg++) {
    for(bg=BLACK; bg<=LIGHTGRAY; bg++) {
      textcolor(fg);
      textbackground(bg);
      cprintf("this is a test ");
    }
```

```
    cprintf("\n\r");
  }
  textcolor(WHITE);
  textbackground(BLACK);
  cprintf("done");
  textmode(LASTMODE);

  return 0;
}
```

An Introduction to Turbo C++'s Graphics Subsystem

Turbo C++'s second screen control subsystem is its graphics package. This package contains a great number of functions that perform tasks ranging from the drawing of lines and circles to the construction of bar graphs and pie charts. While it is beyond the scope of this book to look at every function, this section will introduce you to the most common ones.

The prototypes to the graphics functions are in the file GRAPHICS.H. This file must be included with any program that uses a graphics function because all of the graphics functions are **far** functions, and your program must know this before trying to use them.

 NOTE To try the examples that follow, your computer must be equipped with a graphics adapter and preferably with a color monitor.

A Window by Any Other Name

Like the text screen control functions, all of the graphics functions operate through a window. In Turbo C++ terminology, a graphics window is called a *viewport*, but a viewport has essentially the same qualities as a text window. About the only real difference between a window and a viewport is that the upper-left corner of a viewport is location 0,0 — not 1,1, as it is in a window.

By default, the entire screen is the viewport. However, you can create viewports of other dimensions. You will see how to do this later in this chapter. As you read through the following discussions, keep in mind that all graphic output is relative to the current viewport, which is not necessarily the same as the screen.

Initializing the Video Adapter

Before any of the graphics functions can be used, it is necessary to put the video adapter into one of the graphics modes. By default, the vast majority of systems that have graphics video adapters use 80-column text mode for DOS. Since this is not a graphics mode, the graphics functions cannot work with it. To set the adapter to a graphics mode, use the **initgraph( )** function. Its prototype is shown here:

```
void far initgraph(int far *driver, int far *mode,
                char far *path);
```

The **initgraph( )** function loads a graphics driver that corresponds to the number pointed to by *driver* into memory. Without a graphics driver loaded into memory, no graphics functions can operate. The *mode* parameter points to an integer that specifies the specific video mode used by the graphics functions. Finally, you may specify a path to the driver in the string pointed to by *path*. If no path is specified, the current working directory is searched.

The graphics drivers are contained in .BGI files, which must be available on the system. These drivers are supplied with Turbo C++. However, you need not worry about the actual name of the file because you only have to specify the driver by its number. The header GRAPHICS.H defines several macros that you can use for this purpose. They are shown here:

Macro	*Equivalent*
DETECT	0
CGA	1
MCGA	2
EGA	3
EGA64	4
EGAMONO	5
IBM8514	6
HERCMONO	7
ATT400	8
VGA	9
PC3270	10

When you use **DETECT**, **initgraph( )** automatically detects the type of video hardware present in the system and selects the video mode with the greatest resolution. This causes the values of *driver* and *mode* to be set to appropriate values.

The value of *mode* must be one of the graphics modes shown in Table 14-4. For example, to cause the graphics system to be initialized to CGA four-color, 320×200 graphics, you would use this fragment. It assumes that the graphics driver's .BGI file is in the current working directory.

```
#include <graphics.h>
    .
    .
    .
int driver, mode;

driver = CGA;
mode = CGAC0;

initgraph(&driver, &mode, "");
```

Table 14-4.

Driver	Mode	Equivalent	Resolution
CGA	CGAC0	0	320×200
	CGAC1	1	320×200
	CGAC2	2	320×200
	CGAC3	3	320×200
	CGAHI	4	640×200
MCGA	MCGAC0	0	320×200
	MCGAC1	1	320×200
	MCGAC2	2	320×200
	MCGAC3	3	320×200
	MCGAMED	4	640×200
	MCGAHI	5	640×480
EGA	EGALO	0	640×200
	EGAHI	1	640×350
EGA64	EGA64LO	0	640×200
	EGA64HI	1	640×350
EGAMONO	EGAMONOHI	3	640×350
HERC	HERCMONOHI	0	720×348
ATT400	ATT400C0	0	320×200
	ATT400C1	1	320×200
	ATT400C2	2	320×200
	ATT400C3	3	320×200
	ATT400CMED	4	640×200
	ATT400CHI	5	640×400
VGA	VGALO	0	640×200
	VGAMED	1	640×350
	VGAHI	2	640×480
PC3270	PC3270HI	0	720×350
IBM8514	IBM8514LO	0	640×480
	IBM8514HI	1	1024×768

The Turbo C Graphics Drivers and Modes Macros

Exiting Graphics Mode

To stop using a graphics video mode and return to a text mode, you should use either **closegraph( )** or **restorecrtmode( )**. Their prototypes are shown here:

    void far closegraph(void);

    void far restorecrtmode(void);

The **closegraph( )** function should be used when your program is going to continue executing using text mode. It frees memory used by the graphics functions and resets the video mode to what it was prior to the call to **initgraph( )**. If your program is terminating, you can use **restorecrtmode( )**, which resets the video adapter to the mode it was in prior to the first call to **initgraph( )**.

Colors and Palettes

The type of video graphics adapter you have connected to your system determines what kind and how many colors you have available for use when in a graphics mode. The biggest difference in adapters is between the CGA and the EGA/VGA.

CGA four-color graphics gives you access to four colors per palette and four palettes to choose from. The colors are numbered 0 through 3 with 0 always being the background color. The palettes are also numbered 0 through 3. To select a palette, set the *mode* parameter equal to **CGAC**x, where x is the palette number. The palettes and their associated colors are shown in Table 14-5.

In EGA/VGA 16-color mode, a palette consists of 16 colors, which are selected out of a possible 64 colors.

Table 14-5.

	Color Number			
Palette	*0*	*1*	*2*	*3*
0	background	GREEN	RED	YELLOW
1	background	CYAN	MAGENTA	WHITE
2	background	LIGHTGREEN	LIGHTRED	YELLOW
3	background	LIGHTCYAN	LIGHTMAGENTA	WHITE

The Palettes and Colors in Video Mode 4

To change the palette, use the **setpalette( )** function whose prototype is shown here:

void far setpalette(int *index*, int *color*);

The operation of this function is a little difficult to understand at first. What it does, in essence, is to associate the value of *color* with an index into a table that maps the color actually shown on the screen with that being requested. The values for the *color* codes are shown in Table 14-6.

For CGA modes, only the background color can be changed. The background color is always index 0. So, for CGA modes, this fragment changes the background color to green.

```
setpalette(0, GREEN);
```

The EGA can display 16 colors at a time with the total number of different colors being 64. You can use **setpalette( )** to map a color onto one of the 16 different indexes. For example, this sets the value of color 5 to cyan:

```
setpalette(5, EGA_CYAN);
```

Table 14-6.

CGA (background only)

Macro	Value
BLACK	0
BLUE	1
GREEN	2
CYAN	3
RED	4
MAGENTA	5
BROWN	6
LIGHTGRAY	7
DARKGRAY	8
LIGHTBLUE	9
LIGHTGREEN	10
LIGHTCYAN	11
LIGHTRED	12
LIGHTMAGENTA	13
YELLOW	14
WHITE	15

EGA and VGA

Macro	Value
EGA_BLACK	0
EGA_BLUE	1
EGA_GREEN	2
EGA_CYAN	3
EGA_RED	4
EGA_MAGENTA	5
EGA_BROWN	20
EGA_LIGHTGRAY	7
EGA_DARKGRAY	56
EGA_LIGHTBLUE	57

*The Color Codes for the **setpalette( )** Function*

Table 14-6. *(continued)*

Macro	Value
EGA_LIGHTGREEN	58
EGA_LIGHTCYAN	59
EGA_LIGHTRED	60
EGA_LIGHTMAGENTA	61
EGA_YELLOW	62
EGA_WHITE	63

*The Color Codes for the **setpalette( )** Function*

The Basic Plotting Functions

The most fundamental graphing functions are those that draw a point, a line, and a circle. These functions are called **putpixel( )**, **line( )**, and **circle( )**, respectively. Their prototypes are shown here:

    void far putpixel(int x, int y, int color);

    void far line(int startx, int starty, int endx, int endy);

    void far circle(int x, int y, int radius);

The **putpixel( )** function writes the specified color to the location determined by x and y. The **line( )** function draws a line from the location specified by *startx,starty* to *endx,endy* in the current drawing color. The default drawing color is white. The **circle( )** function draws a circle of radius *radius* in the current drawing color with the center being at the location specified by *x,y*. If any of the coordinates are out of range, then the only output will be that part (if any) of the circle that is in range.

The following program demonstrates these functions:

```
/* Points, lines, circles demonstration. */
#include <graphics.h>
#include <conio.h>

main(void)
{
  int driver, mode;

  register int i;

  driver = DETECT;
  initgraph(&driver, &mode, "");

  line(0, 0, 200, 150);
  line(50, 100, 200, 125);

  /* some points */
  for(i=0; i<319; i+=10) putpixel(i, 100, RED);

  /* draw some circles */
  circle(50, 50, 35);
  circle(100, 160, 100);

  getch(); /* wait until keypress */
  restorecrtmode();

  return 0;
}
```

Changing the Drawing Color

The example just shown draws the lines and circles in white, which is the default drawing color. (Remember, the **putpixel( )** function always draws in the color specified in its third argument.) You can set the current drawing color using **setcolor( )** whose prototype is shown here:

void far setcolor(int *color*);

The value of *color* must be in the range valid for the current graphics mode. Once the color has been changed, subsequent write operations take place in the new color.

Filling an Area

You can fill any enclosed shape using the **floodfill( )** function. Its prototype is shown here:

    void far floodfill(int *x*, int *y*, int *bordercolor*);

To use this function to fill an enclosed shape, call it with the coordinates of a point inside the shape and the color of the lines that make up the shape (its border). You must make sure that the object that you are filling is completely enclosed. If it is not, the area outside the shape will get filled as well. What the object is filled with is determined by the current fill pattern and fill color. By default, the background color is used. However, you can change the way objects are filled by using **setfillstyle( )**, whose prototype is shown here:

    void far setfillstyle(int *pattern*, int *color*);

The values for *pattern* are shown in Table 14-7 along with their macro equivalents (defined in GRAPHICS.H).

The rectangle( ) Function

The **rectangle( )** function draws a box as defined by the coordinates *left,top* and *right,bottom* in the current drawing color. It has this prototype:

    void far rectangle(int *left*, int *top*, int *right*, int *bottom*);

Table 14-7.

Macro	Value	Fill Pattern
EMPTY_FILL	0	Background color
SOLID_FILL	1	Solid color
LINE_FILL	2	Lines
LTSLASH_FILL	3	Light slashes
SLASH_FILL	4	Slashes
BKSLASH_FILL	5	Backslashes
LTBKSLASH_FILL	6	Light backslashes
HATCH_FILL	7	Light hatching
XHATCH_FILL	8	Hatching
INTERLEAVE_FILL	9	Interleaving
WIDEDOT_FILL	10	Widely spaced dots
CLOSEDOT_FILL	11	Closely spaced dots
USER_FILL	12	Custom pattern

The Fill Patterns

Figure 14-3.

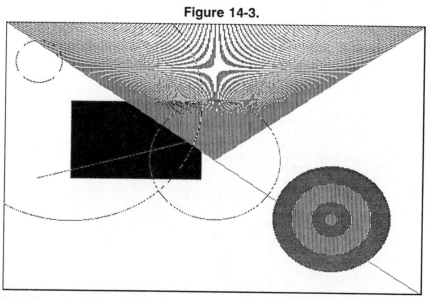

Sample output from the graphics demonstration program

The following program demonstrates all the graphics functions you have learned so far, except for **setpalette( )**. Its output is shown in Figure 14-3. This program requires a VGA adapter; however, you can easily change it to agree with the type of graphics adapter you have.

```
/* Color, rectangle, and fills demonstration program. */
#include <graphics.h>
#include <conio.h>

main(void)
{
  int driver, mode;

  register int i;

  driver = VGA;
  mode = VGAMED;
  initgraph(&driver, &mode, "");

  /* outline the screen */
  rectangle(0, 0, 639, 349);

  setcolor(RED);
  line(0, 0, 639, 349);

  setcolor(GREEN);
  rectangle(100, 100, 300, 200);

  setcolor(BLUE);
  floodfill(110, 110, GREEN); /* fill part of a box */

  setcolor(CYAN);
  line(50, 200, 400, 125);

  /* draw some circles */
  setcolor(RED);

  for(i=0; i<640; i+=3) line(320, 174, i, 0);

  setcolor(GREEN);
  circle(50, 50, 35);
  circle(320, 175, 100);
  circle(500, 250, 90);
  circle(100, 100, 200);
```

```
/* make a bullseye */
setfillstyle(SOLID_FILL, GREEN);
floodfill(500, 250, GREEN); /* fill part of a circle */

setcolor(RED);
circle(500, 250, 60);
setfillstyle(SOLID_FILL, RED);
floodfill(500, 250, RED);

setcolor(GREEN);
circle(500, 250, 30);
setfillstyle(SOLID_FILL, GREEN);
floodfill(500, 250, GREEN); /* fill part of a circle */

setcolor(RED);
circle(500, 250, 10);
setfillstyle(SOLID_FILL, RED);
floodfill(500, 250, RED);

getch(); /* wait until keypress */
restorecrtmode();

return 0;
}
```

Creating Viewports

You can create viewports in graphics mode in a fashion similar to the way windows are created in text mode. As stated earlier, all the graphics output is relative to the coordinates of the active viewport. This means that the coordinate of the upper-left corner of the window is 0,0 no matter where the viewport is on the screen. The function you use to create a graphics viewport is called **setviewport( )**. Its prototype is shown here:

> void far setviewport(int *left*, int *top*, int *right*,
> int *bottom*, int *clipflag*);

To use it, you specify the coordinates of the upper-left and lower-right corners of the screen. If the *clipflag* parameter is nonzero, then automatic truncation of output that would exceed the viewport's boundaries will take place. Otherwise, with clipping turned off, it is possible for output to overrun the viewport. Keep in mind, however, that the clipping of output is not considered an error.

You can find the dimensions of the current viewport by using the **getviewsettings( )** function. Its prototype is

void far getviewsettings(struct viewporttype far *info*)

The structure **viewporttype** is defined in GRAPHICS.H as shown here:

```
struct viewporttype {
  int left, top, right, bottom;
  int clipflag;
}
```

The **left**, **top**, **right**, and **bottom** fields hold the coordinates of the upper-left and lower-right corners of the viewport. When **clipflag** is zero, no clipping of output that overruns the viewport boundaries will occur. Otherwise, clipping will be performed to prevent boundary overrun.

The most important use of **getviewsettings( )** is to allow you to write programs that can automatically adjust to the type of video display adapter in use by examining the viewport dimensions and compensating accordingly. For example, the following program uses **setviewport( )** and **getviewsettings( )** to construct a second viewport that is centered on the screen. In the first viewport, vertical lines are drawn. In the second, horizontal lines are drawn. This program will work with any graphics adapter:

```
/* Demonstrate viewports */
#include <graphics.h>
#include <stdlib.h>
#include <conio.h>
```

```
main(void)
{
  int driver, mode;
  struct viewporttype info;
  int width, height;
  register int i;

  driver = DETECT;
  initgraph(&driver, &mode, "");

  /* Get screen dimensions */
  getviewsettings((struct viewporttype far *) &info);

  /* draw some vertical lines in first viewport */
  for(i=0; i<info.right; i+=20)
    line(i, info.top, i, info.bottom);

  /* create new viewport in the center of the screen */
  height = info.bottom/4;
  width = info.right/4;
  setviewport(width, height, width*3, height*3, 1);
  getviewsettings((struct viewporttype far *) &info);

  /* draw some horizontal lines inside second viewport */
  for(i=0; i<info.right; i+=10)
    line(0, i, info.bottom, i);

  getch(); /* wait for keypress */
  restorecrtmode();

  return 0;
}
```

Keep in mind that this chapter has only been an introduction to the most common text screen and graphics functions. You will want to consult your user manuals for a complete description of all screen and graphics functions.

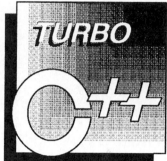

15

The C
Preprocessor

It is possible to include various instructions to Turbo C++ in the source code of a program. These are called preprocessor directives, and although they are not actually part of the C language, they expand the scope of the C programming environment. Preprocessor directives will be examined in this chapter along with Turbo C++'s built-in macros.

The C Preprocessor

The C preprocessor contains the following directives:

#if
#ifdef

```
#ifndef
#else
#elif
#endif
#include
#define
#undef
#line
#error
#pragma
```

As is apparent, all preprocessor directives begin with a **#** sign. Each will be examined now.

#define

Although you have already been introduced to **#define**, let's take a closer look at it here. In its simplest form, **#define** is used to define an identifier and a character sequence that will be substituted for the identifier each time it is encountered in the source file. The identifier is called the macro name and the replacement process is called macro substitution. The general form of the directive is

#define *macro-name character-sequence*

Notice that there is no semicolon in this statement. There may be any number of spaces between the identifier and the character sequence, but once it begins, the character sequence is terminated only by a newline.

For example, you can define the word **MAX** as the value 100.

```
#define MAX 100
```

This will cause the value 100 to be substituted for **MAX** each time the macro name **MAX** is encountered in your source file.

You can also use a macro name in place of a character sequence. For example, this code fragment prints the string "version 2.12."

```
#define VERSION "version 2.12"

printf(VERSION);
```

Remember, however, that no text substitutions will occur if the macro name occurs within a string. For example,

```
printf("HARD DISK VERSION");
```

will be displayed as shown with no substitution of the word "VERSION."

If the character sequence is longer than one line, it may be continued on the next line by placing a backslash at the end of the line, as shown in this example:

```
#define LONG_STRING "this is a how to handle a long \
string using #define statement."
```

It is common practice among C programmers to use capital letters for defined identifiers. This convention enables anyone reading the program to know at a glance that a macro substitution will take place. Also, it is best to put all **#define**s at the start of the file, or perhaps in a separate include file, rather than sprinkling them throughout the program.

The most common use of macro substitutions is to define names for "magic numbers" that occur in a program. For example, you may have a program that defines an array and has several routines that access that array. Instead of hard-coding the array's size with a constant, it is better to define a size and use that name whenever the size of the array is needed. In this way, it only requires a change in one place, plus a recompilation, to alter the size of the array if it needs to be changed. For example:

```
#define MAX_SIZE 100

float balance[MAX_SIZE];
```

The **#define** directive has another powerful feature: The macro name can have arguments. Each time the macro name is encountered, the arguments associated with it are replaced by the actual arguments found in the program. For example:

```
#include <stdio.h>

#define MIN(a,b)  ((a)<(b)) ? (a) : (b)

main(void)
{
  int x, y;

  x = 10;
  y = 20;
  printf("the minimum is: %d", MIN(x,y));

  return 0;
}
```

When this program is compiled, the expression defined by **MIN(a,b)** will be substituted, except that **x** and **y** will be used as the operands. That is, the **printf( )** statement will be substituted to look like this:

```
printf("the minimum is: %d",((x)<(y)) ? (x) : (y));
```

The reason for the parentheses around the **a** and **b** in the macro definition is to ensure that whatever expressions are substituted for **a** and **b** are fully evaluated. In some instances, leaving the parentheses off will cause erroneous results.

The use of macro substitutions in place of real functions has one major benefit: it increases the speed of the code because no overhead for a function call is incurred. However, sometimes increased speed is paid for with an increase in the size of the program because of duplicated code.

#error

The **#error** directive forces the compiler to stop compilation when it is encountered. It is used primarily for debugging. The general form of the directive is

#error *error-message*

The *error-message* is not between double quotes. When the compiler encounters this directive, it displays the following information and terminates compilation:

Error *filename linenum*: *Error directive*: *error-message*

#include

The **#include** preprocessor directive instructs the compiler to include another source file with the one that has the **#include** directive in it. The source file to be read in must be enclosed between double quotes or angle brackets. For example,

```
#include "stdio.h"
#include <stdio.h>
```

both instruct the C compiler to read and compile the header for the disk file library routines.

It is valid for include files to have **#include** directives in them. These are referred to as nested includes.

If explicit pathnames are specified as part of the filename identifier, then only those directories will be searched for the included file. Otherwise, if the filename is enclosed in quotes, first the current working directory is searched. If the file is not found, then any directories specified on the command line are searched. Finally, if the file has still not been found, the standard directories, as defined by the implementation, are searched.

If no explicit pathnames are specified and the filename is enclosed by angle brackets, the file is first searched for in the directories specified in the compiler command line. If the file is not found, then the standard directories are searched. At no time is the current working directory searched.

Conditional Compilation Directives

There are several directives that allow you to selectively compile portions of your program's source code. This process is called *conditional compilation* and is used widely by commercial software houses that provide and maintain many customized versions of one program.

#if, #else, #elif, and #endif

The general idea behind the **#if** is that if the constant expression following the **#if** is true, then the code that is between it and an **#endif** will be compiled; otherwise, it will be skipped over. The

#endif is used to mark the end of an **#if** block.

The general form of **#if** is

```
#if constant-expression
    statement sequence
#endif
```

If the constant expression is true, the block of code will be compiled; otherwise, it will be skipped. For example:

```
/* simple #if example */

#include <stdio.h>

#define MAX 100

main(void)
{
#if MAX>99
  printf("MAX greater than 99\n");
#endif

  return 0;
}
```

This program will display the message on the screen because, as defined in the program, **MAX** is greater than 99. This example illustrates an important point. The expression that follows the **#if** is *evaluated at compile time.* Therefore, it can contain only constants and identifiers that have been previously defined—no variables may be used.

The **#else** works in much the same way as the **else** that forms part of the C language: it establishes an alternative if the **#if** fails. The previous example can be expanded as shown here:

```
/* simple #if/#else example */

#include <stdio.h>
```

```
#define MAX 10

main(void)
{
#if MAX>99
  print("MAX greater than 99\n");
#else
  printf("MAX less than 99\n");
#endif

  return 0;
}
```

In this case, **MAX** is defined to be less than 99 so the **#if** portion of the code is not compiled, but the **#else** alternative is. Therefore, the message "MAX less than 99" is displayed.

Notice that the **#else** is used to mark both the end of the **#if** block and the beginning of the **#else** block. This is necessary because there can be only one **#endif** associated with any **#if**.

The **#elif** means "else if" and is used to establish an if/else/if ladder for multiple compilation options. The **#elif** is followed by a constant expression. If the expression is true, then that block of code is compiled and no other **#elif** expressions are tested. Otherwise, the next in the series is checked. This is the general form:

> #if *expression*
>   *statement sequence*
> #elif *expression 1*
>   *statement sequence*
> #elif *expression 2*
>   *statement sequence*
> #elif *expression 3*
>   *statement sequence*
> #elif *expression 4*
>   .
>   .
>   .

```
#elif expression N
    statement sequence
#endif
```

For example, this fragment uses the value of **ACTIVE**
_COUNTRY to define the currency name.

```
#define US 0
#define ENGLAND 1
#define FRANCE 2

#define ACTIVE_COUNTRY US

#if ACTIVE_COUNTRY==US
  char currency[]="dollar";
#elif ACTIVE_COUNTRY==ENGLAND
  char currency[]="pound";
#else
  char currency[]="franc";
#endif
```

You can nest **#if**s and **#elif**s to any level with the **#endif**,
#else, or **#elif** associating with the nearest **#if** or **#elif**. For example, the following is perfectly valid:

```
#if MAX>100
   #if SERIAL_VERSION
      int port=198;
   #else
      int port=200;
   #endif
#else
   char out_buffer[100];
#endif
```

#ifdef and #ifndef

Another method of conditional compilation uses the directives
#ifdef and **#ifndef**, which mean "if defined" and "if not defined,"
respectively.

The general form of **#ifdef** is

```
#ifdef macro-name
   statement sequence
#endif
```

If the macro name has been previously defined in a **#define** statement, the statement sequence between the **#ifdef** and **#endif** will be compiled.

The general form of **#ifndef** is

```
#ifndef macro-name
   statement sequence
#endif
```

If the macro name is currently undefined by a **#define** statement, then the block of code is compiled.

Both the **#ifdef** and **#ifndef** may use an **#else** statement but they cannot use the **#elif**. For example:

```
#include <stdio.h>

#define JON 10

main(void)
{
#ifdef JON
  printf("Hi Jon\n");
#else
  printf("Hi anyone\n");
#endif
#ifndef RACHEL
  printf("RACHEL not defined\n");
#endif

  return 0;
}
```

This will print "Hi Jon" and "RACHEL not defined." However, if **JON** was not defined, then "Hi anyone" would be displayed, followed by "RACHEL not defined."

You may nest **#ifdef**s and **#ifndef**s to any level in the same way as **#if**s.

#undef

The **#undef** directive is used to remove a previously defined definition of the macro name that follows it. The general form is

   #undef *macro-name*

For example:

```
#define LEN 100
#define WIDTH 100

char array[LEN][WIDTH];

#undef LEN
#undef WIDTH
/* at this point both LEN and WIDTH are undefined */
```

Both **LEN** and **WIDTH** are defined until the **#undef** statements are encountered.

The principle use of **#undef** is to allow macro names to be localized to only those sections of code that need them.

#line

The **#line** directive is used to change the contents of **__LINE__** and **__FILE__**, which are predefined identifiers in the compiler. The basic form of the command is

   #line *number "filename"*

where *number* is any positive integer and the optional *filename* is any valid file identifier. The line number is the number of the current source line and the filename is the name of the source file.

The **#line** directive is primarily used for debugging purposes and special applications. It is ignored by the integrated environment but is used by the command-line compiler.

For example, the following code specifies that the line count will begin with 100. The **printf( )** statement displays the number 102 because it is the third line in the program after the **#line 100** statement.

```
#include <stdio.h>

#line 100    /* reset the line counter */
main(void)        /* line 100 */
{            /* line 101 */
  printf("%d\n",__LINE__);   /* line 102 */

  return 0;
}
```

#pragma

The **#pragma** directive is an implementation-defined directive that allows various instructions, defined by the compiler's creator, to be given to the compiler. The general form of the **#pragma** directive is

    #pragma *name*

where *name* is the name of the **#pragma** you want. Turbo C++ defines these seven **#pragma** statements:

    argsused
    exit
    startup

inline
option
saveregs
warn

Although the use of some of these **#pragma**s requires more knowledge than you now have, each will be described briefly here.

The **argsused** directive must precede a function. It is used to prevent a warning message if an argument to the function that the **#pragma** precedes does not utilize that argument in the body of the function. In general, you won't need to use this **#pragma**.

The **exit** directive specifies one or more functions that will be called when the program terminates. The **startup** directive specifies one or more functions that will be called when the program starts running. They have these general forms:

#pragma exit *function-name priority*
#pragma startup *function-name priority*

The *priority* is a value between 64 and 255. (The values 0 through 63 are reserved.) The priority determines the order in which the functions are called when more than one of each kind exist. If no priority is given, then it is defaulted to 100. All **startup** and **exit** functions must be declared like this:

void *func*(void);

The following example defines a **startup** function called **start( )** and a termination function called **stop( )**.

```
#include <stdio.h>

void stop(void);
void start(void);

#pragma exit stop 101
#pragma startup start 101
main(void)
```

```
{
  printf("In main.\n");
  return 0;
}

void stop(void)
{
  printf("Program is terminating.");
}

void start(void)
{
  printf("Program is starting.\n");
}
```

As this example shows, you must provide a function prototype for all **exit** and **startup** functions prior to the **#pragma** statement. Note that neither **start( )** nor **stop( )** is explicitly called by the program. Instead, they are executed automatically when the program begins and ends execution. When this program runs, it displays this output:

```
Program is starting.
In main.
Program is terminating.
```

Another **#pragma** is **inline**. It has the general form

```
#pragma inline
```

This tells Turbo C++ that inline assembly code is contained in the program. For the greatest efficiency, Turbo C++ needs to know this in advance. (The use of inline assembly code is an advanced topic that is beyond the scope of this book. However, inline assembly code is discussed in my book *Turbo C/C++: The Complete Reference* [Berkeley, Ca.: Osborne/McGraw-Hill, 1990].)

The **option #pragma** allows you to specify command-line options within your program instead of on the command line. It takes this general form:

```
#pragma option option-list
```

You won't need to use this **#pragma** if you are using the Integrated Development Environment.

The **saveregs** directive prevents a function from altering the value of any CPU registers. It is unlikely that you will ever need to use this **#pragma**.

The **warn** directive causes Turbo C++ to override warning message options. It takes the form,

#pragma warn *setting*

where *setting* is one of the various warning error options. See your Turbo C++ user manuals for details about these options.

Predefined Macro Names

The ANSI C standard specifies these five built-in predefined macro names:

```
_ _LINE_ _
_ _FILE_ _
_ _DATE_ _
_ _TIME_ _
_ _STDC_ _
```

In addition to these, Turbo C++ defines these built-in macros:

```
_ _CDECL_ _
_ _COMPACT_ _
_ _HUGE_ _
_ _LARGE_ _
_ _MEDIUM_ _
_ _MSDOS_ _
```

_ _PASCAL_ _
_ _SMALL_ _
_ _TINY_ _
_ _TURBOC_ _
_ _cplusplus
_ _OVERLAY_ _

The _ _**LINE**_ _ and _ _**FILE**_ _ macros were discussed in the **#line** discussion. The others will be examined here.

The _ _**DATE**_ _ macro contains a string of the form *month/day/year* that is the date of the translation of the source file into object code.

The time when compilation of the source code begins is represented as a string in the _ _**TIME**_ _ macro. The form of the string is *hour:minute:second.*

The macro _ _**STDC**_ _ is defined as 1 if you compile a C program with the **ANSI Keywords Only** option on. Otherwise, this macro is undefined.

When a program is compiled using overlays, then the _ _**OVERLAY**_ _ macro will be defined as 1. Otherwise, _ _**OVERLAY**_ _ is undefined. (Overlays are covered in Appendix E.)

The _ _**CDECL**_ _ macro is defined if the standard C calling convention is used—that is, if the **Pascal** option is not in use. If this is not the case, then the macro is undefined.

Only one of these macros is defined, based on the memory model used during compilation:

_ _TINY_ _
_ _SMALL_ _
_ _COMPACT_ _
_ _MEDIUM_ _
_ _LARGE_ _
_ _HUGE_ _

(Memory models are discussed in Appendix C.)

The **_ _MSDOS_ _** macro is defined with the value 1 under all situations when using the MS-DOS version of Turbo C.

The **_ _PASCAL_ _** macro is defined only if the Pascal calling conventions are used to compile a program; otherwise, it is undefined.

The **_ _TURBOC_ _** macro contains the version number of Turbo C/C++. It is represented as a hexadecimal constant. The two rightmost digits represent the minor revision numbers and the leftmost digit represents the major revision number. For example, the number 202 represents version 2.02.

If your program is compiled as a C++ program, then **_ _cplusplus** is defined; otherwise, it is not defined.

The following program illustrates the use of some of these macros:

```
#include <stdio.h>

main(void)
{
  printf("%s %s %s %s\n", __FILE__, __LINE__, __DATE__,
         __TIME__);

  printf("Using version %X of Turbo C++.", __TURBOC__);
  return 0;
}
```

For the most part, these built-in macros are used in fairly complex programming environments when several versions of a program—perhaps running on different types of computers—are developed or maintained. As a beginning C++ programmer, it is good to be aware that these macros are available, although you will probably not need to use one for some time.

Using Turbo C++'s Object Oriented Features

In Part II of this book, you learned about those features C++ has in common with C. (Knowledge of the C language is prerequisite to learning C++.) In Part III you will learn about those features that are unique to C++. For the most part, these features provide specific support for object oriented programming.

Originally called "C with classes," C++ was developed by Bjarne Stroustrup at Bell Laboratories in Murray Hill, New Jersey in 1983. While C is excellent for small-to medium-sized programming projects, it can be stretched beyond its capabilities by truly large projects. C++ was invented to allow large projects to be more easily managed.

C++ is essentially a superset of C; everything you already know about C is therefore applicable to C++. Many of the concepts embodied in C++ will be new, but don't worry, you are starting from a firm base.

CHAPTER

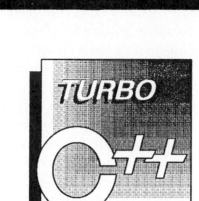

16

An Overview of C++

C++ is an *object oriented* programming language. Before learning anything specific about C++, it is important to understand the basic theory behind object oriented programming.

What Is Object Oriented Programming?

Object oriented programming is a new way of approaching the job of programming. Approaches to programming have changed dramatically since the invention of the computer. The primary reason for change is to accommodate the increasing complexity of programs. For example, when computers were first invented, programming was done by toggling in the binary machine instructions using the front panel. As long as programs were just a few hundred instructions long, this approach worked. As programs grew, assembly language was invented so that a programmer could deal with larger, increasingly complex programs by using symbolic representations of the machine instructions. As programs continued to grow, high-level languages were introduced to give the programmer more tools with which to handle complexity. The first widespread high-level language was, of course, FORTRAN. While FORTRAN was a very impressive first step, it is hardly a language that encourages clear and easy to understand programs.

The 1960s gave birth to *structured* programming. This is the method encouraged by languages such as C and Pascal. Using structured languages, it was for the first time possible to write moderately complex programs fairly easily. However, even with structured programming methods, once a project reaches a certain size it gets uncontrollable. The reason it becomes uncontrollable is that its complexity exceeds that which a programmer can manage using structured programming techniques. At each milestone in the development of programming, methods were created to allow the programmer to deal with increasingly greater complexity. Each step of the way, the new approach took the best elements of the previous methods and moved forward. Today, many projects are near or at the point where the structured approach no longer works. To solve this problem, object oriented programming was invented.

Object oriented programming has taken the best ideas of structured programming and combined them with several powerful, new concepts that encourage looking at the task of programming in a new light. Object oriented programming allows you to more easily decompose a problem into subgroups of related parts of the problem. Then, using the language, you can translate these subgroups into self-contained units called objects.

All object oriented programming languages have three things in common: objects, polymorphism, and inheritance. Let's take a look at these concepts now.

Objects

The single most important feature of an object oriented langauge is the object. Put simply, an *object* is a logical entity that contains data and code that manipulates that data. Within an object, some of the code and/or data may be private to the object and inaccessible directly by anything outside the object. In this way, an object provides a significant level of protection against some other, unrelated part of the program accidentally modifying or incorrectly using the private parts of the object. The linkage of code and data in this way is often referred to as *encapsulation*.

For all intents and purposes, an object is a variable of a user-defined type. It may seem strange at first to think of an object, which links both code and data, to be a variable. However, in object oriented programming, this is precisely the case. When you define an object you are implicitly creating a new data type.

Polymorphism

Object oriented programming languages support *polymorphism,* which essentially means that one name can be used for several related but slightly different purposes. The purpose of polymorphism is to allow one name to be used to specify a general class of actions. However, depending upon what type of data it is dealing with, a specific instance of the general case is executed. For example, you might have a program that defines three different types of stacks. One stack is used for integer values, one for floating-point values, and one for **long**s. Because of polymorphism, you can create three sets of functions for these stacks called **push( )** and **pop( )** and the compiler will select the correct routine depending upon what type of data the function is called with. In this example, the general concept is that of pushing and popping data onto and from a stack. The functions define the specific way in which this is done for each type of data.

The first object oriented programming languages were interpreters, so polymorphism was, of course, supported at run time. However, C++ is a compiled language. Therefore, in C++, both runtime and compile-time polymorphism is supported.

Inheritance

Inheritance is the process by which one object can acquire the properties of another object. This is important because it supports the concept of classification. If you think about it, most knowledge is made manageable by hierarchical classifications. For example, a Red Delicious apple is part of the classification *apple,* which in turn is part of the *fruit* class, which is under the larger class *food.* Without the use of classifications, each object would have to explicitly define all of its characteristics. However, using classifications, an object need only define those qualities that make it unique within its class. It can inherit those qualities it shares with the more general classes. It is the inheritance mechanism that makes it possible for one object to be a specific instance of a more general case.

A Few C++ Fundamentals

Since C++ is a superset of C, most C programs are implicitly C++ programs as well. (There are a few minor differences between

ANSI C and C++ that will prevent a very few C programs from being compiled by a C++ compiler. These differences will be discussed later.) This means that you can write C++ programs that look just like C programs. However, doing this is comparable to driving your car down the highway using second gear. You just are not taking full advantage of its capabilities. Furthermore, although C++ will allow you to write C-like programs, most C++ programmers use a style and certain features that are unique to C++. Since it is important to learn to write C++ programs that look like C++ programs, this section introduces a few of these features before moving on to the "meat" of C++.

Let's begin with an example. Examine this C++ program:

```cpp
#include <iostream.h>

main(void)
{
  int i;
  char str[80];

  cout << "C++ is fun\n";  // this is a single line comment
  /* you can still use C style comments, too */

  printf("You can use printf() if you like\n");

  // input a number using >>
  cout << "enter a number: ";
  cin >> i;

  // now, output a number using <<
  cout << "your number is " << i << "\n";

  // read a string
  cout << "enter a string: ";
  cin >> str;
  // print it
  cout << str;

  return 0;
}
```

As you can see, this program looks much different from the average C program. To begin, the header file IOSTREAM.H is included. This file is defined by C++ and is used to support C++-style I/O operations.

The next line that looks different is shown here:

```
cout << "C++ is fun\n";  // this is a single line comment
```

This line introduces two new C++ features. First, the statement,

```
cout << "C++ is fun\n";
```

causes **C++ is fun** to be displayed on the screen followed by a carriage return, linefeed combination. In C++, the **<<** has an expanded role. It is still the left-shift operator, but when it is used as shown in this example, it is also an output operator. The word **cout** is an identifier that is linked to the screen. (Actually, like C, C++ supports I/O redirection, but for the sake of discussion, you can assume that **cout** refers to the screen.) You can use **cout** and **<<** to output any of the built-in data types plus strings of characters.

It is important to note that you can still use **printf( )** (as the program illustrates) or any other of C's I/O functions. It is just that many programmers feel that using **cout <<** is more in the spirit of C++.

What follows the output expression is a C++ comment. In C++, comments are defined in two ways. First, you may use a C-like comment, which works the same in C++ as in C. However, in C++ you can also define a *single-line* comment by using **//**. When you start a comment by using **//**, whatever follows is ignored by the compiler until the end of the line is reached. In general, C++ programmers use C-like comments when a multiline comment is being created and C++, single-line comments when only a single-line comment is needed.

Next, the program prompts the user for a number. The number is read from the keyboard using this statement:

```
cin >> i;
```

In C++, the **>>** operator still retains its right-shift meaning. However, when used as shown, it also causes **i** to be given a value read from the keyboard. The identifier **cin** refers to the keyboard. In general you can use **cin >>** to load a variable of any of the basic data types (plus strings).

Although not illustrated by the program, you are free to use any of C's input functions, such as **scanf( )**, instead of using **cin >>**. However, as stated, many programmers feel that **cin >>** is more in the spirit of C++.

Another interesting line in the program is shown here:

```
cout << "your number is " << i << "\n";
```

As you can probably tell, this causes

```
your number is 100
```

to be displayed (assuming **i** has the value 100), followed by a carriage return-linefeed. In general, you can run together as many **<<** output operations as you want.

The rest of the program demonstrates how you can read and write a string using **cin >>** and **cout <<**.

Compiling a C++ Program

As you know, Turbo C++ can compile both C and C++. In general, if a program ends in .CPP it will be compiled as a C++ program. If it ends in any other extension, it will be compiled as a C program. Therefore, the simplest way to cause Turbo C++ to compile your C++ program as a C++ program is to give it the .CPP extension.

If you don't want to give your C++ program the .CPP extension, you must change the default settings of the integrated development environment. To do this, first select the **Options** menu; then the **Compiler** option; followed by the **C++** option. You will then be able to set an option that causes the integrated environment to compile all programs as C++ programs.

Introducing Classes and Objects

Now that you know some of the conventions and special features of C++, it is time to introduce its most important feature: the **class**. In C++, to create an object you must first define its general form using the keyword **class**. A **class** is similar to a structure. Let's begin with an example. This **class** defines a type called **queue**, which is used to create a queue object:

```
#include <iostream.h>

// this creates the class queue
class queue {
  int q[100];
  int sloc, rloc;
public:
  void init(void);
  void qput(int i);
  int qget(void);
};
```

Let's look closely at this **class** declaration.

A **class** may contain private as well as public parts. By default, all items defined in the **class** are private. For example, the variables **q**, **sloc**, and **rloc** are private. This means that they cannot be accessed by any function that is not a member of the **class**. This is one way that encapsulation is achieved—access to certain items of data may be tightly controlled by keeping them private. Although not shown in this example, you can also define private functions, which may be called only by other members of the **class**.

To make parts of a **class** public (that is, accessible to other parts of your program), you must declare them after the **public** keyword. All variables or functions defined after **public** are accessible by all other functions in the program. Essentially, the rest of your program accesses an object through its **public** functions and data. It should be mentioned at this time that although you can have **public** variables, philosophically you should try to limit or eliminate their use. Instead, you should make all data private and control access to it through **public** functions. Notice that the **public** keyword is followed by a colon.

The functions **init( )**, **qput( )**, and **qget( )** are called *member functions* because they are part of the **class queue**. Remember that an object forms a bond between code and data. Only those functions declared in the **class** have access to the private parts of that **class**. These functions are referred to as *member functions*.

Once you have defined a **class**, you can create an object of that type by using the **class** name. In essence, the **class** name becomes a new data type specifier. For example, this creates an object called **intqueue** of type **queue**:

```
queue intqueue;
```

You may also create objects when you define the **class** by putting their names after the closing brace, in exactly the same way as you do with a structure.

To review, in C++, a **class** creates a new data type, which may be used to create objects of that type.

The general form of a **class** declaration is

class *class-name* {
    private data and functions
public:
    public data and functions
    } *object list*;

Of course, the *object list* may be empty.

Inside the declaration of **queue**, prototypes to the member functions were used. It is important to understand that in C++, when you need to tell the compiler about a function, you must use its full prototype form. C++ does not support the old, traditional function declaration methods. (Also, in C++, all functions must be prototyped. Prototypes are not optional in C++.)

When it comes time to actually code a function that is a member of a **class**, you must tell the compiler which **class** the function belongs to by qualifying the function name with the **class** name that it is a member of. For example, here is one way to code the **qput**( ) function:

```
void queue::qput(int i)
{
  if(sloc==100) {
    cout << "queue is full";
    return;
  }
  sloc++;
  q[sloc] = i;
}
```

The **::** is called the *scope resolution operator*. It tells the compiler that this version of **qput**( ) belongs to the **queue class**; or, put differently, that this **qput**( ) is in **queue**'s scope. As you will soon see, in C++ several different **class**es can use the same function names. The compiler knows which function belongs to which class because of the scope resolution operator and the **class** name.

To call a member function from a part of your program that is not part of the **class**, you must use the object's name and the dot operator. For example, this calls **init( )** for object **a**:

```
queue a, b;
a.init();
```

It is very important to understand that **a** and **b** are two separate objects. This means, for example, that initializing **a** does not somehow cause **b** to also be initialized. The only relationship **a** has with **b** is that they are objects of the same type.

Another important point is that a member function can call another member function directly, without using the dot operator. It is only when a member function is called by code that does not belong to the **class** that the variable name and the dot operator must be used.

The program shown here puts together all the pieces and missing details and illustrates the **queue class**:

```
#include <iostream.h>

//this creates the class queue
   class queue {
   int q[100];
   int sloc, rloc;
public:
   void init(void);
   void qput(int i);
   int qget(void);
};

void queue::init(void)
{
```

```
   rloc = sloc = 0;
}

void queue::qput(int i)
{
  if(sloc==100) {
    cout << "queue is full";
    return;
  }
  sloc++;
  q[sloc] = i;
}

int queue::qget(void)
{
  if(rloc == sloc) {
    cout << "queue underflow";
    return 0;
  }
  rloc++;
  return q[rloc];
}

main(void)
{
  queue a, b;  // create two queue objects

  a.init();
  b.init();

  a.qput(10);
  b.qput(19);

  a.qput(20);
  b.qput(1);

  cout << a.qget() << " ";
  cout << a.qget() << " ";
  cout << b.qget() << " ";
  cout << b.qget() << "\n";

  return 0;
}
```

 REMEMBER The private parts of an object are accessible only by functions that are members of that object. For example, a statement like,

```
a.rloc = 0;
```

could not be in the **main( )** function of the previous program.

 NOTE By convention, most C programs have the **main( )** function as the first function in the program. However, in the queue program, the member functions of **queue** are defined before the **main( )** function. While there is no rule that dictates this (they could be defined anywhere in the program), this is the most common approach used in writing C++ code. This book follows that convention. (Actually, in real applications the **class**es associated with a program will usually be contained in a header file.)

Function Overloading

One way that C++ achieves polymorphism is through the use of function overloading. In C++, two or more functions can share the same name as long as their parameter declarations are different. In this situation, the functions that share the same name are said to be *overloaded* and the process is referred to as *function overloading*. For example, consider this program:

```
#include <iostream.h>

// sqr_it is overloaded three ways
int sqr_it(int i);
double sqr_it(double d);
long sqr_it(long l);

main(void)
{
  cout << sqr_it(10) << "\n";

  cout << sqr_it(11.0) << "\n";
```

```
    cout << sqr_it(9L) << "\n";

    return 0;
}

int sqr_it(int i)
{
    cout << "Inside the sqr_it() function that uses ";
    cout << "an integer argument.\n";

    return i*i;
}

double sqr_it(double d)
{
    cout << "Inside the sqr_it() function that uses ";
    cout << "a double argument.\n";

    return d*d;
}

long sqr_it(long l)
{
    cout << "Inside the sqr_it() function that uses ";
    cout << "a long argument.\n";

    return l*l;
}
```

This program creates three similar but different functions called **sqr_it( )**, each of which returns the square of its argument. As the program illustrates, the compiler knows which function to use in each case because of the type of the argument. The value of overloading functions is that it allows related sets of functions to be accessed using only one name. In a sense, function overloading lets you create a generic name for some operation with the compiler resolving exactly what function is actually needed to perform the operation.

One reason that function overloading is important is that it can help manage complexity. To understand how, consider this example. Most C compilers contain functions like **atoi( )**, **atof( )**, and **atol( )** in their standard library. Collectively, these functions convert a string of digits into the internal formats of an integer, a **double**, and a **long**, respectively. Even though these functions perform almost identical actions, three slightly different names must be used in C to represent these tasks, which makes the situation more complex, conceptually, than it actually is. Even though the underlying concept of each function is the same, it means that the programmer has three things to remember, not just one. However, in C++ it is possible to use the same name, such as **atonum( )**, for all three functions. Thus, the name **atonum( )** represents the *general action* which is being performed. It is left to the compiler to choose the right *specific* version for a particular circumstance. Thus, the programmer need only remember the general action being performed. Therefore, by applying polymorphism, three things to remember have been reduced to one. Although this example is fairly trivial, if you expand the concept you can see how polymorphism can help you understand very complex programs.

A more practical example of function overloading is illustrated by the following program. As you know, C (and C++) do not contain any library funtions that prompt the user for input and then wait for a response. This program creates three functions called **prompt( )**, which perform this task for data of types **int**, **double**, and **long**:

```
#include <iostream.h>

void prompt(char *str, int *i);
void prompt(char *str, double *d);
void prompt(char *str, long *l);

main(void)
{
  int i;
  double d;
  long l;

  prompt("Enter an integer: ", &i);
  prompt("Enter a double: ", &d);
```

```
    prompt("Enter a long: ", &l);

    cout << i << " " << d << " " << l;

    return 0;
}
void prompt(char *str, int *i)
{
    cout << str;
    cin >> *i;
}

void prompt(char *str, double *d)
{
    cout << str;
    cin >> *d;
}

void prompt(char *str, long *l)
{
    cout << str;
    cin >> *l;
}
```

 CAUTION You can use the same name to overload unrelated functions, but you should not. For example, you could use the name **sqr_it( )** to create functions that return the *square* of an **int** and the *square root* of a **double**. However, these two operations are fundamentally different, and applying function overloading in this manner defeats its entire purpose in the first place. In practice, you should only overload closely related operations.

Operator Overloading

Another way that polymorphism is achieved in C++ is through operator overloading. As you know, in C++ it is possible to use the << and >> operators to perform console I/O operations. The reason for this is that in the IOSTREAM.H header file, these operators are overloaded. When an operator is overloaded it takes on an additional meaning relative to a certain **class**. However, it still retains all of its old meanings.

In general, you can overload any of C++'s operators by defining what they mean relative to a specific **class**. For example, think back to the **queue class** developed earlier in this chapter. It is possible to overload the **+** operator relative to objects of type **queue** so that it appends the contents of one stack to those of another. However, the **+** still retains its original meaning relative to other types of data. You will need to know more about C++ before an actual example can be developed, but this is the general idea.

Inheritance

As stated, inheritance is one of the major traits of an object oriented programming language. In C++, inheritance is supported by allowing one **class** to incorporate another **class** into its declaration. To see how this works, let's start with an example. Here is a **class**, called **road_vehicle**, that broadly defines vehicles that travel on the road. It stores the number of wheels a vehicle has and the number of passengers it can carry:

```
class road_vehicle {
  int wheels;
  int passengers;
public:
  void set_wheels(int num);
  int get_wheels(void);
  void set_pass(int num);
  int get_pass(void);
};
```

This broad definition of a road vehicle can be used to help define specific objects. For example, this code declares a **class** called **truck** using **road_vehicle**:

```
class truck : public road_vehicle {
  int cargo;
public:
  void set_cargo(int size);
  int get_cargo(void);
  void show(void);
};
```

Notice how **road_vehicle** is inherited. The general form for inheritance is shown here:

    class *new-class-name* : *access inherited-class* { . . .

Here, *access* is optional. However, if present it must be either **public**, **private**, or **protected**. You will learn more about these options in a later chapter. For now, all inherited **class**es will use **public**. Using **public** means that all the **public** elements of the ancestor will also be **public** to the **class** that inherits it.

    Therefore, members of the **class truck** have access to the member functions of **road_vehicle** just as if they had been declared inside **truck**. However, the member functions *do not* have access to the private part of **road_vehicle**. Here is a program that illustrates inheritance. It creates two subclasses of **road_vehicle** using inheritance. One is **truck** and the other is **automobile**.

```
#include <iostream.h>

class road_vehicle {
  int wheels;
  int passengers;
public:
  void set_wheels(int num);
  int get_wheels(void);
  void set_pass(int num);
  int get_pass(void);
};

class truck : public road_vehicle {
  int cargo;
public:
  void set_cargo(int size);
```

```
   int get_cargo(void);
   void show(void);
};

enum type {car, van, wagon};

class automobile : public road_vehicle {
  enum type car_type;
public:
  void set_type(enum type t);
  enum type get_type(void);
  void show(void);
};

void road_vehicle::set_wheels(int num)
{
  wheels = num;
}

int road_vehicle::get_wheels(void)
{
  return wheels;
}

void road_vehicle::set_pass(int num)
{
  passengers = num;
}

int road_vehicle::get_pass(void)
{
  return passengers;
}

void truck::set_cargo(int num)
{
  cargo = num;
}

int truck::get_cargo(void)
{
  return cargo;
}

void truck::show(void)
{
  cout << "wheels: " << get_wheels() << "\n";
  cout << "passengers: " << get_pass() << "\n";
  cout << "cargo capacity in cubic feet: " << cargo << "\n";
}
```

```
void automobile::set_type(enum type t)
{
  car_type = t;
}

enum type automobile::get_type(void)
{
  return car_type;
}

void automobile::show(void)
{
  cout << "wheels: " << get_wheels() << "\n";
  cout << "passengers: " << get_pass() << "\n";
  cout << "type: ";
  switch(get_type()) {
    case van: cout << "van\n";
      break;
    case car: cout << "car\n";
      break;
    case wagon: cout << "wagon\n";
  }
}

main(void)
{
  truck t1, t2;
  automobile c;

  t1.set_wheels(18);
  t1.set_pass(2);
  t1.set_cargo(3200);

  t2.set_wheels(6);
  t2.set_pass(3);
  t2.set_cargo(1200);

  t1.show();
  t2.show();

  c.set_wheels(4);
  c.set_pass(6);
  c.set_type(van);

  c.show();

  return 0;
}
```

As this program shows, the major advantage of inheritance is that you can create a base classification that can be incorporated into more specific ones. In this way, each object can precisely represent its own classification.

Notice that both **truck** and **automobile** include member functions called **show( )**, which display information about each object. This is another aspect of polymorphism. Since each **show( )** is linked with its own class, the compiler can easily tell which one to call in any circumstance.

Constructors and Destructors

It is very common for some part of an object to require initialization before it can be used. For example, think back to the **queue class** that was developed earlier in this chapter. Before the queue could be used, the variables **rloc** and **sloc** had to be set to zero. This was performed using the function **init( )**. Because the requirement for initialization is so common, C++ allows objects to initialize themselves when they are created. This automatic initialization is performed through the use of a *constructor* function.

A constructor function is a special function that is a member of the **class** and has the same name as that **class**. For example, here is how the **queue class** looks when converted to use a constructor function for initialization:

```
// this creates the class queue
class queue {
  int q[100];
  int sloc, rloc;
public:
  queue(void);   // constructor
  void qput(int i);
  int qget(void);
};
```

Notice that the constructor **queue( )** has no return type specified. In C++, constructor functions cannot return values.

The **queue( )** function is coded like this:

```
// This is the constructor function.
queue::queue(void)
{
  sloc = rloc = 0;
  cout << "queue initialized\n";
}
```

Keep in mind that the message **queue initialized** is output as a way to illustrate the constructor. In actual practice, most constructor functions will not output or input anything.

An object's constructor is called when the object is created. This means that it is called when the object's declaration is executed. Also, for local objects, the constructor is called each time the object declaration is encountered.

The complement of the constructor is the *destructor*. In many circumstances, an object will need to perform some action or actions when it is destroyed. (Keep in mind that local objects are created when their block is entered and destroyed when their block is left.) For example, an object may need to deallocate memory that it previously allocated. In C++, it is the destructor function that handles deactivation. The destructor has the same name as the constructor but it is preceded by a $\sim$. For example, here is the **queue class** and its constructor and destructor functions. (Keep in mind that the **queue** class does not require a destructor, so the one shown here is just for illustration.)

```
// this creates the class queue
class queue {
  int q[100];
  int sloc, rloc;
public:
  queue(void);  // constructor
  ~queue(void); // destructor
  void qput(int i);
  int qget(void);
```

```
};

// This is the constructor function.
queue::queue(void)
{
  sloc = rloc = 0;
  cout << "queue initialized\n";
}

// This is the destructor function.
queue::~queue(void)
{
  cout << "queue destroyed\n";
}
```

To see how constructors and destructors work, here is a new version of the sample program from earlier in this chapter:

```
#include <iostream.h>

// this creates the class queue
class queue {
  int q[100];
  int sloc, rloc;
public:
  queue(void);  // constructor
  ~queue(void); // destructor
  void qput(int i);
  int qget(void);
};

// This is the constructor function.
queue::queue(void)
{
  sloc = rloc = 0;
  cout << "queue initialized\n";
}

// This is the destructor function.
queue::~queue(void)
{
  cout << "queue destroyed\n";
}

void queue::qput(int i)
{
  if(sloc==100) {
```

```
      cout << "queue is full";
      return;
   }
   sloc++;
   q[sloc] = i;
}

int queue::qget(void)
{
   if(rloc == sloc) {
   cout << "queue underflow";
   return 0;
   }
   rloc++;
   return q[rloc];
}

main(void)
{
   queue a, b;   // create two queue objects

   a.qput(10);
   b.qput(19);

   a.qput(20);
   b.qput(1);

   cout << a.qget() << " ";
   cout << a.qget() << " ";
   cout << b.qget() << " ";
   cout << b.qget() << "\n";

   return 0;
}
```

This program displays the following:

```
queue initialized
queue initialized
10 20 19 1
queue destroyed
queue destroyed
```

The C++ Keywords

In addition to those keywords defined by the C language and those specific to Turbo C itself, the C++ extensions to C add the following keywords:

asm
catch
class
delete
friend
inline
new
operator
private
protected
public
template
this
virtual

Of these, **catch** and **template** are reserved for future use. You cannot use any of them as names for variables or functions.

Now that you have been introduced to many of C++'s major features, the remaining chapters in this book will examine C++ in greater detail.

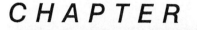

CHAPTER

17

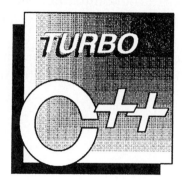

A Closer Look
at Classes

As stated in the previous chapter, the **class** is C++'s most important feature. This chapter examines it and related issues more closely.

Parameterized Constructors

Often, when an object is created it is necessary or desirable to initialize various data elements with specific values. As you saw in

483

the previous chapter, by using a constructor function it is possible to initialize various variables when the object is created. However, in C++, the concept of object initialization is expanded to allow the initialization of specific objects using programmer-defined values. This is accomplished by passing arguments to an object's constructor function. For a simple example, you can enhance the queue **class** that ended the previous chapter to accept an argument that will act as the queue's ID number. First, **queue** is changed to look like this:

```
// this creates the class queue
class queue {
  int q[100];
  int sloc, rloc;
  int who; // holds the queue's ID number
public:
  queue(int id);  // constructor
  ~queue(void); // destructor
  void qput(int i);
  int qget(void);
};
```

The variable **who** is used to hold an ID number, which will identify the queue. Its actual value will be determined by what is passed to the constructor function in **id** when an object of type **queue** is created. The **queue( )** constructor function looks like this:

```
// This is the constructor function.
queue::queue(int id)
{
  sloc = rloc = 0;
  who = id;
  cout << "queue " << who << " initialized\n";
}
```

To pass an argument to the constructor function, you must associate the value or values being passed with an object when it is being declared. C++ supports two ways to accomplish this. The first method is illustrated here:

```
queue a = queue(101);
```

This declaration creates a queue called **a** and passes the value 101 to it. However, this form is seldom used because the second method, sometimes called the *shorthand* method, is shorter and more to the point. In the shorthand method, the argument or arguments must follow the object's name and be enclosed between parentheses. For example, this accomplishes the same thing as the previous declaration:

```
queue a(101);
```

Since the shorthand method is used by virtually all C++ programmers, this book will also use the shorthand form exclusively. The general form of passing arguments to constructor functions is shown here:

  class-type var(arg-list);

Here, *arg-list* is a comma-separated list of arguments that is passed to the constructor.

The following version of the queue program demonstrates passing arguments to constructor functions:

```
#include <iostream.h>

// this creates the class queue
class queue {
  int q[100];
  int sloc, rloc;
  int who; // holds the queue's ID number
public:
  queue(int id);   // constructor
  ~queue(void); // destructor
  void qput(int i);
  int qget(void);
};

// This is the constructor function.
queue::queue(int id)
```

```
{
  sloc = rloc = 0;
  who = id;
  cout << "queue " << who << " initialized\n";
}

// This is the destructor function.
queue::~queue(void)
{
  cout << "queue " << who << " destroyed\n";
}

void queue::qput(int i)
{
  if(sloc==100) {
    cout << "queue is full";
    return;
  }
  sloc++;
  q[sloc] = i;
}

int queue::qget(void)
{
  if(rloc == sloc) {
    cout << "queue underflow";
    return 0;
  }
  rloc++;
  return q[rloc];
}

main(void)
{
  queue a(1), b(2);   // create two queue objects

  a.qput(10);
  b.qput(19);

  a.qput(20);
  b.qput(1);

  cout << a.qget() << " ";
  cout << a.qget() << " ";
  cout << b.qget() << " ";
  cout << b.qget() << "\n";

  return 0;
}
```

This program produces the following output:

```
queue 1 initialized
queue 2 initialized
10 20 19 1
queue 2 destroyed
queue 1 destroyed
```

As you can see by looking at **main( )**, the queue associated with **a** is given the ID number 1 and the queue associated with **b** is given the number 2.

Although the queue example passes only a single argument when an object is created, it is, of course, possible to pass several. For example, here, objects of type **widget** are passed two values:

```
#include <iostream.h>

class widget {
  int i;
  int j;
public:
  widget(int a, int b);
  void put_widget(void);
} ;

widget::widget(int a, int b)
{
  i = a;
  j = b;
}

void widget::put_widget(void)
{
  cout << i << " " << j << "\n";
}

main(void)
{
  widget x(10, 20), y(0, 0);

  x.put_widget();
  y.put_widget();

  return 0;
}
```

This program displays

```
10 20
0 0
```

Friend Functions

It is possible for a nonmember function of a **class** to have access to the private parts of that **class** by declaring it as a **friend** of the **class**. For example, here **frd( )** is declared to be a **friend** of the **class cl**:

```
class cl {
  .
  .
  .
public:
  friend void frd(void);
  .
  .
  .
};
```

As you can see, the keyword **friend** precedes the entire function declaration, which is the case in general.

Although not technically necessary, the reason that **friend** functions are allowed in C++ is to accommodate situations in which, for the sake of efficiency, two classes must share the same function. To see an example, consider a program that defines two **class**es called **line** and **box**. The **class line** contains all necessary data and code to draw a horizontal dashed line of any specified length, beginning at a specified X,Y coordinate and using a specified color. The **box class** contains all code and data to draw a box at the specified upper-left and lower-right coordinates in a specified color. Both **class**es use the **same＿color**( ) function to determine whether both a line and a box are drawn in the same color. These **class**es are declared as shown here:

```
class line;

class box {
  int color; // color of box
  int upx, upy; // upper left corner
  int lowx, lowy; // lower right corner
public:
  friend int same_color(line l, box b);
  void set_color(int c);
  void define_box(int x1, int y1, int x2, int y2);
  void show_box(void);
} ;

class line {
  int color;
  int startx, starty;
  int len;
public:
  friend int same_color(line l, box b);
  void set_color(int c);
  void define_line(int x, int y, int l);
  void show_line();
} ;
```

The **same＿color**( ) function, which is a member of neither but a **friend** of both, returns true if both the **line** object and the **box** object, which form its arguments, are drawn in the same color; it returns zero otherwise. The **same＿color**( ) function is shown here:

```
// return true if line and box have same color.
int same_color(line l, box b)
{
  if(l.color==b.color) return 1;
  return 0;
}
```

As you can see, the **same＿color**( ) function needs access to the private parts of both **line** and **box** to perform its task efficiently. (Remember that **public** interface functions could have been created to return the colors of both **line** and **box** and any function could have compared their colors. However, such an approach requires extra function calls, which in some cases causes too much inefficiency.)

Notice the empty declaration of **line** at the start of the **class** declarations. Since **same_color( )** in **box** references **line** before **line** is declared, **line** must be forward referenced. If this is not done, then the compiler will not know what **line** is when it is encountered in the declaration of **box**. In C++, a forward reference to a **class** is simply the keyword **class** followed by the type name of the **class**. Usually, the only time that forward references are needed is when **friend** functions are involved.

Here is a program that demonstrates the **line** and **box class**es and illustrates how a **friend** function can access the private parts of a **class**. It makes use of various Turbo C++ screen functions.

```
#include <iostream.h>
#include <conio.h>

class line;

class box {
  int color; // color of box
  int upx, upy; // upper left corner
  int lowx, lowy; // lower right corner
public:
  friend int same_color(line l, box b);
  void set_color(int c);
  void define_box(int x1, int y1, int x2, int y2);
  void show_box(void);
} ;

class line {
  int color;
  int startx, starty;
  int len;
public:
  friend int same_color(line l, box b);
  void set_color(int c);
  void define_line(int x, int y, int l);
  void show_line();
} ;
```

```
// return true if line and box have same color.
int same_color(line l, box b)
{

  if(l.color==b.color) return 1;
  return 0;
}

void box::set_color(int c)
{
  color = c;
}

void line::set_color(int c)
{
  color = c;
}

void box::define_box(int x1, int y1, int x2, int y2)
{
  upx = x1;
  upy = y1;
  lowx = x2;
  lowy = y2;
}

void box::show_box(void)
{
  int i;

  textcolor(color);

  gotoxy(upx, upy);
  for(i=upx; i<=lowx; i++) cprintf("-");

  gotoxy(upx, lowy-1);
  for(i=upx; i<=lowx; i++) cprintf("-");

  gotoxy(upx, upy);
  for(i=upy; i<=lowy; i++) {
    cprintf("|");
    gotoxy(upx, i);
  }

  gotoxy(lowx, upy);
  for(i=upy; i<=lowy; i++) {
    cprintf("|");
    gotoxy(lowx, i);
  }
}
```

```
void line::define_line(int x, int y, int l)
{
  startx = x;
  starty = y;
  len = l;
}

void line::show_line(void)
{
  int i;

  textcolor(color);

  gotoxy(startx, starty);

  for(i=0; i<len; i++) cprintf("-");
}

main(void)
{
  box b;
  line l;

  b.define_box(10, 10, 15, 15);
  b.set_color(3);
  b.show_box();

  l.define_line(2, 2, 10);
  l.set_color(2);
  l.show_line();

  if(!same_color(l, b)) cout << "not the same";
  cout << "\npress a key";
  getch();

  // now, make line and box the same color
  l.define_line(2, 2, 10);
  l.set_color(3);
  l.show_line();

  if(same_color(l, b)) cout << "are the same color";

  return 0;
}
```

Default Function Arguments

C++ allows a function to assign a default value to a parameter when no argument corresponding to that parameter is specified in a call to that function. The default value is specified in a manner syntactically similar to a variable initialization. For example, this declares **f( )** as taking one integer variable and declares a default value of 1:

```
void f(int i = 1)
{
   .
   .
   .
}
```

Now **f( )** can be called in one of two ways, as these examples show:

```
f(10);  // pass an explicit value
f();    // let function use default
```

The first call passes the value 10 to **i**. The second call automatically gives **i** the default value 1.

The reason that default arguments are included in C++ is that they provide another method of enabling the programmer to manage greater complexity. In order to handle the widest variety of situations, quite frequently a function contains more parameters than are required for its most common usage. Thus, when the default arguments apply, you need only remember and specify the arguments that are meaningful to the exact situation — not the most general case.

To understand the reason for default arguments, let's develop a practical example. One useful function not found in Turbo C++'s library, called **xyout( )**, is shown here:

```
// Output a string at specified X,Y location.
void xyout(char *str, int x = -1, int y = -1)
{
  if(x==-1) x = wherex();
  if(y==-1) y = wherey();
  gotoxy(x, y);
  cout << str;
}
```

This function displays, in text mode, the string pointed to by **str** beginning at the X,Y location defined by **x** and **y**. If neither **x** nor **y** is specified, then the string is output at the current text mode X,Y location. (You can think of this function as a "souped up" version of **puts( )**.) The functions **wherex( )**, **wherey( )**, and **gotoxy( )** are part of the Turbo C++ library. The **wherex( )** and **wherey( )** functions return the current X and Y coordinates, respectively. The current X,Y coordinates are where the next output operation will begin. The **gotoxy( )** function moves the cursor to the specified X,Y location. (If you have not read Chapter 14, which discusses the Turbo C++ screen control functions, you might want to skim through it.)

The following short program demonstrates **xyout( )**'s use:

```
#include <iostream.h>
#include <conio.h>

void xyout(char *str, int x = -1, int y = -1);

main(void)
{
  xyout("hello", 10, 10);
  xyout(" there");
  xyout("I like C++", 40);   // this is still on line 10

  xyout("This is on line 11.\n", 1, 11);
  xyout("This follows on line 12.\n");
  xyout("This follows on line 13.");

  return 0;
}

void xyout(char *str, int x = -1, int y = -1)
```

```
{
  if(x==-1) x = wherex();
  if(y==-1) y = wherey();
  gotoxy(x, y);
  cout << str;
}
```

Look closely at how **xyout( )** is called inside **main( )**. This program produces output similar to that shown in Figure 17-1. As this program illustrates, although it is sometimes useful to specify the exact location where text will be displayed, often you simply want to continue on from the point at which the last output occurred. By using default arguments, you can use the same function to accomplish both goals—there is no need for two separate functions.

Notice that in **main( )**, **xyout( )** is called with three, two, or one argument. When called with only one argument, both **x** and **y** default. However, when called with two arguments, only **y** defaults. There is no way to call **xyout( )** with **x** defaulting and **y** being specified. More generally, when a function is called, all arguments are matched to their respective parameters in order of left to right. Once all existing arguments have been matched, any remaining default arguments are used.

It is important to understand that all parameters that take default values must appear to the right of those that do not. That is, once you begin to define parameters that take default values,

Figure 17-1.

```
          hello there                    I like C++
This is on line 11.
This follows on line 12.
This follows on the third line 13.
```

*Sample output from the **xyout( )** program*

you may not specify a nondefaulting parameter. For example, it would have been incorrect to define **xyout( )** like this:

```
// wrong!
void xyout(int x = -1, int y = -1, char *str)
```

Here is another incorrect attempted use of default parameters:

```
// wrong !
int f(int i, int j=10, int k)
```

Once the default parameters begin, no nondefaulting parameter may occur in the list.

You can also use default parameters in an object's constructor function. For example, here is a slightly different version of the **queue( )** constructor function shown earlier in this chapter:

```
// This is the constructor function that uses
// a default value.
queue::queue(int id=0)
{
  sloc = rloc = 0;
  who = id;
  cout << "queue " << who << " initialized\n";
}
```

In this version, if an object is declared without any initializing values, then **id** defaults to 0. For example,

```
queue a, b(2);
```

creates two objects, **a** and **b**. Here, **a** has a **who** ID value of 0 and **b**'s value is 2.

Using Default Arguments Correctly

Although default arguments can be a very powerful tool when used correctly, they can actually work against you when misused. Here is why. The entire point of default arguments is to allow a function to perform its job in an efficient and easy-to-use manner while still allowing considerable flexibility. Toward this end, all default arguments should represent the way the function is used most of the time. For example, a default argument makes sense if a parameter will contain the same value 90 percent of the time. However, if a common value will occur in only 10 percent of the calls and the rest of the time the arguments corresponding to that parameter vary widely, then it is probably not a good idea to use a default argument.

The point of default arguments is that their values are those that the programmer will normally associate with a given function. When there is no single value that is normally associated with a parameter, then there is no reason for a default argument. In fact, declaring default arguments when there is insufficient basis de-structures your code because it misleads and confuses anyone reading your program. Where—in between 10 percent and 90 percent—you should elect to use a default argument is, of course, subjective. But 51 percent would seem a reasonable break point.

Classes and Structures Are Related

You might be surprised to learn that in C++, the **struct** has some expanded capabilities compared to its C counterpart. In C++, **class**es and **struct**s are highly related. In fact, with one exception, they are interchangeable because the C++ **struct** can also include data and the code that manipulates that data in just the same way that a **class** can. The difference between a C++ structure and a **class** is that by default the members of a **class** are **private** while, by default, the members of a **struct** are **public**. Aside from this exception, **struct**s and **class**es perform exactly the same function. For example, consider this program:

```
#include <iostream.h>

struct cl {
  int get_i(void); // these are public
  void put_i(int j); // by default
private:
  int i;
} ;

int cl::get_i(void)
{
  return i;
}

void cl::put_i(int j)
{
  i = j;
}

main(void)
{
  cl s;

  s.put_i(10);
  cout << s.get_i();

  return 0;
}
```

This simple program defines a structure type called **cl** in which **get_i( )** and **put_i( )** are **public** and **i** is private. Notice that **struct**s use the keyword **private** to introduce the **private** elements of the structure.

The following program shows an equivalent program that uses a **class** instead of a **struct**:

```
#include <iostream.h>

class cl {
  int i; // private by default
public:
  int get_i(void);
  void put_i(int j);
} ;
```

```
int cl::get_i(void)
{
  return i;
}

void cl::put_i(int j)
{
  i = j;
}

main(void)
{
  cl s;

  s.put_i(10);
  cout << s.get_i();

  return 0;
}
```

For the most part, C++ programmers use a **class** to define the form of an object and a **struct** in the same way that it is used in C. However, from time to time, you will see C++ code that uses the expanded abilities of structures.

Unions and Classes Are Related

You might be surprised to learn that **union**s are also related to **class**es. As far as C++ is concerned, a **union** is essentially a structure in which all elements are stored in the same location. A **union** can contain constructor and destructor functions as well as member and **friend** functions. For example, this program uses a **union** to display the characters that comprise the low- and high-order bytes of an integer (assuming two-byte integers):

```
#include <iostream.h>

union u_type {
```

```
  u_type(int a);   // public by default
  void showchars(void);
  int i;
  char ch[2];
};

// constructor
u_type::u_type(int a)
{
  i = a;
}

// show the characters that comprise an int
void u_type::showchars(void)
{
  cout << ch[0] << " ";
  cout << ch[1] << "\n";
}

main(void)
{
  u_type u(1000);

  u.showchars();

  return 0;
}
```

As you can see, since a **union** resembles a structure, its members are **public** by default. In fact, the keyword **private** cannot be applied to a **union**. (As you will learn later in this chapter, the keyword **protected** cannot be applied to a **union** either.)

 REMEMBER   Just because C++ gives **union**s greater power and flexibilty does not mean that you have to use them this way. In cases where you simply need a C-style **union**, you are free to use one in that manner. However, in cases where you can encapsulate a **union** along with the routines that manipulate it, you will be adding considerable structure to your program.

Inline Functions

While not pertaining specifically to object oriented programming, C++ contains one very important feature that is not found in C. This feature is called an *inline function*. An inline function is a function that is expanded in line when it is called instead of actually being called. This is similar to a parameterized function-like macro in C, but more flexible. There are two ways to create an inline function. The first is to use the **inline** modifier. For example, to create an inline function called **f**, which returns an **int** and takes no parameters, you must declare it like this:

```
inline int f(void)
{
    .
    .
    .
}
```

The general form of **inline** is

inline *function __ declaration*

The **inline** modifier precedes all other aspects of a function's declaration.

The reason for **inline** functions is efficiency. Every time a function is called, a series of instructions must be executed to set up the function call, including pushing any arguments onto the stack and returning from the function. In some cases, many CPU cycles are used to perform these procedures. When a function is expanded in line, no such overhead exists and the overall speed of your program increases. However, in cases where the **inline** function is large, the overall size of your program also increases. For this reason, the best **inline** functions are those that are very small. Larger ones should be left as normal functions.

As an example, the following program uses **inline** to make the program in the previous section more efficient:

```
#include <iostream.h>

class cl {
  int i; // private by default
public:
  int get_i(void);
  void put_i(int j);
} ;

inline int cl::get_i(void)
{
  return i;
}

inline void cl::put_i(int j)
{
  i = j;
}

main(void)
{
  cl s;

  s.put_i(10);
  cout << s.get_i();

  return 0;
}
```

If you compile this version of the program and compare it to a compiled version of the previous program, the **inline** version will be several bytes smaller.

It is important to understand that, technically, **inline** is a *request,* not a *command*, to the compiler to generate inline code. There are various situations that can prevent the compiler from complying with the request. Some of the most common are discussed here. First, for functions returning values, if a loop, a **switch**, or a **goto** exists, the compiler will not generate inline code. For functions not returning values, if a **return** statement exists, inline code will not be generated. You cannot have **inline** recursive functions, nor can you create **inline** functions that contain **static** variables.

Creating an Inline Function Inside a Class

There is another way to create an **inline** function in C++. This is accomplished by defining the code to a function *inside* a **class** definition. Any function that is defined inside a **class** is automatically made into an **inline** function. It is not necessary to precede its declaration with the keyword **inline** (subject to the exceptions just stated). For example, the previous program can be rewritten as shown here:

```
#include <iostream.h>

class cl {
  int i; // private by default
public:
  // automatic inline functions
  int get_i(void) { return i; }
  void put_i(int j) { i = j; }
} ;

main(void)
{
  cl s;

  s.put_i(10);
  cout << s.get_i();

  return 0;
}
```

Notice the way the function code is arranged. For very short functions, this arrangement reflects common C++ style. However, there is no reason you cannot write the functions as shown here:

```
class cl {
  int i; // private by default
public:
  // inline functions
  int get_i(void)
  {
    return i;
  }

  void put_i(int j)
  {
    i = j;
  }
} ;
```

In professionally written C++ code, short functions like those illustrated in the example are commonly defined inside the **class** definition. This convention will be followed in the rest of the C++ examples in this book.

More About Inheritance

As you saw in the previous chapter, it is possible for one **class** to inherit the attributes of another **class**. Some more details relating to inheritance will be examined here.

Let's begin with some terminology. A **class** that is inherited by another **class** is called the *base class*. Sometimes, this is referred to as the *parent class*. The **class** that does the inheriting is called the *derived class,* sometimes called the *child class.* This book will use the terms *base* and *derived* because they are the traditional C++ terms.

In C++, a **class** can categorize its elements into three classifications. An element may be **public**, **private**, or **protected**. As you know, a **public** element may be accessed by any other function in the program. A **private** element may be accessed only by member or **friend** functions. A **protected** element, also, may be accessed only by member or **friend** functions.

When one **class** inherits another **class**, all **private** elements of the base **class** are *inaccessible to the derived class*. For example:

```
class X {
  int i;
  int j;
public:
  void get_ij(void);
  void put_ij(void);
} ;

class Y : public X {
  int k;
public:
  int get_k(void);
  void make_k(void);
} ;
```

Here, the elements of **Y** can access **X**'s **public** functions **get_ij( )** and **put_ij( )**, but they cannot access **i** or **j** because they are **private** to **X**.

You can grant the derived **class** access to a **class**'s **private** elements by making them **protected**. For example:

```
class X {
protected://make protected
  int i;
  int j;
public:
  void get_ij(void);
  void put_ij(void);
} ;

class Y : public X {
  int k;
public:
  int get_k(void);
  void make_k(void);
} ;
```

Now, **Y** has access to **i** and **j** even though they are still inaccessible to the rest of the program. The key point is that when you make an element **protected**, you are restricting its access to only the member functions of the **class** but you are allowing this access to be inherited. When an element is **private**, access will not be inherited.

As you know from the last chapter, the general form for inheriting a **class** is as shown here:

```
class class-name : access class-name {
    .
    .
    .
};
```

Here, *access* must be either **private** or **public**. (It may also be omitted, in which case **public** is assumed if the base class is a structure or **private** if the base class is a **class**.) If *access* is **public**, then all **public** elements of the base **class** remain **public** elements of the derived **class**, and **protected** elements of the base **class** remain **protected** elements of the derived **class**. If *access* is **private**, then all **public** and **protected** elements of the base **class** become **private** elements of the derived **class**. To understand the ramifications of these conversions, let's work through an example. Consider the program shown here:

```
#include <iostream.h>

class X {
protected:
  int i;
  int j;
public:
  void get_ij(void);
  void put_ij(void);
} ;

// In Y, i and j of X become protected members.
class Y : public X {
  int k;
```

```
public:
  int get_k(void);
  void make_k(void);
} ;

// Z has access to i and j of X, but not to
// k of Y, since it is private by default.
class Z : public Y {
public:
  void f(void);
} ;

void X::get_ij(void)
{
  cout << "Enter two numbers: ";
  cin >> i >> j;
}

void X::put_ij(void)
{
  cout << i << " " << j << "\n";
}

int Y::get_k(void)
{
  return k;
}

void Y::make_k(void)
{
  k = i*j;
}

void Z::f(void)
{
  i = 2;
  j = 3;
}

main(void)
{
  Y var;
  Z var2;

  var.get_ij();
  var.put_ij();

  var.make_k();
  cout << var.get_k();
  cout << "\n";
```

```
  var2.f();
  var2.put_ij();

  return 0;
}
```

Since **Y** declares **X** as **public**, the **protected** elements of **X** become **protected** elements of **Y**, which means that they may also be inherited by **Z** and this program compiles and runs correctly. However, changing **X**'s status in **Y**, as shown here, causes **Z** to be denied access to **i** and **j**:

```
#include <iostream.h>

class X {
protected:
  int i;
  int j;
public:
  void get_ij(void);
  void put_ij(void);
} ;

// Now, i and j are converted to private members of Y.
class Y : private X {
  int k;
public:
  int get_k(void);
  void make_k(void);
} ;

// Because i and j are private in Y, they
// may not be accessed by Z.
class Z : public Y {
public:
  void f(void);
} ;

void X::get_ij(void)
{
  cout << "Enter two numbers: ";
  cin >> i >> j;
}

void X::put_ij(void)
```

```
{
  cout << i << " " << j << "\n";
}

int Y::get_k(void)
{
  return k;
}

void Y::make_k(void)
{
  k = i*j;
}

// This function no longer works.
void Z::f(void)
{
//  i = 2;  i and j are no longer accessible
//  j = 3;
}

main(void)
{
  Y var;
  Z var2;

  var.get_ij();
  var.put_ij();

  var.make_k();
  cout << var.get_k();
  cout << "\n";

  var2.f();
  var2.put_ij();

  return 0;
}
```

When **X** is made **private** in **Y**'s declaration, it causes **i** and **j** to be treated as **private** in **Y**, which means that they cannot be inherited by **Z**. Thus, **Z**'s function **f( )** may no longer access them.

One final point about **private**, **protected**, and **public**. These keywords may appear in any order and any number of times in the declaration of **struct** or **class**. For example, this is perfectly valid:

```
class my_class {
protected:
  int i;
  int j;
public:
  void f1(void);
  void f2(void);
protected:
  int a;
public:
  int b;
} ;
```

However, it is usually considered good form to have only one heading inside each **class** or **struct**.

If the use of **public**, **private**, and **protected** seems a bit confusing, be patient, think about the example program, and perhaps try some experiments of your own. With a little effort, it will become clear.

Multiple Inheritance

It is possible for one **class** to inherit the attributes of two or more classes. To accomplish this, use a comma-separated inheritance list in the derived **class**'s base **class** list. The general form is

```
class derived-class-name : base-class list
{
  .
  .
  .
};
```

For example, in this program **Z** inherits both **X** and **Y**:

```
#include <iostream.h>

class X {
protected:
  int a;
public:
  void make_a(int i);
};

class Y {
protected:
  int b;
public:
  void make_b(int i);
} ;

// Z inherits both X and Y
class Z : public X, public Y {
public:
  int make_ab(void);
} ;

void X::make_a(int i)
{
  a = i;
}

void Y::make_b(int i)
{
  b = i;
}

int Z::make_ab(void)
{
  return a*b;
}

main(void)
{
  Z i;

  i.make_a(10);
  i.make_b(12);

  cout << i.make_ab();

  return 0;
}
```

In this example, **Z** has access to the **public** and **protected** portions of both **X** and **Y**.

In the preceding example, **X**, **Y**, and **Z** do not contain constructor functions. However, the situation is more complex when a base **class** contains a constructor function. For example, let's change the preceding example so that **class**es **X**, **Y**, and **Z** each have a constructor function, as shown here:

```
#include <iostream.h>

class X {
protected:
  int a;
public:
  X(void);
};

class Y {
protected:
  int b;
public:
  Y(void);
} ;

// Z inherits both X and Y
class Z : public X, public Y {
public:
  Z(void);
  int make_ab(void);
} ;

X::X(void)
{
  a = 10;
  cout << "initializing X\n";
}

Y::Y(void)
{
  cout << "initializing Y\n";
  b = 20;
}

Z::Z(void)
{
  cout << "initializing Z\n";
```

```
}

int Z::make_ab(void)
{
  return a*b;
}

main(void)
{
  Z i;

  cout << i.make_ab();

  return 0;
}
```

When this program runs, it displays this output:

```
initializing X
initializing Y
initializing Z
200
```

Notice that the base **class**es are constructed in the order they appear in **Z**'s declaration. This result can be generalized because in C++, the constructor functions for any inherited base **class**es will be called in the order in which they appear. Once the base **class** or **class**es have been initialized, the derived **class**'s constructor executes.

As long as no base **class** constructor function takes any arguments, then the derived **class** need not have a constructor function. However, when a base **class** contains a constructor function that uses one or more arguments, any derived class must also contain a constructor function. The reason for this is to allow a means of passing arguments to the base **class**'s or **class**es' constructor function(s). To pass arguments to a base **class**, you specify them after the derived **class**'s constructor function declaration, as shown in this general form:

   derived-constructor(arg-list) :
      base1(arg-list), base2(arg-list), . . ., baseN(arg-list)

```
{
    .
    .
    .
}
```

Here, *base1* through *baseN* are the names of the base **class**es inherited by the derived **class**. Notice that the colon is used to separate the derived **class**'s constructor function from the argument lists of the base **class**es'. It is very important to understand that the argument lists associated with the base **class**es may consist of constants, global parameters, and/or the parameters to the derived **class**'s constructor function. Since an object's initialization occurs at run time, you may use as an argument any identifier that is defined within the scope of the **class**.

The following program illustrates how to pass arguments to the base **class**es of a derived **class** by modifying the preceding program:

```
#include <iostream.h>

class X {
protected:
  int a;
public:
  X(int i);
};

class Y {
protected:
  int b;
public:
  Y(int i);
} ;

// Z inherits both X and Y
class Z : public X, public Y {
public:
  Z(int x, int y);
  int make_ab(void);
} ;
```

```
X::X(int i)
{
  a = i;
}

Y::Y(int i)
{
  b = i;
}

// Initialize X and Y via Z's constructor.
// Notice that Z does not actually use x or y
// itself, but it could, if it so chooses.
Z::Z(int x, int y) : X(x), Y(y)
{
  cout << "initializing\n";
}

int Z::make_ab(void)
{
  return a*b;
}

main(void)
{
  Z i(10, 20);

  cout << i.make_ab();

  return 0;
}
```

Notice how the constructor **Z** does not actually use its parameters directly. Instead, in this example, they are simply passed along to the constructor functions for **X** and **Y**. Keep in mind, however, that there is no reason that **Z** could not use these or other arguments.

Passing Objects to Functions

An object may be passed to a function in the same way as any other data type. Objects are passed to functions using the normal C++

call-by-value parameter-passing convention. This means that a copy of the object is passed to the function, not the actual object itself. Therefore, any changes made to the object inside the function do not affect the object used to call the function. The following program illustrates this point:

```
#include <iostream.h>

class OBJ {
  int i;
public:
  void set_i(int x) { i = x; }
  void out_i() { cout << i << " "; }
};

void f(OBJ x);

main(void)
{
  OBJ o;

  o.set_i(10);
  f(o);
  o.out_i();   // still outputs 10, value of i unchanged

  return 0;
}

void f(OBJ x)
{
  x.out_i();   // outputs 10
  x.set_i(100);  // this affects only local copy
  x.out_i();   // outputs 100
}
```

As you will see later in this book, it is also possible to pass only the address of an object to a function. When an address to an object is passed, then alterations made to the object inside the function will, indeed, affect the object used in the call.

Arrays of Objects

You can create arrays of objects in just the same way that you create arrays of any other data types. For example, the following program establishes a class called **display**, which holds information about the various display monitors that can be attached to a PC. Specifically, it contains the number of colors that can be displayed and the type of video adapter. Inside **main( )**, an array of three **display** objects is created and the objects that comprise the elements of the array are accessed via the normal indexing procedure.

```
// An example of arrays of objects

#include <iostream.h>

enum disp_type {mono, cga, ega, vga};

class display {
  int colors;  // number of colors
  enum disp_type dt; // display type
public:
  void set_colors(int num) {colors = num;}
  int get_colors() {return colors;}
  void set_type(enum disp_type t) {dt = t;}
  enum disp_type get_type() {return dt;}
} ;

char names[4][5] = {
  "mono",
  "cga",
  "ega",
  "vga"
} ;

main(void)
{
  display monitors[3];
  register int i;

  monitors[0].set_type(mono);
  monitors[0].set_colors(1);
```

```
monitors[1].set_type(cga);
monitors[1].set_colors(4);

monitors[2].set_type(vga);
monitors[2].set_colors(16);

for(i=0; i<3; i++) {
  cout << names[monitors[i].get_type()] << " ";
  cout << "has " << monitors[i].get_colors();
  cout << " colors" << "\n";
}

return 0;
}
```

This program produces the following output:

```
mono has 1 colors
cga has 4 colors
vga has 16 colors
```

Although not related to arrays of objects, notice how the two-dimensional character array **names** is used to convert between an enumerated value and its equivalent character string. In all enumerations that do not contain explicit initializations, the first constant has the value 0, the second 1, and so on. Therefore, the value returned by **get_type( )** can be used to index the **names** array, causing the appropriate name to be printed.

Multidimensional arrays of objects are indexed in precisely the same way as arrays of other types of data.

Pointers to Objects

As you know, in C you may access a structure directly or through a pointer to that structure. In like fashion, in C++ you may reference an object either directly (as has been the case in all preceding examples) or by using a pointer to that object. As you will see later on, pointers to objects are among C++'s most important features.

As you know, to access an element of an object when using the actual object itself, you use the dot (.) operator. To access a specific element of an object when using a pointer to the object, you must use the arrow operator (−>). (The use of the dot and arrow operators for objects parallels their use for structures and unions.)

You declare an object pointer by using the same declaration syntax as you do for any other type of data. The following program creates a simple **class** called **P_example** and defines an object of that **class** called **ob** and a pointer to an object of type **P_example** called **p**. It then illustrates how to access **ob** directly and indirectly using a pointer.

```
// A simple example using an object pointer.

#include <iostream.h>

class P_example {
  int num;
public:
  void set_num(int val) {num = val;}
  void show_num();
};

void P_example::show_num()
{
  cout << num << "\n";
}

main(void)
{
  P_example ob, *p; // declare an object and pointer to it

  ob.set_num(1); // access ob directly

  ob.show_num();

  p = &ob; // assign p the address of ob
```

```
    p->show_num();   // access ob using pointer

    return 0;
}
```

Notice that the address of **ob** is obtained by using the **&** (address of) operator in the same way that the address is obtained for any type of variable.

As you know, when a pointer is incremented or decremented, it is increased or decreased in such a way that it will always point to the next element of its base type. The same thing occurs when a pointer to an object is incremented or decremented: the next object is pointed to. To illustrate this, the preceding program has been modified so that **ob** is a two-element array of type **P_example**. Notice how **p** is incremented and decremented to access the two elements in the array.

```
// Incrementing an object pointer
#include <iostream.h>

class P_example {
  int num;
public:
  void set_num(int val) {num = val;}
  void show_num();
};

void P_example::show_num()
{
  cout << num << "\n";
}

main(void)
{
  P_example ob[2], *p;

  ob[0].set_num(10);   // access objects directly
  ob[1].set_num(20);

  p = &ob[0];  // obtain pointer to first element
  p->show_num(); // show value of ob[0] using pointer

  p++;   // advance to next object
```

```
    p->show_num(); // show value of ob[1] using pointer

    p--;  // retreat to previous object
    p->show_num(); // again show value of ob[0]

    return 0;
}
```

The output from this program is 10, 20, 10.

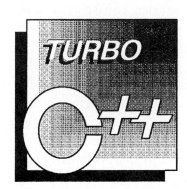

Function and Operator Overloading

In Chapter 16 you were introduced to function overloading. This chapter examines more issues relating to this topic and also discusses operator overloading. These are two of C++'s most important features. In the course of these discussions, other related topics are also introduced.

Overloading Constructor Functions

Although they perform a unique service, constructor functions are not much different from other types of functions and they, too, can be overloaded. To overload a **class**'s constructor function, simply declare the various forms it will take and define its action relative to these forms. For example, the following program declares a **class** called **timer**, which acts as a countdown timer (such as a darkroom timer). When an object of type **timer** is created, it is given an initial time value. When the **run( )** function is called, the timer counts down to zero and then rings the bell. In this example, the constructor has been overloaded to allow the time to be specified as an integer, a string, or as two integers specifying minutes and seconds.

This program makes use of Turbo C++'s **clock( )** function, which returns the number of system clock ticks since the program began running. Dividing this value by the macro **CLK_TCK** converts the return value of **clock( )** into seconds. Both the prototype for **clock( )** and the definition of **CLK_TCK** are found in the header file TIME.H.

```
#include <iostream.h>
#include <stdlib.h>
#include <time.h>

class timer{
  int seconds;
public:
  // seconds specified as a string
  timer(char *t) { seconds = atoi(t); }

  // seconds specified as integer
  timer(int t) { seconds = t; }

  // time specified in minutes and seconds
  timer(int min, int sec) { seconds = min*60 + sec; }
```

```
   void run(void);
} ;

void timer::run(void)
{
  clock_t t1, t2;

  t1 = t2 = clock()/CLK_TCK;
  while(seconds) {
    if(t1/CLK_TCK+1 <= (t2=clock())/CLK_TCK) {
       seconds--;
       t1 = t2;
    }
  }
  cout << "\a"; // ring the bell
}

main(void)
{
  timer a(10), b("20"), c(1, 10);

  a.run(); // count 10 seconds
  b.run(); // count 20 seconds
  c.run(); // count 1 minute, 10 seconds
  return 0;
}
```

As you can see, when **a**, **b**, and **c** are created inside **main( )**, they are given initial values using the three different methods supported by the overloaded constructor functions. Each approach causes the appropriate constructor to be utilized, thus properly initializing all three variables.

In the program just shown, you may see little value in overloading a constructor function because it is not difficult to simply decide on a single way to specify the time. However, if you were creating a library of **class**es for someone else to use, then you might want to supply constructors for the most common forms of initialization to give the user the most flexibility. Also, as you will see shortly, there is one C++ attribute that makes overloaded constructors quite valuable.

Local Variables in C++

Before continuing with the discussion of overloaded functions, a small digression that deals with the declaration of local variables is required.

In C, you must declare all local variables used within a block at the start of that block. You cannot declare a variable in a block after another statement has occurred. For example, in C, this fragment is incorrect:

```
/* incorrect in C */
f()
{
  int i;

  i = 10;

  int j;
    .
    .
    .
}
```

Because the statement **i = 10** intervenes between the declaration of **i** and that of **j**, a C compiler will flag an error and refuse to compile this function. However, in C++, this fragment is perfectly acceptable and will compile without error. For example, the following is a perfectly acceptable C++ program:

```
#include <iostream.h>
#include <string.h>

main(void)
{
  int i;

  i = 10;

  int j = 100; // perfectly legal in C++
```

```
cout << i*j << "\n";

cout << "Enter a string: ";
char str[80];
cin >> str;

// display the string in reverse order
int k;  // declare k where it is needed
k = strlen(str);
k--;
while(k>=0) {
  cout << str[k];
  k--;
}
return 0;
}
```

As this program illustrates, in C++ you may declare local variables anywhere within a block of code. Since much of the philosophy behind C++ is the encapsulation of code and data, it makes sense that you can declare variables close to where they are used instead of just at the beginning of the block. In this example, the declarations of **i** and **j** are separated simply for illustration. However, you can see how the localization of **k** to its relevant code helps encapsulate that routine. Declaring variables close to their use can help you avoid accidental side effects.

Dynamic Initialization

In C++, both local and global variables can be initialized at run time. This is sometimes referred to as *dynamic initialization*. Remember that in C, a variable must be initialized using a constant expression. The reason for this is that a C compiler fixes the initialization code at compile time. However, in C++, a variable can be initialized at run time using any C++ expression that is valid at the time the variable is declared. For example, these are perfectly valid variable initializations in C++:

```
.
.
.
int n = atoi(gets(str));

long pos = ftell(fp);

double d = 1.02 * count / deltax;
```

You can make use of dynamic initialization to improve the example program from the previous section, as shown here:

```
#include <iostream.h>
#include <string.h>

main(void)
{
  int i;

  i = 10;

  int j = 100;

  cout << i*j << "\n";

  cout << "Enter a string: ";
  char str[80];
  cin >> str;

  // initialize k dynamically at runtime
  int k = strlen(str)-1;

  while(k>=0) {
    cout << str[k];
    k--;
  }
  return 0;
}
```

Here, **k** is dynamically initialized because the call to **strlen( )** is resolved at run time.

Applying Dynamic Initialization to Constructors

Like simple variables, objects can be initialized dynamically when they are created. This feature allows you to create exactly the type of object you need using information that is known only at run time. To illustrate how dynamic initialization works, let's rework the timer program from earlier in this chapter.

In the first example of the timer program there is little to be gained by overloading the **timer( )** constructor because all objects of its type were initialized using constants. However, in cases where an object will be initialized at run time, there may be significant advantages in allowing various initialization formats to be used. This allows the programmer the flexibility of using the constructor that most closely matches the format of the data at any given time. For example, in this version of the timer program, two objects, **b** and **c**, are constructed at run time using dynamic initialization:

```
#include <iostream.h>
#include <stdlib.h>
#include <time.h>

class timer{
  int seconds;
public:
  // seconds specified as a string
  timer(char *t) { seconds = atoi(t); }

  // seconds specified as integer
  timer(int t) { seconds = t; }

  // time specified in minutes and seconds
  timer(int min, int sec) { seconds = min*60 + sec; }

  void run(void);
} ;

void timer::run(void)
```

```
{
  clock_t tl, t2;

  tl = t2 = clock()/CLK_TCK;
  while(seconds) {
    if(tl/CLK_TCK+1 <= (t2=clock())/CLK_TCK) {
        seconds--;
        tl = t2;
    }
  }
  cout << "\a"; // ring the bell
}

main(void)
{
  timer a(10);

  a.run();

  cout << "Enter number of seconds: ";
  char str[80];
  cin >> str;
  timer b(str);  // initialize at runtime
  b.run();

  cout << "Enter minutes and seconds: ";
  int min, sec;
  cin >> min >> sec;
  timer c(min, sec);  // initialize at runtime
  c.run();
  return 0;
}
```

As you can see, object **a** is constructed using an integer constant. However, objects **b** and **c** are constructed using information entered by the user. For **b**, since the user enters a string, it makes sense for **timer( )** to be overloaded to accept it. In a similar fashion, object **c** is also constructed at run time using user-input information. In this case, since the time is entered as minutes and seconds, it is logical to use this form to construct object **c**. By allowing various initialization formats, you (the programmer) need not perform any unnecessary conversions from one form to the other when initializing an object.

The point of overloading constructor functions is to help the programmer to handle greater complexity by allowing objects to be constructed in the most natural manner relative to their specific uses. Since there are three common ways to pass timing values to an object, it makes sense that **timer( )** be overloaded to accept each way. However, overloading **timer( )** to accept hours or days, or even nanoseconds, is probably not a good idea because littering your code with constructors to handle seldom-used contingencies has a destabilizing influence on your program. The point here is that you must decide what constitutes valid constructor overloading and what is frivolous.

The this Keyword

Before moving on to operator overloading, it is necessary for you to learn about another of C++'s keywords, called **this**, which is an essential ingredient for many overloaded operators.

Each time a member function is invoked, it is automatically passed a pointer to the object that invoked it. You can access this pointer using **this**. Furthermore, this pointer is automatically passed to a member function when it is called. The **this** pointer is an *implicit* parameter to all member functions.

As you know, a member function may directly access the **private** data of its **class**. For example, given this **class**

```
class cl {
  int i;
  .
  .
  .
};
```

a member function can assign **i** the value 10 using this statement:

```
i = 10;
```

Actually, the preceding statement is shorthand for this statement:

```
this->i = 10;
```

To see how the **this** pointer works, examine the following short program:

```
#include <iostream.h>

class cl {
  int i;
public:
  void load_i(int val) { this->i = val; } // same as i = val
  int get_i(void) { return this->i; } // same as return i
} ;

void main(void)
{
  cl o;

  o.load_i(100);
  cout << o.get_i();
}
```

This program displays the number 100.

While the preceding example is trivial—in fact, no one would actually use the **this** pointer in this way—in the next section you will see why the **this** pointer is so important.

Operator Overloading

Another feature of C++, which is related to function overloading, is called *operator overloading*. With very few exceptions, most of C++'s operators may be given special meanings relative to specific **class**es. For example, a **class** that defines a linked list might use the **+** operator to add an object to the list. Another **class** might use the + operator in an entirely different way. When an operator is overloaded, none of its original meaning is lost. It is simply that a new operation relative to a specific **class** is defined. Therefore, overloading the + to handle a linked list does not cause its meaning relative to integers (that is, addition) to be changed, for example.

To overload an operator you must define what that operation means relative to the **class** that it is applied to. To do this you create an **operator** function, which defines its action. The general form of an **operator** function is shown here:

```
type classname::operator#(arg-list)
{
  // operation defined relative to the class
}
```

Here, *type* is the type of value returned by the specified operation. Often, the return value is of the same type as the **class** (although it could be of any type you choose). The reason that an overloaded operator often has a return value that is of the same type as the **class** for which the operator is overloaded is that it facilitates its use in complex expressions, as you will soon see.

Operator functions must be either members or **friends** of the **class** for which they are being used. Although very similar, there are some differences between the way a member operator function is overloaded and the way a **friend** operator function is overloaded. In this section, only member functions will be overloaded. Later, you will see how to overload **friend** operator functions.

To see how operator overloading works, let's start with a simple example that creates a **class** called **three_d**, which maintains the coordinates of an object in three-dimensional space. This program overloads the + and the = operators relative to the **three_d class**. Examine it closely.

```
#include <iostream.h>

class three_d {
  int x, y, z; // 3-d coordinates
public:
  three_d operator+(three_d t);
  three_d operator=(three_d t);

  void show(void) ;
  void assign(int mx, int my, int mz);
} ;

// Overload the +.
three_d three_d::operator+(three_d t)
{
  three_d temp;

  temp.x = x+t.x;
  temp.y = y+t.y;
  temp.z = z+t.z;
  return temp;
}

// Overload the =.
three_d three_d::operator=(three_d t)
{
  x = t.x;
  y = t.y;
  z = t.z;
  return *this;
}

// show X, Y, Z coordinates
void three_d::show(void)
{
  cout << x << ", ";
  cout << y << ", ";
  cout << z << "\n";
}

// Assign coordinates
void three_d::assign(int mx, int my, int mz)
{
  x = mx;
  y = my;
  z = mz;
}
```

```
main(void)
{
  three_d a, b, c;

  a.assign(1, 2, 3);
  b.assign(10, 10, 10);

  a.show();
  b.show();

  c = a+b;   // now add a and b together
  c.show();

  c = a+b+c; // add a, b and c together
  c.show();

  c = b = a;   // demonstrate multiple assignment
  c.show();
  b.show();
  return 0;
}
```

This program produces the following output:

```
1, 2, 3
10, 10, 10
11, 12, 13
22, 24, 26
1, 2, 3
1, 2, 3
```

As you examined this program, you may have been surprised to see that both operator functions had only one parameter each, even though they overloaded binary operations. The reason for this apparent contradiction is that when a binary operator is overloaded using a member function, only one argument need be passed to it explicitly. The other argument is implicitly passed using the **this** pointer. Thus, in the line

```
temp.x = x + t.x;
```

the **x** refers to **this** —> **x**, which is the **x** associated with the object that prompted the call to the operator function. In all cases, it is the object on the left side of an operation that causes the call to the operator function. The object on the right side is passed to the function.

In general, when you are using a member function, no parameters are needed for overloading a unary operator, and only one parameter is required for overloading a binary operator. (You cannot overload the **?** ternary operator.) In either case, the object that causes the activation of the operator function is implicitly passed by the **this** pointer.

To understand how operator overloading works, let's examine this program carefully, beginning with the overloaded **+** operator. When two objects of type **three _ d** are operated on by the **+** operator, the magnitudes of their respective coordinates are added together, as shown in the **operator +** ( ) function associated with this **class**. Notice, however, that this function does not modify the value of either operand. Instead, an object of type **three _ d** is returned by the function that contains the result of the operation. This is an important point.

To understand why the **+** operation must not change the contents of either object, think about the standard arithmetic **+** operation 10 + 12. The outcome of this operation is 22, but neither 10 nor 12 is changed by it. Although there is no rule that states that an overloaded operator must perform in the same way as it does for any of C++'s built-in types, it usually makes sense to stay within the spirit of its original use.

Another key point about how the **+** operator is overloaded is that it returns an object of type **three _ d**. Although the function could have returned any valid C++ type, the fact that it returns a **three _ d** object allows the **+** operator to be used in more complex expressions, such as **a + b + c**.

Contrasting with the **+** operator, the assignment operator does, indeed, cause one of its arguments to be modified. (This is, after all, the very essence of assignment.) Since the **operator =** ( )

function is called by the object that occurs on the left side of the assignment, it is this object that is modified by the assignment operation. However, even the assignment operation must return a value because, in C++ (as well as in C), the assignment operation produces the value that occurs on the right side. Thus, to allow statements like

```
a = b = c = d;
```

it is necessary for **operator=( )** to return the object pointed to by **this**, which will be the object that occurs on the left side of the assignment statement. This allows a string of assignments to be made.

You may also overload unary operators, such as **+ +** or **− −**. As stated earlier, when overloading a unary operator, no object is explicitly passed to the operator function. Instead, the operation is performed on the object that generates the call to the function through the implicitly passed **this** pointer. For example, here is an expanded version of the previous example program that defines the increment operation for objects of type **three＿d**:

```
#include <iostream.h>

class three_d {
  int x, y, z; // 3-d coordinates
public:
  three_d operator+(three_d op2);  // op1 is implied
  three_d operator=(three_d op2);  // op1 is implied
  three_d operator++(void); // op1 is also implied here

  void show(void) ;
  void assign(int mx, int my, int mz);
} ;

three_d three_d::operator+(three_d op2)
{
  three_d temp;

  temp.x = x+op2.x;  // these are integer additions
```

```
      temp.y = y+op2.y;   // and the + retains its original
      temp.z = z+op2.z;   // meaning relative to them
      return temp;
}

three_d three_d::operator=(three_d op2)
{
  x = op2.x; // these are integer assigments
  y = op2.y; // and the = retains its original
  z = op2.z; // meaning relative to them
  return *this;
}

// Overload a unary operator.
three_d three_d::operator++(void)
{
  x++;
  y++;
  z++;
  return *this;
}

// show X, Y, Z coordinates
void three_d::show(void)
{
  cout << x << ", ";
  cout << y << ", ";
  cout << z << "\n";
}

// Assign coordinates
void three_d::assign(int mx, int my, int mz)
{
  x = mx;
  y = my;
  z = mz;
}

main(void)
{
  three_d a, b, c;

  a.assign(1, 2, 3);
  b.assign(10, 10, 10);

  a.show();
  b.show();
```

```
    c = a+b;   // now add a and b together
    c.show();

    c = a+b+c; // add a, b and c together
    c.show();

    c = b = a;  // demonstrate multiple assignment
    c.show();
    b.show();

    c++;  // increment c
    c.show();
    return 0;
}
```

One important point to keep in mind when you overload **+ +** or **− −** is that it is not possible to determine from within the **operator** function whether the operator precedes or follows its operand. That is, your **operator** function cannot know whether the expression that causes the call to the function is

```
++OBJ;
```

or

```
OBJ++;
```

where **OBJ** is the object being subjected to the operation.

The action of an overloaded operator as applied to the **class** for which it is defined need not bear any relationship to that operator's default usage as applied to C++'s built-in types. For example, << and >> as applied to **cout** and **cin** have nothing in common with the same operators applied to integer types. However, for the purposes of the structure and readability of your code, an overloaded operator should reflect, when possible, the spirit of the operator's original use. For example, + relative to **three _ d** is conceptually similar to + relative to integer types. There is little benefit, for example, in defining the + operator relative to some **class** in such a way that it acts in some completely unexpected way. The key concept here is that while you may give an overloaded operator any meaning you like, it is best, for clarity, when that new meaning is related to its original meaning.

Some restrictions to overloading operators also apply. First, you may not alter the precedence of any operator. Second, you cannot alter the number of operands required by the operator, although your **operator( )** function could choose to ignore an operand. Finally, except for the =, overloaded operators are inherited by any derived **class**es. (Of course, you may overload operators relative to the derived **class** if necessary.) Each **class** must explicitly define its own overloaded = operator if one is needed.

The only operators you may not overload are shown here:

.   ::   .*   ?

Friend Operator Functions

It is possible for an operator function to be a **friend** of a **class** rather than a member. As you learned earlier in this chapter, **friend** functions do not have the implied argument **this**. Therefore, when a **friend** is used to overload an operator, both operands are passed explicitly to an operator when overloading binary operators, and a single operand is passed when overloading unary operators. The only operators that cannot use **friend** functions are =, ( ), [], and −>. The rest may use either member or **friend** functions to implement the specified operation relative to its **class**. For example, here is a modified version of the preceding program that uses a **friend** instead of a member function to overload the + operation:

```
#include <iostream.h>

class three_d {
```

```
      int x, y, z; // 3-d coordinates
  public:
      friend three_d operator+(three_d op1, three_d op2);
      three_d operator=(three_d op2);  // op1 is implied
      three_d operator++(void); // op1 is implied here, too

      void show(void) ;
      void assign(int mx, int my, int mz);
  } ;

  // This is now a friend function.
  three_d operator+(three_d op1, three_d op2)
  {
      three_d temp;

      temp.x = op1.x + op2.x;  // these are integer additions
      temp.y = op1.y + op2.y;  // and the + retains its original
      temp.z = op1. z+ op2.z;  // meaning relative to them
      return temp;
  }

  three_d three_d::operator=(three_d op2)
  {
      x = op2.x; // these are integer assigments
      y = op2.y; // and the = retains its original
      z = op2.z; // meaning relative to them
      return *this;
  }

  // Overload a unary operator.
  three_d three_d::operator++(void)
  {
      x++;
      y++;
      z++;
      return *this;
  }

  // show X, Y, Z coordinates
  void three_d::show(void)
  {
      cout << x << ", ";
      cout << y << ", ";
      cout << z << "\n";
  }

  // Assign coordinates
  void three_d::assign(int mx, int my, int mz)
  {
      x = mx;
```

```
   y = my;
   z = mz;
}

main(void)
{
  three_d a, b, c;

  a.assign(1, 2, 3);
  b.assign(10, 10, 10);

  a.show();
  b.show();

  c = a+b;   // now add a and b together
  c.show();

  c = a+b+c; // add a, b and c together
  c.show();

  c = b = a;   // demonstrate multiple assignment
  c.show();
  b.show();

  c++;   // increment c
  c.show();
  return 0;
}
```

As you can see, now both operands are passed to **operator+( )**. The left operand is passed in **op1** and the right operand in **op2**.

In many cases, there is no benefit to using a **friend** function instead of a member function when overloading an operator. However, there is one situation in which you must use a **friend** function. Here is why. As you know, a pointer to the object that invokes a member operator function is passed in **this**. In the case of binary operators, the object on the left invokes the function. This is fine provided that the object on the left defines the specified operation. For example, assuming some object called **O** has assignment and addition defined for it, then this is a perfectly valid statement:

```
O = O + 10; // will work
```

Since the object **O** is on the left of the + operator, it invokes its overloaded operator function, which is presumably capable of adding an integer value to some element of **O**. However, this statement will not work:

```
O = 10 + O; // won't work
```

The reason is that the object on the left is an integer, which is a built-in type for which no operation involving an integer and an object of **O**'s type is defined.

The problem of built-in types on the left side of an operation can be eliminated if + is overloaded using two **friend** functions. In this case, the operator function is explicitly passed both arguments and it is invoked like any other overloaded function, based on the types of its arguments. Overloading the + (or any other binary operator) using a **friend** allows a built-in type to occur on the left side of the operator. The following program illustrates how to accomplish this:

```
#include <iostream.h>

class CL {
public:
  int count;
  CL operator=(int i);
  friend CL operator+(CL ob, int i);
  friend CL operator+(int i, CL ob);
};

CL CL::operator=(int i)
{
  count = i;
  return *this;
}

// This handles ob + int.
CL operator+(CL ob, int i)
{
  CL temp;
```

```
    temp.count = ob.count + i;
    return temp;
}

// This handles int + ob.
CL operator+(int i, CL ob)
{
  CL temp;

  temp.count = ob.count + i;
  return temp;
}

main(void)
{
  CL obj;

  obj = 10;
  cout << obj.count << " "; // outputs 10

  obj = 10 + obj; // add object to integer
  cout << obj.count << " "; // outputs 20

  obj = obj + 12; // add integer to object
  cout << obj.count;         // outputs 32
  return 0;
}
```

As you can see, the **operator+( )** function is overloaded twice to accommodate the two ways in which an integer and an object of type **CL** may occur in the addition operation.

Although you may use a **friend** function to overload a unary operator such as **+ +**, you first need to know about another feature of C++ called the *reference,* which is the subject of the next section.

References

By default, C and C++ pass arguments to a function using call-by-value. As you know, passing an argument using call-by-value causes a copy of that argument to be used by the function and prevents the argument used in the call from being modified by the function. In C (and optionally in C++), when a function needs to be able to alter the values of the variables used as arguments, the parameters need to be explicitly declared as pointer types and the function must operate on the calling variables using the * pointer operator. For example, the following program implements a function called **swap( )** that exchanges its two integer arguments:

```
#include <iostream.h>

void swap(int *a, int *b);

main(void)
{
  int i, j;

  i = 10;
  j = 20;

  cout << i << " " << j << "\n";

  swap(&i, &j); // exchange their values

  cout << i << " " << j << "\n";
  return 0;
}

// C-like, explicit pointer version of swap().
void swap(int *a, int *b)
{
  int t;

  t = *a;
  *a = *b;
  *b = t;
}
```

When calling **swap( )**, the variables used in the call must be preceded by the **&** operator in order to produce a pointer to each argument. This is the way that a call-by-reference is generated in C. However, even though C++ still allows this syntax, it supports a cleaner, more transparent method of generating a call-by-reference using what is called a *reference parameter.*

In C++, it is possible to tell the compiler to automatically generate a call-by-reference rather than a call-by-value for one or more parameters of a particular function. This is accomplished by preceding the parameter name in the function's declaration by the **&**. For example, here is a function called **f( )**, which takes one reference parameter of type **float**:

```
void f(int &f)
{
  f = rand(); // this modifies calling argument
}
```

This declaration form is also used in the function's prototype. Notice that the statement **f = rand( )** does not use the * pointer operator. When you declare a reference parameter, the C++ compiler automatically knows that it is a pointer and dereferences it for you.

Once the compiler has seen this declaration, it will automatically pass **f( )** the *address* of any variable it is called with. For example, given this fragment

```
int val;

f(val);   // get random value
printf("%d", val);
```

the address of **val**, *not its value,* will be passed to **f( )**. Thus, **f( )** may modify the value of **val**.

If you are familar with Pascal, it may help to know that a reference parameter in C++ is similar to a **VAR** parameter in Pascal.

To see reference parameters in actual use, the **swap( )** function is rewritten using references in this version of the program. Look carefully at how **swap( )** is declared and called.

```
#include <iostream.h>

void swap(int &a, int &b); // declare as reference parameters

main(void)
{
  int i, j;

  i = 10;
  j = 20;

  cout << i << " " << j << "\n";

  swap(i, j); // exchange their values

  cout << i << " " << j << "\n";
  return 0;
}

// Here, swap() is defined as using call-by-reference,
// not call-by-value.
void swap(int &a, int &b)
{
  int t;

  t = a;
  a = b;   // this swaps i
  b = t;   // this swaps j
}
```

Stylistic Note: Some C++ programmers associate the **&** with the type rather than the variable. For example, here is another way to write the prototype to **swap( )**:

```
void swap(int& a, int& b);
```

Furthermore, some C++ programmers also specify pointers by associating the ***** with the type rather than the variable, as shown here:

```
float* p;
```

These types of declarations reflect the desire by some programmers for C++ to contain a separate pointer type. However, the trouble with associating the **&** or * with the type rather than the variable is that, according to the C++ syntax, neither the **&** nor the * is transitive over a list of variables and can lead to confusing declarations. For example, the following declaration creates one, not two, integer pointers. Here, **b** is declared as an integer because, as specified by the C++ syntax, when used in a declaration, the * and **&** are linked to the individual variable that they precede, not to the type that they follow.

```
int* a, b;
```

It is important to understand that as far as the C++ compiler is concerned, it does not matter whether you write **int *p** or **int* p**. Thus, if you prefer to associate * or **&** with the type rather than the variable, feel free to do so. However, to avoid confusion, this book will continue to associate * and **&** with the variable that is modified rather than the type.

Non-Parameter Reference Variables

Even though references are included in C++ primarily for supporting call-by-reference parameter passing, it is possible to declare a reference variable that is not a parameter to a function. It must be stated at the outset, however, that non-parameter reference variables are seldom a good idea because they tend to confuse and destructure your program. With these reservations in mind, let's take a short look at them here.

Non-parameter reference variables are sometimes called *independent* or *stand-alone references*. Since a reference variable must point to some object, an independent reference must be initialized when it is declared. Generally, this means that it will be assigned the address of a previously declared variable. Once this is done, the reference variable may be used anywhere that the variable it references may be used. In fact, there is virtually no distinction between the two. For example, consider this program:

```
#include <iostream.h>

main(void)
{
  int j, k;
  int &i = j;

  j = 10;

  cout << j << " " << i; // outputs 10 10

  k = 121;
  i = k; // copies k's value into j
         // not k's address

  cout << "\n" << j;  // outputs 121
  return 0;
}
```

The program displays this output:

```
10 10
121
```

The key point is that the object pointed to by the reference variable is fixed. Thus, when the statement **i = k** is evaluated, it is **k**'s value that is copied into **j** (pointed to by **i**), not its address. In other words, references are not pointers.

There are several restrictions that apply to stand-alone reference variables. First, you cannot reference a reference variable.

That is, you cannot take its address. Second, references are not allowed on bit-fields. Third, you cannot create arrays of references. Finally, you cannot create a pointer to a reference.

You may also use an independent reference to point to a constant. For example, this is valid:

```
int &i = 100;
```

In this case, **i** references the location in your program's constant table where the value 100 is stored.

As stated earlier, in general it is not a good idea to use independent references because they are not necessary and tend to confuse your code.

Using a Reference to Overload a Unary Operator

In the final version of the timer program from the preceding section, the **++** operator was not overloaded using a **friend** function because it required the use of a reference. In this section you will learn why.

To begin, think back to the original version of the overloaded **++** operator relative to the **three_d class**. It is shown here for your convenience:

```
// Overload a unary operator.
three_d three_d::operator++(void)
{
  x++;
  y++;
  z++;
  return *this;
}
```

As you know, all member functions have as an implicit argument a pointer to themselves, which is referenced inside the member function using the keyword **this**. This is why, when overloading a unary operator using a member function, no argument is explicitly declared. The only argument needed in this situation is the implicit pointer to the object that activated the call to the overloaded operator function. Since **this** is a pointer to the object, any changes made to the object's private data will affect the object that generates the call to the operator function. Unlike member functions, **friend** functions do not receive a **this** pointer and therefore cannot reference the object that activated it. For this reason, trying to create a **friend operator + +( )** function as shown here will not work:

```
// THIS WILL NOT WORK
three_d operator++(three_d op1)
{
  op1.x++;
  op1.y++;
  op1.z++;
  return op1;
}
```

The reason this function will not work is because only a *copy* of the object that activated the call to **operator + +( )** is passed to the function in parameter **op1**. Thus, the changes inside **operator + +( )** will not affect the called object.

You might at first think that the solution to this program is to define the **friend** operator function as shown here, using a pointer to the object that activates the call:

```
// THIS WILL NOT WORK
three_d operator++(three_d *op1)
{
  op1->x++;
  op1->y++;
  op1->z++;
```

```
    return *opl;
}
```

While this function is correct as far as it goes, C++ does not know
how to correctly activate it. For example, assuming this version of
the **operator+ +( )** function, this code fragment will not compile:

```
three_d ob(l, 2, 3);

&ob++;  // will not compile
```

The trouble here is that the statement **&ob+ +** is inherently
ambiguous.

The way to use a **friend** when overloading a unary **+ +** or **− −**
is to use a reference parameter. In this way the compiler knows in
advance that it must generate an address when it calls the
function. This avoids the ambiguity introduced by the previous
attempt. Here is the entire **three_d** program using a **friend
operator+ +( )** function:

```
// This version uses a friend operator++() function.
#include <iostream.h>

class three_d {
  int x, y, z; // 3-d coordinates
public:
  friend three_d operator+(three_d opl, three_d op2);
  three_d operator=(three_d op2);  // opl is implied
  // use a reference to overload the ++
  friend three_d operator++(three_d &opl);

  void show(void) ;
  void assign(int mx, int my, int mz);
} ;

// This is now a friend function.
three_d operator+(three_d opl, three_d op2)
{
  three_d temp;

  temp.x = opl.x + op2.x;  // these are integer additions
  temp.y = opl.y + op2.y;  // and the + retains its original
  temp.z = opl.z + op2.z;  // meaning relative to them
  return temp;
```

```
}

three_d three_d::operator=(three_d op2)
{
  x = op2.x; // these are integer assigments
  y = op2.y; // and the = retains its original
  z = op2.z; // meaning relative to them
  return *this;
}

// Overload a unary operator using a friend function.
// This requires the use of a reference parameter.
three_d operator++(three_d &op1)
{
  op1.x++;
  op1.y++;
  op1.z++;
  return op1;
}

// show X, Y, Z coordinates
void three_d::show(void)
{
  cout << x << ", ";
  cout << y << ", ";
  cout << z << "\n";
}

// Assign coordinates
void three_d::assign(int mx, int my, int mz)
{
  x = mx;
  y = my;
  z = mz;
}

main(void)
{
  three_d a, b, c;

  a.assign(1, 2, 3);
  b.assign(10, 10, 10);

  a.show();
  b.show();

  c = a+b;  // now add a and b together
  c.show();

  c = a+b+c; // add a, b and c together
```

```
    c.show();

    c = b = a;   // demonstrate multiple assignment
    c.show();
    b.show();

    c++;  // increment c
    c.show();
    return 0;
}
```

Keep in mind one important point: In general, you should use member functions to implement overloaded operators. Remember that **friend** functions are allowed in C++ mostly to handle some special-case situations.

Another Example of Operator Overloading

To close this chapter, another example of operator overloading will be developed. This example implements a string type and defines several operations relative to that type. As you might know, many newcomers to C (and C++) complain about the lack of an explicit string type. Even though C's approach to strings is more flexible and efficiently implemented as character arrays rather than as a type unto itself, to beginners it can still lack the conceptual clarity of the way strings are implemented in languages such as BASIC. However, using C++ it is possible to combine the best of both worlds by defining a string **class** and operations that relate to that class.

To begin, the following **class** declares the type **str_type**:

```
#include <iostream.h>
#include <string.h>

class str_type {
```

```
      char string[80];
public:
      str_type(char *str = "\0") { strcpy(string, str); }

      str_type operator+(str_type str); // concatenate
      str_type operator=(str_type str); // assign

      // output the string
      void show_str(void) { cout << string; }
} ;
```

As you can see, **str _ type** declares one string in its private portion. For the sake of this example, no string can be longer than 80 bytes. The **class** has one constructor function, which can be used to initialize the array **string** with a specific value, or to assign it a null string in the absence of any initializer. It also declares two overloaded operators that will perform concatenation and assignment. Finally, it declares the function **show _ str( )**, which outputs **string** to the screen. The overloaded operator functions are shown here:

```
// Concatenate two strings.
str_type str_type::operator+(str_type str) {
  str_type temp;

  strcpy(temp.string, string);
  strcat(temp.string, str.string);
  return temp;
}

// Assign one string to another.
str_type str_type::operator=(str_type str) {
  strcpy(string, str.string);
  return *this;
}
```

Given these definitions, the following **main( )** function illustrates their use:

```
main(void)
{
  str_type a("Hello "), b("There"), c;
```

```
  c = a + b;

  c.show_str();
  return 0;
}
```

This program outputs "Hello There" on the screen. It first concatenates **a** with **b** and then assigns this value to **c**. Keep in mind that both = and the + are defined only for objects of type **str_type**. For example, this statement is invalid because it tries to assign object **a** a normal C++ string:

```
a = "this is currently wrong";
```

However, the **str_type class** can be enhanced to allow such a statement, as you will see next.

To expand the types of operations supported by the **str_type class** so that you can assign strings to objects or concatenate a string with an object, you will need to overload the + and = operations a second time. First, the **class** declaration is changed, as shown here:

```
class str_type {
  char string[80];
public:
  str_type(char *str = "\0") { strcpy(string, str); }

  str_type operator+(str_type str); // concatenate objects
  str_type operator+(char *str);   // concatenate object with
                                   // a string

  str_type operator=(str_type str); // assign object to
                                   // object
  char *operator=(char *str); // assign string to object

  void show_str(void) { cout << string; }
} ;
```

Next, the overloaded **operator+( )** and **operator=( )** are implemented, as shown here:

```
// Assign a string to an object
str_type str_type::operator=(char *str)
{
  str_type temp;

  strcpy(string, str);
  strcpy(temp.string, string);
  return temp;
}

// Add a string to an object
str_type str_type::operator+(char *str)
{
  str_type temp;

  strcpy(temp.string, string);
  strcat(temp.string, str);
  return temp;
}
```

Look carefully at these functions. Notice that the right-side argument is not an object of type **str _ type** but rather simply a pointer to a null-terminated character array—that is, a normal string in C++. However, notice that both functions return an object of type **str _ type**. Although the functions could, in theory, have returned some other type, it makes the most sense to return an object since the targets of these operations are also objects. The advantage to defining string operations that accept normal C++ strings as the right-side operand is that it allows some statements to be written in a natural way. For example, these are now valid statements:

```
str_type a, b, c;

a = "hi there";  // assign an object a string

c = a + " George";  // concatenate an object with a string
```

The following program incorporates the additional meanings for the **+** and **=** operations and illustrates their use:

```
// Expanding the string type.
#include <iostream.h>
#include <string.h>
```

```
class str_type {
  char string[80];
public:
  str_type(char *str = "\0") { strcpy(string, str); }

  str_type operator+(str_type str);
  str_type operator+(char *str);

  str_type operator=(str_type str);
  str_type operator=(char *str);

  void show_str(void) { cout << string; }
} ;

str_type str_type::operator+(str_type str) {
  str_type temp;

  strcpy(temp.string, string);
  strcat(temp.string, str.string);
  return temp;
}

str_type str_type::operator=(str_type str) {
  strcpy(string, str.string);
  return *this;
}

str_type str_type::operator=(char *str)
{
  str_type temp;

  strcpy(string, str);
  strcpy(temp.string, string);
  return temp;
}

str_type str_type::operator+(char *str)
{
  str_type temp;

  strcpy(temp.string, string);
  strcat(temp.string, str);
  return temp;
}

main(void)
{
  str_type a("Hello "), b("There"), c;
```

```
    c = a + b;

    c.show_str();
    cout << "\n";

    a = "to program in because";
    a.show_str();
    cout << "\n";

    b = c = "C++ is fun";

    c = c+" "+a+" "+b;
    c.show_str();
    return 0;
}
```

The program displays this on the screen:

```
Hello There
to program in because
C++ is fun to program in because C++ is fun
```

Before continuing, you should make sure that you understand how this output is created. Also, on your own, try creating other string operations. For example, you might try defining the − − so that it performs a substring deletion. For example, if object **A**'s string is "This is a test" and object **B**'s string is "is", then **A − B** yields "th a test". In this case, all occurrences of the substring are removed from the original string.

Inheritance,
Virtual Functions,
and Polymorphism

Crucial to object oriented programming is the concept of polymor
phism. As applied to C++, polymorphism is the term used to
describe the process by which different implementations of a
function can be accessed using the same name. For this reason,
polymorphism is sometimes characterized by the phrase "one
interface, multiple methods." This means that a general class of

operations may be accessed in the same fashion even though the specific actions associated with each operation may differ.

In C++, polymorphism is supported both at run time and at compile time. Operator and function overloading are examples of compile-time polymorphism. However, as powerful as operator and function overloading are, they cannot perform all tasks required by a true, object oriented language. Therefore, C++ also allows runtime polymorphism through the use of derived **class**es and *virtual functions*, and these are the major topics of this chapter.

This chapter begins with a short discussion of pointers to derived types because they are needed to support runtime polymorphism.

Pointers to Derived Types

Pointers to base types and derived types are related. Assume that you have a base type called **B_class** and a type called **D_class**, which is derived from **B_class**. In C++, any pointer declared as a pointer to **B_class** *may also be a pointer to* **D_class**. For example, given,

```
B_class *p; // pointer to object of type B_class
B_class B_ob; // object of type B_class
D_class D_ob; // object of type D_class
```

then the following is perfectly valid:

```
p = &B_ob;   // p points to object of type B_class
p = &D_ob;   /* p points to object of type D_class,
                which is an object derived from B_class. */
```

Using **p**, all elements of **D_ob** inherited from **B_ob** may be accessed. However, elements specific to **D_ob** may not be referenced using **p** (unless a type cast is employed).

For a concrete example, consider this short program, which defines a base class called **B_class** and a derived class called **D_class**. The derived class implements a simple automated telephone book.

```
// Using pointers on derived class objects.

#include <iostream.h>
#include <string.h>

class B_class {
  char name[80];
public:
  void put_name(char *s) {strcpy(name, s); }
  void show_name() {cout << name << " ";}
} ;

class D_class : public B_class {
  char phone_num[80];
public:
  void put_phone(char *num) {
  strcpy(phone_num, num);
  }
  void show_phone() {cout << phone_num << "\n";}
};

main(void)
{
  B_class *p;
  B_class B_ob;

  D_class *dp;
  D_class D_ob;

  p = &B_ob; // address of base

  // Access B_class via pointer.
  p->put_name("Thomas Edison");

  // Access D_class via base pointer.
  p = &D_ob;
  p->put_name("Albert Einstein");

  // Show that each name went into proper object.
  B_ob.show_name();
  D_ob.show_name();
  cout << "\n";
```

```
/* Since put_phone and show_phone are not part of the
   base class, they are not accessible via the base
   pointer p and must be accessed either directly,
   or, as shown here, through a pointer to the
   derived type.
*/
dp = &D_ob;
dp->put_phone("555 555-1234");
p->show_name(); // either p or dp can be used in this line
dp->show_phone();
return 0;
}
```

In this example, the pointer **p** is defined as a pointer to **B_class**. However, it can point to an object of the derived **class D_class** and can be used to access those elements of the derived **class** that are defined by the base class. However, remember that a base pointer cannot access those elements specific to the derived **class** without the use of a type cast. This is why **show_phone( )** is accessed using the **dp** pointer, which is a pointer to the derived **class**.

If you want to access elements defined by a derived type using a base type pointer, you must cast it into a pointer of the derived type. For example, the following line of code will properly call the **show_phone( )** function of **D_ob**:

```
((D_class *)p)->show_phone();
```

The outer set of parentheses is necessary to associate the cast with **p** and not the return type of **show_phone( )**. While there is technically nothing wrong with casting a pointer in this manner, it is probably best avoided because it adds confusion to your code.

Another point to understand is that while a base pointer can be used to point to any type of derived object, the reverse is not true. That is, you cannot use a pointer to a derived **class** to access an object of the base type.

One final point: a pointer is incremented and decremented relative to its base type. Therefore, when a pointer to a base **class** is pointing at a derived **class**, incrementing or decrementing it will *not* make it point to the next object of the derived **class**. Therefore, you should consider it invalid to increment or decrement a pointer when it is pointing to a derived object.

The fact that a pointer to a base type may be used to point to any object derived from that base is extremely important and fundamental to C++. In fact, as you will soon learn, it is crucial to the way C++ implements runtime polymorphism.

Virtual Functions

Runtime polymorphism is achieved through the use of derived types and virtual functions. In short, a virtual function is a function that is declared as **virtual** in a base **class** and redefined in one or more derived **class**es. What makes **virtual** functions special is that when one is accessed using a base **class** pointer to an object of a derived **class**, C++ determines which function to call at run time based on the type of object *pointed to*. Thus, when different objects are pointed to, different versions of the **virtual** function are executed.

A **virtual** function is declared as **virtual** inside the base **class** by preceding its declaration with the keyword **virtual**. However, when a **virtual** function is redefined by a derived **class**, the keyword **virtual** need not be repeated (although it is not an error to do so).

As a first example of **virtual** functions, examine this short program:

```
// A short example that uses virtual functions.
#include <iostream.h>

class Base {
public:
```

```
  virtual void who() { // specify a virtual
    cout << "Base\n";
  }
};

class first_d : public Base {
public:
  void who() { // define who() relative to first_d
    cout << "First derivation\n";
  }
};

class second_d : public Base {
public:
  void who() { // define who() relative to second_d
    cout << "Second derivation\n";
  }
};

main(void)
{
  Base base_obj;
  Base *p;
  first_d first_obj;
  second_d second_obj;

  p = &base_obj;
  p->who();  // access Base's who

  p = &first_obj;
  p->who(); // access first_d's who

  p = &second_obj;
  p->who();  // access second_d's who

  return 0;
}
```

The program produces the following output:

```
Base
First derivation
Second derivation
```

Let's examine it in detail to understand how it works.

As you can see, in **Base**, the function **who( )** is declared as **virtual**. This means that the function may be redefined by a derived **class**. Inside both **first_d** and **second_d**, **who( )** is redefined relative to each **class**. Inside **main( )**, four variables are declared—**base_obj**, which is an object of type **Base**; **p**, which is a pointer to **Base** objects; and **first_obj** and **second_obj**, which are objects of the two derived **class**es. Next, **p** is assigned the address of **base_obj** and the **who( )** function is called. Since **who( )** is declared as **virtual**, C++ determines at run time which version of **who( )** is referred to by the type of object pointed to by **p**. In this case, it is an object of type **Base**, so it is the version of **who( )** declared in **Base** that is executed. Next, **p** is assigned the address of **first_obj.** Remember that a base **class** pointer may be used to reference any derived **class**. Now, when **who( )** is called, C++ again examines what type of object is pointed to by **p** to determine which version of **who( )** to call. Since **p** points to an object of type **first_d**, that version of **who( )** is used. Likewise, when **p** is assigned the address of **second_obj**, the version of **who( )** declared inside **second_d** is executed.

The key point to using **virtual** functions to achieve runtime polymorphism is that you must access those functions through the use of a pointer declared as a pointer to the base **class**. Although you can call a **virtual** function explicitly using the object name in the same way you would call any other member function, it is only when a **virtual** function is accessed through a pointer to the base **class** that runtime polymorphism is achieved.

The redefinition of a **virtual** function in a derived **class** is a special form of function overloading. However, the reason that this term is not used in the preceding discussion is that several restrictions apply. First, the prototypes for **virtual** functions must match. As you know, when overloading normal functions, the return type and the number and type of parameters may differ. However, when overloading a **virtual** function, these elements must be unchanged. If the prototypes of the functions differ, then the function is simply considered overloaded and its **virtual** nature is lost. Also, it is an error if only the return types of the function differ. (Functions that differ only in their return types are inherently ambiguous.) Another restriction is that a **virtual** function must be a member, not a **friend**, of the **class** for which it is defined. However, a **virtual** function can also be a **friend** of another **class**. In addition, it is permissible for destructor functions to be **virtual**, but constructors may not.

Because of the restrictions and differences between overloading normal functions and overloading **virtual** functions, the term *overriding* is used to describe the **virtual** function redefinition.

Once a function is declared as **virtual** it stays **virtual** no matter how many layers of derived **class**es it may pass through. For example, if **second_d** is derived from **first_d** instead of **Base**, as shown here, **who( )** is still **virtual** and the proper version is still correctly selected.

```
// Derive from first_d, not Base
class second_d : public first_d {
public:
  void who() { // define who() relative to second_d
  cout << "Second derivation\n";
  }
};
```

When a derived **class** does not override a **virtual** function, then the version of the function in the base class is used. For example, try this version of the preceding program:

```
#include <iostream.h>

class Base {
public:
  virtual void who() {
    cout << "Base\n";
  }
};

class first_d : public Base {
public:
  void who() {
```

```
      cout << "First derivation\n";
   }
};

class second_d : public Base {
// who() not defined
};

main(void)
{
  Base base_obj;
  Base *p;
  first_d first_obj;
  second_d second_obj;

  p = &base_obj;
  p->who(); // access Base's who()

  p = &first_obj;
  p->who(); // access first_d's who()

  p = &second_obj;
  p->who(); /* access Base's who() because
                second_d does not redefine it */

  return 0;
}
```

This program now outputs the following:

```
Base
First derivation
Base
```

Keep in mind that inherited characteristics are hierarchical. Therefore, if **second_d** is derived from **first_d** instead of **Base**, then when **who( )** is referenced relative to an object of type **second_d**, it is the version of **who( )** declared inside **first_d** that is called since it is the **class** closest to **second_d**—not the **who( )** inside **Base**.

Why Use Virtual Functions?

As stated at the start of this chapter, **virtual** functions in combination with derived types allow C++ to support runtime polymorphism. And polymorphism is essential to object oriented programming for one reason: It allows a generalized **class** to specify those functions that will be common to any derivative of that **class** while allowing a derived **class** to specify the specific implementation of some or all of those functions. Sometimes this idea is expressed like this: The base **class** dictates the general *interface* that any object derived from that **class** will have, but lets the derived **class** define the actual *method*, itself. This is why the phrase "one interface, multiple methods" is often used to describe polymorphism.

Part of the key to successfully applying polymorphism is understanding that base and derived **class**es form a hierarchy that moves from greater to lesser generalization (base to derived). Hence, when used correctly, the base **class** provides all elements that a derived **class** can use directly, plus those functions that the derived **class** must implement on its own. However, since the form of the interface is defined by the base **class**, any derived **class** will still share that common interface. When properly designed, using **virtual** functions the base **class** defines the generic interface, which will be used by all derived **class**es.

At this point, you might be asking yourself why a consistent interface with multiple implementations is important. The answer, again, goes back to the central driving force behind object oriented programming: it helps the programmer handle increasingly complex programs. For example, if you develop your program correctly, then you know that all objects you derive from some base **class** are accessed in the same general way, even if the specific actions vary from one derived **class** to the next. This means that you need to remember only one interface rather than several. Furthermore, the separation of interface and implementation allows the creation of *class libraries,* which can be provided by a third party. If these libraries are implemented correctly, then they will provide a common interface that you can use to derive **class**es of your own to meet your specific needs.

To get an idea of the power of the "one interface, multiple methods" concept, examine this short program. It creates a base **class** called **figure**. This class is used to store the dimensions of various two-dimensional objects and to compute their areas. The function **set_dim( )** is a standard member function because this operation will be common to all derived **class**es. However, **show_area( )** is declared as **virtual** because the way the area of each object is computed will vary. The program uses **figure** to derive two specific **class**es called **square** and **triangle**.

```
#include <iostream.h>

class figure {
protected:
  double x, y;
public:
  void set_dim(double i, double j) {
    x = i;
    y = j;
  }
  virtual void show_area() {
    cout << "No area computation defined ";
    cout << "for this class.\n";
  }
} ;

class triangle : public figure {
  public:
    void show_area() {
      cout << "Triangle with height ";
      cout << x << " and base " << y;
      cout << " has an area of ";
      cout << x * 0.5 * y << ".\n";
    }
};

class square : public figure {
  public:
    void show_area() {
      cout << "Square with dimensions ";
      cout << x << "x" << y;
```

```
          cout << " has an area of ";
          cout << x * y << ".\n";
      }
};

main(void)
{
  figure *p; /* create a pointer to base type */

  triangle t; /* create objects of derived types */
  square s;

  p = &t;
  p->set_dim(10.0, 5.0);
  p->show_area();

  p = &s;
  p->set_dim(10.0, 5.0);
  p->show_area();

  return 0;
}
```

As you can see by examining this program, the interface to both **square** and **triangle** is the same even though both provide their own methods for computing the area of each of their objects.

Given the declaration for **figure**, is it possible to derive a **class** called **circle** that will compute the area of a circle given its radius? The answer is yes. All that you need do is create a new derived type that computes the area of a circle. The power of **virtual** functions is based on the fact that you can easily derive a new type that will still share the same common interface as other related objects. For example, here is one way to do it:

```
class circle : public figure {
  public:
    void show_area() {
      cout << "Circle with radius ";
      cout << x;
      cout << " has an area of ";
      cout << 3.14 * x * x;
    }
} ;
```

Before trying to use **circle**, look closely at the definition to **show‿area( )**. Notice that it uses only the value of **x**, which is assumed to hold the radius. (Remember, the area of a circle is computed using the formula πr^2.) However, the function **set‿dim( )** as defined in **figure** assumes that it will be passed not one, but two values. Since **circle** does not require this second value, what course of action can you take?

There are two ways to resolve this problem. First and worst, you could simply call **set‿dim( )** using a dummy value as the second parameter when using a **circle** object. This has the disadvantage of being sloppy as well as requiring you to remember a special exception, which violates the "one interface, many methods" approach.

A better way to resolve this problem is to give the **y** parameter inside **set‿dim( )** a default value. In this way, when calling **set‿dim( )** for a circle, you need specify only the radius. When calling **set‿dim( )** for a triangle or a square, you would specify both values. The expanded program is shown here:

```
#include <iostream.h>

class figure {
protected:
  double x, y;
public:
  void set_dim(double i, double j=0) {
    x = i;
    y = j;
  }
  virtual void show_area() {
    cout << "No area computation defined ";
    cout << "for this class.\n";
  }
} ;

class triangle : public figure {
  public:
    void show_area() {
      cout << "Triangle with height ";
      cout << x << " and base " << y;
      cout << " has an area of ";
      cout << x * 0.5 * y << ".\n";
```

```
      }
};

class square : public figure {
  public:
    void show_area() {
      cout << "Square with dimensions ";
      cout << x << "x" << y;
      cout << " has an area of ";
      cout << x * y << ".\n";
    }
};

class circle : public figure {
  public:
    void show_area() {
      cout << "Circle with radius ";
      cout << x;
      cout << " has an area of ";
      cout << 3.14 * x * x;
    }
} ;

main(void)
{
  figure *p;   /* create a pointer to base type */

  triangle t;   /* create objects of derived types */
  square s;
  circle c;

  p = &t;
  p->set_dim(10.0, 5.0);
  p->show_area();

  p = &s;
  p->set_dim(10.0, 5.0);
  p->show_area();

  p = &c;
  p->set_dim(9.0);
  p->show_area();

  return 0;
}
```

This illustrates a very important point about defining base **class**es: be as flexible as possible. Don't make unnecessarily harsh restrictions.

Pure Virtual Functions and Abstract Types

When a **virtual** function that is not overridden in a derived **class** is called for an object of that derived **class**, the version of the function as defined in the base **class** is used. However, in many circumstances there will be no meaningful definition of a **virtual** function inside the base **class**. For example, in the base **class** **figure** used in the preceding example, the definition of **show‗area( )** is simply a placeholder. It will not compute and display the area of any type of object. As you will see as you create your own **class** libraries, it is not uncommon for a **virtual** function to have no meaningful definition in the context of its base **class**. When this occurs, there are two ways you can handle it. One way, as shown in the example, is to have it report a warning message. While this approach can be useful in certain situations, it will not be appropriate for all circumstances. For example, there may be **virtual** functions that must be defined by the derived **class** in order for the derived **class** to have any meaning. Consider the **class triangle**; it has no meaning if **show‗area( )** is not defined. In this sort of case, you want some method to ensure that a derived **class** does, indeed, define all necessary functions. C++'s solution to this problem is the *pure* **virtual** function.

A pure **virtual** function is a function declared in a base **class** that has no definition relative to the base. Thus, any derived type must define its own version—it cannot simply use the version defined in the base. To declare a pure **virtual** function, use the general form,

virtual *type func‗name(parameter list)* = 0;

where *type* is the return type of the function and *func‗name* is the name of the function. For example, in this version of **figure**, **show‗area( )** is a pure **virtual** function.

```
class figure {
protected:
  double x, y;
public:
  void set_dim(double i, double j=0) {
    x = i;
    y = j;
  }
  virtual void show_area() = 0; // pure
} ;
```

By declaring a **virtual** function as pure, you force any derived **class** to define its own implementation. If a **class** fails to do so, Turbo C++ will report an error. For example, try to compile this modified version of the figures program in which the definition for **show＿area( )** has been removed from the **circle class**:

```
/*
   This program will not compile because the class
   circle does not override show_area().
*/
#include <iostream.h>

class figure {
protected:
  double x, y;
public:
  void set_dim(double i, double j) {
    x = i;
    y = j;
  }
  virtual void show_area() = 0; // pure
} ;

class triangle : public figure {
  public:
    void show_area() {
      cout << "Triangle with height ";
      cout << x << " and base " << y;
      cout << " has an area of ";
      cout << x * 0.5 * y << ".\n";
    }
};
```

```
class square : public figure {
  public:
    void show_area() {
      cout << "Square with dimensions ";
      cout << x << "x" << y;
      cout << " has an area of ";
      cout << x * y << ".\n";
    }
};

class circle : public figure {
// no definition of show_area() will cause an error
};

main(void)
{
  figure *p;   /* create a pointer to base type */

  triangle t; /* create objects of derived types */
  square s;

  p = &t;
  p->set_dim(10.0, 5.0);
  p->show_area();

  p = &s;
  p->set_dim(10.0, 5.0);
  p->show_area();

  return 0;
}
```

If a **class** has at least one pure **virtual** function, then that class is said to be *abstract*. Abstract **class**es have one important feature: there can be no objects of that **class**. Instead, an abstract **class** must be used only as a base that other **class**es will inherit. The reason that an abstract **class** cannot be used to declare an object is, of course, that one or more of its functions have no definition. However, even if the base **class** is abstract, you still may use it to declare pointers, which are needed to support runtime polymorphism.

Early Versus Late Binding

There are two terms that are commonly used when discussing object oriented programming languages: *early binding* and *late binding*. Relative to C++, these terms refer to events that occur at compile time and events that occur at run time, respectively.

In object oriented terms, early binding means that an object is bound to its function call at compile time. That is, all information necessary to determine which function will be called is known when the program is compiled. Examples of early binding include standard function calls, overloaded function calls, and overloaded operator function calls. The principal advantage to early binding is efficiency—it is faster and often requires less memory. Its disadvantage is lack of flexibility.

Late binding means that an object is bound to its function call at run time. This means that precisely which function relates to an object will be determined on the fly at run time. As you now know, late binding is achieved in C++ by using **virtual** functions and derived types. The advantage to late binding is that it allows greater flexibility. It can be used to support a common interface while allowing various objects that utilize that interface to define their own implementations. Furthermore, it can be used to help you create **class** libraries, which may be reused and extended.

Whether your program uses early or late binding depends on what your program is designed to do. (Actually, most large programs will use a combination of both.) Late binding is one of C++'s most powerful additions to the C language. However, the price you pay for this power is that your program will run slightly slower. Therefore, it is best to use late binding only when it meaningfully adds to the structure and manageability of your program. (In essence, use, but don't abuse the power.) Keep in mind that the loss of performance is very small, so when the situation calls for late binding, you should most definitely use it.

Constructors and Destructors in Derived Classes

Since elements of C++'s polymorphism rely heavily on derived **class**es, it is appropriate to take a closer look at them at this time. One important feature of a derived **class** is seen when its constructor and destructor functions are executed. Let's begin with constructors.

It is possible for a base **class** and a derived **class** to each have a constructor function. (In fact, in the case of multiple inheritance, it is possible for all involved **class**es to have constructors, but let's start with the simplest case.) When a derived **class** contains a constructor, the base constructor is executed before the constructor in the derived **class**. For example, consider the following short program:

```
#include <iostream.h>

class Base {
public:
  Base() {cout << "\nBase created\n";}
};

class D_class1 : public Base {
public:
  D_class1() {cout << "D_class1 created\n";}
};

main(void)
{
  D_class1 d1;

  // do nothing but execute constructors
  return 0;
}
```

The program creates an object of type **D_class1**. It displays this output:

```
Base created
D_class1 created
```

Here, **d1** is an object of type **D_class1**, which is derived using **Base**. Thus, when **d1** is created, first **Base( )** is executed, and then **D_class1( )** is called.

If you think about it, it makes sense for constructors to be called in the same order in which the derivation takes place. Because the base **class** has no knowledge of the derived **class**, any initialization that it needs to perform is obviously separate from and possibly a prerequisite to any derived **class**, so it must be executed first.

On the other hand, a destructor function in a derived **class** is executed before the destructor in the base. The reason for this is also easy to understand. Since the destruction of the base **class** implies the destruction of the derived **class**, the derived destructor must be executed before it is destroyed. This program illustrates the order in which constructors and destructors are executed:

```
#include <iostream.h>

class Base {
public:
  Base( {cout << "\nBase created\n";}
  ~Base() {cout << "Base destroyed\n\n";}
};

class D_class1 : public Base {
public:
  D_class1() {cout << "D_class1 created\n";}
  ~D_class1() {cout << "D_class1 destroyed\n";}
};

main(void)
{
  D_class1 d1;

  cout << "\n";
```

```
   return 0;
}
```

It produces this output:

```
Base created
D_class1 created

D_class1 destroyed
Base destroyed
```

As you know, it is possible for a derived **class** itself to be used as a base **class** in the creation of another derived **class**. When this happens, constructors are executed in the order of the derivation and destructors in the reverse order. For example, consider this program, which uses **D_class1** to derive **D_class2**:

```
#include <iostream.h>

class Base {
public:
  Base() {cout << "\nBase created\n";}
  ~Base() {cout << "Base destroyed\n\n";}
};

class D_class1 : public Base {
public:
  D_class1() {cout << "D_class1 created\n";}
  ~D_class1() {cout << "D_class1 destroyed\n";}
};

class D_class2 : public D_class1 {
public:
  D_class2() {cout << "D_class2 created\n";}
  ~D_class2() {cout << "D_class2 destroyed\n";}
};

main(void)
{
  D_class1 d1;
  D_class2 d2;

  cout << "\n";
```

```
  return 0;
}
```

It produces this output:

```
Base created
D_class1 created

Base created
D_class1 created
D_class2 created

D_class2 destroyed
D_class1 destroyed
Base destroyed

D_class1 destroyed
Base destroyed
```

Multiple Base Classes

It is possible to specify more than one base **class** when creating a derived type. To do so, use a comma-separated list of the **class**es that will be inherited. For example, consider this program:

```
#include <iostream.h>

class Base1 {
public:
  Base1() {cout << "\nBase1 created\n";}
  ~Base1() {cout << "Base1 destroyed\n\n";}
};

class Base2 {
public:
  Base2() {cout << "Base2 created\n";}
  ~Base2() {cout << "Base2 destroyed\n";}
};

// multiple base classes
class D_class1 : public Base1, public Base2 {
```

```
public:
  D_class1() {cout << "D_class1 created\n";}
  ~D_class1() {cout << "D_class1 destroyed\n";}
};

main(void)
{
  D_class1 d1;

  cout << "\n";

  return 0;
}
```

In this program, **D _ class1** is derived from both **Base1** and **Base2**. It produces this output:

```
Base1 created
Base2 created
D_class1 created

D_class1 destroyed
Base2 destroyed
Base1 destroyed
```

As you can see, when a list of base **class**es is used, the constructors are called in order from left to right. Destructors are called in order from right to left.

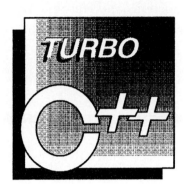

20

Using C++'s I/O Class Library

Since beginning Part III, this book has been performing console input and output using C++'s overloaded operators >> and <<. Although Turbo C++ supports all of C's rich set of I/O functions, the past few chapters have ignored them in favor of C++'s I/O operators. There is one main reason for this: Using C++'s method of I/O helps you to think in an object oriented manner and to see the value of the "one interface, multiple methods" philosophy. In this chapter you will learn more about C++'s I/O system, including how to overload the << and >> operators so that you can input or output objects of **class**es that you design. C++'s I/O system is very large and it is not possible to cover every function and feature, but this chapter will introduce you to the most important and commonly used functions and features. Let's begin with a quick look at why C++ defines its own I/O system.

Why C++ *Has Its Own I/O System*

If you have programmed in other languages, you know that C has one of the most flexible, yet powerful I/O systems. (In fact, it may be safe to say that among the world's structured languages, C's I/O system is unparalleled.) Given the power of C's I/O functions, you might ask why C++ defines its own I/O functions, which (as you will see) in a large part duplicate those already contained in C. The answer is that the C I/O system provides no support for user-defined objects. In C, for example, if you create the structure

```
struct my_struct {
   int count;
   char s[80];
   double balance;
} cust;
```

there is no way to customize or extend C's I/O system so that it knows about and can perform I/O operations directly on a variable of **my_struct**. You cannot create a new format specifier that is defined for data of type **my_struct** and use it in a call to **printf( )**. For example, this will simply not work:

```
printf("%my_struct", cust);
```

Because **printf( )** can only recognize the built-in types, there is no way to extend its capabilities relative to new data types.

However, using C++'s approach to I/O it is possible to overload the **<<** and **>>** operators so that they know about classes that you create. This includes both the console I/O operations you have been using for the past four chapters as well as file I/O. (As you will see, console and file I/O are linked in C++ as they are in C and are really just two sides of the same coin.)

Although there is no I/O operation that you can perform using C++'s I/O system that you cannot perform using C's, the fact that C++'s system can be made aware of user-defined types greatly increases its flexibility and helps to prevent bugs. To see how, consider this call to **printf( )**:

```
printf("%d%s", "Hello", 10);
```

In this call, the string and the integer are inverted in the argument list; the **%d** will be matched with **Hello** and the **%s** with the **10**. However, this is not technically an error in C. (It is conceivable that in some highly unusual situation, you might actually *want* to use a call to **printf( )** like that shown. After all, C was designed to allow you to do anything you can do in assembly language.) However, it is most likely the case that this call to **printf( )** is, indeed, an error. In short, when calling **printf( )**, C has no means of providing strong type checking. However, in C++ I/O operations for all built-in types are defined relative to the **<<** and **>>** operators so that there is no way for such an inversion as shown in the **printf( )** call to take place. Instead, the correct operation is automatically determined by the type of the operand. This feature can also be extended to user-defined objects. (By the way, you can still cause something like the weird **printf( )** call to be generated in C++ by typecasting. Plus, you can always use **printf( )**.)

C++ Streams

You will be happy to know that the C and C++ I/O systems have one important thing in common: they both operate on *streams,* which you learned about in Part II of this book. That discussion will not be repeated here. (See Chapter 10 for details.) The fact that C and C++ streams are similar means that what you know about streams is completely applicable to C++. Also, and maybe more important, with a few small exceptions, you can mix C and C++ I/O operations in the same program. Therefore, you can begin to evolve existing C programs towards C++ without having to convert every I/O operation at the outset.

The C++ Predefined Streams

Like C, C++ contains several predefined streams that are automatically opened when your C++ program begins execution. These are **cin**, **cout**, **cerr**, and **clog**. As you know, **cin** is the stream associated with standard input and **cout** is the stream associated with standard output. The **cerr** stream is linked to standard output and so is **clog**. The difference between **cerr** and **clog** is that **cerr** is not buffered; therefore, any output sent to it is immediately output. In contrast, **clog** is buffered, and output is only written when a buffer is full.

By default, the C++ standard streams are linked to the console, but they may be redirected to other devices or files by your program. Also, they may be redirected by the operating system.

The C++ Stream Classes

The Turbo C++ I/O system is defined by a hierarchy of **class**es that relate to streams. These definitions are found in the header file IOSTREAM.H. The lowest level class is called **streambuf** and it provides the basic stream operations but no formatting support. The next **class** in the hierarchy is called **ios**. The **ios class** provides the basic support for formatted I/O. It is also used to derive three **class**es, which you can use to create streams. They are **istream**, **ostream**, and **iostream**. Using **istream** you can create an input stream; using **ostream** you can create an output stream; and using **iostream** you can create a stream capable of both input and output.

Creating Your Own Insertors and Extractors

Up to this point, when a program needed to output or input the data associated with a **class**, special member functions were created whose only purpose was to output or input the **class**'s data. While there is nothing wrong with this approach, C++ allows a much better way of performing I/O operations on **class**es by overloading the << and the >> operators.

In the language of C++, the << operator is usually referred to as the *insertion* operator because it inserts characters into a stream. Likewise, the >> operator is called the *extraction* operator because it extracts characters from a stream. The operator functions that overload the insertion and extraction operators are generally called *insertors* and *extractors,* respectively.

The insertion and extraction operators are already overloaded (in IOSTREAM.H) so that they are capable of performing stream I/O on any of C++'s built-in types. However, as the beginning of the chapter indicated, it is possible to define these operators relative to **class**es that you create. In this section you will see how.

Creating Insertors

One of the nicest features of C++ is how easily you can make insertors for **class**es that you create. As a simple first example, let's create an insertor for the **three _ d class** (first defined in Chapter 18), shown here:

```
class three_d {
public:
  int x, y, z; // 3-d coordinates
  three_d(int a, int b, int c) {x=a; y=b, z=c;}
} ;
```

To create an insertor function for an object of type **three _ d**, you must define an insertion operation relative to it. To do this, you must overload the **<<** operator, as shown here:

```
// Display X, Y, Z coordinates (three_d's insertor).
ostream &operator<<(ostream &stream, three_d obj)
{
  stream << obj.x << ", ";
  stream << obj.y << ", ";
  stream << obj.z << "\n";
  return stream;  // return the stream
}
```

Let's look closely at this function because many of its features are common to all insertor functions. First, notice that it is declared as returning a reference to an object of type **ostream**. This is necessary to allow several insertors of this type to be strung together. Next, the function has two parameters. The first is the reference to the stream, which occurs on the left side of the **<<** operator. The second parameter is the object that occurs on the right side. Inside the function, the three values contained in an object of type **three _ d** are output, and **stream** is returned. Here is a short program that demonstrates the insertor:

```
#include <iostream.h>

class three_d {
public:
  int x, y, z; // 3-d coordinates
  three_d(int a, int b, int c) {x=a; y=b, z=c;}
} ;

// Display X, Y, Z coordinates - three_d insertor
ostream &operator<<(ostream &stream, three_d obj)
{
  stream << obj.x << ", ";
  stream << obj.y << ", ";
  stream << obj.z << "\n";
  return stream;  // return the stream
}

main(void)
{
  three_d a(1, 2, 3), b(3, 4, 5), c(5, 6, 7);

  cout << a << b << c;

  return 0;
}
```

If you eliminate the code that is specific to the **three _ d class** you are left with the skeleton for an insertor function, as shown here:

```
ostream &operator<<(ostream &stream, class_type obj)
{
  // type specific code goes here
  return stream;  // return the stream
}
```

Within wide boundaries, what an insertor function actually does is up to you. Just make sure that you return **stream**.

You might be wondering why the function was not coded as shown here:

```
// Limited version - don't use.
ostream &operator<<(ostream &stream, three_d obj)
{
  cout << obj.x << ", ";
  cout << obj.y << ", ";
  cout << obj.z << "\n";
  return stream;   // return the stream
}
```

In this version, the **cout** stream is hard coded into the function. However, remember that the **<<** operator can be applied to *any stream*. Therefore, you must use the stream passed to the function if it is to work correctly in all cases.

In the preceding program, the overloaded insertor function is not a member of **three_d**. In fact, neither insertor nor extractor functions can be members of a **class**. The reason for this is that when an **operator** function is a member of a **class**, the left operand (implicitly passed using the **this** pointer) is assumed to be an object of the **class** that generated the call to the **operator** function. There is no way to change this. However, when overloading insertors, the left argument is a stream and the right argument is an object of the **class**. Therefore, overloaded insertors must be nonmember functions.

The fact that insertors must not be members of the **class** they are defined to operate on raises a serious question: How can an overloaded insertor access the private elements of a **class**? In the previous program, the variables **x**, **y**, and **z** were made **public** so that the insertor could access them. But hiding data is an important part of OOP, and forcing all data to be **public** is a serious inconsistency. However, there is a solution: an insertor may be a **friend** of a **class**. As a **friend** of the **class** it is defined for, it has access to private data. To see an example of this, the **three_d class** and sample program are reworked here, with the overloaded insertor declared as a **friend**.

```
#include <iostream.h>

class three_d {
  int x, y, z; // 3-d coordinates - - now private
public:
  three_d(int a, int b, int c) {x=a; y=b, z=c;}
  friend ostream &operator<<(ostream &stream, three_d obj);
} ;

// Display X, Y, Z coordinates - three_d insertor
ostream &operator<<(ostream &stream, three_d obj)
{
  stream << obj.x << ", ";
  stream << obj.y << ", ";
  stream << obj.z << "\n";
  return stream;  // return the stream
}

main(void)
{
  three_d a(1, 2, 3), b(3, 4, 5), c(5, 6, 7);

  cout << a << b << c;
  return 0;
}
```

Notice that the variables **x**, **y**, and **z** are now **private** to **three_d**, but they can still be directly accessed by the insertor. Making insertors (and extractors) **friend**s of the **class**es for which they are defined preserves the data-hiding principle of OOP.

Overloading Extractors

To overload an extractor, use the same general approach as when overloading an insertor. For example, this extractor inputs 3-D coordinates. Notice that it also prompts the user.

```
// Get three dimensional values - extractor.
istream &operator>>(istream &stream, three_d &obj)
{
  cout << "Enter X,Y,Z values: ";
```

```
    stream >> obj.x >> obj.y >> obj.z;
    return stream;
}
```

Extractors must return a reference to an object of type **istream**.
Also, the first parameter must be a reference to an object of type
istream. Notice that the second parameter is a reference. This is
necessary so that its value can be modified.

The general form of an extractor is shown here:

```
istream &operator>>(istream &stream, object_type &obj)
{
  // put your extractor code here
  return stream;
}
```

Here is a program that demonstrates the extractor for objects
of type **three _ d**:

```
#include <iostream.h>

class three_d {
  int x, y, z; // 3-d coordinates
public:
  three_d(int a, int b, int c) {x=a; y=b, z=c;}
  friend ostream &operator<<(ostream &stream, three_d obj);
  friend istream &operator>>(istream &stream, three_d &obj);
} ;

// Display X, Y, Z coordinates - insertor.
ostream &operator<<(ostream &stream, three_d obj)
{
  stream << obj.x << ", ";
  stream << obj.y << ", ";
  stream << obj.z << "\n";
  return stream; // return the stream
}

// Get three dimensional values - extractor
istream &operator>>(istream &stream, three_d &obj)
{
```

```
   cout << "Enter X,Y,Z values: ";
   stream >> obj.x >> obj.y >> obj.z;
   return stream;
}

main(void)
{
   three_d a(1, 2, 3);

   cout << a;

   cin >> a;
   cout << a;

   return 0;
}
```

Like insertors, extractor functions may not be members of the **class** they are designed to operate on. They may, as shown in the example, be **friend**s or simply independent functions.

Except for the fact that you must return a reference to an object of type **istream**, you may do anything you like inside an extractor function. However, for the sake of structure and clarity, it is best to limit the actions of an extractor to the input operation.

Formatting I/O

As you know, by using **printf( )** you can control the format of information displayed on the screen. For example, you can specify field widths and left or right justification. Using C++'s approach to I/O, you can also accomplish the same type of formatting. There are two ways to format output. The first uses member functions of the **ios class**. The second uses a special type of function called a *manipulator*. Let's begin by looking at formatting using the member functions of **ios** and then discuss the manipulators.

Formatting Using the ios Member Functions

In IOSTREAM.H the following enumeration is defined:

```
// formatting flags
enum {
  skipws = 0x0001,
  left = 0x0002,
  right = 0x0004,
  internal = 0x0008,
  dec = 0x0010,
  oct = 0x0020,
  hex = 0x0040,
  showbase = 0x0080,
  showpoint = 0x0100,
  uppercase = 0x0200,
  showpos = 0x0400,
  scientific = 0x0800,
  fixed = 0x1000,
  unitbuf = 0x2000,
  stdio = 0x4000
};
```

The values defined by this enumeration are used to set or clear flags that control some of the ways information is formatted by a stream.

When the **skipws** flag is set, leading white-space characters (spaces, tabs, and newlines) are discarded when performing input on a stream. When **skipws** is cleared, white-space characters are not discarded.

When the **left** flag is set, output is left-justified. When **right** is set, output is right-justified. When the **internal** flag is set, then a numeric value is padded to fill a field by inserting spaces between any sign or base character. (You will learn how to specify a field width shortly.)

By default, numeric values are output in the base in which they are represented. However, you can override this default. For example, to output in decimal, set the **dec** flag. Setting **oct** causes output to be displayed in octal. Setting **hex** causes output to be displayed in hexadecimal. Setting **showbase** causes the base of numeric values to be shown.

By default, when scientific notation is displayed, the "e" is in lowercase. Also, when a hexadecimal value is displayed, the "x" is in lowercase. When **uppercase** is set, these characters are displayed in uppercase.

Setting **showpos** causes a leading plus sign to be displayed before positive integer values. Setting **showpoint** causes a decimal point and trailing zeros to be displayed for all floating-point output—whether needed or not.

By setting the **scientific** flag, floating-point numeric values are displayed using scientific notation. When **fixed** is set, floating-point values are displayed using normal notation, and by default, six decimal places are displayed. When neither flag is set, the compiler chooses an appropriate method.

For reasons that are beyond the scope of this book, when **unitbuf** is set, the C++ I/O system performance is improved. This flag is on by default in Turbo C++.

When **stdio** is set, each stream is flushed after each output. Flushing a stream causes output to be written to the physical device linked to the stream.

The format flags are held in a **long** integer. To set a flag, use the **setf( )** function, whose most common form is shown here:

long setf(long *flags*);

This function returns the previous settings of the format flags and turns on those flags specified by *flags*. For example, to turn on the **showbase** flag, you can use this statement:

```
stream.setf(ios::showbase);
```

Here, *stream* is the stream you wish to affect. For example, this program turns on both the **showpos** and **scientific** flags.

```
#include <iostream.h>

main(void)
{
  cout.setf(ios::showpos);
  cout.setf(ios::scientific);
  cout << 123 << " " << 123.23 << " ";

  return 0;
}
```

The output produced by this program is shown here:

```
+123 +1.2323e+02
```

You may OR together as many flags as you like in a single call. For example, you can change the program so that only one call is made to **setf( )** by ORing together **scientific** and **showpos**, as shown here:

```
cout.setf(ios::scientific | ios::showpos);
```

To turn off a flag, use the **unsetf( )** function whose prototype is shown here:

long unsetf(long *flags*);

The function returns the previous flag settings and turns off those flags specified by *flags*.

Sometimes it is useful to know the current flag settings. You can retrieve the current flag values by using the **flags( )** function, whose prototype is shown here:

long flags(void);

This function returns the current value of the flags relative to the associated stream.

This form of **flags( )** sets the flag values to those specified by *flags* and returns the previous flag values:

```
long flags(long flags);
```

To see how **flags( )** and **unsetf( )** work, examine this program. It includes a function called **showflags( )** that displays the state of the flags:

```
#include <iostream.h>

void showflags(long f);
main(void)
{
  long f;

  f = cout.flags();

  showflags(f);
  cout.setf(ios::showpos);
  cout.setf(ios::scientific);

  f = cout.flags();
  showflags(f);

  cout.unsetf(ios::scientific);

  f = cout.flags();
  showflags(f);

  return 0;
}

void showflags(long f)
{
  long i;

  for(i=0x4000; i; i = i >> 1)
```

```
      if(i & f) cout << "1 ";
      else cout << "0 ";

   cout << "\n";
}
```

When run, the program produces this output:

```
0 1 0 0 0 0 0 0 0 0 0 0 0 0 0 1
0 1 0 1 1 0 0 0 0 0 0 0 0 0 0 1
0 1 0 0 1 0 0 0 0 0 0 0 0 0 0 1
```

In addition to the formatting flags, you can set the field width, the fill character, and the number of digits displayed after a decimal point, using these functions:

> int width(int *len*);
> char fill(char *ch*);
> int precision(int *num*);

The **width( )** function returns the current field width and sets the field width to *len*. By default the field width varies, depending on the number of characters it takes to represent the data. The **fill( )** function returns the current fill character, which is a space by default, and makes the current fill character the same as *ch*. The fill character is the character used to pad output to fill a specified field width. The **precision( )** function returns the number of digits displayed after a decimal point and sets that value to *num*. Here is a program that demonstrates these three functions:

```
#include <iostream.h>

main(void)
{
  cout.setf(ios::showpos);
  cout.setf(ios::scientific);
  cout << 123 << " " << 123.23 << "\n";
```

```
    cout.precision(2); // two digits after decimal point
    cout.width(10);    // in a field of ten characters
    cout << 123 << " " << 123.23 << "\n";

    cout.fill('#');    // fill using #
    cout.width(10);    // in a field of ten characters
    cout << 123 << " " << 123.23;

    return 0;
}
```

The program displays this output:

```
+123 +1.2323e+02
      +123 +1.23e+02
##### +123 +1.23e+02
```

Using Manipulators

The C++ I/O system includes a second way in which you may alter the format parameters of a stream. This way uses special functions called manipulators, which can be included in an I/O statement. The standard manipulators are shown in Table 20-1. To access these manipulators, you must include IOMANIP.H in your program.

All manipulators have the stream they are currently affecting as an argument and they return that stream. In this way, a manipulator can be used as part of an I/O expression. Here is an example program that uses manipulators to change the format of output:

```
#include <iostream.h>
#include <iomanip.h>

main(void)
{
  cout << setprecision(2) << 1000.243 << endl;
```

Table 20-1.

Manipulator	Purpose	Input/Output
dec	Format numeric data in decimal	Input and output
endl	Output a newline character and flush the stream	Output
ends	Output a null	Output
flush	Flush a stream	Output
hex	Format numeric data in hexadecimal	Input and output
oct	Format numeric data in octal	Input and output
resetiosflags(long f)	Turn off the flags specified in **f**	Input and output
setbase(int base)	Set the number base to **base**	Output
setfill(int ch)	Set the fill character to **ch**	Input and output
setiosflags(long f)	Turn on the flags specified in **f**	Input and output
setprecision(int p)	Set the number of digits displayed after a decimal point	Input and output
setw(int w)	Set the field width to **w**	Input and output
ws	Skip leading white-space characters	Input

The C++ Manipulators

```
    cout << setw(20) << "Hello there.";

    return 0;
}
```

It produces this output:

```
1000.24
        Hello there.
```

Notice how the manipulators occur in the chain of I/O operations. Also, notice that when a manipulator does not take an argument, such as **endl( )** in the example, it is not followed by parentheses. The reason for this is that it is the address of the function that is passed to the overloaded **<<** operator.

This program uses **setiosflags( )** to set the **scientific** and **showpos** flags:

```
#include <iostream.h>
#include <iomanip.h>

main(void)
{
  cout << setiosflags(ios::showpos);
  cout << setiosflags(ios::scientific);
  cout << 123 << " " << 123.23;

  return 0;
}
```

This program uses **ws** to skip any leading white-space characters when inputting a string into **s**:

```
#include <iostream.h>

main(void)
{
  char s[80];

  cin >> ws >> s;
  cout << s;
}
```

Creating Your Own Manipulator Functions

You can create your own manipulator functions. The easiest ones to create are those that don't take arguments and it is these types of manipulators that you will learn to create here. (The creation of parameterized manipulators is beyond the scope of this book.)

All non-argument manipulator output functions have this skeleton:

```
ostream &manip-name(ostream &stream)
{
  // your code here
  return stream;
}
```

Here, *manip-name* is the name of the manipulator. It is important to understand that even though the manipulator has as its single argument a pointer to the stream on which it is operating, no argument is used when the manipulator is inserted in an output operation.

This program creates a manipulator called **setup( )** that turns on left justification, sets the field width to 10, and specifies that the dollar sign will be the fill character:

```
#include <iostream.h>
#include <iomanip.h>

ostream &setup(ostream &stream)
{
  stream.setf(ios::left);
  stream << setw(10) << setfill('$');
  return stream;
}

main(void)
{
  cout << 10 << " " << setup << 10;

  return 0;
}
```

Custom manipulators are useful for two reasons. First, you might need to perform an I/O operation on a device for which none of the predefined manipulators apply—a plotter, for example. In this case, creating your own manipulators will make it more convenient when outputting to the device. Second, you may find that you are repeating the same sequence of operations many times. You can consolidate these operations into a single manipulator, as the previous program illustrated.

All non-argument input manipulator functions have the skeleton shown here:

```
istream &manip-name(istream &stream)
{
  // your code here
  return stream;
}
```

For example, this program creates the **prompt( )** manipulator, which converts to hexadecimal input and prompts the user to enter a value using hexadecimal:

```
#include <iostream.h>
#include <iomanip.h>

istream &prompt(istream &stream)
{
  cin >> hex;
  cout << "Enter number using hex format: ";

  return stream;
}

main(void)
{
  int i;
```

```
    cin >> prompt >> i;
    cout << i;

    return 0;
}
```

File I/O

You can use the C++ I/O system to perform file I/O. Although the end result is the same, C++'s approach to file I/O differs in places from the ANSI C I/O system discussed in Part II. For this reason, you will want to pay special attention to this section.

In order to perform file I/O, you must include the header file FSTREAM.H in your program. It defines several important **class**es and values.

Opening and Closing a File

In C++, a file is opened by linking it to a stream. There are three types of streams: input, output, and input/output. To open an input stream, you must declare the stream to be of **class ifstream**. To open an output stream, it must be declared as **class ofstream**. Streams that will be performing both input and output operations must be declared as **class fstream**. For example, this fragment creates one input stream, one output stream, and one stream capable of both input and output:

```
ifstream in;  // input

ofstream out; // output
```

```
fstream both; // input and output
```

Once you have created a stream, one way to associate it with a file is by using the function **open( )**. This function is a member of each of the three stream **class**es. Its prototype is shown here:

void open(char *filename, int mode, int access);

Here, *filename* is the name of the file, which may include a path specifier. The value of *mode* determines how the file is opened. It must be one (or more) of these values (defined in FSTREAM.H):

ios::app
ios::ate
ios::in
ios::nocreate
ios::noreplace
ios::out
ios::trunc

You can combine two or more of these values by ORing them together. Let's see what each of these values means.

Including **ios::app** causes all output to that file to be appended. This value can be used only with files capable of output. Including **ios::ate** causes a seek to the end of the file to occur when the file is opened.

The **ios::in** specifies that the file is capable of input. The **ios::out** specifies that the file is capable of output. However, creating a stream using **ifstream** implies input and creating a stream using **ofstream** implies output, so in these cases it is unnecessary to supply these values.

Including **ios::nocreate** causes the **open( )** function to fail if the file does not already exist. The **ios::noreplace** value causes the **open( )** function to fail if the file already exists.

The **ios::trunc** value causes the contents of a preexisting file by the same name to be destroyed and the file to be truncated to zero length.

The value of *access* determines how the file can be accessed. This value corresponds to DOS's file attribute codes, shown here:

Attribute	Meaning
0	Normal file—open access
1	Read-only file
2	Hidden file
4	System file
8	Archive bit set

You can OR two or more of these together.

The following fragment opens a normal output file:

```
ofstream out;

out.open("test", ios::out, 0);
```

However, you will seldom (if ever) see **open( )** called as shown because both the *mode* and *access* parameters have default values. For both **ifstream** and **ofstream** the *mode* parameter has a default value. For **ifstream** it is **ios::in**, and for **ofstream** it is **ios::out**. The *access* parameter also has a default value of 0 (normal file). Therefore, the preceding statement will usually look like this:

```
out.open("test");  // defaults to output and normal file
```

To open a stream for input and output, you must specify both the **ios::in** and the **ios::out** *mode* values, as shown in this example:

```
fstream mystream;

mystream.open("test", ios::in ¦ ios::out);
```

If **open( )** fails, **mystream** will be 0.

Although it is entirely proper to open a file using the **open( )** function, most of the time you will not do so because the **ifstream**, **ofstream**, and **fstream class**es have constructor functions that automatically open the file. The constructor functions have the same parameters and defaults as the **open( )** function. Therefore, the most common way you will see a file opened is as shown in this example:

```
ifstream  mystream("myfile"); // open file for input
```

If, for some reason, the file cannot be opened, the value of the associated stream variable will be zero. Therefore, to confirm that the file has actually been opened, you will use code like that shown here:

```
ifstream  mystream("myfile"); // open file for input
if(!mystream) {
  cout << "cannot open file";
  //  process error
}
```

To close a file, use the member function **close( )**. For example, to close the file linked to a stream called **mystream**, use this statement:

```
mystream.close();
```

The **close( )** function takes no parameters and returns no value.

Reading and Writing Text Files

To read from or write to a text file is a simple matter because you can simply use the << and >> operators. For example, this program writes an integer, a floating-point value, and a string to a file called TEST.

```
#include <iostream.h>
#include <fstream.h>

main(void)
{
  ofstream out("test");
  if(!out) {
  cout << "Cannot open file";
    return 1;
   }

  out << 10 << " " << 123.23 << "\n";
  out << "This is a short text file.";

  out.close();

  return 0;
}
```

The following program reads an integer, a **float**, a character, and a string from the file created by the previous program:

```
#include <iostream.h>
#include <fstream.h>

main(void)
{
  char ch;
  int i;
  float f;
  char str[80];

  ifstream in("test");
  if(!in) {
    cout << "Cannot open file";
    return 1;
  }

  in >> i;
  in >> f;
  in >> ch;
  in >> str;

  cout << i << " " << f << " " << ch << "\n";
  cout << str;
```

```
    in.close();
    return 0;
}
```

When reading text files using the **>>** operator, keep in mind that certain character translations will occur. For example, white-space characters are omitted. If you want to prevent any character translations, you must use C++'s binary I/O functions, which are discussed in the next section.

Binary I/O

There are two ways to write and read binary data to or from a file. First, you may write a byte using the member function **put( )** and read a byte using the member function **get( )**. The **get( )** function has many forms, but the most commonly used version is shown here along with **put( )**:

istream &get(char &*ch*);
ostream &put(char *ch*);

The **get( )** function reads a single character from the associated stream and puts that value in *ch*. It returns the stream. The **put( )** function writes *ch* to the stream and returns the stream.

This program will display the contents of any file on the screen. It uses the **get( )** function.

```
#include <iostream.h>
#include <fstream.h>

main(int argc, char *argv[])
{
  char ch;
```

```
if(argc!=2) {
  cout << "Usage: PR <filename>\n";
  return 1;
}

ifstream in(argv[1]);

if(!in) {
  cout << "Cannot open file";
  return 1;
}

while(in) { // in will be 0 when eof is reached
  in.get(ch);
  cout << ch;
}

return 0;
}
```

When **in** reaches the end of the file it will be zero, causing the **while** loop to stop.

There is actually a more compact way to code the loop that reads and displays a file, as shown here:

```
while(in.get(ch))
  cout << ch;
```

This works because **get( )** returns the stream **in**, and **in** will be zero when the end of the file is encountered.

This program uses **put( )** to write a string to a file:

```
#include <iostream.h>
#include <fstream.h>

main(void)
{
  char *p = "hello there";

  ofstream out("test");
  if(!out) {
    cout << "Cannot open file";
```

```
    return 1;
  }

  while(*p) out.put(*p++);

  out.close();

  return 0;
}
```

To read and write blocks of binary data, use C++'s **read( )** and **write( )** member functions. Their prototypes are shown here:

istream &read(unsigned char *buf, int num);
ostream &write(const unsigned char *buf, int num);

The **read( )** function reads num bytes from the associated stream and puts them in the buffer pointed to by buf. The **write( )** function writes num bytes to the associated stream from the buffer pointed to by buf.

The following program writes and then reads an array of integers:

```
#include <iostream.h>
#include <fstream.h>

main(void)
{
  int n[5] = {1, 2, 3, 4, 5};
  register int i;

  ofstream out("test");
  if(!out) {
    cout << "Cannot open file";
    return 1;
  }

  out.write((unsigned char *) &n, sizeof n);

  out.close();

  for(i=0; i<5; i++) // clear array
```

```
   n[i] = 0;

 ifstream in("test");
 in.read((unsigned char *) &n, sizeof n);

 for(i=0; i<5; i++) // show values read from file
   cout << n[i] << " ";

 in.close();

 return 0;
}
```

Note that the type casts inside the calls to **read( )** and **write( )** are necessary when operating on a buffer that is not defined as a character array.

If the end of the file is reached before *num* characters have been read, then **read( )** simply stops and the buffer contains as many characters as were available. You can find out how many characters have been read by using another member function called **gcount( )**, which has this prototype:

   int gcount( );

It returns the number of characters read by the last binary read operation.

Detecting EOF

You can detect when the end of the file is reached by using the member function **eof( )**, which has this prototype:

   int eof( );

It returns nonzero when the end of the file has been reached; otherwise, it returns zero.

Random Access

In C++'s I/O system you perform random access by using the
seekg( ) and **seekp( )** functions. Their most common forms are
shown here:

> istream &seekg(streamoff *offset,* seek_dir *origin*);
> ostream &seekp(streamoff *offset,* seek_dir *origin*);

Here, **streamoff** is a type defined in IOSTREAM.H that is capable
of containing the largest valid value that *offset* can have. **seek_dir**
is an enumeration that may have these values:

> ios::beg
> ios::cur
> ios::end

The C++ I/O system manages two pointers associated with a
file. One is the *get pointer,* which specifies where in the file the next
input operation will occur. The other is the *put pointer,* which
specifies where in the file the next output operation will occur.
Each time an input or output operation takes place, the appropriate pointer is automatically advanced. However, using the
seekg( ) and **seekp( )** functions, it is possible to access the file in a
nonsequential fashion.

The **seekg( )** function moves the associated file's current get
pointer *offset* number of bytes from the specified *origin,* which
must be one of these three values:

ios::beg	beginning of file
ios::cur	current location
ios::end	end of file

The **seekp( )** function moves the associated file's current put
pointer *offset* number of bytes from the specified *origin,* which
must be one of the values just shown.

This demonstrates the **seekp( )** function. It allows you to specify a filename on the command line followed by the specific byte in the file you want to change. It then writes an "X" at the specified location:

```
#include <iostream.h>
#include <fstream.h>
#include <stdlib.h>

main(int argc, char *argv[])
{
  if(argc!=3) {
    cout << "Usage: CHANGE <filename> <byte>\n";
    return 1;
  }

  ofstream out(argv[1]);
  if(!out) {
    cout << "Cannot open file";
    return 1;
  }

  out.seekp(atoi(argv[2]), ios::beg);

  out.put('X');
  out.close();

  return 0;
}
```

This program uses **seekg( )**. It displays the contents of a file, beginning with the location you specify:

```
#include <iostream.h>
#include <fstream.h>
#include <stdlib.h>

main(int argc, char *argv[])
{
  char ch;

  if(argc!=3) {
    cout << "Usage: PR <filename> <starting location>\n";
```

```
    return 1;
}

ifstream in(argv[1]);
if(!in) {
  cout << "Cannot open file";
  return 1;
}

in.seekg(atoi(argv[2]), ios::beg);

while(in.get(ch))
  cout << ch;

return 0;
}
```

You can determine the current position of each file pointer using these functions:

```
streampos tellg( );
streampos tellp( );
```

Here, **streampos** is a type defined in IOSTREAM.H that is capable of holding the largest value that either function can return.

As you have seen, C++'s I/O system is both powerful and flexible. Although this chapter discussed the most important and commonly used functions, C++ includes several other I/O functions. You should consult your Turbo C++ user manuals to see what other goodies are contained within the C++ I/O system.

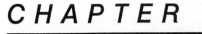

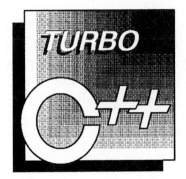

Miscellaneous C++ Topics

If you have read and worked through the examples of the preceding 20 chapters, then you can definitely call yourself a C++ programmer. This final chapter of the book discusses several aspects of C++ that were not covered in the previous chapters. It also looks at some differences between C and C++ as well as some design philosophy.

Dynamic Allocation Using new and delete

As you know, C uses the functions **malloc( )** and **free( )** (among others) to dynamically allocate memory and to free dynamically allocated memory. However, C++ contains two operators that perform the function of allocating and freeing memory in a better and easier way. The operators are **new** and **delete**. Their general form is shown here:

pointer＿var = new *var＿type*;
delete *pointer＿var*;

Here, *pointer＿var* is a pointer of type *var＿type*. The **new** operator allocates sufficient memory to hold a value of type *var＿type* and returns an address to it. Any valid data type may be allocated using **new**. The **delete** operator frees the memory pointed to by *pointer＿var*.

Like **malloc( )**, **new** returns a null pointer if the allocation request fails. Therefore, you must always check the pointer produced by **new** before using it. Also, like **malloc( )**, **new** allocates memory from the heap.

Because of the way dynamic allocation is managed, you can only use **delete** with a pointer to memory that was allocated using **new**. Using **delete** with any other type of address will cause serious problems.

There are several advantages to using **new** over **malloc( )**. First, **new** automatically computes the size of the type being allocated. You don't have to make use of the **sizeof** operator, which saves you some effort. More importantly, it prevents the wrong amount of memory from being accidentally allocated. Second, it automatically returns the correct pointer type—you don't need to use a type cast. Third, as you will soon see, it is possible to initialize the object being allocated using **new**. Finally, it is possible to overload **new** (and **delete**) relative to a **class.**

Here is a simple example of **new** and **delete**:

```
#include <iostream.h>

main(void)
{
  int *p;

  p = new int; // allocate memory for int
  if(!p) {
    cout << "allocation failure\n";
    return 1;
  }

  *p = 20; // assign that memory the value 20
  cout << *p; // prove that it works by displaying value

  delete p; // free the memory

  return 0;
}
```

This program assigns to **p** an address in memory that is large enough to hold an integer. It then assigns to that memory the value 20 and displays the contents of that memory on the screen. Finally, it frees the dynamically allocated memory.

As stated, you can initialize the memory using the **new** operator. To do this, specify the initial value inside parentheses after the type name. For example, this program uses initialization to give the memory that **p** points to, the value 99.

```
#include <iostream.h>

main(void)
{
  int *p;

  p = new int (99);  // initialize with 99
  if(!p) {
    cout << "allocation failure\n";
    return 1;
```

```
   }

   cout << *p;

   delete p;

   return 0;
}
```

You can allocate arrays using **new**. The general form for a singly dimensioned array is shown here:

pointer _ var = new *var _ type* [*size*];

Here, *size* specifies the number of elements in the array.

When you free a dynamically allocated array, you must use this form of **delete**:

delete [*size*] *pointer _ var*;

Again, *size* specifies the number of elements in the array. The reason you must specify the size of the array is that when you free the memory of an array containing objects, the destructor function (if existent) for each object must be executed. (You will see an example of this soon.)

This program allocates space for ten **float**s, assigns the array the values 100 to 109, and displays the contents of the array on the screen:

```
#include <iostream.h>

main(void)
{
  float *p;
  int i;

  p = new float [10]; // get a 10-element array
  if(!p) {
    cout << "allocation failure\n";
    return 1;
```

```
  }

  // assign the values 100 through 109
  for(i=0; i<10; i++) p[i] = 100.00 + i;

  // display the contents of the array
  for(i=0; i<10; i++)  cout << p[i] << " ";

  delete [10] p; // delete the entire array

  return 0;
}
```

There is one important point to remember about allocating an array: you cannot initialize it.

You can allocate memory for any valid type. This includes objects. For example, in this program, **new** allocates memory for an object of type **three_d**:

```
#include <iostream.h>

class three_d {
public:
  int x, y, z; // 3-d coordinates
  three_d(int a, int b, int c);
  ~three_d() {cout << "destructing\n";}
} ;

three_d::three_d(int a, int b, int c)
{
  cout << "constructing\n";
  x = a;
  y = b;
  z = c;
}

// Display X, Y, Z coordinates - three_d insertor
ostream &operator<<(ostream &stream, three_d obj)
{
  stream << obj.x << ", ";
  stream << obj.y << ", ";
  stream << obj.z << "\n";
  return stream;  // return the stream
}

main(void)
```

```
{
  three_d *p;

  p = new three_d (5, 6, 7);
  if(!p) {
    cout << "allocation failure\n";
    return 1;
  }

  cout << *p;

  delete p;

  return 0;
}
```

Notice that this program makes use of the insertor function for the **three _ d class** created in Chapter 20. When you run the program, you will see that **three _ d**'s constructor function is called when **new** is encountered and that its destructor function is called when **delete** is reached. Also note that the initializers are automatically passed to the constructor by **new**.

As this program illustrates, you may allocate an array of user-defined objects using **new**:

```
#include <iostream.h>
class three_d {
public:
  int x, y, z; // 3-d coordinates
  three_d(int a, int b, int c) ;
  three_d(){cout << "constructing\n";} // needed for arrays
  ~three_d() {cout << "destructing\n";}
} ;

three_d::three_d(int a, int b, int c)
{
  cout << "constructing\n";
  x = a;
  y = b;
  z = c;
}

// Display X, Y, Z coordinates - three_d insertor
ostream &operator<<(ostream &stream, three_d obj)
```

```
{
  stream << obj.x << ", ";
  stream << obj.y << ", ";
  stream << obj.z << "\n";
  return stream;  // return the stream
}

main(void)
{
  three_d *p;
  int i;

  p = new three_d [10];
  if(!p) {
    cout << "allocation failure\n";
    return 1;
  }

  for(i=0; i<10; i++) {
    p[i].x = 1;
    p[i].y = 2;
    p[i].z = 3;
  }

  for(i=0; i<10; i++) cout << *p;

  delete [10] p;

  return 0;
}
```

Notice that a second constructor function has been added to the **three_d class**. Because allocated arrays cannot be initialized, a constructor function that does not have any parameters is needed. If you don't supply this constructor, an error message will be displayed. In this example, it performs no service, but in other **class**es it might.

Overloading new and delete

It is possible to overload **new** and **delete**. One reason you might want to do this is because you want to use some special allocation method. For example, you may want allocation routines that automatically begin using a disk file as virtual memory when the heap has been exhausted. Whatever the reason, it is a very simple matter to overload these operators.

The skeletons for the functions that overload **new** and **delete** are shown here:

```
void *operator new(size_t size)
{
  // perform allocation
  return pointer_to_memory;
}

void operator delete(void *p)
{
  // free memory pointed to by p
}
```

The type **size_t** is defined by Turbo C++ as a type capable of containing the largest single piece of memory that can be allocated; **size_t** is an integer type. The parameter *size* will contain the number of bytes needed to hold the object being allocated. The overloaded **new** function must return a pointer to the memory that it allocates or zero if an allocation error occurs. Beyond these constraints, the overloaded **new** function can do anything else you require.

The **delete** function receives a pointer to the region of memory to free.

The **new** and **delete** operators may be overloaded globally so that all uses of these operators call your custom versions, or they can be overloaded relative to one or more **class**es. Let's begin with an example of overloading **new** and **delete** relative to the **three_d** type. For the purposes of illustration, no new allocation scheme will be used. Instead, the overloaded functions will simply invoke **malloc( )** and **free( )**. However, you are free to implement any alternative allocation scheme you like.

To overload the **new** and **delete** operators relative to a **class**, simply make the overloaded operator functions **class** members. For example, here the **new** and **delete** operators arc overloaded relative to the **three _ d class**:

```cpp
#include <iostream.h>
#include <stdlib.h>
class three_d {
public:
  int x, y, z; // 3-d coordinates
  three_d(int a, int b, int c) ;
  ~three_d() {cout << "destructing\n";}
  void *operator new(size_t size);
  void operator delete(void *p);
} ;

three_d::three_d(int a, int b, int c)
{
  cout << "constructing\n";
  x = a;
  y = b;
  z = c;
}

// Overload new relative to three_d
void * three_d::operator new(size_t size)
{
  cout << "in three_d new\n";
  return malloc(size);
}

// Overload delete relative to three_d
void three_d::operator delete(void *p)
{
  cout << "in three_d delete\n";
  free(p);
}

// Display X, Y, Z coordinates - three_d insertor
ostream &operator<<(ostream &stream, three_d obj)
{
```

```
    stream << obj.x << ", ";
    stream << obj.y << ", ";
    stream << obj.z << "\n";
    return stream;   // return the stream
}

main(void)
{
  three_d *p, *pl;

  p = new three_d (1, 2, 3);
  pl = new three_d (4, 5, 6);
  if(!p || !pl) {
    cout << "allocation failure\n";
    return 1;
  }

  cout << *p << *pl;

  delete p;
  delete pl;

  return 0;
}
```

It is important to understand that when **new** and **delete** are overloaded relative to a specific **class**, the use of these operators on any other type of data causes the original **new** or **delete** to be employed. The overloaded operators are only applied to the types for which they are defined. This means that if you add this line to **main()**, the global **new** will be executed:

```
int *i = new int;
```

You can overload **new** and **delete** globally by overloading them outside of any **class** declaration. When **new** and **delete** are overloaded globally, C++'s original **new** and **delete** are ignored and the new operators are used for all allocation requests. Of course, if you have defined any versions of **new** and **delete** relative to one or more **class**es, then the **class**-specific versions are used when allocating objects of the **class** for which they are defined. In other words, when either **new** or **delete** is encountered, the compiler first checks to see whether they are defined relative to the class they are operating on. If so, then those specific versions are used. If not, then C++ uses the globally defined **new** and **delete**. However, if these have been overloaded, then the overloaded versions are used.

To see an example of overloading **new** and **delete** globally, examine this program:

```cpp
#include <iostream.h>
#include <stdlib.h>
class three_d {
public:
  int x, y, z; // 3-d coordinates
  three_d(int a, int b, int c) ;
  ~three_d() {cout << "destructing\n";}
} ;

three_d::three_d(int a, int b, int c)
{
  cout << "constructing\n";
  x = a;
  y = b;
  z = c;
}

// Overload new globally.
void * operator new(size_t size)
{
  cout << "in new new\n";
  return malloc(size);
}

// Overload delete globally.
void operator delete(void *p)
{
  cout << "in new delete\n";
  free(p);
}

// Display X, Y, Z coordinates - three_d insertor
ostream &operator<<(ostream &stream, three_d obj)
{
  stream << obj.x << ", ";
  stream << obj.y << ", ";
```

```
     stream << obj.z << "\n";
     return stream;  // return the stream
   }

main(void)
{
   three_d *p, *pl;

   p = new three_d (1, 2, 3);
   pl = new three_d (4, 5, 6);
   if(!p || !pl) {
     cout << "allocation failure\n";
     return 1;
   }

   cout << *p << *pl;

   delete p;
   delete pl;

   int *i = new int;
   if(!i) {
     cout << "allocation failure\n";
     return 1;
   }

   *i = 10;
   cout << *i << "\n";
   return 0;
}
```

You should run this program to prove to yourself that the built-in
new and **delete** operators have, indeed, been overloaded.

Static Class Members

The keyword **static** can be applied to members of a **class**. Its
meaning in this context is similar to its meaning in C. When you
declare a member of a **class** as **static**, you are telling the compiler
that no matter how many objects of the **class** are created, there is

only one copy of the **static** member. A **static** member is *shared* by all objects of the **class**. All **static** data is initialized to zero when the first object of its **class** is created, and no other initialization is allowed.

As a first example, examine the following program and try to understand how it works:

```
#include <iostream.h>

class counter {
  static int count;
public:
  void setcount(int i) {count = i;};
  void showcount() {cout << count << " ";}
};

main(void)
{
  counter a, b;

  a.showcount(); // prints 0
  b.showcount(); // prints 0

  a.setcount(10); // set static count to 10

  a.showcount(); // prints 10
  b.showcount(); // also prints 10
}
```

Turbo C++ initializes **count** to 0. This is why the first calls to **showcount( )** both display 0. Next, object **a** sets **count** to 10. Next, both **a** and **b** use **showcount( )** to display its value. Because there is only one copy of **count** shared by both **a** and **b**, both cause the value 10 to be displayed.

 REMEMBER   When you declare a member of a **class** as **static**, you are causing only one copy of that member to be created and then shared by all objects of that **class**.

You can also have **static** member functions. When a member function is declared as **static**, then only one copy of it exists and it is used by all objects of the **class** it belongs to. **static** member functions have access to all **static** data and other **static** functions declared in a **class**, but they have two important restrictions: they cannot manipulate non-**static** data nor call non-**static** functions. The reason for this is that a **static** member function does not have a **this** pointer. This means that it has no way of knowing which object's non-**static** data to access. For example, if there are two objects of a **class** that contains a **static** function called **f( )**, and if **f( )** attempts to access a non-**static** variable called **var** defined in the **class**, which copy of **var** should the call be routed to? The compiler has no way of knowing. This is why **static** functions can only access other **static** functions or data.

To see an example of **static** functions, here is a short program that gives you the flavor of their usage. It is not uncommon for a object to require access to some scarce resource, such as a shared file in a network. As the program illustrates, the use of **static** data and functions provides a method by which an object can check on the status of the resource and access it if it is available:

```
#include <iostream.h>

enum access_t {shared, in_use, locked, unlocked};

// a scarce resource control class
class access {
  static enum access_t acs;
  // ...
public:
  static void set_access(enum access_t a) {acs = a;}
  static enum access_t get_access()
  {
    return acs;
  }
  // ...
};

main(void)
{
  access  obj1, obj2;

  obj1.set_access(locked);

  // ... intervening code

  // see if obj2 can access resource
```

```
    if(obj2.get_access()==unlocked) {
      obj2.set_access(in_use);
      cout << "access resource\n";
    }
    else cout << "locked out\n";

   // ...
}
```

If you compile this skeleton, you will see that "locked out" is displayed. You might want to play with the program a little, until you are sure you understand the effect of **static** on both data and functions.

As stated, **static** functions can only access other **static** functions or **static** data within the same **class**. To prove this, try compiling this version of the program:

```
#include <iostream.h>

enum access_t {shared, in_use, locked, unlocked};

// a scarce resource control class
class access {
  static enum access_t acs;
  int i;   // non-static
  // ...
public:
  static void set_access(enum access_t a) {acs = a;}
  static enum access_t get_access()
  {
    i = 100; // this will not compile
    return acs;
  }
  // ...
};

main(void)
{
  access  obj1, obj2;

  obj1.set_access(locked);

  // ... intervening code

  // see if obj2 can access resource
```

```
if(obj2.get_access()==unlocked) {
    obj2.set_access(in_use);
    cout << "access resource\n";
}
else cout << "locked out\n";

// ...
}
```

Turbo C++ will issue an error message and not compile your program because **getaccess( )** is attempting to access a non-**static** variable.

Although you may not see an immediate need for **static** members, as you continue to write programs in C++, you will find them very useful in certain situations because they allow you to avoid the use of global variables.

Differences Between C and C++

For the most part, C++ is a superset of ANSI standard C and virtually all C programs are also C++ programs. However, a few differences do exist, the most important of which are discussed here.

One of the most important yet subtle differences between C and C++ is the fact that in C, a function declared as

```
int f();
```

says *nothing* about any parameters to that function. That is, when there is nothing specified between the parentheses following the function's name, in C this means that nothing is being stated, one way or the other, about any parameters to that function. It might have parameters; it might not have parameters. However, in C++, a function declaration like this means that the function *does not* have parameters. That is, in C++, these two declarations are equivalent:

```
int f();

int f(void);
```

In C++, the **void** is optional. Many C++ programmers include the **void** as a means of making it completely clear to anyone reading the program that a function does not have any parameters. But this is technically unnecessary.

In C++, all functions must be prototyped. This is an option in C, although good programming practice suggests full prototyping be used in a C program.

A small but potentially important difference between C and C++ is that in C a character constant is automatically elevated to an integer. In C++, it is not.

In C, it is not an error to declare a global variable several times, even though this is bad programming practice. In C++, this is an error.

As you learned earlier, in C, an identifier may be up to 31 characters long. In C++, no such limit exists. However, from a practical point of view, extremely long identifiers are unwieldy and are seldom needed.

Turbo C++'s Complex and BCD Classes

In addition to the **class**es and overloaded operators defined by IOSTREAM.H and its derivatives, Turbo C++ includes two additional **class** libraries that perform complex and BCD arithmetic. Let's take a quick look at these now.

As you may know, a *complex* number has two parts: a real half and an imaginary half. The real half is an ordinary number; the imaginary part is a multiple of the square root of −1. To use complex numbers, you must include COMPLEX.H in your program.

To construct a complex number, use the **complex** constructor function. It has this prototype:

complex(double *real_part,* double *imaginary_part*);

The << and >> operators are overloaded relative to complex numbers. For example, this program constructs an imaginary number and displays it on the screen:

```
#include <iostream.h>
#include <complex.h>

main(void)
{
  complex num(10, 1);

  cout << num;

  return 0;
}
```

The program outputs the following:

```
(10, 1)
```

This output also illustrates the general format used when displaying complex numbers.

You may mix complex numbers with any other type of number, including integers, **floats**, and **doubles**. The arithmetic operators +, −, *, and / are overloaded relative to complex numbers as are the relational operators == and !=. This program illustrates how complex and regular numbers can be mixed in an expression.

```
#include <iostream.h>
#include <complex.h>

main(void)
{
  complex num(10, 1);

  num = 123.23 + num / 3;

  cout << num;

  return 0;
}
```

Turbo C++ has overloaded many mathematical functions, such as **sin( )** (which returns the sine of its argument) relative to complex numbers. It also defines several functions that apply specifically to complex numbers. The complex functions are shown in Table 21-1.

Turbo C++ also defines the **bcd class**. As you may know, real numbers can be represented inside the computer in a number of different ways. The most common is as binary floating-point values. However, another way to represent a real number is to use *Binary Coded Decimal,* or *BCD*. In BCD, base 10—rather than base 2—is used to represent a number. The major advantage to the BCD representation is that no round-off errors occur. For example, using binary floating point, the number 100.23 cannot be accurately represented and is rounded to 100.230003. However, using BCD, no rounding occurs. For this reason, BCD numbers are often used in accounting programs and the like. The major disadvantage to BCD numbers is that BCD calculations are slower than binary floating-point calculations. To use BCD numbers, you must include BCD.H in your programs.

The **bcd class** has these constructor functions:

bcd(int *n*);
bcd(double *n*);
bcd(double *n*, int *digits*);

The first two are self-explanatory. The last one creates a BCD

Table 21-1.

Function	Returns
complex abs(complex *n*)	The absolute value of *n*
double acos(complex *n*)	The arc cosine of *n*
double arg(complex *n*)	The angle of *n* in the complex coordinate plane
complex asin(complex *n*)	The arc sine of *n*
complex atan(complex *n*)	The arc tangent of *n*
complex atan2(complex *n*)	The arc tangent2 of *n*
double conj(complex *n*)	The conjugate of *n*
complex cos(complex *n*)	The cosine of *n*
complex cosh(complex *n*)	The hyperbolic cosine of *n*
complex exp(complex *n*)	e^n
double imag(complex *n*)	The imaginary part of *n*
complex log(complex *n*)	The natural log of *n*
complex log10(complex *n*)	The log base 10 of *n*
double norm(complex *n*)	The square of *n*
complex polar(double magnitude, double angle)	The complex number given its polar coordinates
complex pow(complex x, complex y)	
complex pow(complex x, double y)	
complex pow(double x, complex y)	x^y
double real(complex *n*)	The real part of *n*
complex sin(complex *n*)	The sine of *n*
complex sinh(complex *n*)	The hyperbolic sine of *n*
complex sqrt(complex *n*)	The square root of *n*
complex tan(complex *n*)	The tangent of *n*
complex tanh(complex *n*)	The hyperbolic tangent of *n*

The Complex Functions

Table 21-2.

Function	Returns
bcd abs(bcd n)	The absolute value of n
bcd acos(bcd n)	The arc cosine of n
bcd asin(bcd n)	The arc sine of n
bcd atan(bcd n)	The arc tangent of n
bcd cos(bcd n)	The cosine of n
bcd cosh(bcd n)	The hyperbolic cosine of n
bcd exp(bcd n)	e^n
bcd log(bcd n)	The natural log of n
bcd log10(bcd n)	The log base 10 of n
bcd pow(bcd x, bcd y)	x^y
bcd sin(bcd n)	The sine of n
bcd sinh(bcd n)	The hyperbolic sine of n
bcd sqrt(bcd n)	The square root of n
bcd tan(bcd n)	The tangent of n
bcd tanh(bcd n)	The hyperbolic tangent of n

The BCD Functions

number that uses *digits* (number of digits) after the decimal point.

In Turbo C++, BCD numbers range from 10^{-125} to 10^{125} with 17 digits of precision.

To convert a number from BCD format to normal binary floating-point format, use **real( )**, whose prototype is shown here:

long double real(bcd n);

The **bcd class** overloads the arithmetic and relational operators as well as the functions shown in Table 21-2.

Here is a sample program that illustrates the advantage of BCD numbers when prevention of round-off errors is important.

```
#include <iostream.h>
#include <bcd.h>
```

```
main(void)
{
  float f = 100.23, f1 = 101.337;
  bcd b(100.23), b1(101.337);

  cout << f+f1 << " " << b+b1;

  return 0;
}
```

This program displays

```
201.567001 201.567
```

on the screen.

The Message-Based Philosophy

Before concluding this book, a few words are in order about a programming philosophy that fits very well with OOP in general and C++ in particular. This programming philosophy is based on the concept of *messages*. In a message-based approach, most data is held privately inside a **class**. To retrieve or alter an item of data, you send the object a message to this effect. Code outside the **class** never operates directly on any data privately held by the **class**. Instead, the only things capable of altering data are the member (or **friend**) functions of the object that contains the data. This approach reduces the possibility of accidental side effects. It also lets you govern precisely what values the private data of an object may have because the member functions that access the data can filter out incorrect values.

In C++, to send an object a message means to call a member (or **friend**) function. To better understand this concept, think about a **class** that manages access to a database. In normal C code, to modify an entry in the database, you would simply write a line of code such as this:

```
database[record].balance = 100.75;
```

(assuming that **database** is an array of some sort of C-like structures).

However, using a message-based approach and C++, you would call a member function with the record number and new value as arguments. For example, you would use a statement such as this:

```
database.newbalance(record, 100.75);
```

(Here, **database** is an object.) In this case, no other code actually "touches" the data protected within the object.

To see how the message-based approach works in practice, here is a **class** that emulates a stopwatch along with a short **main( )** to illustrate its usage:

```
#include <iostream.h>
#include <time.h>
#include <conio.h>

class stopwatch {
  clock_t time1, time2;
public:
  stopwatch() {time1 = time2 = 0;}
  void reset() {time1 = time2 = 0;}
  void start() {time1 = clock()/CLK_TCK;}
  void stop() {time2 = clock()/CLK_TCK;}
  clock_t elapsed() {return time2 - time1;}
} ;

main(void)
{
  stopwatch timer;

  cout << "wait a while, then press a key\n";
  timer.start();

  while(!kbhit()) ; // wait for keypress

  timer.stop();
  cout << (long) timer.elapsed();
```

```
cout << " seconds have elapsed\n";

return 0;
}
```

This program displays the number of seconds between the time it starts running and the time you press a key. It uses Turbo C++'s **clock( )** function. This function returns a value which, when divided by **CLK_TCK**, is the number of seconds since the program started running. The type **clock_t** is defined in the TIME.H header file required by the **clock( )** function. This type is essentially a **long** integer. The macro **CLK_TCK** is also defined in this file.

The **stopwatch class** declares the variables **time1** and **time2** as private members. The only access to them is by sending messages through the member functions. For example, to start the stopwatch, send the message "start the clock" by calling the **start( )** function. This function then sets the value of **time1**. To stop the clock, send the message "stop the clock" by calling **stop( )**. To obtain the elapsed time, call the **elapsed( )** function. The key point here is that at no time does any other part of the program access **time1** or **time2** directly.

Although the implementation of **stopwatch** is correct as far as it goes, it does not provide all the protection for **time1** and **time2** that it might. For example, there is nothing that prevents the **start( )** function from being called a second time before a call to **stop( )**. Also, there is nothing that prevents **stop( )** from being called before **start( )** has been called. However, using the message-based architecture, it is possible to closely regulate access to private data and to prevent it from being misused. For example, here is an improved version of the program that prevents the accidental misuse of the stopwatch:

```
#include <iostream.h>
#include <time.h>
#include <conio.h>

class stopwatch {
```

```
    clock_t time1, time2;
    int ready;
public:
    stopwatch() {time1 = time2 = 0; ready = 1;}
    void reset() {time1 = time2 = 0; ready = 1;}
    void start();
    void stop();
    clock_t elapsed();
} ;

void stopwatch::start()
{
  if(!ready)
    cout << "timer has not been reset\n";
  else {
    time1 = clock()/CLK_TCK;
    ready = 0;
  }
}

void stopwatch::stop()
{
  if(ready)
    cout << "timer has not been started\n";
  else {
    time2 = clock()/CLK_TCK;
    ready = 1;
  }
}

clock_t stopwatch::elapsed()
{
  if(!ready) {
    cout << "timer has not been stopped\n";
    return -1;
  }
  else
    return time2 - time1;
}

main(void)
{
  stopwatch timer;

  cout << "wait a while, then press a key\n";
  timer.start();

  while(!kbhit()) ; // wait for keypress
  getch(); // read and dispose of keystroke
```

```
    timer.stop();
    cout << (long) timer.elapsed();
    cout << " seconds have elapsed\n";

    timer.stop(); // this will cause error message because
                  // the timer is not currently running

    timer.start();
    cout << "now running, wait a while, then press a key\n";

    while(!kbhit()) ; // wait for keypress

    timer.stop(); // now, this will work
    cout << (long) timer.elapsed();
    cout << " seconds have elapsed\n";

    return 0;
}
```

In this version, it is not possible to accidentally misuse the stopwatch because the **ready** flag is turned on only when the stopwatch is not currently running.

Although you don't have to use a message-based approach to programming in C++, you will be ignoring much of C++'s power if you don't. If you master this method, you will be writing programs that are more bug-free, extensible, and flexible.

Final Thoughts

If you are new to object oriented programming, but want to become proficient, the best approach is to write many object oriented programs. Programming is best learned by doing. Also, look at examples of C++ programs written by other people. If possible, study the C++ code written by several different programmers, paying attention to how the program is designed and implemented. Look for shortcomings as well as strong points. This will broaden the way you think about programming. Finally, experiment. Push your limits. You will be surprised how quickly you become an expert C++ programmer!

Some Common C Library Functions

As you know, C++ is built upon C. Much of the power of C is provided by its library functions. C++ includes these same functions and they are equally important to C++ programs. For this reason, a number of common library functions are examined here. If you have looked through the *Turbo C++ Library Reference*, you are no doubt aware of the large number of library functions. It is far beyond the scope of this book to cover each one. However, those discussed here, along with the class libraries discussed in the body of the book, are the ones you will need for most programming tasks.

The library functions that for the most part have not been covered in this book, can be grouped into these categories:

- string and character functions
- mathematical functions
- operating-system-related functions
- miscellaneous functions

This chapter will look at each of the categories in turn. Some of the functions discussed here have been presented in passing in earlier chapters. They are included here for a more formal treatment.

Each of the function descriptions begins with the header file required by the function followed by its prototype. Keep in mind that the prototype provides you with a quick way of knowing the type and number of arguments the function takes and what type of value it returns. All functions are listed alphabetically within each category.

This chapter only scratches the surface. You should leaf through the *Turbo C++ Library Reference* to see what other functions are available.

String and Character Functions

The Turbo C++ standard library has a rich and varied set of string and character handling functions. In C, a *string* is a null-terminated array of characters. The declarations for the string functions are found in the header file **string.h**. The character functions use **ctype.h** as their header file.

Because C has no bounds-checking on array operations, it is the programmer's responsibility to prevent an array overflow.

In Turbo C++, a *printable character* is one that can be displayed on a terminal. These are the characters between the space (0x20) and the tilde (0x7E). *Control characters* have values between 0 and 0x1F, as well as DEL (0x7F).

The character functions are declared to take an integer argument. While this is true, only the low-order byte is used by the function. Generally, you are free to use a character argument because it is automatically elevated to **int** at the time of the call.

#include <ctype.h>
int isalnum(int ch)

Description   The **isalnum( )** function returns nonzero if its argument is either a letter of the alphabet or a digit. If the character is not alphanumeric, then 0 is returned.

Example

This program checks each character read from the keyboard and reports all alphanumeric ones:

```
#include <ctype.h>
#include <stdio.h>
#include <conio.h>

main(void)
{
  char ch;

  for(;;) {
    ch = getche();
    if(ch==' ') break;
    if(isalnum(ch)) printf("%c is alphanumeric\n", ch);
```

```
  }
  return 0;
}
```

#include <ctype.h>
int isalpha(int ch)

Description   The **isalpha( )** function returns nonzero if *ch* is a letter of the alphabet; otherwise, 0 is returned.

Example

This program checks each character read from the keyboard and reports all those that are letters of the alphabet:

```
#include <ctype.h>
#include <stdio.h>
#include <conio.h>

main(void)
{
  char ch;
  for(;;) {
    ch = getche();
    if(ch==' ') break;
    if(isalpha(ch)) printf("%c is a letter\n", ch);
  }
  return 0;
}
```

#include <ctype.h>
int iscntrl(int ch)

Description   The **iscntrl( )** function returns nonzero if *ch* is between 0 and 0x1F or is equal to 0x7F (DEL); otherwise, 0 is returned.

Example

This program checks each character read from the keyboard and reports all those that are control characters:

```
#include <ctype.h>
#include <stdio.h>
#include <conio.h>

main(void)
{
  char ch;

  for(;;) {
    ch = getche();
    if(ch==' ') break;
    if(iscntrl(ch)) printf("%c is a control character\n", ch);
  }
  return 0;
}
```

#include <ctype.h>
int isdigit(int ch)

Description   The **isdigit( )** function returns nonzero if *ch* is a digit, that is, 0 through 9; otherwise, 0 is returned.

Example

This program checks each character read from the keyboard and reports all those that are digits:

```
#include <ctype.h>
#include <stdio.h>
#include <conio.h>
```

```
main(void)
{
  char ch;

  for(;;) {
    ch = getche();
    if(ch==' ') break;
    if(isdigit(ch)) printf("%c is a digit\n", ch);
  }
  return 0;
}
```

#include <ctype.h>
int isgraph(int ch)

Description   The **isgraph( )** function returns nonzero if *ch* is any printable character other than a space; otherwise, 0 is returned. Printable characters are in the range 0x21 through 0x7E.

Example

This program checks each character read from the keyboard and reports all those that are printable characters:

```
#include <ctype.h>
#include <stdio.h>

main(void)
{
  char ch;
  for(;;) {
    ch = getche();
    if(ch==' ') break;
    if(isgraph(ch)) printf("%c is a printing character\n",ch);
  }
  return 0;
}
```

#include <ctype.h>
int islower(int ch)

Description   The **islower( )** function returns nonzero if *ch* is a lowercase letter (a through z); otherwise, 0 is returned.

Example

This program checks each character read from the keyboard and reports all those that are lowercase letters:

```
#include <ctype.h>
#include <stdio.h>
#include <conio.h>

main(void)
{
  char ch;

  for(;;) {
    ch = getche();
    if(ch==' ') break;
    if(islower(ch)) printf("%c is lowercase\n", ch);
  }
  return 0;
}
```

#include <ctype.h>
int isprint(int ch)

Description   The **isprint( )** function returns nonzero if *ch* is a printable character, including a space; otherwise, 0 is returned. Printable characters are often in the range 0x20 through 0x7E.

Example

This program checks each character read from the keyboard and reports all those that are printable:

```
#include <ctype.h>
#include <stdio.h>
#include <conio.h>

main(void)
{
  char ch;

  for(;;) {
    ch = getche();
    if(ch==' ') break;
    if(isprint(ch)) printf("%c is printable\n", ch);
  }
  return 0;
}
```

#include <ctype.h>
int ispunct(int ch)

Description   The **ispunct( )** function returns nonzero if *ch* is a punctuation character, excluding the space; otherwise, 0 is returned. The term *punctuation,* as defined by this function, includes all printable characters that are neither alphanumeric nor a space.

Example

This program checks each character read from the keyboard and reports all those that are punctuation:

```
#include <ctype.h>
#include <stdio.h>
#include <conio.h>

main(void)
{
  char ch;

  for(;;) {
    ch = getche();
    if(ch==' ') break;
    if(ispunct(ch)) printf("%c is punctuation\n", ch);
  }
  return 0;
}
```

#include < ctype.h >
int isspace(int ch)

Description   The **isspace( )** function returns nonzero if *ch* is one of the following: a space, a tab, a vertical tab, a form feed, a carriage return, or a newline character; otherwise, 0 is returned.

Example

This program checks each character read from the keyboard and reports all those that are white-space:

```
#include <ctype.h>
#include <stdio.h>
#include <conio.h>

main(void)
{
  char ch;

  for(;;) {
    ch = getche();
```

```
    if(ch==' ') break;
    if(isspace(ch)) printf("%c is white-space\n", ch);
  }
  return 0;
}
```

#include <ctype.h>
int isupper(int ch)

Description   The **isupper( )** function returns nonzero if *ch* is an uppercase letter (A through Z); otherwise, 0 is returned.

Example

This program checks each character read from the keyboard and reports all those that are uppercase letters:

```
#include <ctype.h>
#include <stdio.h>
#include <conio.h>

main(void)
{
  char ch;

  for(;;) {
    ch = getche();
    if(ch==' ') break;
    if(isupper(ch)) printf("%c is uppercase\n", ch);
  }
  return 0;
}
```

#include <ctype.h>
int isxdigit(int ch)

Description   The **isxdigit( )** function returns nonzero if *ch* is a hexadecimal digit; otherwise, 0 is returned. A hexadecimal digit will be in one of these ranges: A through F, a through f, or 0 through 9.

Example

This program checks each character read from the keyboard and reports all those that are hexadecimal digits:

```
#include <ctype.h>
#include <stdio.h>
#include <conio.h>

main(void)
{
  char ch;

  for(;;) {
    ch = getche();
    if(ch==' ') break;
    if(isxdigit(ch)) printf("%c is hexadecimal \n", ch);
  }
  return 0;
}
```

#include < string.h >
char *strcat(char *str1, const char *str2)

Description   The **strcat( )** function concatenates a copy of *str2* to *str1* and terminates *str1* with a null. The null terminator originally ending *str1* is overwritten by the first character of *str2*. The string *str2* is untouched by the operation. The **strcat( )** function returns the string *str1*.

Remember, no bounds-checking takes place, so it is the programmer's responsibility to ensure that *str1* is large enough to hold both its original contents and those of *str2*.

Example

This program appends the first string read from the keyboard to the second. For example, assuming the user enters **hello** and **there**, the program will print "therehello."

```
#include <string.h>
#include <stdio.h>

main(void)
{
  char s1[80], s2[80];

  printf("enter two strings: ");
  gets(s1);
  gets(s2);

  strcat(s2, s1);
  printf(s2);
  return 0;
}
```

#include *<string.h>*
char *strchr(const char *str, int ch)

Description   The **strchr( )** function returns a pointer to the first occurrence of the low-order byte of *ch* in the string pointed to by *str*. If no match is found, a null pointer is returned.

Example

This program prints the string "is a test":

```
#include <string.h>
#include <stdio.h>

main(void)
{
  char *p;

  p = strchr("this is a test", (int) ' ');
  printf(p);
  return 0;
}
```

#include <string.h>
int strcmp(const char *str1, const char *str2)

Description The **strcmp( )** function compares two null-terminated strings and returns an integer based on the outcome, as shown here:

Value	Meaning
less than 0	*str1* is less than *str2*
0	*str1* is equal to *str2*
greater than 0	*str1* is greater than *str2*

Example

The following function can be used as a password-verification routine. It will return 0 upon failure and 1 upon success.

```
#include <string.h>

password()
{
  char s[80];

  printf("enter password: ");
  gets(s);

  if(strcmp(s,"pass")) {
    printf("invalid password\n");
    return 0;
  }
  return 1;
}
```

#include <string.h>
char *strcpy(char *str1, const char *str2)

Description The **strcpy( )** function is used to copy the contents of *str2* into *str1,* where *str2* must be a pointer to a null-terminated string. The **strcpy( )** function returns a pointer to *str1.*

If *str1* and *str2* overlap, the behavior of **strcpy( )** is undefined.

Example

The following code fragment will copy "hello" into string **str**:

```
char str[80];
strcpy(str, "hello");
```

#include <string.h>
*unsigned int strlen(const char *str)*

Description   The **strlen( )** function returns the length of the null-terminated string pointed to by *str.* The null is not counted.

Example

The following code fragment will print the number 5 on the screen:

```
strcpy(s, "hello");
printf("%d", strlen(s));
```

#include <stdio.h>
*char *strstr(const char *str1,*
*const char *str2)*

Description   The **strstr( )** function returns a pointer to the first occurrence in the string pointed to by *str1* of the string pointed to by *str2* (except *str2*'s null terminator). It returns a null pointer if no match is found.

Example

This program displays the message "is a test":

```
#include <string.h>
#include <stdio.h>

main(void)
{
  char *p;

  p = strstr("this is a test","is");
  printf(p);
  return 0;
}
```

#include <string.h>
char *strtok(char *str1, const char *str2)

Description   The **strtok( )** function returns a pointer to the next token in the string pointed to by *str1*. The characters making up the string pointed to by *str2* are the delimiters that determine the token. A null pointer is returned when there is no token to return.

The first time **strtok( )** is called, *str1* is actually used in the call. Subsequent calls use a null pointer for the first argument. In this way the entire string can be reduced to its tokens.

It is important to understand that the **strtok( )** function modifies the string pointed to by *str1*. Each time a token is found, a null is placed where the delimiter was found. In this way **strtok( )** can continue to advance through the string.

It is possible to use a different set of delimiters for each call to **strtok( )**.

Example

This program tokenizes the string "The summer soldier, the sunshine patriot" with spaces and commas being the delimiters. The output will be

The | summer | soldier | the | sunshine | patriot

```
#include <string.h>
#include <stdio.h>

main(void)
{
  char *p;

  p = strtok("The summer soldier, the sunshine patriot", " ,");
  printf(p);
  do {
    p = strtok('\0', " ,");
    if(p) printf("|%s", p);
  } while(p);
  return 0;
}
```

#include <ctype.h>
int tolower(int ch)

Description The **tolower**( ) function returns the lowercase equivalent of *ch* if *ch* is a letter; otherwise, *ch* is returned unchanged.

Example

This fragment displays "q":

```
putchar(tolower('Q'));
```

#include <ctype.h>
int toupper(int ch)

Description The **toupper**( ) function returns the uppercase equivalent of *ch* if *ch* is a letter; otherwise *ch* is returned unchanged.

Example

This code fragment displays "A":

```
putchar(toupper('a'));
```

Mathematics Functions

Turbo C++ contains several mathematical functions that take **double** arguments and return **double** values. These functions fall into the following categories:

- trigonometric functions
- hyperbolic functions
- exponential and logarithmic functions
- miscellaneous

All the math functions require the header **math.h** to be included in any program using them. In addition to declaring the math functions, this header defines macros called **EDOM**, **ERANGE**, and **HUGE_VAL**. If an argument to a math function is not in the domain for which it is defined, then a 0 is returned and the global **errno** is set equal to **EDOM**. If a routine produces a result that is too large to be represented by a **double**, an overflow occurs. This causes the routine to return **HUGE_VAL**, and **errno** is set to **ERANGE**, indicating a range error. If an underflow happens, the routine returns 0 and sets **errno** to **ERANGE**.

Many of the math functions are overloaded to operate with complex numbers. The complex versions of those functions are discussed in Chapter 21. Here, only the C-like versions are examined.

#include <math.h>
double acos(double arg)

Description   The **acos( )** function returns the arc cosine of *arg*. The argument to **acos( )** must be in the range −1 to 1; otherwise, a domain error will occur.

Example

This program prints the arc cosines, in one-tenth increments, of the values −1 through 1:

```
#include <math.h>
#include <stdio.h>

main(void)
{
  double val = -1.0;

  do {
    printf("arc cosine of %f is %f\n", val, acos(val));
    val += 0.1;
  } while(val<=1.0);
  return 0;
}
```

#include <math.h>
double asin(double arg)

Description   The **asin( )** function returns the arc sine of *arg*. The argument to **asin( )** must be in the range −1 to 1; otherwise, a domain error will occur.

Example

This program prints the arc sines, in one-tenth increments, of the values −1 through 1:

```
#include <math.h>
#include <stdio.h>

main(void)
{
  double val=-1.0;
  do {
    printf("arc sine of %f is %f\n", val, asin(val));
    val += 0.1;
  } while(val<=1.0);
  return 0;
}
```

#include < math.h >
double atan(double arg)

Description   The **atan( )** function returns the arc tangent of *arg*.

Example

This program prints the arc tangents, in one-tenth increments, of the values −1 through 1:

```
#include <math.h>
#include <stdio.h>

main(void)
{
  double val=-1.0;

  do {
    printf("arc tangent of %f is %f\n", val, atan(val));
```

```
    val += 0.1;
  } while(val<=1.0);
  return 0;
}
```

#include <math.h >
double atan2(double y, double x)

Description   The **atan2( )** function returns the arc tangent of *y/x*. It uses the signs of its arguments to compute the quadrant of the return value.

Example

This program prints the arc tangents, in one-tenth increments, of *y* from −1 through 1:

```
#include <math.h>
#include <stdio.h>

main(void)
{
  double y=-1.0;

  do {
    printf("atan2 of %f is %f\n", y atan2(y, 1.0));
    y += 0.1;
  } while(y<=1.0);
  return 0;
}
```

#include <math.h >
double ceil(double num)

Description   The **ceil( )** function returns the smallest integer represented as a **double** not less than *num*. For example, given 1.02, **ceil( )** would return 2.0. For −1.02, **ceil( )** would return −1.

Example

This fragment prints "10" on the screen:

```
printf("%f", ceil(9.9));
```

#include <math.h>
double cos(double arg)

Description   The **cos( )** function returns the cosine of *arg*. The value of *arg* must be in radians.

Example

This program prints the cosines, in one-tenth increments, of the values −1 through 1:

```
#include <math.h>
#include <stdio.h>

main(void)
{
  double val=-1.0;

  do {
    printf("cosine of %f is %f\n", val, cos(val));
    val += 0.1;
  } while(val<=1.0);
  return 0;
}
```

#include <math.h>
double cosh(double arg)

Description   The **cosh( )** function returns the hyperbolic cosine of *arg*. The value of *arg* must be in radians.

Example

This program prints the hyperbolic cosines, in one-tenth increments, of the values −1 through 1:

```
#include <math.h>
#include <stdio.h>

main(void)
{
  double val=-1.0;

  do {
    printf("hyperbolic cosine of %f is %f\n", val, cosh(val));
    val += 0.1;
  } while(val<=1.0);
  return 0;
}
```

#include < math.h >
double exp(double arg)

Description   The **exp( )** function returns the natural logarithm *e* raised to the *arg* power.

Example

This fragment displays the value of *e* (rounded to 2.718282):

```
printf("value of e to the first: %f", exp(1.0));
```

#include < math.h >
double fabs(double num)

Description   The **fabs( )** function will return the absolute value of *num*.

Example

This program prints "1.0 1.0" on the screen:

```
#include <math.h>
#include <stdio.h>

main(void)
{
  printf("%1.1f %1.1f", fabs(1.0), fabs(-1.0));
  return 0;
}
```

#include <math.h>
double floor(double num)

Description   The **floor( )** function returns the largest integer (represented as a **double**) not greater than *num*. For example, given 1.02, **floor( )** would return 1.0. Given −1.02, **floor( )** would return −2.0.

Example

This fragment prints "10" on the screen:

```
printf("%f", floor(10.9));
```

#include <math.h>
double log(double num)

Description   The **log( )** function returns the natural logarithm for *num*. A domain error occurs if *num* is negative, and a range error occurs if the argument is 0.

Example

This program prints the natural logarithms for the numbers 1 through 10:

```
#include <math.h>
#include <stdio.h>

main(void)
{
  double val=1.0;

  do {
    printf("%f %f\n", val, log(val));
    val++;
  } while (val<11.0);
  return 0;
}
```

#include <math.h>
double log10(double num)

Description   The **log10( )** function returns the base 10 logarithm for *num*. A domain error occurs if *num* is negative, and a range error occurs if the argument is 0.

Example

This program prints the base 10 logarithms for the numbers 1 through 10:

```
#include <math.h>
#include <stdio.h>

main(void)
{
```

```
double val=1.0;

do {
  printf("%f %f\n", val, log10(val));
  val++;
} while (val<11.0);
return 0;
}
```

#include <math.h>
double pow(double base, double exp)

Description   The **pow( )** function returns *base* raised to the *exp* power (*base*^{exp}). A domain error occurs if *base* is 0 and *exp* is less than or equal to 0. It may also happen if *base* is negative and *exp* is not an integer. An overflow produces a range error.

Example

This program prints the first ten powers of 10:

```
#include <math.h>
#include <stdio.h>

main(void)
{
  double x=10.0, y=0.0;

  do {
    printf("%f",pow(x, y));
    y++;
  } while(y<11);
  return 0;
}
```

#include <math.h>
double sin(double arg)

Description   The **sin( )** function returns the sine of *arg*. The value of *arg* must be in radians.

Example

This program prints the sines, in one-tenth increments, of the values −1 through 1:

```
#include <math.h>
#include <stdio.h>

main(void)
{
  double val=-1.0;

  do {
    printf("sine of %f is %f\n", val, sin(val));
    val += 0.1;
  } while(val<=1.0);
  return 0;
}
```

#include <math.h>
double sinh(double arg)

Description   The **sinh( )** function returns the hyperbolic sine of *arg*. The value of *arg* must be in radians.

Example

This program prints the hyperbolic sines, in one-tenth increments, of the values −1 through 1:

```
#include <math.h>
#include <stdio.h>

main(void)
{
  double val=-1.0;
```

```
do {
  printf("hyperbolic sine of %f is %f\n", val, sinh(val));
  val += 0.1;
} while(val<=1.0);
return 0;
}
```

#include <math.h>
double sqrt(double num)

Description   The **sqrt( )** function returns the square root of *num*. If it is called with a negative argument, a domain error will occur.

Example

This fragment prints "4" on the screen:

```
printf("%f", sqrt(16.0));
```

#include <math.h>
double tan(double arg)

Description   The **tan( )** function returns the tangent of *arg*. The value of *arg* must be in radians.

Example

This program prints the tangent, in one-tenth increments, of the values −1 through 1:

```
#include <math.h>
#include <stdio.h>

main(void)
{
  double val=-1.0;

  do {
    printf("tangent of %f is %f\n", val, tan(val));
    val += 0.1;
  } while(val<=1.0);
  return 0;
}
```

#include <math.h>
double tanh(double arg)

Description   The **tanh( )** function returns the hyperbolic tangent of *arg*. The value of *arg* must be in radians.

Example

This program prints the hyperbolic tangent, in one-tenth increments, of the values −1 through 1:

```
#include <math.h>
#include <stdio.h>

main(void)
{
  double val=-1.0;

  do {
    printf("Hyperbolic tangent of %f is %f\n", val, tanh(val));
    val += 0.1;
  } while(val<=1.0);
  return 0;
}
```

Operating-System-Related Functions

This section covers those functions that in one way or another are more operating-system sensitive than others. Of the functions found in Turbo C++'s library, these include the time and date functions as well as those functions that allow direct operating-system interfacing.

The time and date functions require the header **time.h** for their prototypes. The header file also defines two types. The **time_t** type is capable of representing the system time and date as a long integer. This is called the *calendar time*. The structure type **tm** holds the date and time broken down into its elements. The **tm** structure is defined as shown here:

```
struct tm {
  int tm_sec;   /* seconds, 0-59 */
  int tm_min;   /* minutes, 0-59 */
  int tm_hour;  /* hours, 0-23 */
  int tm_mday;  /* day of the month, 1-31 */
  int tm_mon;   /* months since Jan, 0-11 */
  int tm_year;  /* years from 1900 */
  int tm_wday;  /* days since Sunday, 0-6 */
  int tm_yday;  /* days since Jan 1, 0-365 */
  int tm_isdst  /* Daylight Savings Time indicator */
}
```

The value of **tm_isdst** will be positive if Daylight Savings Time is in effect, 0 if it is not in effect, and negative if no information is available. Time represented in this way is referred to as *broken-down time*.

The DOS interfacing functions defined by Turbo C++ require the header **dos.h**. The **dos.h** file defines a union that corresponds to the registers of the 8088/86 CPU and is used by some of the system interfacing functions. It is defined as the union of two structures in order to allow each register to be accessed by word *or* by byte.

```
/*      dos.h

        Defines structs, unions, macros, and functions
        for dealing  with MSDOS and the Intel iAPX86
        microprocessor family.

        Copyright (c) Borland International Inc. 1987, 1988,
        1990 All Rights Reserved.
*/
struct WORDREGS
        {
        unsigned int      ax, bx, cx, dx, si, di, cflag, flags;
        };

struct BYTEREGS
        {
        unsigned char     al, ah, bl, bh, cl, ch, dl, dh;
        };
union   REGS      {
        struct    WORDREGS x;
        struct    BYTEREGS h;
        };
```

#include <time.h>
char *asctime(const struct tm *ptr)

Description   The **asctime( )** function returns a pointer to a string that converts the information stored in the structure pointed to by *ptr* into the following form:

day month date hours:minutes:seconds year\n\0

For example:

Wed Jun 19 12:05:34 1999

The structure pointer passed to **asctime( )** is usually obtained from either **localtime( )** or **gmtime( )**.

The buffer used by **asctime( )** to hold the formatted output string is a statically allocated character array and is overwritten each time the function is called. If you wish to save the contents of the string, it is necessary to copy it elsewhere.

Example

This program displays the local time defined by the system:

```
#include <time.h>
#include <stdio.h>

main(void)
{
  struct tm *ptr;
  time_t lt;
  lt = time(NULL);
  ptr = localtime(&lt);
  printf(asctime(ptr));
  return 0;
}
```

#include <dos.h>
int bdos(int fnum, unsigned dx, unsigned al)

Description   This function is not part of the ANSI C Standard.

The **bdos( )** function is used to access the DOS system call specified by *fnum*. It first places the value *dx* into the DX register and the value *al* into the AL register. It then executes an INT 21H instruction.

The **bdos( )** function returns the value of the AX register, which is used by DOS to return information.

The **bdos( )** function can be used to access only those system calls that either take no arguments or require only DX and/or AL for their arguments.

Example

This program reads characters directly from the keyboard, by-passing all of C's I/O functions, until a **q** is typed:

```
/* do raw keyboard reads */
#include <dos.h>

main(void)
{
  char ch;

  while((ch=bdos(1,0,0))!=\q) ;
  return 0;
}
```

#include <time.h>
char *ctime(const time_t *time)

Description   The **ctime( )** function returns a pointer to a string of the form

day month date hours:minutes:seconds year\n\0

given a pointer to the calendar time. The calendar time is generally obtained through a call to **time( )**. The **ctime( )** function is equivalent to

```
asctime(localtime(time))
```

The buffer used by **ctime( )** to hold the formatted output string is a statically allocated character array and is overwritten each time the function is called. If you wish to save the contents of the string, it is necessary to copy it elsewhere.

Example

This program displays the local time defined by the system:

```
#include <time.h>
#include <stdio.h>
main(void)
{
  time_t lt;

  lt = time(NULL);
  printf(ctime(&lt));
  return 0;
}
```

#include <time.h>
double difftime(time_t time2, time_t time1)

Description   The **difftime( )** function returns the difference, in seconds, between *time1* and *time2* — that is, *time2* minus *time1*.

Example

This program times the number of seconds that it takes for the empty **for** loop to go from 0 to 500000:

```
#include <time.h>
#include <stdio.h>

main(void)
{
  time_t start,end;
  long unsigned int t;

  start = time(NULL);
  for(t=0; t<500000L; t++) ;
  end = time(NULL);
```

```
    printf("loop required %f seconds\n", difftime(end, start));
    return 0;
}
```

#include <time.h>
struct tm *gmtime(const time _ t *time)

Description   The **gmtime( )** function returns a pointer to the broken-down form of *time* in the form of a **tm** structure. The time is represented in Greenwich mean time. The *time* value is generally obtained through a call to **time( )**.

The structure used by **gmtime( )** to hold the broken-down time is statically allocated and is overwritten each time the function is called. If you wish to save the contents of the structure, it is necessary to copy it elsewhere.

Example

This program prints both the local time and the Greenwich mean time of the system:

```
#include <time.h>
#include <stdio.h>

/* print local and GM time */
main(void)
{
   struct tm *local, *gm;
   time_t t;

   t = time(NULL);
   local = localtime(&t);
   printf("Local time and date: %s", asctime(local));
   gm = gmtime(&t);
```

```
    printf("Greenwich mean time and date: %s", asctime(gm));
    return 0;
}
```

#include <dos.h>
int int86(int int_num, union REGS *in_regs,
union REGS *out_regs)

Description   This function is not part of the ANSI C Standard.

The **int86( )** function is used to execute a software interrupt specified by *int_num*. The contents of the union *in_regs* are first copied into the register of the processor and then the proper interrupt is executed.

Upon return, the union *out_regs* will contain the values of the registers that the CPU has returning from the interrupt.

The union **REGS** is defined in the header **dos.h**.

Example

The **int86( )** function is often used to call ROM routines in the IBM PC. For example, this function executes an INT 10H function code 0 that causes the video mode to be set to that specified by the argument **mode**:

```
#include <dos.h>

set_mode(char mode)
{
  union REGS in, out;

  in.h.al = mode;
  in.h.ah = 0;  /* set mode function number */

  int86(0x10, &in, &out);
}
```

#include <dos.h>
int intdos(union REGS *in _regs,
union REGS *out _regs)

Description   This function is not part of the ANSI C Standard.

The **intdos( )** function is used to access the DOS system call specified by the contents of the union pointed to by *in _regs*. It executes an INT 21H instruction and the outcome of the operation is placed in the union pointed to by *out _regs*. The **intdos( )** function returns the value of the AX register, which is used by DOS to return information.

The **intdos( )** function is used to access those system calls that either require arguments in registers other than only DX and/or AL or that return information in a register other than AX.

The union **REGS** defines the registers of the 8088/86 family of processors and is found in the **dos.h** header file.

Example

This program reads the time directly from the system clock, bypassing all of C's time functions:

```
#include <dos.h>
#include <stdio.h>

main(void)
{
  union REGS in, out;

  in.h.ah = 0x2c;  /* get time function number */
  intdos(&in, &out);
  printf("time is %.2d:%.2d:%.2d",out.h.ch, out.h.cl, out.h.dh);
  return 0;
}
```

#include <time.h>
struct tm *localtime(const time_t *time)

Description   The **localtime( )** function returns a pointer to the broken-down form of *time* in the form of a **tm** structure. The time is represented in local time. The *time* value is generally obtained through a call to **time( )**.

The structure used by **localtime( )** to hold the broken-down time is statically allocated and is overwritten each time the function is called. If you wish to save the contents of the structure, it is necessary to copy it elsewhere.

Example

This program prints both the local time and the Greenwich mean time of the system:

```
#include <time.h>
#include <stdio.h>

/* print local and Greenwich mean time */
main(void)
{
  struct tm *local;
  time_t t;

  t = time(NULL);
  local = localtime(&t);
  printf("Local time and date: %s", asctime(local));
  local = gmtime(&t);
  printf("Greenwich mean time and date: %s", asctime(local));
  return 0;
}
```

#include <time.h>
time_t time(time_t *time)

Description   The **time( )** function returns the current calendar time of the system. If the system has no time, then −1 is returned.

The **time( )** function can be called either with a null pointer or with a pointer to a variable of type **time_t**. If the latter is used, then the argument will also be assigned the calendar time.

Example

This program displays the local time defined by the system:

```
#include <time.h>
#include <stdio.h>

main(void)
{
  struct tm *ptr;
  time_t lt;

  lt = time(NULL);
  ptr = localtime(&lt);
  printf(asctime(ptr));
  return 0;
}
```

Miscellaneous Functions

The functions discussed in this section are those standard functions that do not easily fit into another category.

#include <stdlib.h>
void abort(void)

Description   The **abort( )** function causes immediate termination of a program. No files are flushed and the value 3 is returned to the calling process (usually the operating system).

The primary use of **abort( )** is to prevent a runaway program from closing active files.

Example

In this program, if the user enters an **A**, the program will terminate:

```
#include <stdlib.h>
#include <stdio.h>
#include <conio.h>

main(void)
{
  for(;;)
    if(getche()=='A') abort();
  return 0;
}
```

#include < stdlib.h >
int abs(int num)

Description   The **abs( )** function returns the absolute value of the integer *num*.

Example

This function converts the user-entered numbers into their absolute values:

```
#include <stdlib.h>
#include <stdio.h>
```

```
get_abs(void)
{
  char num[80];

  gets(num)

  return abs(atoi(num));
}
```

#include <stdlib.h>
double atof(const char *str)

Description   The **atof( )** function converts the string pointed to by *str* into a **double** value. The string must contain a valid floating-point number. If this is not the case, the returned value is 0.

The number may be terminated by any character that cannot be part of a valid floating-point number. This includes whitespace, punctuation (other than periods), and characters other than "E" or "e." This means that if **atof( )** is called with "100.00HELLO," the value 100.00 will be returned.

Example

This program will read two floating-point numbers and will display their sum:

```
#include <stdlib.h>
#include <stdio.h>

main(void)
{
  char num1[80], num2[80];

  printf("enter first: ");
  gets(num1);
```

```
      printf("enter second: ");
      gets(num2);
      printf("the sum is: %f",atof(num1)+atof(num2));
      return 0;
    }
```

#include < stdlib.h >
int atoi(const char *str)

Description   The **atoi( )** function converts the string pointed to by *str* into an **int** value. The string must contain a valid integer number. If this is not the case, the returned value is 0.

The number may be terminated by any character that cannot be part of an integer number. This includes white-space, punctuation, and other characters. This means that if **atoi( )** is called with "123.23", the integer value 123 will be returned and the 0.23 ignored.

Example

This program reads two integer numbers and displays their sum:

```
#include <stdlib.h>
#include <stdio.h>

main(void)
{
  char num1[80], num2[80];

  printf("enter first: ");
  gets(num1);
  printf("enter second: ");
  gets(num2);
  printf("the sum is: %d",atoi(num1)+atoi(num2));
  return 0;
}
```

#include <stdlib.h>
int atol(const char *str)

Description   The **atol( )** function converts the string pointed to by *str* into a **long int** value. The string must contain a valid long integer number. If this is not the case, the returned value is 0.

The number may be terminated by any character that cannot be part of an integer number. This includes white-space, punctuation, and other characters. This means that if **atol( )** is called with "123.23", the integer value 123 will be returned and the 0.23 ignored.

Example

This program reads two long integer numbers and displays their sum in the following manner:

```
#include <stdlib.h>
#include <stdio.h>

main(void)
{
  char num1[80], num2[80];

  printf("enter first: ");
  gets(num1);
  printf("enter second: ");
  gets(num2);
  printf("the sum is: %ld",atol(num1)+atol(num2));
  return 0;
}
```

#include <stdlib.h>
void *bsearch(const void *key,
const void *base,
unsigned num, unsigned size,
int (*compare) (const void *,
const void *))

Description   The **bsearch( )** function performs a binary search on the sorted array pointed to by *base*, and returns a pointer to the first member that matches the key pointed to by *key*. The number of elements in the array is specified by *num*, and the size (in bytes) of each element is described by *size*.

The function pointed to by *compare* is used to compare an element of the array with the key. The form of the compare function must be

func__name(const void *arg1*, const void *arg2*)

It must return the following values:

- If *arg1* is less than *arg2*, then return less than 0.
- If *arg1* is equal to *arg2*, then return 0.
- If *arg1* is greater than *arg2*, then return greater than 0.

The array must be sorted in ascending order with the lowest address containing the lowest element.

If the array does not contain the key, then a null pointer is returned.

Example

This program reads characters entered at the keyboard (assuming buffered keyboard I/O) and determines whether they belong to the alphabet:

```
#include <stdlib.h>
#include <ctype.h>
#include <stdio.h>
int comp();

char *alpha="abcdefghijklmnopqrstuvwxyz";

main(void)
{
```

```
   char ch;
   char *p;
   int comp();

   do {
     printf("enter a character: ");
     scanf("%c%*c",&ch);
     ch = tolower(ch);
     p = (char *) bsearch(&ch,alpha, 26, 1, comp);
     if(p) printf("is in alphabet\n");
     else printf("is not in alphabet\n");
   } while(p);
   return 0;
}

/* compare two characters */
comp(const char *ch, const char *s)
{
  return *ch-*s;
}
```

#include <stdlib.h>
void exit(int status)

Description   The **exit( )** function causes immediate, normal termination of a program.

The value of *status* is passed to the calling process—usually the operating system—if the environment supports it. By convention, if the value of *status* is 0, normal program termination is assumed. A nonzero value may be used to indicate an error.

Example

This function performs menu selection for a mailing list program. If **Q** is selected, the program is terminated.

```
menu(void)
{
  char choice;
```

```
do {
  printf("Enter names (E)\n");
  printf("Delete name (D)\n");
  printf("Print (P)\n");
  printf("Quit (Q)\n");
} while(!strchr("EDPQ",toupper(ch)));
if(ch=='Q') exit(0);
return ch;
}
```

#include <stdlib.h>
char *itoa(int num, char *str, int radix)

Description   This function is not currently defined by the ANSI
C standard.

The **itoa( )** function converts the integer *num* into its string
equivalent and places the result in the string pointed to by *str*. The
base of the output string is determined by *radix*, which may be in
the range 2 through 36.

The **itoa( )** function returns a pointer to *str*. Generally, str has
no error return value. Be sure to call **itoa( )** with a string of
sufficient length to hold the converted result.

The main use of **itoa( )** is to transform integers into strings so
that they can be sent to a device not directly supported by the
normal C I/O system — that is, a nonstream device. The same thing
may be accomplished using **sprintf( )**. The reason **itoa( )** is included here is that its use is prevalent throughout older existing
code.

Example

This program displays the value of 1423 in hexadecimal (58F):

```
#include <stdlib.h>
#include <stdio.h>

main(void)
{
  char p[20];

  itoa(1423, p, 16);

  printf(p);
  return 0;
}
```

#include <stdlib.h>
long labs(long num)

Description   The **labs( )** function returns the absolute value of the **long int** *num*.

Example

This function converts the user-entered numbers into their absolute values:

```
#include <stdlib.h>
#include <stdio.h>

long int get_labs()
{
  char num[80];

  gets(num)

  return labs(atol(num));
}
```

#include <setjmp.h>
void longjmp(envbuf, val)
jmp_buf envbuf; int val

Description   The **longjmp( )** function causes program execution to resume at the point of the last call to **setjmp( )**. These two functions are Turbo C++'s way of providing for a jump between functions. Notice that the header **setjump.h** is required.

The **longjmp( )** function operates by resetting the stack as described in *envbuf,* which must have been set by a prior call to **setjmp( )**. This causes program execution to resume at the statement following the **setjmp( )** invocation. That is, the computer is tricked into thinking that it never left the function that called **setjmp( )**. As a somewhat graphic explanation, the **longjmp( )** function warps across time and (memory) space to a previous point in your program without having to perform the normal function return process.

The buffer *envbuf* is of type **jmp _ buf**, which is defined in the header **setjmp.h**. The buffer must have been set through a call to **setjmp( )** prior to calling **longjmp( )**.

The value of *val* becomes the return value of **setjump( )** and may be interrogated to determine where the long jump came from. The only value not allowed is 0.

It is important to understand that the **longjmp( )** function must be called before the function that called **setjmp( )** returns. If not, the result is technically undefined. (Actually, a crash will almost certainly occur.)

By far, the most common use of **longjmp( )** is to return from a deeply nested set of routines when a catastrophic error occurs.

Example

This program prints **1 2 3**:

```
#include <setjmp.h>
#include <stdio.h>

void f2(void);
```

```
jmp_buf ebuf;

main(void)
{
  char first=1;
  int i;
  printf("1 ");
  i = setjmp(ebuf);
  if(first) {
    first = !first;
    f2();
    printf("this will not be printed");
  }
  printf("%d", i);
  return 0;
}

void f2(void)
{
 printf("2 ");
 longjmp(ebuf, 3);
}
```

#include <stdlib.h>
void qsort(void *base, size_t num,
size_t size,
int (*compare)
(const *void, const *void))

Description   The **qsort( )** function sorts the array pointed to by *base* using a quicksort (developed by C.A.R. Hoare). The quicksort is generally considered the best general-purpose sorting algorithm. Upon termination, the array will be sorted. The number of elements in the array is specified by *num* and the size (in bytes) of each element is described by *size*.

The function pointed to by *compare* is used to compare an element of the array with the key. The form of the compare function must be *func* __ *name*(const void *arg1*, const void *arg2*)

It must return the following values:

- If *arg1* is less than *arg2,* then return less than 0.
- If *arg1* is equal to *arg2,* then return 0.
- If *arg1* is greater than *arg2,* then return greater than 0.

The array is sorted into ascending order with the lowest address containing the lowest element.

Example

This program sorts a list of integers and displays the result:

```
#include <stdlib.h>
#include <stdio.h>

int comp();

int num[10]= {
   1,3,6,5,8,7,9,6,2,0
};

main(void)
{
  int i;

  printf("original array: ");
  for(i=0; i<10; i++) printf("%d ", num[i]);

  qsort(num, 10, sizeof(int), comp);

  printf("sorted array: ");
  for(i=0; i<10; i++) printf("%d ", num[i]);
  return 0;
}

/* compare the integers */
```

```
comp(const int *i, const int *j)
{
  return *i-*j;
}
```

#include < stdlib.h >
int rand(void)

Description   The **rand( )** function generates a sequence of pseudorandom numbers. Each time it is called, an integer between 0
and **RAND _ MAX** is returned.

Example

This program displays ten pseudorandom numbers:

```
#include <stdlib.h>
#include <stdio.h>

main(void)
{
  int i;

  for(i=0; i<10; i++)
    printf("%d ",rand());
  return 0;
}
```

#include < setjmp.h >
int setjmp(jmp _ buf envbuf)
jmp _ buf envbuf

Description   The **setjmp( )** function saves the contents of the
system stack in the buffer *envbuf* for later use by **longjmp( )**.

The **setjmp( )** function returns 0 upon invocation. However, a **longjmp( )** passes an argument to **setjmp( )** when it executes, and it is this value (always nonzero) that will appear to be **setjmp( )**'s value after a call to **longjmp( )**.

See **longjmp( )** for additional information.

Example

This program prints **1 2 3**:

```
#include <setjmp.h>
#include <stdio.h>

void f2(void)

jmp_buf ebuf;

main(void)
{
  char first=1;
  int i;

  printf("1 ");
  i = setjmp(ebuf);
  if(first) {
    first = !first;
    f2();
    printf("this will not be printed");
  }
  printf("%d",i);
  return 0;
}

void f2(void)
{
 printf("2 ");
 longjmp(ebuf, 3);
}
```

#include < stdlib.h >
void srand(unsigned seed)

Description The **srand( )** function is used to set a starting point for the sequence generated by the **rand( )** function, which returns pseudorandom numbers.

The **srand( )** function is generally used to allow multiple program runs using different sequences of pseudorandom numbers.

Example

This program uses the system time to randomly initialize the **rand( )** function using **srand( )**:

```
#include <stdio.h>
#include <stdlib.h>
#include <time.h>

/* Seed rand with the system time
   and display the first 10 numbers.
*/
main(void)
{
  int i,utime;
  long  ltime;

  /* get the current calendar time */

  ltime = time(NULL);
  utime = (unsigned int) ltime/2;
  srand(utime);
  for(i=0; i<10; i++) printf("%d ", rand());
  return 0;
}
```

Using Turbo C++'s Debugger

Turbo C++ includes a built-in source-level debugger in its integrated development environment. This appendix introduces the debugger and explores some of its most important features.

Preparing Your Programs for Debugging

Although Turbo C++'s debugger is available for use at the press of a key, you must make sure that your programs are compiled for a debugging session. For the debugger to work, you must include debugging information in your program's executable file. By default, the proper debugging information is automatically included in your program. The option that controls the inclusion of debugging information is found under the **Debugger** entry of the **Options** main menu entry. Make sure that **Source Debugging** is on. The debugging information contained in the compiled version of your program helps Turbo C++ link your source code to its object code.

What Is a Source-Level Debugger?

To understand what a source-level debugger is and why it is so valuable, it is necessary to understand how a traditional debugger works. A traditional debugger is designed to provide object code debugging in which you monitor the contents of the CPU's registers or memory. To use a traditional debugger, the linker generates a symbol table that shows the memory address of each function and variable in memory. To debug a program, you use this symbol table and begin executing your program, monitoring the contents of various registers and memory locations. Most debuggers allow you to single step your program one instruction at a time and to set break points in the object code. The biggest drawback to a traditional debugger is that the object code of your program generally bears little resemblance to the source code. Thus, it is difficult, even with the use of a symbol table, to know exactly what is actually happening.

A source-level debugger is a vast improvement over the older, traditional form. A source-level debugger allows you to debug your program using the original source code. The debugger automatically links the compiled object code associated with each line in your program with its corresponding source code. You no longer need to use a symbol table. You can control the execution of your program by setting break points in the source code. You can watch the values of various variables by using the variables' names. You can single step your program one statement at a time and watch the contents of the program's call stack. Also, communication with Turbo C++'s debugger is accomplished using C-like expressions, so there is nothing new to learn.

Debugger Basics

This section introduces the most common debugging commands. Before getting started, enter the following program at this time. It will be used for demonstration.

```
#include <iostream.h>

void sqr_it(int n);

main(void)
{
  int i;

  for(i=0; i<10; i++) {
    cout << i << " ";
    sqr_it(i);
  }
  return 0;
}

void sqr_it(int n)
{
  cout << n*n << " ";
}
```

After you have entered the program, compile and run it to make sure that you entered it correctly. It prints the values 0 through 9 along with their squares.

Single Stepping

Single stepping is the process by which you execute your program a single statement at a time. To accomplish this using Turbo C++, press the F7 key. The F7 key is called the Trace key by Turbo C++. Press F7 at this time. Notice that the line containing the **main( )** function declaration is highlighted. This is where your program begins execution. Note also that the line **#include <iostream.h>** and **sqr_it( )**'s prototype are skipped over. Statements that do not generate code, such as the preprocessor directives, obviously cannot be executed, so the debugger automatically skips them. The same is true of variable declaration statements. A variable declaration is not an action statement that can be traced. Hence, variable declaration statements are also skipped when single stepping. (A variable declaration that provides an intialization is traced, however.)

NOTE   Pressing F7 is the same as selecting the **Trace into** option of the **Run** main menu option.

Press F7 several times. Notice how the highlight moves from line to line as you would expect. Also notice that when the function **sqr_it( )** is called, the highlight moves into the function and then returns from it. The F7 key causes the execution of your program to be traced into function calls. However, there can be times when you want to watch the performance of the code within only one function. To accomplish this, use the F8 (Step over) key. Each time this key is pressed, another statement is executed, but calls to functions are not traced. The F8 key is very useful when you only want to watch what is happening inside one function. Pressing F8 is the same as selecting the **Step over** entry on the **Run** option's menu.

Experiment with the F8 key at this time. Notice that the highlight never enters the **sqr_it( )** function.

Setting Break Points

As useful as single stepping is, it can be very tedious in a large program — especially if the piece of code that you want to debug is well into the program. Instead of pressing F7 or F8 repeatedly to get to the part you want to debug, it is easier — and better — to set a *break point* at the beginning of the critical section. A break point is, as the name implies, a break in the execution of your program. When execution reaches the break point, your program stops running and control returns to the debugger, allowing you to check the value of certain variables or to begin single stepping the routine.

To set a break point, move the cursor to the line in your program that will become the break point. Next, invoke the **Debug** menu and select the **Toggle breakpoint** option. (You can also use the hot key CTRL-F8.) The line of code at which the break point is set will be shown in either high-intensity video or in another color, depending on the type of video adapter and monitor in your system. Remember that you can have several active break points in a program.

Once you have defined one or more break points, execute your program using the **Run/Run** option. Your program will run until it encounters the first break point. To see this in action, set a break point at the line

```
cout << n*n << "  ";
```

inside **sqr_it( )** and then run the program. As you can see, execution stops at that line.

To remove a break point, position the cursor on the line containing the break point that you want to remove and select the **Debug/Toggle breakpoint** option (or press CTRL-F8). You can toggle break points on or off repeatedly if needed.

Watching Variables

One of the most common needs you will have while debugging is to see the value of one or more variables as your program executes. This is very easy to do using Turbo C++'s debugger. To define a variable to watch, select the **Debug/Watches** option and then select **Add watch** (or simply press CTRL-F7). You will see a small window pop up. In this window enter the name of the variable you want to watch. The debugger will automatically display the value of the variable, in the watch window, as the program executes. If the variable is global, then its value will always be available. However, if the variable is local, then its value will only be able to be reported when the function containing that variable is being executed. When execution moves to a different function, the variable's value is unknown. Keep in mind that if two functions both use the same name for a variable, then the value you see displayed will relate to the function currently executing.

Let's try an example. Activate the **Watches** entry at this time. To watch the value of **i** in the example program, enter **i** at this time. If you are not currently running the program, or if execution has been stopped inside the **sqr_it( )** function, then you will first see the message

```
Undefined symbol 'i'
```

However, when execution is inside the **main( )** function, the value of **i** will be displayed.

You are not limited to watching only the contents of variables. You can watch any valid C expression involving those variables with these two restrictions: First, the expression may not call a function; second, it cannot use any **#define** values.

Watched Expression Format Codes

Turbo C++'s debugger allows you to format the output of a watched expression by using format codes. To specify a format code, use this general form:

expression,format-code

The format codes are shown in Table B-1. If you don't specify a format code, then the debugger automatically provides a default format, which is usually correct.

Table B-1.

Format Code	Meaning
C	Display as a character with no translation
D	Display in decimal
F	Display in floating point
H	Display in hexadecimal
M	Show memory
P	Display pointer
R	Display structure or union names and values
S	Display as a character with appropriate character translations
X	Display in hexadecimal (same as H)

Debugger Format Codes

You can display integers in two different ways: in decimal or in hexadecimal. The debugger automatically knows the difference between **long** and **short** integers because it has access to the source code.

When specifying a floating-point format, you can tell the debugger to show a certain number of significant digits after the decimal point by adding a number to the **F** format. For example, if **average** is a **float**, then this tells the debugger to show five significant digits:

```
average,F5
```

Remember that the number is optional. The debugger automatically knows the difference between **float**s and **double**s.

Pointers are displayed using segment/offset notation. However, a **near** pointer does not display a value for the segment. Instead, **DS** is substituted because all **near** pointers reside in the data segment. On the other hand, **far** pointers are shown using the full segment/offset. You can display the value pointed to by using the * operator in front of the pointer in the watched expression.

Character arrays are displayed as strings. By default, the debugger translates non-ASCII characters into codes. For example, a CTRL-D is displayed as **\4**. However, if you specify the **C** format code, then all characters are displayed as is, using the PC's extended character set.

When a structure or a union is displayed, the values associated with each field are shown using an appropriate format. By including the **R** format command, the name of each field is also shown. To see an example, enter the following program. Try watching both **sample** and **sample,R**.

```
#include <string.h>
struct inventory {
  char item [10];
```

```
   int  count;
   float cost;
} sample;

main(void)
{
  strcpy(sample.item,  "hammer");
  sample.count = 100;
  sample.cost = 3.95;

  return 0;
}
```

As you might expect, you can also watch an object. When you watch an object, you will be shown the current value(s) of any data that is contained within the object. As with structures and unions, if you use the **R** format specifier, the name of each data item will also be displayed.

Using the **Debug/Watches** menu, it is possible to delete a watched expression, modify a watched expression, or remove all watched expressions. By default, when modifying an expression, the one modified is the last one entered. You can specify which watched expression to modify. First switch to the watch window and then move the highlight to the expression you want to modify. Finally, invoke the **Edit watch** option on the **Watches** menu.

Watching the Stack

During the execution of your program, you can display the contents of the call stack by using the **Call stack** option under the **Debug** menu. This option displays the order in which the various functions in your program were called. It does not display any local variables or return addresses. It also displays the value of any function parameters at the time of the call. To see how this feature works, enter this program.

```
#include <iostream.h>
void f1(void), f2(int i);
main(void)
{
  f1();
  return 0;
}

void f1(void)
{
  int i;
  for(i=0; i<10; i++) f2(i);
}

void f2(int i)
{
  cout << "in f2, value is " << i << " ";
}
```

Set a break point at the line containing the **cout** statement in
f2( ). The first time the break point is encountered, the call stack
will look like this:

```
f2(0)
f1()
main()
```

Evaluating an Expression

You can evaluate any legal C expression by selecting the option,
Evaluate/modify, on the **Debug** menu. You can use variables
defined in the program you are debugging as part of the
expression. You can also use this option to change the value of a

variable. You cannot call any function or use any **#define**d value, however.

Inspecting a Variable

Although watching a variable using the **Watches** option is generally sufficient, in the most demanding of circumstances, you may need to monitor more closely what is happening to a variable. To do this, use the **Inspect** option on the **Debug** menu. This option causes the contents and address of a variable to be displayed. Knowing a variable's address can be of value when bugs involve things like wild pointers.

Using the Register Window

One final debugging tool at your disposal is Turbo C++'s register window. If you select the **Window** main menu option and then select the **Register** entry, a small window will pop up that displays the contents of each register in the CPU as well as the state of each flag. When you trace, or each time a break point is encountered, the contents of the register window will change to reflect the values contained in the CPU registers.

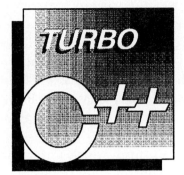

Turbo C++'s
Memory Models

For reasons that will become clear, you can compile a Turbo C++ program using any of the six different *memory models* defined by the 8086 family of processors. Each model organizes the memory of the computer differently and governs the size of the code, or the data, or both that a program may have. It also determines how quickly your program will execute. Because the model used has a profound effect on your program's speed of execution and on the way a program may access the system resources, this appendix discusses in detail the various memory models.

The 8086 Family of Processors

Before you can understand the way the various memory models work, you need to understand how the 8086 family of processors addresses memory. For the rest of this appendix, the CPU will be referred to as the 8086, but the information applies to all processors in this family, including the 8088, 80186, 80286, and 80386. (For the 80286 and 80386, the information that follows is applicable only when the processor is running in 8086 emulation mode.)

The 8086 contains 14 registers into which information is placed for processing or program control. The registers fall into the following categories:

- General-purpose registers

- Base pointer and index registers

- Segment registers

- Special-purpose registers

All the registers in the 8086 CPU are 16 bits (two bytes) wide.

The *general-purpose registers* are the "workhorse" registers of the CPU. It is in these registers that values are placed for processing, including arithmetic operations, such as adding or multiplying; comparisons, including equality, less than, greater than, and the like; and branch (jump) instructions. Each of the general-purpose registers may be accessed in two ways, either as a 16-bit register or as two 8-bit registers.

The *base pointer* and *index registers* provide support for such things as relative addressing, the stack pointer, and block move instructions.

The *segment registers* help implement the 8086's segmented memory scheme. The CS register holds the current code segment; the DS holds the current data segment; the ES holds the extra segment; and the SS holds the stack segment.

Finally, the *special-purpose registers* include the flag register, which holds the state of the CPU, and the instruction pointer, which points to the next instruction for the CPU to execute.

Address Calculation

The 8086 has a total address space of one megabyte. (The more powerful CPUs in the family can address more memory, but not when used in their 8086 emulation mode.) To access a megabyte of RAM requires a 20-bit address. However, on the 8086 no register is larger than 16 bits. This means that the 20-bit address must be divided between two registers. Unfortunately, the way the 20 bits are divided is a little more complex than one might assume.

For the 8086, all addresses consist of a *segment* and an *offset*. In fact, the addressing method used by the 8086 is generally referred to as the *segment/offset* method. A segment is a 64K region of RAM that must start on an even multiple of 16. In 8086 jargon, 16 bytes is called a *paragraph*; hence, you will sometimes encounter the term *paragraph boundary* used to reference these even multiples of 16 bytes. The 8086 defines four segments: one for code, one for data, one for the stack, and one extra segment. (These segments may overlap each other or they may be separate.) The location of any byte within a segment is determined by the offset. Put differently, the value of the segment register determines which 64K segment is referred to and the value of the offset determines which byte, within that segment, is actually being addressed. Thus, the 20-bit physical address of any specific byte within the computer is the combination of the segment and the offset.

Near Versus Far Pointers

As long as you are only accessing addresses within the segment currently loaded in a segment register, then only the offset of the address needs to be loaded into a register. This means that any object referenced using only a 16-bit address must be within the currently loaded segment. This is referred to as a *near address,* or a *near pointer.*

To access an address that is not in the current segment, both the segment and the offset of the desired address must be loaded. This is called a *far address* or a *far pointer.* A far pointer can access any address within the one megabyte address space.

Only the 16-bit offset must be loaded to access memory within the current segment. However, if you wish to access memory outside that segment, then both the segment and the offset must be loaded with the proper values into their respective registers. Since it takes twice as long to load two 16-bit registers as it does to load one, it takes longer to load a far pointer than it does to load a near pointer. Hence, your programs run much slower using far pointers than they do using near pointers. Also, using far pointers causes your program to be bigger. However, far pointers do allow you to have larger programs and/or data. The exact relationship between program speed and size and the trade-offs involved are the subject of the next section.

Memory Models

Turbo C++ for the 8086 family of processors can compile your program in six different ways and each way organizes the memory in the computer differently. Each organization affects different aspects of your program's performance. The six models are called tiny, small, medium, compact, large, and huge. Let's look at how these differ.

Tiny Model

The tiny model compiles a program so that all the segment registers are set to the same value and all addressing is done using 16 bits (near pointers). This means that the code, data, and stack must all be within the same 64K segment. This method of compilation produces the smallest, fastest code. Programs compiled using this memory model may be converted to .COM files using the /**t** option to the Turbo C++ linker. The tiny model produces the fastest run times.

Small Model

The small model is Turbo C++'s default mode of compilation and is useful for a wide variety of tasks. Although all addressing is done using only the 16-bit offset, the code segment is separate from the data, stack, and extra segments, which are in their own segment. This means that the total size of a program compiled this way is 128K split between code and data. Since the small model uses only near pointers, the execution speed is as good as it is for the tiny model but the program can be twice as big (more or less).

Medium Model

The medium model is for large programs where the code exceeds the one-segment restriction of the small model. Here, the code may use multiple segments and requires 20-bit (far) pointers, but the stack, data, and extra segments are in their own segment and use 16-bit (near) addressing. This is good for large programs that use little data. Your programs will run slower as far as function calls are concerned, but references to data will be as fast as the small model.

Compact Model

The complement of the medium model is the compact model. In this version, program code is restricted to one segment but data may occupy several segments. This means that all accesses to data require 20-bit (far) addressing but the code uses 16-bit (near) addressing. This is good for programs that require large amounts of data but little code. Your program will run as fast as the small model except when referencing data, when it will be slower.

Large Model

The large model allows both code and data to use multiple segments. However, the largest single item of data, such as an array, is limited to 64K. This model is used when you have both large code and large data requirements. It runs much slower than any of the previous models.

Huge Model

The huge model is the same as the large model with the exception that individual data items may exceed 64K. This makes runtime speed degrade further. (You will see why in the next section.)

Selecting a Model

Generally, you should use the small model unless there is a reason to do otherwise. Select the medium model if you have a lot of program but not much data. Use the compact model if you have a lot of data and not much program. If you have both a large amount of code and a lot of data, then use the large model—unless you need single data items to be larger than 64K, in which case you will need to use the huge model. Remember that both the large and huge models run substantially slower than the others.

There is another consideration that may affect how you compile your program. If you are compiling your program for either the compact or large memory model, then all pointer references to data will be through far pointers. However, this creates two problems. First, most pointer comparisons will not generate correct results. The reason for these incorrect results is that more than one segment/offset pair can map onto the same physical address. When far pointers are compared, only the offset is checked. This means that two pointers may actually point to the same physical address but compare as unequal, or point to different addresses and compare as equal. The only comparison that is guaranteed to be valid for far pointers is equality with 0 (the null pointer).

The second problem with far pointers is that when a far pointer is incremented or decremented, only the offset is altered. This means that a pointer will "wrap" when incremented (or decremented) past a segment boundary.

Pointers generated when compiling from the huge model are called *huge pointers*. They are similar to far pointers in that they use a full 20-bit address, but they do not suffer from the limitations of far pointers. First, huge pointers can be correctly compared. The reason for this is that they are *normalized*. The normalization process ensures that there is only one segment/offset address for each physical address. Thus, all comparisons are valid. However, the normalization process takes time, thus slowing execution speed. Second, when a pointer is incremented or decremented past a segment boundary, the segment is adjusted accordingly and the "wrap around" problem experienced with far pointers is eliminated. This is how access to a single data object that is larger than 64K is achieved.

The Memory Model Compiler Options

Turbo C++ compiles your program using the small model by default. To cause Turbo C++ to use a different model you must give it the proper instructions. In the integrated environment version, you select the memory model through the use of the **Options/Compiler** menu. For the command-line version, you use one of the following command-line options:

Option	*Memory model*
-mc	compact
-mh	huge
-ml	large
-mm	medium
-ms	small (default)
-mt	tiny

Overriding a Memory Model

You may have been thinking during the previous discussion how unfortunate it is that even a single reference to data in another segment would require that the compact rather than small model be used, for example. In this case, the execution speed of the entire program degrades even though only an isolated part of it actually needs a far pointer. In general, this sort of situation can present itself in a variety of ways. For example, it is necessary to use 20-bit addressing to access the video RAM of a PC even though the rest of the program might only need near pointers. The solution to this and other related problems is the *segment override* type modifiers, which are enhancements provided by Turbo C++. They are **near, far**, and **huge**.

When these modifiers are applied to pointers, they affect the way data is accessed. It is also possible to apply the **near** and **far** modifiers to functions. In this case, they affect the way the function is called and returned.

These modifiers follow the base type and precede the variable name. For example, this declares a **far** pointer called **f_pointer**:

```
char far *f_pointer;
```

In this example, the function **myfarfunc( )** is declared as **far:**

```
void far myfarfunc(int *p);
```

Let's look at these type modifiers now.

far

The most common memory model override is **far**. The reason for this is that it is very common to want to access some region of memory that is (or may be) outside the data segment. However, if the program is compiled for one of the large data models, all access to data becomes very slow—not just the one. The solution to this problem is to explicitly declare the pointers to data that is outside the current data segment as **far** and compile using the small memory model. In this way, only those references to the object actually outside the default data segment will incur the additional overhead.

The use of **far** functions is less common and is generally restricted to specialized programming situations where a function may lie outside the current code segment, such as a ROM-based routine. In these cases, the use of **far** ensures that the proper calling and returning sequence is used.

Explicitly declared **far** pointers suffer from the same trouble as those implicitly generated when compiling for one of the large data models. First, pointer arithmetic only affects the offset and can cause "wrap around." This means that if a **far** pointer with the value 0000:FFFF is incremented, its new value will be 0000:0000, not 1000:0000. The value of the segment is never changed. Second, two **far** pointers should not be used in a relational expression because only their offsets will be checked. As stated earlier, it is possible to have two different pointers actually contain the same physical address but have different segments and offsets. If you need to compare 20-bit pointers, you must use **huge** pointers. However, you can compare a **far** pointer against the null pointer.

near

A **near** pointer is a 16-bit offset that uses the value of the appropriate segment to determine the actual memory location. The **near** modifier to data forces Turbo C++ to treat the pointer as a 16-bit offset to the segment contained in DS. You will use a **near** pointer when you have compiled a program using the medium, large, or huge memory model.

Using **near** on a function causes that function to be treated as if it were compiled using the small code model. (The address of the function is computed using the CS register.) When a function is compiled using the tiny, small, or compact models, all calls to the function place a 16-bit return address on the stack. A function compiled with a large code model causes a 20-bit address to be pushed onto the stack. Therefore, in programs that are compiled for the large code model, a highly recursive function should be declared as **near** (if possible) to conserve stack space and decrease execution time.

huge

The **huge** modifier may only be applied to data, not to functions. A **huge** pointer is like a pointer generated when compiling for the huge memory mode. It is normalized so that comparisons between **huge** pointers are meaningful. When a **huge** pointer is incremented, both the segment and the offset may change—it does not suffer from the "wrap around" problem of **far** pointers. Using a **huge** pointer, you can access objects larger than 64K.

Turbo C++'s Segment Specifiers

In addition to **near**, **far**, and **huge**, Turbo C++ supports these four additional addressing modifiers:

    _cs
    _ds
    _ss
    _es

When these type modifiers are applied to a pointer's declaration they cause the pointer to become a 16-bit offset into the specified segment. For example, given the statement

```
int _es *ptr;
```

ptr will cause the extra segment to contain a 16-bit offset.

Turbo C++ also includes the **_seg** modifier, which creates pointers that are 16 bits long and contain only the segment address. The offset is assumed to be zero. There are several restrictions to **_seg** pointers. You cannot increment or decrement them. In an expression that adds or subtracts an integer value from a **_seg** pointer, a **far** pointer is generated. When dereferencing a **_seg** pointer, it is converted into a **far** pointer. You can add a **near** pointer with a **_seg** pointer and the result is a **far** pointer.

The use of these modifiers is generally reserved for only the most exotic applications.

Keep in mind that Turbo C++'s **near, far, huge, _es, _cs, _ds, _ss,** and **_seg** modifiers are not defined by the ANSI standard and are not fully portable. However, most 8086-based C compilers support some, if not all, of these modifiers.

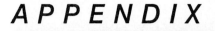

D

Using the VROOMM Overlay Technology

With the introduction of Turbo C++, Borland has made available its VROOMM (Virtual Runtime Object-Oriented Memory Manager) technology to all programmers. As you probably know, overlays are a time-honored method of dealing with a program that is too big to fit in available memory. When overlays are used, pieces of your program are stored on disk and swapped into memory only when needed. This reduces the amount of memory required by the program. However, it slows down execution speed because of the time it takes to load a module.

In general, to use overlays you need an overlay manager, which will swap parts of your program into memory from disk. You also need to break your program into several smaller pieces suitable for overlays. What makes the VROOMM technology special is that it automatically handles the details of overlays for you. You don't need to calculate any sizes or determine any calling dependencies. In fact, to let your large programs take advantage of VROOMM you simply change a few compiler options. Nothing else needs to change.

When compiling for overlays, you must use the medium, large, or huge memory model. If you forget to do this, the linker will not link your program.

Since you will only use VROOMM on a very large program, most likely that program will be split among several files. To make your program use VROOMM, first make sure that full menus are active and select the **Options** entry on the main menu. Next, select **Compiler** followed by **Code**. Turn on the **Overlays** check box. Also, select the medium, large, or huge memory model. Return to the main menu. Now activate the **Options** entry a second time and select **Linker**. Turn on the **Overlays** check box. Finally, from the main menu select the **Project** entry and **Local options**. This will let you specify what files you want to compile as overlays.

If you are using the command-line version of Turbo C++, you must specify the **−Yo** option before the file(s) that you want to be overlays. Also, if there is a part of your program that you want to stay resident, precede its filename using just **−Y**. Since you must compile any program using overlays for the medium, large, or huge memory model, you must also specify the **−mm**, **−ml**, or **−mh** option. For example, this series of command lines compiles a program consisting of the files PROG.CPP, PROG1.CPP, and PROG2.CPP for overlays. Notice that PROG.CPP is resident all the time. The other two files will be overlaid.

```
tcc -ml  -c -Yo prog1.cpp
tcc -ml  -c -Yo prog2.cpp
tcc -ml  -Y prog.cpp prog2.obj prog3.obj
```

The VROOMM overlay manager works like this: When a piece of code is called that is not currently in memory, it is read from disk into a buffer set aside for overlays. If the buffer is already full, then another module is discarded. By default, the size of the buffer that Turbo C++ sets aside for overlaying is twice the size of the largest overlayable module. However, you can increase the size of the buffer (and thereby increase performance) by setting the global variable **_ovrbuffer**. The size of the buffer is specified in paragraphs (16 bytes). Experimentation may prove the easiest way to determine what buffer size is best for your program. Remember that except for running out of memory, there is nothing wrong with making the buffer as large as you can because it reduces disk accesses.

When using overlays, keep in mind that you will almost certainly want to keep parts of your program resident and other parts as overlays. The best candidate modules to make into overlays are those parts of your programs that are executed infrequently, for example, a help system or a sort. However, you should not make into an overlay any module that depends upon timing.

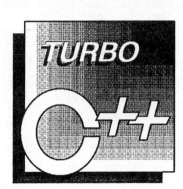

Using the Command-Line Compiler

If you are new to Turbo C and C++, there is no doubt that you will find Turbo C++'s integrated environment the easiest way to develop programs. However, if you have been programming for some time using your own editor, you might find the command-line version of Turbo C++ more to your liking. For experienced programmers, the command-line version represents the traditional method of compilation and linking. The name of the command-line compiler is TCC.EXE. This appendix takes a brief look at the command-line compiler.

Compiling Using the Command-Line Compiler

Assume that you have a program called X.CPP. To compile this program using the command-line version of Turbo C++, your command line will look like this:

```
C>TCC X.CPP
```

Assuming that there are no errors in the program, this causes X.CPP to be compiled and linked with the proper library files. This is the simplest form of the command line.

The general form of the command line is

TCC [*option1 option2 . . . optionN*] *fname1 fname2 . . . fnameN*

where *option* refers to a compiler or linker option and *fname* is a C or C++ source file, an .OBJ file, or a library.

All compiler/linker options begin with a minus sign. Generally, following an option with a minus sign turns that option off. Table E-1 shows the options available in the command-line version of Turbo C++. Keep in mind that the options are case sensitive.

For example, to compile X.CPP with the stack checked for overflow, your command line will look like this:

```
C>TCC -N X.CPP
```

What's in a Filename?

The Turbo C++ command-line compiler automatically adds the .C extension to any filename if no extension is specified. For example, both of these command lines are functionally the same:

Table E-1.

Option	*Meaning*
−A	Recognize only ANSI keywords
−AK	Recognize only K&R keywords
−AU	Recognize only UNIX C keywords
−a	Use word alignment for data
−a-	Use byte alignment for data
−B	Inline assembly code in source file
−C	Accept nested comments
−c	Compile to .OBJ only
−Dname	Define a macro name
−Dname=string	Define and give a value to a macro name
−d	Merge duplicate strings
−d-	Do not merge duplicate strings
−E*xxx*	Specify name of assembler
−efname	Specify executable filename
−f	Use floating-point emulation
−ff	Optimize for fast floating point
−f-	No floating point
−f87	Use 8087
−f287	Use 80287
−G	Optimize code for speed
−g*N*	Stop after *N* warning errors
−Ipath	Specify the path to the include directory
−i*N*	Specify identifier length *N*
−j*N*	Stop after *N* fatal errors
−K	char unsigned
−K-	char signed
−k	Use standard stack frame
−Lpath	Specify library directory
−lx	Pass an option to the linker
−M	Create map file

Turbo C++'s Command-Line Options

Table E-1. (*continued*)

Option	Meaning
−mc	Use compact memory model
−mh	Use huge memory model
−ml	Use large memory model
−mm	Use medium memory model
−ms	Use small memory model
−mt	Use tiny memory model
−N	Check for stack overflows
−npath	Specify output directory
−O	Optimize jumps
−P	Compile as a C++ program
−p	Use Pascal calling conventions
−p-	Use C calling conventions
−Qe	Use all EMS memory
−Qe-	Use no EMS memory
−Qx	Similar to −Qe
−r	Use register variables
−r-	Don't use register variables
−rd	Use only declared register variables
−S	Generate assembly code output
−T	Pass an option to the assembler
−Uname	Undefine a macro name
−u	Generate underscores
−Vx	Specify virtual table options
−v	Include debug information
−w	Display warning errors (see Turbo C++ Reference Guide)
−w-	Do not display warning errors
−Y	Program contains overlay modules
−Yo	Compile as an overlay

Turbo C++'s Command-Line Options

Table E-1. *(continued)*

Option	Meaning
−y	Embed line numbers into object code
−Z	Register optimization on
−z	Specify segment names (see Turbo C++ Reference Guide)
−1	Generate 80186/80286 instructions
−1-	Do not generate 80186/80286 instructions
−2	Generate 80286 protected mode instructions

Turbo C++'s Command-Line Options

```
C>TCC X.C
C>TCC X
```

This causes the program to be compiled as a C rather than a C++ program. If you want to compile your program using C++, the file must use the .CPP extension (and you must explicitly specify it) or you must use the −P compiler option.

You can compile a file with an extension other than .C or .CPP by specifying its extension. For example, to compile X.TMP, the command line will look like this:

```
C>TCC X.TMP
```

Files that don't have the .C or .CPP extensions will be compiled as C programs.

You may specify additional object files that will be linked in with the source file you are compiling by specifying them after the source file. All included files must have been previously compiled and have an .OBJ extension. For example, if your program consists of the files P1.CPP, P2.CPP, and P3.CPP, and if P2 and P3 have already been compiled to .OBJ files, then the following command line will first compile P1.CPP and then link it with P2.OBJ and P3.OBJ.

```
C>TCC P1.CPP P2.OBJ P3.OBJ
```

In this example, it is assumed that P2.OBJ and P3.OBJ exist. The way to produce these files starting from their .CPP source files is to compile each using the −c compiler option. This option causes the compiler to create .OBJ files but no link process takes place.

If you have additional libraries other than those supplied with Turbo C++, you can specify them by using the .LIB extension.

The executable output file produced by the linker is generally the name of the source file being compiled with an .EXE extension. However, you can specify a different name using the −e option. The name that follows the −e is the name the compiler will use as the executable file. There can be no spaces between the −e and the filename. For example, the following compiles the file TEST.CPP and creates an executable file called RUN.EXE:

```
C>TCC -eRUN TEST.CPP
```

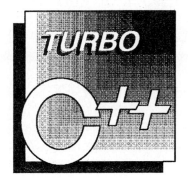

Compiling Multiple File Programs

Most real world C++ programs are too large to easily fit into one file. Extremely large files are difficult to edit. Also, making a small change in the program requires that the entire program be recompiled. Although Turbo C++ is very fast at compiling, at some point—no matter how fast the compiler—the time it takes to compile will become unbearable.

The solution to these types of problems is to break the program into smaller pieces, compile these pieces, and then link them together. This process is known as *separate compilation and linking* and it forms the backbone of most development efforts.

Projects and the Project Option

In the Turbo C++ integrated environment, multiple file programs are called *projects*. Each project is associated with a *project file*, which determines what files are part of the project. The **Project** main menu option lets you manage project files. All project files must end with a .PRJ extension.

When you select the **Project** option, you are presented with these choices:

```
Open project...
Close project
Add item...
Delete item
Local options...
Include files...
```

To create a project, you must first select **Open project**. You will then be prompted for the name of the project, which must have the extension .PRJ. To clear a project, use **Close project**. Once you have created a project file, use **Add item** to put into the project file the names of the files that form the project. For example, if the project file is called MYPROJ.PRJ and your project contains the two files TEST1.CPP and TEST2.CPP, then you would enter the two files TEST1.CPP and TEST2.CPP. To remove an item, select **Delete item**. You specify various options using **Local options**. The **Include files** option lets you see what include files are used by your project.

For the sake of discussion, assume that you have a project file that contains the files TEST1.CPP and TEST2.CPP. Further assume that neither TEST1.CPP nor TEST2.CPP has yet been compiled. There are two ways to compile and link these files together. First, you can select the **Run** main menu option. When there is a .PRJ file specified in the **Project** option, this file is used to guide Turbo C++ in compiling your program. The content of the .PRJ file is read and each file that needs to be compiled is compiled to an .OBJ file. Next, those files are linked together and the program is executed.

The second way you can compile a project is to use the built-in **Make** facility. By pressing F9, or by selecting the **Make** option under the **Compile** main menu option, you cause Turbo C++ to compile and link all files specified in the project file. The only difference between this and the **Run** option is that the program is not executed. In fact, you can think of the **Run** option as first performing a **Make** and then executing the .EXE file.

Whenever you **Make** a program, only those files that need to be compiled will actually be compiled. Turbo C++ determines this by checking the time and date associated with each source file and its .OBJ file. If the .CPP file is newer than the .OBJ file, then Turbo C++ knows that the .CPP file has been changed and it recompiles it. Otherwise, it simply uses the .OBJ file. In this situation, the *target* .OBJ file is said to be *dependent* on the .CPP file. The same sort of thing is true of the .EXE file. As long as the .EXE file is newer than all of the .OBJ files in the project, then nothing is recompiled. Otherwise, the necessary files are compiled and the project relinked.

In addition to checking the dates on .CPP, .OBJ, and .EXE files, Turbo C++ checks to see if any header files used by your program have changed. If this is the case, then any file that uses a changed header file is automatically recompiled.

Without a doubt, the project capabilities of Turbo C++ are among its most important aspects because they let you manage multiple source file programs with little difficulty.

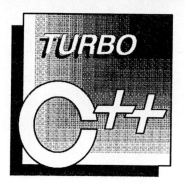

Index

The manuscript for this book was prepared and submitted to Osborne/McGraw-Hill in electronic form. The acquisitions editor for this project was Jeffrey Pepper, the technical reviewers were Jim Turley and Chris Ohlsen, and the project editor was Judith Brown.

Text design by Stefany Otis and Valerie Haynes-Perry, using Baskerville for text body and Swiss boldface for display.

Cover art by Bay Graphics Design, Inc. Color separation and cover supplier, Phoenix Color Corporation. Screens produced with InSet, from Inset Systems, Inc. Book printed and bound by R.R. Donnelly & Sons Company, Crawfordsville, Indiana.